JOAN COLLINS

Also by Graham Lord

Novels
Marshmallow Pie
A Roof Under Your Feet
The Spider and the Fly
God and All His Angels
The Nostradamus Horoscope
Time Out of Mind
A Party to Die For
Sorry, We're Going to Have to Let You Go

Autobiography
Ghosts of King Solomon's Mines

Biography
Just the One: The Wives and Times of Jeffrey Bernard
James Herriot: The Life of a Country Vet
Dick Francis: A Racing Life
Arthur Lowe
Niv: The Authorised Biography of David Niven
John Mortimer: The Devil's Advocate

JOAN COLLINS

THE BIOGRAPHY OF AN ICON

GRAHAM LORD

First published in Great Britain in 2007
by Orion Books Ltd
The Orion Publishing Group Ltd
Orion House
5 Upper Saint Martin's Lane
London, WC2H 9EA
An Hachette Livre UK Company

1 3 5 7 9 10 8 6 4 2

A CIP catalogue record for this book
is available from the British Library.

ISBN: 978 0 7528 6753 3

Typeset by Deltatype Ltd, Birkenhead, Merseyside

Printed in Great Britain by Clays Ltd, St Ives plc

The Orion Publishing Group's Policy is to use papers that
are natural, renewable and recyclable products and made
from wood grown in sustainable forests. The logging and
manufacturing processes are expected to conform to the
environmental regulations of the country of origin.

For Juliet

CONTENTS

PREFACE

When I told Joan that I wanted to write this book she was understandably wary and decided not to co-operate. Some of those I contacted had been asked not to talk to me. My previous biography, of Sir John Mortimer, was not entirely flattering and Joan suspected that I might be planning to do a hatchet job on her. But none of my biographies has been a hatchet job and nothing could have been further from my mind. Joan Collins is an international icon, a superstar admired and even loved by men as well as women all over the world, and nothing I could ever discover or write about her would change that.

I have long admired her beauty, impish wit, independence, optimism, *joie de vivre* and dogged courage and self-confidence in the face of many adversities and challenges. She has often been ridiculed unfairly for her acting, yet even in her worst films – and there have been plenty of stinkers – she has usually been the best ingredient, and in some (*Sea Wife, The Wayward Bus, Quest For Love, Revenge, The Bawdy Adventures of Tom Jones, The Big Sleep, Decadence, The Clandestine Marriage*) she has been extremely good.

She has huge flaws, of course, but boldly she has admitted to most of them. All in all I believe that she is a Good Thing who has brightened our lives with her sense of fun, triumphs and even her disasters. I have written what in my opinion is an honest, accurate and sometimes critical but also warm and affectionate biography because I think she deserves it.

CHAPTER ONE

A GENTEEL LITTLE GYPSY

{ 1933–1949 }

When Joan Collins was a girl she dreamed of becoming a detective like her favourite fictional radio hero of the 1940s, Dick Barton, or a dress designer, or a journalist. In fact she could hardly have become anyone other than an actress, for the greasepaint ran thick in her family's veins. Her South African Jewish cockney father, Joe, was a successful London theatrical agent, a partner of Lew (later Lord) Grade, his clients including Max Miller, Flanagan and Allen, Vera Lynn, Elsie and Doris Waters. Joan's aunts Pauline and Lalla were dancers and Pauline – who was bold enough to pose for topless photographs at a time when nice girls didn't – also became an agent. Joan's paternal grandfather, Isaac Hart, was a theatre manager and impresario who changed his name to Will Collins. Her paternal grandmother, Hettie (Henrietta) Assenheim, was a saucy vaudeville actress, singer and dancer. So were Hettie's sisters Hannah and Bessie. And Joan herself was such a pretty, photogenic, green-eyed baby that her mother hung on her pram a sign that read PLEASE DO NOT KISS ME. Joan was not yet two when she was given her first part in a film, which starred Stewart Granger, but she yelled so much that she was sacked. She was not yet three when she went to the first of many dancing schools and still only three when she made her first stage appearance, as a fairy in a school production of a musical called *Why the Fairies Cried*. From then on she appeared regularly in school plays and shows and it would have been remarkable had she *not* become an actress.

She was born in London in the early hours of 23 May 1933 at 268 Gloucester Terrace, a five-storey nursing home (now converted into five flats) less than half a mile from the bustle of Paddington railway station and backing onto the above-ground Underground line at

I

Royal Oak and the noisy Great Western line that snakes out of the city towards Berkshire and the south-western counties of England. Her thirty-year-old father was not impressed by the 7lb baby when he and Lew Grade first saw her that late spring morning. She was 'just a dark little nothing', Joe wrote in his autobiography, *A Touch of Collins*, fifty-three years later, 'a scruffy little child with a few tufts of hair. Very ordinary.' 'What's that bit of scrag you've got there?' he joked with his twenty-seven-year-old wife of just over a year, Elsie Bessant, a blonde, blue-eyed London nightclub hostess/dance partner whom Joe started calling Elsa as soon as the baby was born. They named the infant Joan Henrietta (after his mother) and took her back to their rented home half a mile away at 133 Castellain Mansions in Maida Vale – a bright, airy four-roomed apartment on the first floor of an elegant, four-storey terrace of genteel, red-brick mansion flats with wrought-iron balconies in a quiet, wide, tree-lined avenue.

Joan's parents were sufficiently well-off to employ the first of a series of maids or nannies, a girl whom they sacked a few weeks later after she dropped a lighted cigarette into the baby's cot while the family was out one Sunday afternoon and set fire to the flat. It was so badly damaged that they had to be taken in for a while by a neighbour, Jock Jacobson. Joan said later that she had an idyllic childhood with plenty of love, comfort and security and for the rest of her life she was grateful to her parents for insisting on high standards of behaviour, manners and politeness. 'If I'd so much as thrown a sweet paper out of the car my father would have made me get out and pick it up,' she told Richard Barber of the *Mail on Sunday* in 1998. 'And he was right. Each small incident like that is part of a larger picture. Abandon your standards and you're on a slippery slope.' When she was a toddler she threw a tantrum in Selfridges department store because her mother would not buy her a doll that she wanted, and lay on the ground drumming her heels on the carpet. Elsa shrugged and walked on until Joan became worried and ran after her. When she misbehaved she was made to stand in the corner, which embarrassed her. 'Childcare was based around instilling discipline,' she told the *Daily Mail* with approval in 2006. 'Such instances led to me being a disciplined person today – not the sort of tearaway child so often seen nowadays. You don't even need to smack children to keep the peace in the house – I never slapped my children and I was never slapped.' She was also extremely grateful to her father for teaching her that life could be tough and unfair, that the world did not owe her a living, and that she had to work hard and stand on her own feet if she was ever to make anything of her life. That early grounding built an inner strength and resilience that was to give her the will to survive triumphantly all the obstacles and setbacks that she would face in life. It was also to make her a lifelong political Conservative. 'I was lucky to have Joe and Elsa Collins as parents,' she said years later.

Joan adored both her parents even though her father, who could be utterly charming and was attractive to women, was also an extremely strict, dogmatic and adulterous male chauvinist who dominated her mother and expected to be obeyed in everything. 'The attitude in those days was "I'm a man – and men are the boss",' she told Lynda Lee-Potter of the *Daily Mail* in 1999. She was genuinely frightened when he flew into one of his rages, shouted, and threw things. Even so, 'I don't think that did us any harm at all,' she said. Her younger sister, Jackie, who was born in 1937, was less forgiving. 'I loved my father,' she said, 'but he was a total male chauvinist pig.' She claimed that he was mean as well: 'He made a lot of money but spent it on himself,' she said, and added that he had had 'a kind of gangster mentality'. He was also sexually unfaithful. Joan thought her mother was totally faithful, she told Gyles Brandreth in a *Sunday Telegraph* interview in 2001, but 'my father was quite a naughty lad in his time. Daddy did his bit for heterosexuality, as I have tried to do mine.' During the week he rarely returned from work (or his latest girlfriend) before the girls were asleep and on Fridays and Saturdays he went off to fish or to watch football and then played cards with his cronies late into the night. Her mother, by contrast, was quiet, sweet, domesticated, and so loving that she would put little Joanie's ice-cream in the oven first to take the chill off it. She worshipped her macho husband but was afraid of most other men, terrified of leaving doors or windows unlocked, and utterly subservient to her husband, which later irritated both her daughters so deeply that they rebelled by becoming strong, independent, assertive feminists.

Joe Collins came to realise that both Joan and Jackie were appalled by the domineering way that he treated them and their mother, but he blamed his behaviour on the stiff-upper-lip English boarding school that he had attended as a boy. 'I did shout at my children, quite a lot,' he wrote in his autobiography. 'Shouting was my way of getting my children to behave themselves, and it worked. Yet for all the noise I made, they never appeared scared of me.' He said in his defence that he had never smacked any of his children or resorted to foul language and added mischievously: 'Today [1986], when I hear Joan use bad language I'm shocked.' As for Elsa, she 'never wavered in her role of the supportive wife, and we loved each other'. Neither Joan nor Jackie ever doubted it: despite their father's faults, and even though their mother kept warning them that men were the enemy, Elsa adored Joe for all of their thirty years together, and those contradictions and tensions were to build an extremely complex relationship between Joan and her father. He was 'totally unloving', she told Roald Dahl's daughter Tessa, who had a similar relationship with her father and interviewed her for the *Mail on Sunday* in 1988. 'He was detached, cold, hard, critical, difficult, acerbic, and everybody had to please him.' And did she ever please him? 'No,' said Joan sadly. Ms Dahl knew exactly what Joan meant and wrote: 'This desperate need to satisfy an emotionally unavailable man is exhausting, and doting daughters will go on and on striving to please their unreachable love object.' That conflict was to cause most of Joan's problems with men throughout her life. 'I never really felt he cared about me,' she said in 1988, and in her first autobiography, *Past Imperfect*, she wrote that after her first six or seven years, when he had adored her, he had terrified her for many years and had never been a proper father figure. Because of him, she said, she was to spend decades chasing difficult men in the hope of recapturing Daddy.

Before he became allegedly an ogre Joan's earliest years were filled with fun, laughter and variety. The Collins flat often rang to the merriment of his theatrical friends and clients and she revelled in the warmth of her extended family. On Sundays Joe, Elsa and Joanie would drive off to the south coast to spend the day with her adoring grandmothers and aunts. In Brighton they would visit her grandmother, Hettie, five spinster aunts, and great-grandmother Leah. In Bognor Regis they would see her other grandmother, stern, unsmiling Ada, and aunt Renee. Cheerful, vivacious Hettie was a particularly strong influence on the little girl, encouraging her, despite Joe's disapproval, to act, dance and sing, passing on tricks of the trade and fuelling her dreams by telling her glamorous stories from her own theatrical past. Joan loved dressing up in her grannies' and aunts' old clothes and when she was six Joe found her preening in front of a mirror, balancing matchsticks on her eyelashes because Granny Hettie had told her that this would make her lashes longer and thicker.

In 1937, when Joan was four, the family moved two miles north of Castellain Mansions to an ugly but modern six-storey block of flats near Kilburn tube station on Shoot Up Hill, where they rented a quiet, five-room apartment at the back of the third floor at 20 Hillcrest Court, perhaps because Elsa was about to have her second baby and the flat had an extra room and a lift. Joan's sister, Jacqueline Jill, was born just around the corner in a nursing home at 87 Fordwych Road on 4 October 1937, but the family did not stay long in the area, which was probably then even bleaker and more rundown than it is today. They moved back to Maida Vale the following year, to 61 Maida Vale, to rent a much smarter, bigger, three-bedroom, second-floor flat on the corner of St John's Wood Road overlooking a small garden at the back of Alexandra Court. It was an upmarket, six-storey, red-brick mansion block set back from the broad leafy avenue with an ornate, imposing façade, spacious hallways, a lift and small wrought-iron balconies. Joe's agency was obviously thriving and in later years he was to represent and promote a host of big names, among them Shirley Bassey, the Beatles, Johnny Dankworth, Lonnie Donegan, Diana Dors, Rolf Harris, Benny Hill, Tom Jones, Danny La Rue, Roger Moore, Des O'Connor, Ronnie Scott, Peter Sellers, Frankie Vaughan, Jimmy Young – and Bruce Forsyth, whom he billed in 1954 as 'The New Style Funster'. Nice to see him: to see him, nice.

At five Joan began to go to her first school but her cosy, ordered childhood was to be disrupted by the outbreak of the Second World War on 3 September 1939 and for the next six years she moved constantly from one flat to another, eight of them in all, and from one new school to another, so that she never had time to settle into any of them or down to any serious studies. 'We were like gypsies,' she told Gyles Brandreth. 'That's why I'm incredibly adjustable.' That summer Joe realised that war was inevitable and that if his wife and little daughters stayed in London they would soon be threatened by German bombs. While he decided to stay in the city himself to keep his business going, in August he moved his family to a rented house with a garden near Elsa's mother in Bognor Regis. The move bewildered Joan, who wondered why she was being sent away, but it soon became obvious that German raids along the south coast made Bognor just as dangerous as London, so the family moved again, this time to a small, rented riverside flat twenty-five miles to the west of London, in Maidenhead. After a while there seemed to be a lull in the German blitz on London and the family moved back to Alexandra Court, only to find themselves in the middle of a ferocious bombing raid during which they sheltered with hundreds of others in the nearby Underground station at Warwick Avenue, where seven-year-old Joan felt a deep pride in the courage and fortitude of those who took refuge there. 'I remember the air raids,' she told Brandreth, 'and Nanny zipping Jackie and me into our siren suits and taking us into the bowels of the Underground, which was always jolly, people with mouth organs, singing songs.' She was also vividly impressed by the kindness of the air-raid wardens and policemen in charge, and the frightened but courteous and indomitable public, who shared their flasks of tea and handfuls of biscuits. The memory of their calm fortitude kindled in her breast an English patriotism that was to last all her life.

Joe's sister Pauline was now married and living in Portsea Hall in Portsea Place, an elegant eight-storey mansion block just off the busy Edgware Road near Marble Arch. She persuaded Joe and Elsa that it would be safer if they and the girls spent each night in her block's own air-raid shelter in the basement as the Nazi aircraft roared overhead, the bombs exploded, and the buildings crashed down around them. One morning Joe, Elsa and the girls went back to Alexandra Court and found to their horror that their flat had been destroyed completely. For a while they moved in permanently with Pauline, and eight-year-old Joan began at yet another school a few streets away in Gloucester Place, her first co-educational school. As she picked her way to school each morning, through the rubble and broken glass of the bombed-out streets, she would collect interesting pieces of German shrapnel. At school she launched her lifelong career of amusing the boys by drawing cheeky cartoons of Adolf Hitler and singing a cockney song that began, ''Oo's this geezer 'itler? 'Oo's 'e fink 'e is?' Another of her specialities was to goose-step around the playground pretending to have a silly little black moustache and trilling a popular bawdy ditty about the Nazis' testicles, which she warbled to the tune of 'Colonel Bogey':

Hitler has only got one ball.
Goering has two but very small.
Himmler's are something sim'lar
But Goebbels has no balls at all.

Yet behind the girlish bravado Joan was so frightened by the noise and terror of life in London that she could not sleep unless the light was left on. Elsa, Jackie and the nanny were all so nervous too that Joe decided to move them as far from the war as possible. He chose the quiet seaside resort of Ilfracombe in north Devon, a hundred and sixty miles away, where his sister Lalla and her husband lived, and there rented a flat above a seafront sweet shop. It was a wise choice. Thousands of other children from the cities were evacuated to the Ilfracombe area that year and although the Luftwaffe regularly and heavily bombed the docks and factories of Cardiff and Swansea on the other side of the Bristol Channel, Ilfracombe itself was never attacked. Joan had to start as a day girl at yet another school, Hereford House, a devoutly Christian establishment for 'girls of gentlefolk' that was run by spinster sisters Doris and Ethel Theake, but here she quickly made friends and began to enjoy the peace of the timeless English seaside. Despite all the wartime shortages and rationing – no fruit, few sweets, little sugar or milk – she found magic in Ilfracombe, where she and Jackie loved running on the downs, playing on the sandy beaches, and climbing across the rocks by the sea. Gilbert Ralph, an old soldier whose parents had lived near the Collinses, remembered in 2002 that Joan was very pretty and that she and Jackie were nice girls who were always laughing and playing outside with friends.

Joe was rejected by the army as unfit for service because of his chronic stomach ulcers and carried on working in London, moving his agency into new offices in Regent Street and joining a *Dad's Army* Home Guard platoon which was lucky enough to have its headquarters nearby at the luxurious Grosvenor House hotel. Cleverly he managed to lay his hands on enough black-market petrol to drive down to Devon every two or three weeks to see the family in Ilfracombe, where Joan was doing well at school. She hated most sports, especially netball and lacrosse, but was above average at drama, English and art. Elsa and Lalla opened a small drinking club, the Odd Spot, for the soldiers stationed in Ilfracombe and for most of the war Joe's family lived in peace and far from danger. But one price that his daughters paid was that they rarely saw him. For two vital, formative years they barely had a father at all and deep down they felt that he had rejected them.

As the girls grew up they developed completely different looks and characters. Both inherited their father's impatience and quick temper, both were good at English, and both wrote stories from the age of eight – Joan's had titles such as *The Little Ballerinas* and *The Gypsy and the Prince* – but otherwise they had little in common. Joan was tiny – she was never to grow taller than 5ft 5ins – and an extrovert who loved dressing up, showing off, flicking through film magazines, writing letters to famous actors, collecting their autographs, sticking their photographs in her bulging scrapbook, and using her little detective kit to fingerprint everyone who came to the flat. She was so restless and full of energy that Elsa called her 'Miss Perpetual Motion', though she was never prepared to help with any housework and told her mother imperiously that that was *her* job. Jackie was much bigger, quieter, more sensitive and thoughtful, a loner who hated children's parties, preferred to read Enid Blyton, and decided at the age of eight not only to write stories but to become an author. Indeed, she began to make money from her writing by copying dirty limericks into her diary and charging her schoolfriends to read them. 'I love my daughters,' wrote Joe in his autobiography, 'but I am not the kind of parent who deludes himself that his children are superior to everyone else's. I did not think of them as outstanding in any way.' Even as late as 1986, when Joan was at the peak of her worldwide fame in *Dynasty* and Jackie had written a dozen international bestsellers, he confessed that he did not think they were particularly special. 'We were never told we were beautiful, clever, funny, witty or good people,' Joan told Peregrine Worsthorne of the *Sunday Telegraph* sadly in 1994.

After a year in Ilfracombe Joe moved his family yet again, this time to Brighton, where he rented a fifth-floor flat on the seafront so that they could again be near his mother, who was now in her seventies. Yet again ten-year-old Joan had to settle into a new school, an all-girls establishment called St Wilfred's, but she was able to join the Brownies. It was here that she started going to the cinema at least once a week and finally decided that she wanted to be an actress – even though she fainted with terror in the middle of one hospital movie when a doctor advanced on his patient wielding a huge syringe. Already she knew how to flirt with men and in one school concert – in which she wore a short flouncy frock and sang a cheeky little French song – she turned her back on the audience and waggled her bottom. The men in the audience cheered. She was to waggle her bottom at men for more than fifty years.

In 1944 Joe realised that the war was nearly over and Elsa, Joan and Jackie returned to the West End of London to live with him again at last in yet another rented mansion-block flat, at 37 Portland Court in Great Portland Street, just north of Oxford Street. They were there when Germany finally surrendered on 8 May 1945 and the streets of London exploded with joyful relief instead of bombs. The city went wild and the Collinses joined the ecstatic crowds in Trafalgar Square and outside Buckingham Palace to cheer the royal family on the balcony above.

Joe still wished that he had a son and Joan tried to make up for being a girl by going to Arsenal football matches with him on Saturday afternoons, attempting to look enthusiastic by wearing the club scarf and twirling a soccer rattle. But she was bored rigid by the game and frozen on the icy winter terraces, so when Elsa became pregnant again she, too, prayed that the baby would be a boy. Still determined at the age of twelve to go onto the stage, she persuaded Joe to send her to the Cone-Ripman theatrical day school in London, at Chiswick, where the pupils spent the mornings in normal classes and the afternoons acting, dancing, singing and learning elocution. Joe tried constantly to dissuade her from becoming an actress because he knew how insecure a profession it was and doubted whether she would ever succeed, but almost immediately she was chosen to appear in a small part in her first professional West End play as one of the three children in *A Doll's House* by Henrik Ibsen in a minor production at the small Arts Theatre. The entire Collins, Bessant and Assenheim dynasties, from proud Granny Hettie to all the aunts and great-aunts, turned out to see the girl's triumphant first night, but the third night was a disaster: she missed her cue because she was engrossed in reading *Girls' Crystal* magazine backstage and was sacked in tears by the enraged director, John Fernald. She then persuaded her father to send her to Cone-Ripman's new boarding school in an old manor house at Tring in Buckinghamshire, twenty-five miles north-west of London, but she hated boarding, the food, having to make her own bed and clean her room, and she was disgusted by the sexual crudity of the other girls, and after just six weeks she begged her parents to take her home again.

Elsa's baby – a boy, praise be – was born on 1 May 1946 at Queen Charlotte's Hospital, Hammersmith, named William Richard, and was inevitably always called Bill. Joan agreed that he was adorable and he became immediately his father's favourite child. 'In analysing the success of Jackie and me,' Joan told the *TV Times* in 1988, 'a lot of it stems in some strange way from the daddy who never really thought much of either of us girls. We were just a bunch of scruffy kids as far as my father was concerned.' As soon as Bill started talking he gave Joan her family nickname, Dodo, which was the closest he could get to saying 'Joan'.

Now that Joe and Elsa had a third child – and Joan and Jackie were twelve and eight – they needed a bigger place to live where each girl could have a room of her own. They found it less than a mile away: a large, shady basement flat with four bedrooms, two bathrooms and two big reception rooms in an imposing, elegant, seven-storey, honey-coloured block at 15 Harley House in the Marylebone Road near Madame Tussaud's famous waxworks exhibition. With its wrought-iron gates, ornate stonework, hallway chandeliers and full-time porters, it was the most impressive of all the flats that Joe had rented, yet because the rental was officially controlled he had to pay only £10 a week – a tiny amount for such a stylish flat, about £260 a week in 2007 values. To make it even more of a bargain, it was just a hundred and fifty yards from the York Gate entrance to the huge green open spaces of Regent's Park, where the family could enjoy hundreds of fresh, leafy acres of formal gardens, trim walkways, fountains, ponds, bridges, boating lake, bandstand and fields for hockey, netball and tennis. After years of roaming southern England, Joe had at last found his family a permanent, stylish nest where he was to live for nearly thirty years, and half a mile away he found an excellent school for all three of his children, Francis Holland, at Clarence Gate.

Joan and Jackie started there at the end of 1946, strolling each day from Harley House in their grey blazers, grey felt hats, and pink-and-white candy-striped dresses in the summer – or grey skirts in winter – along the quiet outer circle of Regent's Park with its scurrying squirrels and strutting pigeons, or along the elegant row of Nash buildings on York Terrace, or along the busy, noisy Marylebone Road past Madame

Tussaud's and Baker Street Underground Station. Francis Holland was a genteel, expensive, terribly correct Church of England day school, founded on religious principles by a canon of Canterbury in 1878 and named after him. It had been badly damaged by bombs during the war and dusty workmen were still crawling all over the building to repair it, but the hundred and eighty girls were still expected to wear hats and gloves at all times in public, to have immaculate manners, to speak with perfect en-un-ci-a-tion, and to eat pudding with a fork – *not* a vulgar spoon, thank you *very* much. 'The other girls were all very proper and had fathers who were doctors or bank managers and they spent their weekends in the country,' said Jackie in an interview with Pamela Coleman of *The Times* in 1994. 'We were a showbiz family and so we were different. My homelife involved mixing with people who were jugglers, acrobats, singers and comedians – the acts my father managed.' The school song was Rudyard Kipling's 'Children's Song' from *Puck of Pook's Hill*, which begins:

> *Father in Heaven, who lovest all,*
> *O help Thy children when they call,*
> *That they may build from age to age*
> *An undefiled heritage.*

'It was quite a strict but happy school,' I was told by one of Jackie's contemporaries, Julia Campion, who joined the school three years after Joan left. Sally Adams, who was two forms lower than Joan, told me that 'the teaching was very old-fashioned. God was very central, all the books in the library were locked away, and we had to read poetry aloud.' The school motto was adapted from Psalm 144 – 'That Our Daughters May Be As The Polished Corners Of The Temple' – and its Old Girls still call themselves Polished Corners. 'That gentility bred people of great character, resolve and strength, like Joan Collins,' I was told in 2006 by the headmistress, Vivienne Durham. 'Old Francis Holland girls all look beautiful, immaculate and well groomed.'

Except Jackie. 'She was a quiet, neat little girl with pigtails and freckles until she reached the age of twelve or thirteen,' I was told by her contemporary Dr Barbara Simcock (née Truscoe). 'She grew in height very quickly and was much taller than Joan, ending up at least 5ft 10ins. She took to wearing her hair in a long, thick pony-tail and seemed too big for her clothes. At that time I was going through a scruffy, bolshie and mildly miserable time myself and would occasionally get sent out of class for some minor misdemeanour only to find Jackie had also been sent out of her class. On one occasion we went down to the girls' cloakroom to have a chat and she began to change out of her clothes and was down to her bra and shorts when we heard some wolf whistles and, on looking up, saw three or four men peeping down into the cloakroom through the pavement-level oriel windows. She was only thirteen but very well-developed and we had a good laugh together. Like me she was bored in class but for different reasons and I believe that she often skipped school and went to see a movie instead. She read a lot of books but not school books and she didn't like exams.' As Jackie grew older she became increasingly untidy, unhappy and rebellious, but perhaps the whistling lechers were to inspire the first of all her future raunchy novels.

Joan enjoyed her three years at Francis Holland much more than Jackie and said later that they were some of the best years of her life. 'It was wonderful to be in a school where I was actually able to spend more than one term or a term and a half,' she said in a speech when she returned to the school as its most famous old girl to open its new swimming pool in 1999. 'We did have a lot of fun here and I really had a wonderful time.' Asked by one of the pupils what values she had picked up at Francis Holland, she replied: 'Discipline, hard work, and nothing much happens unless you do it for yourself.' In later life she may also have taken rather too literally the last line of the school song:

Teach us delight in simple things . . .
And love to all men 'neath the sun.

At thirteen Joan was gawky, spotty and still wearing pigtails. 'I wasn't pretty when I was young,' she said once. 'I always wanted to be older.' One of her classmates, Belinda Poolman, now Webster, told me that 'she wasn't especially good-looking at school. She had very thin plaits, in fact very thin hair, but she became better and better looking as she grew older. She invited me to her flat for her thirteenth birthday party and I remember distinctly seeing a photograph of her on the wall and thinking how striking she looked in it. The camera loved her.' Joan was already trying to look as good as possible, loved clothes and fashion, and was reprimanded for coming to school one day with forbidden frills along the hem of her grey school tunic. 'Wartime skirts were very short because of the shortage of materials,' I was told by Rona Blythe (née Cove-Smith), who was in the same thirteen-girl form as Joan. 'When the New Look arrived in 1947 dresses suddenly went down to ballerina length and the next day Joan arrived at school with a circle of white material, possibly from a sheet, inserted below her skirt to make it six or eight inches longer. That was typical of her. She was very fashion conscious.' She was also 'terribly sophisticated and used to wear make-up', Mrs Blythe's sister, Dr Penny Newall-Price, who was three years younger than Joan, told me. From an early age Joan was extremely conscious of the need to protect her skin from the cold and grime of London. 'My mother had the most wonderful English skin, and she had me putting cream on my face from about thirteen or fourteen,' she said years later. She always loved chocolate but to keep her complexion clear of spots 'she held an auction to sell her sweet coupons', said Mrs Webster. Perhaps it was a deficiency of sugar that made Joan faint regularly during morning assembly. 'During prayers she used to go down with a terrible thud,' said Mrs Webster, 'and we'd all think "There goes Joan Collins again!"'

Joan quickly made friends at Francis Holland. 'She was very popular,' I was told by another of her classmates, Diana Truscoe, now Hall. 'We were best friends for all the three years we were there. There was nobody else like her in the class. She was great fun, not timid at all, and good at swimming. We were both wickeder than the others but the teachers still liked her.' One teacher, Beryl Lester, told me that 'Joan was notorious, such a bright spark, so full of beans, such a nice girl with such a pleasant manner. We were all very fond of her, and she was also popular with the girls.' Joan was 'lovely, kind and very friendly', said Dr Newall-Price.

Her headmistress, Miss Ivy Joslin, who was renowned for being strict but also for her great sense of humour, remembered that Joan was 'both clever and charming, perhaps a little naughty', and one of Joan's classmates, Beryl Isaacs, told the *Daily Mirror* in 1985 that 'Joan was always game for a laugh and she had us all in giggles on school outings because she pulled such funny faces behind the teacher's back. By fourteen she was a real beauty and full of confidence. By fifteen she was coming to school in make-up and tight sweaters. In those days none of the other girls would have dared do that at such a posh school.' The first time Joan wore make-up her father yelled at her to wash it off because he hated to think that she was growing up so quickly. He was right to be apprehensive: she had suddenly realised that boys fancied her when the pimply newsboy from the local corner shop asked her out for a date and she told him not to be cheeky. 'She had an early interest in boys and wasn't at all shy with men,' said Belinda Webster. 'She was very keen on the English actor Maxwell Reed and stuck his photograph on the inside of her desk.'

Joan and Diana Truscoe would go to the cinema two or three times a week and she was stunned by the performances of Laurence Olivier and Ralph Richardson in *Henry IV, Part I* at the New Theatre in St Martin's Lane. She and Belinda Poolman loved reading and went together regularly to the public library, where she developed a taste for sexy books, one of them *Forever Amber* by Kathleen Winsor, from which she read choice paragraphs to the other girls. 'She was sharp rather than academic but she was very good at English,' said Diana Hall. 'It was her best subject at school. If we were in a boring lesson she'd write chapter one of a novel and pass it on to me and I'd write chapter two, though we never got very far.' Belinda Poolman told me that 'everyone thought Joan would be a writer because she was terrific at essays. One, about the school fête, was so good that it was put in the school magazine' in January 1947, when Joan was thirteen. Before long she was producing her own Upper Fourth Form magazine, which she called *Much-Binding-in-the-Form* after the title of the famous radio comedy *Much-Binding-in-the-Marsh*. 'I thought that was frightfully witty,' she told the Francis Holland girls in her speech in 1999, but 'I always knew she would be an actress,' Diana Hall told me. 'She always wanted to be an actress and she was in all the mid-term, end-of-term and Christmas plays.' The younger girls used 'to long for the plays because she was so good in them', said Dr Newall-Price. Beryl Lester and Rona Blythe thought straight away that Joan would become an actress and Ivy Joslin quickly spotted her thespian potential – perhaps even as a Shakespearean actress, she said – and encouraged her to appear in as many plays as possible. 'We acted together a great deal in school and class plays,' Belinda Webster told me. 'In the first I was Mary Tudor and Joan was Elizabeth I and I remember she jumped up and down excitedly and said "she's my favourite queen". She played the lead in J. M. Barrie's play *Quality Street*, Phoebe, a girl who was still unmarried at thirty. She was very good in that.' Joan also distinguished herself in July 1948 in the part of a Dominican nun, Sister Marcella, in *The Cradle Song* by the Spanish dramatists Gregorio and Maria Martinez Sierra, and was acclaimed in January 1950 for her performance in Euripides' *The Alcestis*, in which she played the Ancient Greek queen who volunteers to die instead of her beloved husband Admetus but is rescued from Death by Heracles and brought back to life. 'It is not easy to interpret the characters in this play, since the Greek conception of tragedy is so far removed from our own,' reported the school magazine. 'She was very moving in that,' said Belinda Webster. 'She was a good actress then – much better then than later on, to be absolutely frank. And she was very ambitious. I remember us sitting together on the steps up to the rostrum in the assembly hall and she suddenly blurted out: "One day, Belinda, I am going to be a world-famous actress." I didn't laugh because I saw from the serious look on her face that she really meant it. She told me her father was dead set against her going into acting. "So I am going to do it all on my own," she said defiantly.'

In June 1949 she sat her final examinations at Francis Holland for the School Certificate, which were much more difficult than the equivalent British GCSE exams are today. Not only were the papers much more testing, it was also not possible to take one subject at a time, as it is now: to win a School Certificate a candidate had to pass within the space of a couple of weeks at least five specified subjects, including English language and literature, mathematics, a foreign language and a general paper that tested a broader range of knowledge. Should you fail just one of those subjects you failed the entire exam, no matter how high were your marks in all the other subjects. Not surprisingly, given Joan's shambolic schooling, she failed the exam even though her headmistress had said she was clever, and she left Francis Holland without any qualifications. 'She wasn't stupid, she just enjoyed other things,' said Rona Blythe, and Belinda Webster reckoned that 'even though she was very good at English she failed the English exam because she wrote six essays instead of answering all the questions. She shouldn't have failed her School Certificate. She wasn't a fool.'

Joe tried to persuade her to take a secretarial course and become his assistant, but she was adamant that she wanted to try to enter

Britain's most distinguished theatrical college, the Royal Academy of Dramatic Art (RADA). Convinced that she would fail the RADA entrance exam too, he allowed her to apply. For her audition she chose a simple white dress with blue polka dots, a flirty Cleopatra speech from George Bernard Shaw's *Caesar and Cleopatra*, and a speech from Thornton Wilder's *Our Town*. When she saw who the judges were – John Gielgud, Flora Robson, and several other distinguished actors as well as RADA's principal, Sir Kenneth Barnes – she was all but paralysed with terror. Afterwards, convinced that she had failed, she went off on holiday with Elsa and Jackie to stay with her Aunt Lalla and Uncle Godfrey at their flat in the South of France, at Cannes, where she consoled herself by wearing one of the naughty new black bikinis, sunbathing, swimming, window-shopping, flirting with and teasing all the boys who suddenly seemed to notice her, and falling in love for the first time. He was a curly-haired French boy called Bernard whom she met when she bought an ice-cream cone at his father's shop, but neither could speak the other's language and they went no further than to walk hand-in-hand along the beach. It was then too that she fell in love with the South of France. 'It was fantastically beautiful,' she told David Wigg of the *Daily Mail* in 2002. 'There was no pollution, there were the beaches with the umbrellas like they are today at the Carlton and the Martinez hotels, but they weren't covered with millions of people. I thought it was the most wonderful place I had ever been.' She was to love the Côte d'Azur, eventually to buy two houses there, and to return to it every year.

Back in London Joan was ecstatic to receive a letter offering her a place at RADA. Her father was not only astonished but also immensely proud and at last decided to support and encourage her dream of becoming an actress and to pay her RADA fees. In her second autobiography, *Second Act*, she claimed that more than a thousand candidates had applied to join RADA that year. In fact, no more than two hundred and fifty had done so and Joan was lucky that the academy had decided to accept as many as two hundred new pupils because it was desperately short of funds and needed their fees. 'RADA was at that period still a private school,' the academy's official historian, Peter Fiddick, told me, 'and almost totally dependent on students' fees for its income. In the immediate post-war period, when Joan Collins was there, the financial situation was worse than ever, since the academy's theatre was destroyed in an air-raid in 1941 and after the war every available penny and money-raising effort went into creating a rebuilding fund. And given post-war shortages of material, the government building licence wasn't granted until 1951, and the new theatre was not opened until 1954. So Joan was there when the place was in a pretty hand-to-mouth state and very crowded. Closure had been faced more than once, and since Sir Kenneth Barnes' first response when finances were hard was to pack in as many fee-paying students as possible, more than two hundred students were packed into a site that started out as two Georgian family town-houses. Nowadays, considerably expanded, it takes just thirty-four acting students a year.'

No matter that Joan had perhaps been extremely lucky, she had won a place at the world's most famous acting academy. It was the first small step up a steep ladder that was to take her to the very top of the glitzy world that she had always dreamed about.

CHAPTER TWO

RADA, RANK AND REED

{ 1949–1952 }

Joan joined RADA in October 1949 when she was sixteen and a half. Among her fellow students at the academy – in Central London's Gower Street – were twenty-year-old Gerald Harper, later to star on television in *Adam Adamant Lives!* and *Hadleigh*; sixteen-year-old David McCallum, who was to appear in scores of films and TV programmes, most notably *The Man From U.N.C.L.E.*; and eighteen-year-old Margaret Tyzack, who would play numerous regal ladies on television, among them Queen Anne, George V's Queen Mary, and Elizabeth II.

The students were encouraged to study plays by Shakespeare, Marlowe, Johnson and Shaw; to read theatrical biographies, and to rehearse and perform two plays a term, culminating in performances on the academy's little stage at the end of each term that were attended by the principal, Sir Kenneth Barnes. Diane Cilento, who joined RADA at the age of seventeen during Joan's last term, recalled in her autobiography that performances were often interrupted by Sir Kenneth's loud whispers of concern about his dog, Marsha:

SIR KENNETH to Sargeant, the doorman: Did she *do* it?
SARGEANT: Yes, Sir Kennuf.
SIR KENNETH: *Both* of them?
SARGEANT: I'm not sure if it was both of them, Sir Kennuf.
SIR KENNETH (vehemently): Then take her out *again* and make *sure* this time!'

The students were encouraged to go to the theatre as often as possible, where Joan was excited to see the stars of the age – Laurence Olivier,

John Gielgud, Ralph Richardson, Edith Evans, Michael Redgrave – and was mesmerised by Richard Burton's performance in Christopher Fry's play *The Lady's Not For Burning*. She thought that he, his eyes and voice were so gorgeous that she queued at the stage door afterwards for his autograph, saw the play several times, and wrote him a fan letter asking successfully for an autographed photograph, never dreaming that six years later she would be playing opposite him in the film *Sea Wife*. Back at RADA the students were taught to talk in the posh, clipped, perfectly en-un-ci-a-ted accent that Joan was to adopt for the rest of her life. They were taught to breathe properly, make up, walk, mime, dance, fence – even how to sit on a chair – and among the plays in which Joan had parts were *Macbeth*, in which she played the third witch; *The Merchant of Venice* (Shylock's daughter, Jessica); *The Taming of the Shrew* (a very small part as the widow); Noël Coward's *Present Laughter* (Joanna); and Coward's *Private Lives*, in which she was the French maid, Louise, though she hankered to play the lead, Amanda – a role she was eventually to achieve forty years later in the West End and on Broadway. Sir Ian Holm, who was a student at RADA just after Joan left, wrote in his autobiography that the quality of tuition there was not particularly high but added: 'I do believe that some kind of grounding is important, and going to stage school – as opposed to starting at the bottom, for example by sweeping floors in a local repertory company – was as good a foundation as any other.'

The RADA building was cold, draughty and chaotic, with dreadful plumbing, but Joan loved student life. 'She was very friendly, honest, upfront and straightforward,' I was told by her classmate Margaret Tyzack. 'We hung out a bit and I met all her family. Her mother was lovely but her father was a bit strict. One night I went out with them to a dance and Joan gave me her big earrings to keep in my pocket until we got there because she thought he would disapprove of them.' At RADA Joan discovered her power over men, beginning with the actor Roger Livesey's son, Tony. She adopted the dark look of the beautiful, intense, twenty-two-year-old French singer and actress Juliette Gréco, the sultry bohemian darling of Paris's post-war Left Bank intellectuals, and grew her fringe low over her eyes, circled them with thick black pencil, and wore a ponytail, black polo-neck sweaters, short tight black skirts, black stockings, black ballet shoes, huge gold earrings and a jangle of bracelets. Men were stunned. 'She was like a beautiful little Labrador puppy, coltish and young,' said Gerald Harper. David McCallum agreed: 'She was really the embodiment of everything female that I'd ever thought of. She was gorgeous in every respect.' When a photographer from the Rosemary Chance modelling agency was looking for girls to model teenage clothes and illustrate short stories for *Woman* and *Woman's Own* magazines he chose Joan as one of them. 'She fell in love at least once a week,' said her old schoolfriend Beryl Isaacs, and Belinda Poolman, who followed Joan to RADA a term later, said that 'she had a devastating, hypnotic effect on all the men. RADA was full of good-looking women but Joan was one of those whom men take one look at and go crazy. She had them dangling on a string. All the boys at RADA chased her. They fetched her coffee, carried her bags and rushed to open doors for her. She loved the adoration.'

'Sex can be the best and the worst thing in the world,' Joan told Lynda Lee-Potter in 2002. 'It can be wonderful and it can be frightful. My mother always told me it was ghastly. I gradually discovered it wasn't necessarily so.' Her mother often warned her that men want 'only one thing', and in those days a nice half-Jewish girl would never 'go all the way' until she was married, so Joan apparently remained a virgin until she was nearly nineteen, but she had so many boyfriends in the time she was at RADA that she spent most of it dreaming about the current beloved rather than working. She had no interest in men who pursued her but was always the pursuer herself, choosing moody, difficult men who played hard to get, chasing them ruthlessly, and eventually dumping them with callous regularity. It was, she believed, a classic example of a girl with a father complex who kept trying to prove to herself that she was irresistibly attractive.

While she was still sixteen she tried desperately to lose her virginity to a gorgeous twenty-two-year-old blond called Barry but despite several torrid bedroom encounters he failed to come up to the mark, beat and bruised her in his frustration, and the deed was never done. Typically Joan blamed herself for not being desirable or lovable enough to make him want her, but eventually she discovered that he was homosexual. Two more of her admirers that year were the up-and-coming twenty-nine-year-old British film star Anthony Steel and a nineteen-year-old American Air Force serviceman, Larry Hagman, who had recently been appearing onstage with his mother, Mary Martin, in the musical *South*

Pacific and was later to achieve worldwide fame in the TV series *Dallas*. Joan was 'so breathtakingly beautiful that I thought she made Elizabeth Taylor look like a boy', wrote Hagman in his autobiography fifty years later. 'I was a lark for her, since she normally dated older men, in their twenties and thirties. But we had some fun. I also went out with her sister Jackie, who was just as stunning. I never got anywhere with them, but boy, they were lots of fun.'

Had he known that Jackie was only just thirteen he would have run for the hills, for by now she was jailbait personified: four inches taller than Joan's petite 5ft 5ins, sexually more mature, astonishingly shapely, and much more knowing and streetwise. She looked eighteen and jeered at Joan's prim behaviour when she was out on a date, calling her 'Goody Two Shoes'. Feeling a misfit at home and at school, Jackie had started smoking, breaking the rules, playing truant from Francis Holland, wearing thick make-up and high heels, sneaking out of the flat at night, camouflaging her bed with a bolster under the blankets, and climbing out of her window to meet men and enjoy Soho discos and nightclubs and the bright lights of Piccadilly and Leicester Square. She drank, smoked marijuana, even tried cocaine, and was once nearly arrested by two policemen who thought she was a runaway. Eventually they sent her back home and luckily did not contact her parents. 'I was a "try anything girl",' she told Pamela Coleman. 'If I'd been growing up in the 1990s rather than the fifties I'd probably be dead by now.' In the summer of 1951, before she was fourteen, she went with Joan to Cannes for a holiday with their Auntie Lalla, had a fling with an American sailor from the USS *Coral Sea*, and Elsa made her write to the unsuspecting matelot to confess how young she was. Already she loved everything American: she claimed at school to be American, that her father was a spy, wrote fan letters to American film stars like Tony Curtis and Rock Hudson and covered her bedroom walls with their pictures, and she discovered early and relished American novels by Mickey Spillane, Harold Robbins and Henry Miller, the sort of raunchy books that she was later to write herself. Her fling in Cannes with the sailor was only the first of several steamy encounters with American servicemen, though she also found time to step out with the teenage Michael Winner, the future film director, who recalled nearly fifty years later how 'unbelievably beautiful and fresh' Joan was. When Joe and Elsa discovered how wild Jackie had become they locked her in her room and burned her trendy clothes, but they failed to tame her and she escaped time and again. 'I was utterly uncontrollable,' she confessed.

Joan was remarkably staid, naïve and virginal by comparison but she too loved dancing and West End nightclubs, especially Humphrey Lyttelton's jazz club at 100 Oxford Street, where she would dance with a young art gallery assistant and up-and-coming jazz singer, George Melly. She and her latest boyfriend, John Turner, were even photographed wearing jeans and plaid shirts at a jazz party aboard a Thames river boat for an article in *Picture Post* magazine that described them as 'the couple who dress "très Jazz"'. She claimed that her father used to spy on her, peering suspiciously into nightclubs to check up on her. In fact he was now so keen to help her succeed on the stage that in March 1950 he started a repertory company at the Palace Theatre in Maidstone, the Eros Players, to give her more experience. For six months the Players presented several productions with which Joan helped out, doing odd jobs, painting scenery, and for six weeks during RADA's summer vacation acting as assistant stage manager, for which Joe paid her £3–10s a week, the equivalent of about £85 in 2007. One of her jobs was to lower the curtain several times at the end of a play, a task that ended in disaster one night during a performance of *Dangerous Corner* by J. B. Priestley when she found that she could not lower it the final time and left the embarrassed cast of six stranded onstage in front of a sniggering audience. She understudied several parts and in the last production of the season, in September, appeared in a small role as the maid in the Terence Rattigan comedy *French Without Tears*. The Eros Players were not particularly successful and Joe lost money on the venture, but it allowed him to buy a half-page advertisement for Joan in the autumn edition of the thick theatrical casting directory *Spotlight* with a big, flirty photograph of her on page 1055 and a line saying that she was with a Maidstone repertory company. A leading agent, Bill Watts, was looking for a fresh face to play the lead in a film about beauty queens, spotted the photograph, thought Joan looked great, and asked if she could attend an audition on the next Wednesday afternoon at a time when she would normally be on her way to Maidstone to appear that evening. To allow her to take the audition Joe simply cancelled the Eros Players' performance that night and refunded everyone who had bought tickets. Joan went to the audition at Shepperton studios to compete with several other girls, among them Anne Heywood (who was to go on to make more than thirty films) and Jean Marsh (who was to create and star in the TV series *Upstairs, Downstairs*) and although they failed to win the lead part in the film, *Lady Godiva Rides Again*, all three were given small roles as runners-up in the beauty contest. So was a pretty, twenty-four-year-old brunette, Ruth Ellis, who was to shoot her unfaithful boyfriend four years later and to be hanged for murder in 1955, the last woman to suffer the death penalty in Britain. Joan's career was launched at last and Joe disbanded the Eros Players: they had served their purpose.

Lady Godiva Rides Again was a cheery, very English romp about a competition to choose a girl to play the legendary naked lady of Coventry in a medieval pageant and maybe to win a film contract that might make her a star. It was shot in May 1951 at Shepperton studios and Folkestone town hall with a cast of highly accomplished comic actors: Dora Bryan, George Cole, Diana Dors, Stanley Holloway, Sid James, Kay Kendall, Dennis Price and Alastair Sim. Joan appeared only very briefly as one of the beauty competition contestants, had no dialogue and was not credited, but she looked so good on the screen that Bill Watts quickly found other jobs for her, and she may well have learned a valuable lesson by taking to heart two lines from the film when Kay Kendall, playing the daughter of cockney newsagent Stanley Holloway, remarks that 'you don't always have to have talent to be a film star, you know, Dad' and Holloway replies: 'No, but you have to look as though you have.' Joan was never to be a great actress but she was always to look and behave like a star.

Since Joe specialised as an agent in variety and music hall he knew that he was not the right man to handle Joan's career in theatre and films and handed her over to Bill Watts, who signed her up to make a short cinema advertisement for Swedish chocolates, for which she was paid £5, which was worth about £111 in 2007 – and in the rest of this book equivalent 2007 currency values will be shown in square brackets, thus [£111]. Watts followed up with another cinema advertisement, for a local gas board, and parts in two more movies for Associated British Films: the first a small role as a Greek maid in *The Woman's Angle*, for which she was paid £50 for two days' work [£1,110]; and a slightly more substantial role in *Judgment Deferred*, playing the part of 'a once-beautiful girl being dragged downhill by drink and degradation', the first of Joan's many early parts as a bad girl, for which she earned £300 [£6,663].

In an article that she wrote for the Sunday newspaper the *People* seven years later she made no mention at all of the generous and loving help that her father had given her to kick-start her career, pretending that she had paid for the *Spotlight* advertisement herself. She said nothing about it either in her first autobiography nearly thirty years later: nothing about the Eros Players or her six weeks as an assistant stage manager or Joe's advertisement in *Spotlight*. Instead, she claimed that Bill Watts had seen her photograph in *Woman's Own*, telephoned her, and promised that he could make her a film star. At first, she said, she resisted his blandishments because at RADA she had been made to believe that the theatre was the only place for a proper actress. Indeed, one of her RADA reports, criticising the weakness of her voice, warned that she had to learn to project it much better if she was to work in the theatre, 'otherwise it is "the Films" for her and that would be such a pity'. Watts, however, persuaded her that a few film roles would help rather than damage her theatre career and she agreed that he should become her agent. 'I always thought that film might be her first choice and that possibly she wasn't going to be a classical actress,' Margaret Tyzack told me. Joe must have been deeply upset that Joan seemed to be so ungrateful for his help and it was not until eight years after his death that she told the true story in her second autobiography, *Second Act*, in 1996, and said how generous he had been and how grateful she was.

Joan, Elsa and Jackie went off to Cannes again for a summer holiday with Auntie Lalla and Joan fell even more in love with the Côte d'Azur, especially Juan-les-Pins, which throbbed with jazz clubs, musicians playing in the square and good-looking boys, and she swore that one day she would buy a house somewhere along this magical coast. Back in England she did a film test at Elstree for *The Red Beret* with the diminutive American actor Alan Ladd, who was so short that when they were filmed together he had to wear high heels and she had to walk in a trench. She did not get the part.

Her role in *Judgment Deferred* was very small but she still had to ask RADA for twelve days' leave to shoot the film. Sir Kenneth Barnes was adamant that she could not make movies and stay on at the college. Films were not for serious actors, he insisted: serious actors went into the theatre, so she made the film surreptitiously by pretending to be ill.

It was a very bad movie indeed – slow, dreary and quite unbelievable – in which she played the teenage mistress of a rich, ruthless drug dealer who has used her to plant drugs on her father and frame him for a crime for which he has been sent to prison. The only enjoyment to be derived from the film are two appearances by the music hall singer Bud Flanagan and the band leader Edmundo Ros playing themselves. Joan's melodramatic performance was embarrassingly stagey and her voice thin and squeaky, but because she looked moody, pouty and sulky the reviewers suddenly hailed her as 'Britain's best bet since Jean Simmons' and 'England's answer to Ava Gardner and Marilyn Monroe'. The weekly paper *Reveille* gushed that Joan 'has the come-hither eyes of Ava Gardner, the sultry look of Lauren Bacall, a Jane Russell figure and more sex appeal at her age than any other film actress I've met'. The British Photographers' Association voted her The Most Beautiful Girl in Films and Joe reacted typically by saying he was amazed: 'She's a good-looking girl but nothing special,' he said. The directors Basil Dearden and Michael Relph, who had recently made *The Blue Lamp, Cage of Gold, Pool of London* and *Kind Hearts and Coronets*, disagreed and auditioned her for their next major film. 'Bill Watts specialised in having a stable of pretty girls, so one rather knew what to expect from Bill Watts girls,' Relph told Susan Crimp and Patricia Burstein for their book *Hollywood Sisters*. 'But Joan had something extra. She was a sensationally beautiful young girl and my partner Basil Dearden was scared off. Joan was very self-possessed, and I think that was what made Basil hesitant. She had an amazing sophistication [and] she was sharp and intelligent. We felt like we were taking a bit of a chance. But I felt she had star quality.'

Dearden and Relph signed her up for £300 [£6,663] to play the juvenile lead in the film, which was titled appropriately *I Believe in You*. She begged Barnes to give her twelve weeks' leave of absence to make the film at Ealing but he was angry that she had deceived him over *Judgment Deferred* and told her bluntly that she had to choose between films or being a proper actress. Bill Watts urged her to choose films and reluctantly she left RADA in 1951 without completing her course. *I Believe in You* was her first big chance and she grabbed it. She played Norma, another squeaky-voiced, teenage, working-class delinquent. Celia Johnson played her probation officer and took Joan under her wing – 'Forget most of what they taught you at RADA, dear,' she said – though privately she thought Joan was 'rather precocious'. The other actors were equally distinguished: a bumbling but kind-hearted Cecil Parker as another probation officer; Godfrey Tearle as a magistrate; twenty-two-year-old Laurence Harvey as one of Norma's spivvy boyfriends; Harry Fowler as another; Sid James as a police sergeant. Today the film seems slow, amateurish and unconvincing but its story of how young working-class tearaways might be rehabilitated seemed important at the time and some of Joan's reviews were so good that she became famous almost overnight. 'Joan Collins makes a tremendous impression as the wayward girl,' wrote Jympson Harman. 'She has a dark, luscious kind of beauty which puts her in the Jane Russell class, but Joan already seems to be an actress of greater ability. On the showing of this first big film part, she looks like the most impressive recruit to British films for many a moon.' The *News of the World* agreed, praising the 'fire and spirit in her acting and that odd combination of allure and mystery that spells eventual world stardom'.

The J. Arthur Rank Organisation, the biggest film conglomerate in Britain, was so impressed by her performance that it offered her a rare five-year contract starting at £50 [£1,110] a week and rising to £100 [£2,220] a week after a year. Diana Dors, a busty, brassy, twenty-year-old platinum blonde who had already made sixteen films and had appeared with Joan in *Lady Godiva Rides Again*, reckoned that Joan's sudden success had gone to her head. One evening Diana and her husband Dennis Hamilton were due to pick Joan up by car at Harley House to go to a charity première. Joan kept them waiting for a while and eventually emerged from the flat with her mother and in a foul temper, Dors reported twenty-seven years later in her autobiography. Joan had had an accident with some nail varnish, and instead of apologising for being late, 'she proceeded to seethe and grumble about it, even blaming her unfortunate mother for the accident. When the poor woman tried to remonstrate with her [Joan] snapped, "Don't sit near my dress, you're creasing it."' Dennis and Diana were not impressed by Joan's performance, reckoned she had become very spoiled, and decided that she needed to be taken down a peg or two so he rang her the next day, pretended to be a cinema manager, invited her to a première, asked if she would make a speech, and promised that she would be picked up by limousine. Joan accepted and on the appointed night, said Dors, the car arrived to pick her up and off she went, accompanied again by her mother. Hamilton then telephoned the cinema's real manager to warn him that a stagestruck young woman was about to arrive at his cinema pretending to be an actress attending a première and that her delusions had been causing a lot of trouble for some time. We can only imagine the rumpus when Joan arrived at the cinema expecting a red carpet, but early the next day Joan telephoned Dors in a rage, accused her angrily of being behind the practical joke, and 'screamed' that Dors should pay for the car or she would sue her. Dors told her to send her the bill: 'The laugh was well worth the price.'

The Rank Organisation's famous Charm School, which taught its young actors and actresses how to dress and behave, had just been disbanded but Joan and her Rank contemporaries were still nagged never to go out in public unless they were carefully groomed, elegantly dressed, fully made-up and wearing gloves. She was also taken in hand by young Laurence Harvey, a Lithuanian South African who had also been to RADA and become a good friend. Joan thought he was polite, amusing and stylish, adored his elegant and expensive lifestyle, developed a crush on him, and introduced him to her parents, who both approved of him. He escorted her around town, took her to fancy restaurants, clubs and parties, taught her about food and wine, and polished up some of the corners that Francis Holland and RADA had left unpolished. But they did not become lovers because Harvey was living as a gigolo in Chester Square with (and off) a rich, ugly, forty-six-year-old actress who was more than twice his age: the ferocious, chain-smoking, curly redheaded Hermione Baddeley, who kept a sharp, jealous eye on him. When he invited Joan to a party at Baddeley's house, without telling Joan that he was Baddeley's lover, the drunken old dragon went for her immediately. 'So this is the one you're seeing, Larry, is it?' she sneered. 'This is "the new Jean Simmons". Let me tell you, my dear, Jean has absolutely nothing to worry about. You don't have her looks. You don't have her talent. And you certainly don't have half the things the newspapers have been saying you have.' Joan burst into tears and ran sobbing from the house. 'That's right,' jeered Baddeley. 'Leave! No guts. That's the trouble with you young ones today: no guts at all.' Harvey ran after Joan, put her in a taxi, returned to the party, and when Baddeley mocked him for his poor taste in girls he hit her hard in front of their guests.

In Baddeley's autobiography, published in 1984 when Joan was the most famous television actress in the world because of *Dynasty*, the old hag wrote loftily: 'There was a film actress, at that time, called Joan Collins who had a "thing" about Larry. She thought she was in love with him, but he wanted to cool the situation and try and find someone else for Joan. We invited a young actor called Maxwell Reed to our party and he and Joan hit it off splendidly. We congratulated each other that everyone was happy again.' In fact Harvey introduced Joan to Reed over dinner at a smart Curzon Street drinking club, La Rue, in November 1951.

Max Reed was a tall, dark, brooding, thirty-two-year-old Anglo-Irish actor, a handsome star of the late 1940s with an American accent and 'lips cruel, thick and wet' as starstruck Joan put it. The Rank publicity department called him 'The Beautiful Beast' and even thirty-six years later, decades after he and Joan had married and had an acrimonious divorce, she admitted that 'he was the most devastatingly beautiful man I'd ever met. And those gorgeous eyes just melted my heart.' Reed had already made fourteen films and he had been one of her movie heart-throbs for several years. She had written him fan letters, mooned over his photographs, stuck one of his pictures up on her bedroom wall, and still at the age of eighteen had a huge crush on him, so when Harvey introduced them she was mesmerised. He had just returned from making a film in Hollywood and bowled her over with his flirty chat, charm and man-of-the-world *savoir-faire*. Joan should have realised right from the start that he was likely to be bad news because with blatant callousness he simply dumped the girl he was dining with that night so that he could join Joan and Harvey at their table. The following Sunday evening he picked her up in his huge, flashy, blue American car and – according to Joan's first autobiography – instead of taking her out to dinner he drove her straight to his fourth-floor flat in the West End, at 14 St George Street, off Hanover Square, and gave her a doctored whisky and coke and a book of pornographic pictures while he had a bath. She passed out, came round vomiting, and realised that he had raped her while she had been unconscious. He then put his penis into her mouth and raped her again before driving her home at 3.30 a.m. In her book Joan claimed that she was terrified and revolted by the experience – yet the very next night she agreed to meet him for dinner at the Caprice because, she explained, she was flattered that he wanted to see her again.

Is it really credible that an eighteen-year-old virgin who has just been raped twice would agree to have dinner with the rapist the very next night, and then marry him six months later, as Joan did? Or is it more likely that she had too much to drink, allowed Reed to ravish her, and was afterwards overcome by remorse and disgust? Joan would not have been the first young girl to cry 'rape!' unjustly. She even reported that during dinner at the Caprice the next night Reed was handsome, witty, kept her in fits of laughter all night, and regaled her with fascinating stories about Hollywood. Afterwards he took her home, gave her a chaste, gentlemanly goodnight kiss, and for the next month they were rarely apart. They went dancing, to theatres, the cinema, boating, and despite his black, sadistic moods she fell in love with him although, she said, she was never to enjoy sex with him. When they made love, she said, it was usually on a sofa in the living room, which allowed her to watch television over his shoulder. She claimed that eventually Reed became increasingly cruel and sexually sadistic, insisted that she should pose for nude photographs and succumb to beatings and perversions, belittled her all the time and sneered at her acting.

Do young, innocent virgins fall in love with rapists and marry them? It seems unlikely, and thirty-four years later Reed's twenty-two-year-old niece Bebe Reed, a singer with the pop group Real Macabre, defended his reputation in an article in the *People* that was headlined I can't believe my uncle raped joan collins. In it she asked why Joan had not 'shot through the door' as soon as she saw Reed's pornographic book and why she had made no attempt to fight or escape, although she was with Reed for hours after the alleged rape. 'I don't believe any of these stories,' wrote Ms Reed. 'Not even Auntie Joan would be stupid enough to wed a man who had treated her like that.' Bebe's view of her uncle was completely different: 'Uncle Max was often at our house playing games with my sister, my brother and myself. We had a pony and he used to come out riding. He was an artistic man, a keen model-maker and a great raconteur about his film days.' It certainly seems bizarre that Joan made no mention at all of this 'rape' when she came to write her second autobiography in 1996, in which she wrote just two sentences about Reed's courtship, reporting revealingly that she had 'done the deed' with Reed and then 'paid the price in guilt'. That sounds much more like the truth.

As a Rank starlet Joan had to pose for dozens of glamorous publicity photographs – in bikinis, tight sweaters, brief shorts, fishnet stockings – and had to attend numerous boring parties, lunches and every Rank première. She was coached in every aspect of stardom, from how to deal with the Press to how to climb in and out of a car, and in her first year with Rank she made four films – *Decameron Nights*, *Cosh Boy*, *The Square Ring* (with Reed) and *Turn the Key Softly*. She and Reed also appeared together in three plays at the tiny but highly regarded Q Theatre in Richmond, near Kew Bridge, where many famous actors made their debuts, among them Dirk Bogarde, Vivien Leigh, Margaret Lockwood and Anthony Quayle. Each play ran for a week. The first, in March, was *The Seventh Veil*, in which Joan played the part of a young pianist and Reed a vicious piano teacher. Also in the cast was thirty-year-old Peter Sallis, who was later to play Norman Clegg in the TV series *Last of the Summer Wine*. 'I came out of my dressing room one evening,' Sallis told me, 'and saw this extremely impressive gentle-man coming along the corridor wearing a black coat with an astrakhan collar, a Homburg hat and carrying a cane. "What do you think of the girl?" he asked me, referring to Joan. I hadn't the faintest idea who he was, but I said, "oh, she's fine." He thanked me and we moved on. It was only the following day that it dawned on me: of *course*, that was J. Arthur Rank himself; he was obviously going to see her.' He was equally obviously there to check up on his investment, this seventeen-year-old girl whom someone in his organisation had seen fit to pay a hefty £50 a week.

In *The Seventh Veil* Max Reed as the piano teacher had to whack Joan on the hand and snarl, 'If you won't play for me you won't play for anyone,' and in the second play, *Jassy*, they had an equally tense relationship that she said later could have been based on their own, in which a frightened young girl is dominated by a charismatic but sadistic older man. It was not a good omen for her first marriage.

CHAPTER THREE

THE COFFEE-BAR JEZEBEL

{ 1952–1954 }

Joan married Max Reed at Caxton Hall register office just after noon on 24 May 1952, the day after her nineteenth birthday. He was thirty-three but pretended on the marriage certificate to be only thirty. Joan too was to fib for many years that she was younger than she was, allowing *Who's Who* and *Debrett's People of Today* – which rely on their subjects to write their own entries – to record as much as fifty years later that she married Reed in 1954, not 1952, so that she could claim to be two years younger than she was. Joan's father objected strongly to the marriage, partly because Reed was fourteen years older, partly because he did not trust 'this flashy, worldly man', but Elsa was charmed by Reed, impressed by his fame, and when Joan threatened to live in sin with him if Joe withheld his permission her father agreed reluctantly, telling her brutally that if the marriage failed he would never see or speak to her again. In several newspaper interviews Joan later claimed that one or two nights before the wedding she burst into tears, admitted to her parents that she was making a mistake, and begged to cancel the wedding but was told that she had to go ahead because everything was arranged. The story varied each time she told it and strangely she made no mention of it in her autobiographies. Nor did Joe in his, and it is difficult not to suspect that she was trying to shift some of the blame for her doomed first marriage away from herself and onto her parents. She certainly looked extremely happy in the wedding photographs and told the *Daily Mirror* boldly that she intended to work full time and had no intention of cooking, cleaning or having children for several years. 'Why should I slave domestically?' she said. 'We pay a daily for that.'

After the wedding the happy couple were cheered by a crowd of fans and Joe gave them a generous reception at Ciro's nightclub with its red plush walls and chandeliers, where Joan's old headmistress, Ivy Joslin, was one of the guests. 'She was always intrigued and interested and thoroughly amused by Joan's success,' Miss Joslin's ex-secretary, Maureen Simmons, told Crimp and Burstein. 'She always said Joan was an actress.' Pictures of the wedding appeared in the national newspapers the next morning and the newlyweds drove south to Cannes for a sunny honeymoon, but it turned into a nightmare, Joan claimed later, because Reed was extremely jealous, screamed at her and slapped her when she flirted with a couple of photographers on the beach, yet suggested often that she could earn good money by sleeping with the rich men that they met. She was also beginning to feel embarrassed to be seen with him because he dyed and permed his hair and wore make-up, tiny white shorts, sandals with thongs that laced halfway up his legs, and gold medallions dangling from his neck. 'He got more wolf whistles in the South of France than I did,' she said. She was embarrassed too by his posturing and fake transatlantic accent, and much to her relief the honeymoon had to be cut short after only a week when Rank lent her to Columbia to make *Decameron Nights* with Joan Fontaine and Louis Jourdan, a film of four linked Boccaccio stories of war-torn, fourteenth-century Italy. She flew to Spain to play three small parts in it: a simpering, virginal handmaiden who cries ecstatically when first she sees Boccaccio, 'There's a man coming!'; an exotic Moroccan dancer; and finally an inn-keeper's melodramatic daughter. It was a silly film and Joan hated making it, claiming that Segovia, where she stayed, stank and her hotel was filthy.

Back in London she moved into Reed's flat, a small apartment in fashionable Mayfair, just off Hanover Square, but right at the top of a dilapidated old building. 'The furniture looked to me like second-hand junk from film sets,' wrote Joe Collins in his autobiography. 'He kept an unusual pet, too – a monkey. The creature, who was not house-trained, had a huge cage in the living room, and the stink in that flat was appalling ... It was altogether a most unsavoury set-up.'

As soon as Joan returned to London she started work on *Cosh Boy*, a ridiculous, stilted film about a sixteen-year-old yob, Roy Walsh, who runs a gang of teenage London muggers. Joan looked gorgeous as his sixteen-year-old girlfriend, Rene Collins, but when she becomes pregnant he refuses to marry her, she tries to commit suicide, and loses the baby. Roy kills a man during an attempted robbery but is merely belted by his stepfather in one of the feeblest climaxes in the entire history of films. *Cosh Boy* – renamed *The Slasher* and *The Tough Guy* when it was released in the United States – was obviously intended to be a serious study of violent, anti-social, teenage behaviour but it was mannered, melodramatic and quite unbelievable, and notable only for the facts that Rene's mother was played by Joan's old enemy Hermione Baddeley, Sid James was again a police sergeant, and the film was the first ever to be given an X-certificate rating in Britain. In Birmingham and Sweden it was banned altogether.

For a few months the newlyweds tried to make their marriage work. Joan attempted in vain to learn how to cook, Reed bought a boat and they went sailing together, and in November they appeared together in a third play at the Q Theatre, Thornton Wilder's *The Skin of Our Teeth*, with Joan as the sexy flirt Sabina and Reed as a sixty-year-old man, a performance that Joan admitted reluctantly was not at all bad. In the first scene Joan had to dust furniture and polish silver, and on the first night Elsa had to leave her seat for a while because she was laughing so much at the astonishing sight of her daughter doing housework. Joan enjoyed the play more than any film she had made, and she and Reed appeared together again in *The Square Ring*, an Ealing Studios film about bribery and corruption in English boxing that was shot early in 1953. This time the cast was excellent. Reed – tall, dark and saturnine – played the part of a brooding, corrupt heavyweight with beetling eyebrows and a Teddy boy haircut. Joan as his nervous moll managed to look appropriately coarse, almost ugly, and was suitably frightened when pursued by vicious crooks, though part of her fear was inspired by Reed's angry accusations that she was upstaging him in their scenes together. Jack Warner played a boxing coach, Alfie Bass his amusingly pessimistic assistant, Robert Beatty an old ex-champ making a comeback, Bill Owen a wonderfully perky lightweight, Sid James a promoter, Joan Sims a bubbly groupie, Kay Kendall a manager's wife.

By now Joan was already beginning to feel restless as a Rank starlet. She felt unhappy about the sort of films she was making and the incompetence of hairdressers and make-up girls. 'I was appalled by all the make-up they plastered on,' she told Pearson Phillips of the *Telegraph Sunday Magazine* in 1980. 'They used to put about three inches of horrid slop on my face. A lot of actresses never take it off properly and have terrible skins as a result. So I learned to clean my face properly and insisted that I do my own make-up. I have done it myself ever since.' Her hair, always thin and mousy, was a more difficult problem and 'when I first went into the business I was actually given a huge complex about my hair by hairdressers', she told Nigel Farndale of the *Sunday Telegraph Magazine* in 2004. 'They said, "You've got a tiny pin head and terrible hair. We're going to have to pin a wig on you." They did! I was a teenager – imagine!' For the rest of her life she was to wear so many huge wigs that some gossips insisted that she had become bald.

After Joan had made three films in which she had played bad girls Rank cast her in yet another, *Turn the Key Softly*, this time as a teenage prostitute, one of three women released simultaneously from London's Holloway prison for women, who tries to go straight but is seduced by the glamour of London's West End. The film was shot on the London streets during the icy winter of 1952–3 with Joan shivering in a flimsy, low-cut sweater, skirt slit almost to the waist, black stockings and strappy shoes. The movie confirmed her reputation as the naughty girl of British films, and after making a personal appearance at a provincial cinema to publicise the film one newspaper photograph showed so much of her cleavage that she was deluged with angry letters accusing her of immorality. Newspapers and magazines started to call her 'Britain's Bad Girl', 'The Coffee-Bar Jezebel' and 'The Esses Girl – Sultry! Sexy! A Siren!' The Press wrote about her so often that the National Union of Journalists voted her Miss Press Clippings of 1952, and old Granny Hettie was appalled when she went to see one of Joan's films in Brighton and the audience greeted her granddaughter's appearance on screen with lewd wolf whistles. Joan began to grumble openly about the sort of delinquent parts that Rank was making her play, accused it of not guiding her career properly, and complained that she was much better at playing light comedy than she was in gritty, social-realism roles. 'I never had to make up my mind about anything,' she told Clive Hirschhorn of the *Sunday Express* in 1979. 'There was always someone there to do it for me – you know, telling me what film to be in, what to wear, whom to go out with. And this sort of laziness carried right on into my career. That's why my movies were so lousy. Because I wasn't used to making decisions for myself. I always did as I was told. I was a real glamour-puss ninny without a brain in my head; a typical charm-school product.' Just a year after joining Rank she was saying openly that she would do much better if she went to Hollywood. 'If she takes my advice she will turn her back on California – and concentrate on Kew,' snapped Donald Zec in the *Daily Mirror*. 'She will learn a little more about the art of acting; of growing up ... and how to scratch along contentedly on a hundred quid a week.'

Rank seems to have listened to her complaints because it lent her next to Renown Pictures to replace Jane Russell (who had just backed out of the role) in a daft little comedy about a spoiled, bossy but beautiful rich girl, Sadie, who is shipwrecked on a tropical island with three lecherous men who keep trying to seduce her but pretend to be perfect gentlemen. The film, *Our Girl Friday*, which was shot mainly in Majorca in June 1953 and renamed *The Adventures of Sadie* in the United States, was the first in which her name appeared above the title. What's more, her three co-stars were already big names: thirty-eight-year-old Kenneth More, who played a rough Irish stoker; twenty-eight-year-old George Cole as a journalist; and sixty-one-year-old Robertson Hare as a pompous, fussy little professor of economics. Eight lorries loaded with cameras, lights, imitation palm trees, false flowers and stuffed parrots drove from England to the Mediterranean, where the movie was to be made in a pretty little bay near the village of Paguera. To make the beach look more like a Pacific island some of the trees were painted red, two acres of rocks were painted purple, and false flowers, foliage and rubber palm trees were planted all along the shore – an operation that led to the startled crew digging up two mysterious skeletons. The cast stayed in an hotel where one of the guests was a handsome Swedish astrologer who claimed that he could answer any question about Joan's future within twenty-four hours if she would give him her exact time, date and place of birth. She did and asked: 'When will I get a mink coat?' The following day he gave her his answer: 'You're not far away from it, my dear, not far at all.' He was right: little more than a year later she landed a fat contract to work in Hollywood and bought herself her first mink coat. She was to believe fervently in astrology for the rest of her life.

The actors had great fun making *Our Girl Friday*. When the shipwrecked four had to abandon their sinking lifeboat the boat refused to go down, even when huge lumps of concrete were fixed to the keel, and they had to pretend to 'swim for their lives' with the lifeboat still bobbing merrily on the surface. When Kenneth More and George Cole had to walk naked up the beach one of the prim Spanish extras looked up from her knitting, crossed herself, and fainted. The sun was so hot that the crew had to take it in turns to hold leaves over Robertson Hare's bald head to stop it frying. And there was a randy white parrot that exploded regularly with a filthy cackle whenever Joan undressed – an unforgettably manic cackle provided by Peter Sellers.

Because her co-stars were so much older, Joan felt lonely on location but she enjoyed the company of a practical-joking props man, Eddie Fowlie. When she asked him one day where the ladies' portaloo was he suggested that she should ask one of a nearby group of young Spanish electricians and told her how to ask the question in Spanish. Joan approached the group and enquired of one of them in Spanish 'fancy a quickie, big boy?' She escaped his enthusiastic response only by smacking his face, but she came to love the island and revel in her freedom from Max Reed, who she claimed had been urging her to let him watch her having sex with other men. Had he been with her on location in Majorca he could have done so, for while she was there she embarked on her first adulterous affair and began to enjoy sex for the first time. She also loved playing the 'absolutely gorgeous' part of Sadie and claimed that the script was hilarious. Sadly the film is much less fun to watch, although she did look highly desirable in her skimpy, tattered frocks, tiny hotpants and sexy, homemade bikinis. But her impossibly posh accent made her sound like Princess Margaret and her constantly pouty mouth resembled that of a gormless goldfish. Kenneth More's 'Irish' accent was about as Celtic as Japanese whiskey and managed to incorporate traces of cockney and Zummerzet. The acting was stilted, the dialogue unfunny, the slapstick plot ludicrously melodramatic, and the music – especially the galumphing boom of a farting bassoon – was atrocious. The New York Times reported accurately that 'Joan Collins is perfect for the bikini suit in which she swims and in which she undulates across the beach. And she doesn't make a bad impression in a properly tattered dress, either. She makes no impression as an actress.' No matter: the public flocked to see the film, both in Britain and the US, and it made a lot of money. Most important of all for Joan, her fresh, feisty beauty caught the lecherous eye of the head of 20th Century-Fox, Darryl F. Zanuck, who would offer her a fat Hollywood contract a year later.

She also caught the eye of an Italian director, Renato Castellani, who was about to film *Romeo and Juliet* and wanted her to play Juliet (because he thought she had an innocent face) and Laurence Harvey to play Romeo. The possibility that the sultry Coffee-Bar Jezebel might play sweet, virginal little Juliet caused much merriment in the newspapers, but the deal fell through when Castellani insisted that she should shave her eyebrows completely, cap her teeth, and have an operation to give her a Roman nose. Joan refused. Years later she confessed that when she was twenty-one she had not liked her looks at all but she was still not prepared to have them altered completely. She did, however, make another film that year with Laurence Harvey, *The Good Die Young*, an excellent thriller directed by Lewis Gilbert, who had directed her in *Cosh Boy* and was later to make *Reach for the Sky*, *Sink the Bismarck!* and three James Bond movies. In *The Good Die Young*, which was set in London just after the war, Harvey played a thirty-year-old war-hero aristocrat, Miles Ravenscourt, a smooth lounge lizard with gambling debts, a rich but stingy father (played by Robert Morley) and a wealthy wife (played by Margaret Leighton, whom Harvey was to marry four years later). Ravenscourt persuades three poor but honest men to help him rob a Post Office van: an ex-boxer, played by Stanley Baker; an American war hero with an unfaithful wife; and another American whose sexy, pregnant wife is played very well by Joan. During the raid Ravenscourt kills a policeman and all three of his fellow gangsters, the ending was memorably bleak, and the film did deservedly well at the box office.

Joan's marriage was equally bleak. She claimed in her first autobiography that Reed often threatened to have her face razor-slashed if ever she left him, and that the end came when he took her one night in the autumn of 1953 to dine and dance at Les Ambassadeurs nightclub and fell into conversation with a fat, elderly Arab with the unlikely name of Sheik Abdul Ben Kafir who offered to pay £10,000 [£203,000] if Joan would spend just one night with him. 'And I can even watch!' crowed Reed allegedly. Joan said that she burst into tears, screamed 'never!', rushed out of the club and took a taxi back to her parents' flat at Harley House. Yet she made no mention of this episode in her second autobiography, nor did her father in his. Why not? Neither needed to worry about Reed suing for libel since both books were published after his death. So did it happen at all? Astonishingly – if

Reed did indeed try to make her sleep with the Arab – she returned to him for a while to try a reconciliation but by now, she said, his sexual demands were increasingly perverted and sadistic and she had come to hate him. One day Joan telephoned her parents and sobbed that Reed had been hitting her. Joe told her not even to pack her clothes but to get into a taxi immediately and come to Harley House. She did, and he collected her things from Reed's flat. After eighteen months the marriage was over and she moved back into her old bedroom in Harley House. Magnanimously Joe admitted that Reed deserved some sympathy because his career was declining just as Joan's was taking off.

Fifty years later Joan boasted exaggeratedly that the £10,000 that 'Sheik Abdul Ben Kafir' had offered for one night with her would by then have been worth £250,000 .

Joe and Elsa Collins faced another family crisis that year: Jackie, now fifteen, was expelled from Francis Holland, ostensibly for smoking while wearing school uniform but also because she had been ignoring all the school rules and playing truant for months. 'She was a white-faced, unhappy-looking girl,' Beryl Lester told me, and Dr Penny Newall-Price said that 'Jackie really was a misfit. She was not at all happy, an obviously naughty girl, very scruffy and with decayed, black teeth.' Years later Jackie admitted that as a teenager she had been foul-mouthed and totally uncontrollable, and when she was expelled her rebellious reaction was to take her uniform to Westminster Bridge and throw it into the Thames. 'It was a wonderful feeling watching it float away,' she told Pamela Coleman. Julia Campion told me that 'Jackie always looked dishevelled and untidy, with long, straggly hair. She was always getting into trouble and being given detentions.' Another contemporary, Ella Bland, told me that Jackie was incredibly untidy and unsavoury: 'She was dreadful. I remember that she came to tea with my younger sister once and her shirt and skirt were so dirty that my mother said, "She's not coming here again."' Diana Hall told me that 'Jackie wasn't like Joan and they were not all that close at school. Of course she was four years younger than Joan but she never stuck to the rules and she wasn't a good advertisement for the school.' The headmistress's ex-secretary Maureen Simmons told Crimp and Burstein that Jackie was 'a very ordinary girl, nondescript, just a sort of ill-mannered, finicky girl, living under the shadow of Joan who had been a clever and charming little girl'. Years later, Jackie confessed that as a girl she was so jealous of Joan that she used to cut the buttons off her clothes. None of the teachers ever imagined that Jackie might one day become a writer, let alone an international bestseller. Legend has it that years later her English mistress borrowed one of her raunchy novels from the library and was so appalled by it that she returned it in a paper bag. In later years Joan returned regularly to Francis Holland but Jackie was never to be seen there again.

Jackie later claimed in an interview with Lester Middlehurst of the *Daily Mail* that as soon as she was expelled she left home and never took a further penny from her father. 'I never sought his opinion and I never asked for his approval,' she said. 'I just got on with my life. I never had an ounce of encouragement from him but I never expected it.' Her father, however, told a very different story in his autobiography. When Jackie left Francis Holland she wanted to become a journalist, he said, but since he had no useful contacts in the Press he persuaded her to become an actress instead, and although he was furious that she had left school without any qualifications he promised to help her break into films. 'She seemed quite amenable to the idea,' he said, 'and as she loved the movies I was convinced she had aspirations in that line. It never crossed my mind, nor Elsa's, that Jackie might spend frustrating years in a profession where she was always in Joan's shadow. Jackie had the right attributes: good looks, a superb figure and acting talent too. But throughout her acting career she was always tagged "Joan Collins' younger sister".' Jackie also told interviewers that when she was fifteen her parents threatened her with reform school and then packed her off to live with Joan in Hollywood, where she had an under-age affair with Marlon Brando. 'They stuck me on a plane as fast as they could get rid of me,' she lied. In fact Joan did not go to Hollywood for another eighteen months, at the end of 1954, and Jackie was still living at home. She did not follow Joan to Hollywood until 1956, when she was nearly nineteen, and after eleven months returned to live with her parents. When she reached the age of twenty-one and became eligible to vote her father put her name on the electoral register, and she was still living at Harley House at the end of 1960 when she was twenty-three and left at last to get married. Years of writing fiction had obviously affected her memory.

For many years, like Joan, she was to claim harmlessly that she was much younger than she really was, but it was cruel and disloyal of her to accuse both her parents falsely of trying to get rid of her and not caring about her or supporting her. In the meantime she took her father's advice, stayed in England, and became an actress. Joe persuaded his friend Carroll Levis, who presented talent shows in theatres all over England, to hire her as a compère, and she worked for a while on the stage with a repertory company in Ilfracombe and then between 1955 and 1958 played small bit-parts in one TV drama and six black-and-white British films, mostly short B-movies. The Canadian director Alvin Rakoff, who directed her in 1958 in *Passport to Shame*, in which she played a prostitute, told me that 'Jackie was never as attractive as Joan but she had something. She knew she was no Judi Dench as an actress but she was a pleasant, thoughtful girl', and Joe Collins could not understand why Jackie was so unhappy about her brief acting career because he believed that although she never became a star she did well enough.

Back in London, Joan was excited to be asked to do a film test at Pinewood for the comedy *Doctor At Sea* with the most popular British movie star of the day, thirty-three-year-old Dirk Bogarde, 'The Idol of the Odeons'. She wore a pink babydoll nightie and they writhed and kissed on a silky double bed, but they shared no chemistry, probably because Bogarde was homosexual, and the part went eventually to Brigitte Bardot. Years later, when Joan was at the peak of her *Dynasty* fame, Bogarde remarked that 'she couldn't act her way out of a paper bag and she still can't'. Her next screen test, however, was eventually to take her to Hollywood. She tested in Paris and although she failed again to land the part she met the Hollywood producer Howard Hawks, who had just made *Gentlemen Prefer Blondes* with Jane Russell and Marilyn Monroe and was to remember Joan a few months later when he suddenly needed a quick replacement for the leading actress in his next big film.

To avoid Max Reed, Joan asked Bill Watts to find her a part in a play that would take her on tour out of London, and he came up with *The Praying Mantis*, in which she was a young Byzantine empress who seduces young men and then has them executed. After a week at the Q Theatre in March it went on to Brighton, Wimbledon and Folkestone. The reviews were bad and the play did not do well but Joan loved being back in the theatre and as soon as the tour ended she began to rehearse another with Donald Houston, *Claudia and David*, an American comedy about marriage.

In May Joan turned twenty-one – her parents gave her a small string of pearls that she was still wearing forty years later – and she was appearing at the Q Theatre in *Claudia and David* when Hawks suddenly summoned her to Rome, where he was making *Land of the Pharaohs*, a huge, lavish but hilariously ludicrous pyramids-and-camels epic about Ancient Egypt. Jack Hawkins was starring as the rapaciously greedy Pharaoh Khufu; James Robertson Justice was the fat slave architect Vashtar, who is building the Pharaoh's vast pyramid tomb; Charlie Chaplin's second son, Sydney, was the captain of the guard; and there were more than nine thousand extras teeming across the desert. Hawks had just sacked his leading actress, Ivy Nicholson, who had been playing the devious Princess Nellifer but making too many unacceptable demands. He needed a replacement quickly, remembered Joan from their meeting in Paris, and eight hours after leaving the stage at the Q Theatre she was on a plane to Rome and plunged into her first major role and her first big American film.

Even though the screenplay was said to have been co-written by the acclaimed American novelist William Faulkner, who had won the Nobel Prize for Literature in 1949 and was about to win the Pulitzer Prize for 1955, the dialogue was atrocious and the whole project gloriously over-the-top with marching armies, chanting slaves and raucous, portentous music. The bizarre costumes would have been perfect for *The Mikado* or *Star Wars*. The Chief High Priest appeared in several nifty off-the-shoulder numbers and Jack Hawkins looked absurd in a succession of frocks and necklaces that would not have disgraced *Dynasty* – and at times in a square helmet that made him look like Kryten, the android from the science-fiction TV series *Red Dwarf*. As with so many of her films, Joan was the best thing in it – a dark, sultry, scheming, gorgeously sexy villainess – but understandably she later called the film 'a turkey', Hawkins called it 'perfectly ridiculous' and Howard Hawks himself disowned it and begged the British National Film Theatre not to include it in its 1963 retrospective of his films. Much of the dialogue was quite atrocious, according to Hawkins' autobiography. He had agreed to make the film partly because he was told that Faulkner had written the screenplay, but the script was so bad that he did not believe Faulkner had written any of it. Consequently Hawkins worried constantly about his dialogue. 'Don't worry,' said Hawks breezily when Hawkins objected to a particular line. 'I'll find you another. I have more used lines at my fingertips than anyone you know.' Hawks was quite honest about it, said Hawkins: 'When he was short of dialogue, he would borrow lines from some old movie. I am quite sure that I ended up speaking words that Clark Gable had used in some quite different film.'

Despite the movie's myriad absurdities, Hawkins thought that Joan was very good in it, his widow Doreen told me, and 'she was always great fun'. Some of it was shot in Egypt – in Luxor, Giza and the Valley of the Kings – but Joan's part was filmed in Rome over three summer months and she loved it, not least because her onscreen affair with the tall, dark, twenty-eight-year-old Sydney Chaplin spilled over into their own lives. Until a few weeks previously Chaplin had been living with Kay Kendall, who told her friend Carol Saroyan, the wife of the American author William Saroyan, that 'God, he's terrible in bed and he's fat' but admitted that he was 'a sweet person'. Joan loved his zest for life and outrageously scurrilous sense of humour. They sped in one of his two expensive sports cars to the beaches at Ostia and Fregene, and lounged about in bars, discos and nightclubs, and relished the wonderful Roman restaurants. They drank, danced, gambled, stayed up until dawn, and made love, and she thought she would never be as happy again. She enjoyed the pasta restaurants too much and put on so much weight that the fake ruby that she had to wear in her navel as part of her exotic Ancient Egyptian costume kept popping out and she had to go on a diet. Elsa spent much of that summer with her in Rome as her chaperone but Joan and Sydney were so blatant about their affair, even though she was still married, that they held hands openly on set, though 'they were always having rows', Mrs Hawkins told me, 'and he got into trouble for having her in his hotel room.' Inevitably Italian reporters and paparazzi started chasing them around town and newspapers claimed that Chaplin had broken up her marriage to Reed. She denied it. 'How could he have smashed my marriage?' she asked in the *People* three years later. 'Max and I had separated four months before I ever met Sydney Chaplin.' Reed's niece Bebe Reed was deeply cynical about Joan's denial that Chaplin had had anything to do with the break-up of her marriage. In her article in the *People* in 1986 she wrote: 'If it hadn't been for Maxwell Reed she wouldn't be where she is today. Marrying him I think was the first advantageous career move of her life.' It was Bebe's view that when she couldn't use him any more she dumped him.

Joan could certainly be ruthlessly ambitious when she chose. Alvin Rakoff married one of Joan's RADA contemporaries, Jacqueline Hill, and told me that Joan urged her to dump him 'since at the time I was a penniless BBC director. Joan was never one to take her eye off the ball.'

Rome was a major centre of the European film industry in the early 1950s and at the Hôtel de la Ville one night Joan was riveted to see the irresistibly sexy, nineteen-year-old Brigitte Bardot wearing a girly little dress, a flirty little smile and a come-hither expression that had all the men slavering to join her at the bar. Less welcome was a meeting with Max Reed, who was in Rome playing a small part in another movie, *Helen of Troy*. Legally she was unable to divorce him until they had been wed for three years, and she claimed in *Past Imperfect* that he approached her on the beach at Fregene one day, told her he was broke, reminded her that he had taken some nude photographs of her, and threatened to sell them to an Italian magazine unless she gave him a signed blank cheque and returned the engagement, wedding and topaz rings he had given her. In the early 1950s an actress's career might well be destroyed if nude photos appeared in a magazine, so she did as he asked on the understanding that he would return the photos. He agreed, she said, but then refused to return them once she had paid him.

When Joan and Chaplin finished work on *Land of the Pharaohs* they moved together into the Hôtel Tremoille in Paris and enjoyed an idyllic, hedonistic autumn of cafés, bars, shopping, long lunches, nightclubs, sex, hangovers, and at last the offer to Joan of a seven-year contract to go to Hollywood. Darryl Zanuck, the tiny, randy boss of 20th Century-Fox in Los Angeles, was still inflamed by the memory of her in a bikini on the beach in *Our Girl Friday* and now by the vision of her semi-naked in *Land of the Pharaohs* and was prepared to pay Rank £15,000 [£296,000] to buy her from them and to pay her $350 a week [£1,300] for the first year. Joan had dreamed for years of going to Los Angeles but had read somewhere that even lowly Hollywood technicians were paid $350 a week and that young contract actors could earn as much as $1,250 a week [£4,630], so she told her new agent, John Shepbridge, to demand $1,250. He warned her that she was mad to risk losing the offer but she was adamant, partly because she was now so besotted with Sydney Chaplin that she did not want to leave him in Europe while she went off to California. Nervously Shepbridge put Joan's demand to Zanuck and was astonished when the miniature mogul, by now trembling with lust, agreed to pay what she wanted.

Before she flew to Los Angeles she and Sydney spent a weekend with his sixty-five-year-old father, Charlie, his young wife Oona, and their large tribe of children at their huge house in Switzerland on the edge of Lake Geneva and the village of Vevey. Joan found that Sydney treated his father with careful respect because Charlie was very much the stern paterfamilias, like her own father, was still paying him an allowance, and tended at times to bully him even in public. But Charlie was also charming, funny and surprisingly shy. On the final evening, however, she aroused his ire when she was tiddly with drink. Sydney's playwright and lyricist friend Adolph Green told a joke about Adolf Hitler, and she started giggling helplessly, telling Charlie that she thought that Hitler had been hilariously funny. 'You really think so?' said Chaplin coldly. He fetched a book of dreadful photographs of victims in Auschwitz concentration camp and forced her to look at page after page of horrifying atrocities – starving people, mass graves, terrified children, grinning Nazi guards – until eventually she wept. 'Maybe now you'll realise how extremely *unfunny* Adolf Hitler was,' said Chaplin, and then attacked the Duke of Windsor and 'all of you English' for encouraging Hitler's rise to power. It was a bizarre tirade considering that Chaplin was English himself and had in 1940 made a comic film about Hitler, *The Great Dictator.*

After meeting Sydney's family Joan took him to London to meet hers. Joe was not impressed when Sydney complained that his father had not helped him to build his film career.

Back in Paris she sobbed when she kissed Sydney goodbye, even though he promised to follow her to Los Angeles as soon as he could, and she wept again in London when she said goodbye to her parents, seventeen-year-old Jackie and eight-year-old Bill. It was November 1954. She was only twenty-one but had already bought herself the full-length mink coat that the Swedish astrologer had foretold. 'I had no doubt she would hold her own against the other pretty and talented young actresses in Hollywood,' wrote her father. 'But I could not quell my misgivings about how she would conduct her personal life. At twenty-one, to my mind, Joan was still very childlike.' She wore the mink on the flight west across the Atlantic to New York, Chicago and LA, a twenty-four hour, 9,000-mile journey into the sunset and the dawn of her new life as a Hollywood star.

CHAPTER FOUR

HOLLYWOOD

{ 1954–1956 }

'Hollywood was unbelievably glamorous,' Joan told Melvyn Bragg on ITV's *South Bank Show* in 1999, and just what she had expected. Although it was winter when she arrived she said that it was really warm, with the sun blazing, the shops were amazing, the people looked stunning and everyone was very welcoming. 'Within the first two or three days after I'd arrived I had a telephone message from every eligible man, young, middle-aged and old, in Hollywood because I was the new, young, pretty kid in town.' When she appeared on BBC Radio's *Desert Island Discs* in 1989 she told Sue Lawley: 'Within a week I met Gene Kelly, Judy Garland, Humphrey Bogart, Frank Sinatra and Marilyn Monroe. It was quite astonishing. I just used to sit with my mouth open.'

None of this was necessarily true. According to a newspaper series that she wrote just three years later for the *People*, in 1957, she arrived in Los Angeles on a grey, drizzly day, checked into a bleak Beverly Hills hotel, and spent night after night for three weeks alone, watching television or playing Frank Sinatra records in her room, lonely, bored, homesick and pining for Sydney. She went daily to the 20th Century-Fox studio, where twenty-seven-year-old Marilyn Monroe was the reigning queen, to pose for hundreds of publicity photographs, and in the canteen she gazed goggle-eyed at Richard Burton, Susan Hayward, Lana Turner, Joanne Woodward and Robert Wagner. She met some of the studio bosses and although she was a shapely 38–23–37 and weighed only 126lbs they ordered her to lose 7lbs pronto and put her on a banana and cottage cheese diet. When she failed to lose weight they sent her to the studio doctor, who gave her a course of little green 'slimming pills' that worked miraculously quickly but made her hyperactive and turned out to be a dangerous drug, dexedrine, otherwise known as speed. She was so unhappy that after three weeks she flew back to Paris to see Sydney, but she cheered up quickly when the studio called her back to Los Angeles to start work on her first Hollywood movie, *The Virgin Queen*, set in 1581, in which forty-five-year-old Bette Davis was to play Queen Elizabeth I and Joan one of her Ladies in Waiting. It was a surprisingly meaty part considering Joan's inexperience, and she acquitted herself well as a pretty tease who wears lots of lavish costumes. Secretly she marries Sir Walter Raleigh (played by the British actor Richard Todd), which so angers the jealous Queen that she sends Raleigh to the Tower of London and releases him only when Joan pleads for his life because she is pregnant.

Bette Davis, who had played Elizabeth I already in 1939 with Errol Flynn in *The Private Lives of Elizabeth and Essex*, was ferocious enough just playing herself but as Elizabeth I for the second time she became a bald, glowering monster, tetchy, squeaky and alarmingly melodramatic, who terrified everyone, including Joan. To play the part of the queen, Bette's hair had been shaved off and she wore a red wig. She chain-smoked all day, and Joan and the other young girls in the cast kept apprehensively out of her way as much as possible. Bette Davis 'was one of those people who came from the school of hard knocks', Joan told Lawley. 'She always had to fight.' Davis's regal manner upset almost everyone and she caused numerous rows with the crew, notably with the chief cameraman, Charles Clark, whom she accused of not light-ing her scenes properly. To be fair, her eyes and skin were extremely sensitive to bright lights, her marriage was going through an unhappy period, and she was deeply worried about her little adopted daughter Margot, who was not only mentally handicapped but also frighteningly hostile.

Richard Todd would not hear a word against Bette Davis. She was 'the supreme professional', he wrote in his autobiography. 'Always first on the set in the morning, after long and tedious make-up and ward-robe sessions; always word-perfect; always full of energy and never flagging even at the end of a hard day – she was exemplary. I had heard that she could be fearsome if things did not go as she wanted, but soon I found that although she certainly did not suffer fools gladly, she was never unpleasant in the way some lesser actors and actresses can be ... I really loved working with her.' She could also be remarkably kind and gentle. In one scene she had to deliver a long, difficult speech in the council chamber that had to be interrupted at the very end by one line from a doddery old courtier, but the aged actor playing the part kept getting his line wrong. After several takes it would have been understandable had she blown her top but she kept calm and agreed when the director, Henry Koster, suggested quietly that to save the old boy's feelings they should run through the scene once more, without any film in the camera, and pretend to print it so that he could go away happy, and they would then film the same scene the next day with someone else. They played the scene again, the old actor fouled up again, Koster shouted 'Cut! Print!' and congratulated him on getting it right at last. Half an hour later, said Todd, the guard on the studio's main gate telephoned Koster to say that the old boy had just dropped dead, so 'one man departed this life on cloud nine and not in misery'.

Todd was surprised to find Joan cast as his wife. 'I had never seen her on the screen and knew her only from brief glimpses of her quite startling vital statistics in the restaurant at Pinewood Studios or at film premières. Not at all my idea of a demure English rose and scion of an ancient and noble family [but] in the event, Joan was splendid: a real professional, a very competent actress, a nice person and excellent in the role of Mistress Throgmorton.'

Word eventually spread in Los Angeles that a gorgeous new limey chick had arrived in town and she was deluged with invitations. At first she said no to all the Hollywood wolves, determined to stay faithful to Sydney, but in due course she began to accept dates and to meet some of the most famous stars. At Gene Kelly's house one night she approached a blonde girl without any make-up, bra or jewellery who was scruffily dressed in a grubby sweater and sitting alone on a sofa. 'Hi,' said the girl. 'I'm Marilyn.' Overawed, Joan sat and talked to her and was amazed to discover that Monroe was sweet and shy and not at all like her idea of the sex-goddess everyone thought she was. Without make-up she had a funny little pug nose and looked nothing special. Her hair was messy and showed dark roots and she told Joan that Hollywood was 'all crap' and that every actress was just a piece of meat as far as the studios were concerned. 'Don't let them push you around,' she said. 'They tried to push me around and I didn't believe in myself enough so I made a lot of crappy movies.' Less enjoyable was an encounter at another party with Frank Sinatra and Humphrey Bogart when Sinatra kept teasing Joan by twanging the elastic of her off-the-shoulder blouse. Joan retaliated by remarking that Sinatra looked like some Mafia gangster who had just stepped out of *Guys and Dolls*. Bogart, she said, grabbed the front of her dress, yanked her towards him, and snarled: 'Don't you *ever* talk about a pal of mine like that.'

The studio wanted her to do a screen test with one of its handsome new stars, the charming, twenty-four-year-old Robert ('RJ') Wagner, for an eighteenth-century costume drama, *Lord Vanity*. 'We had this scene where we had to kiss,' recalled Wagner, 'and as we broke apart there was a piece of saliva that was strung right across the camera and we laughed so hard that we never could get it back.' The film was never made but Joan and RJ were to become good friends. Another friend was the moody, twenty-four-year-old James Dean, who had just finished making *Rebel Without a Cause* and was filming his final movie, *Giant*. One night in July, after Joan, Dean, his girlfriend Ursula Andress and a group of young people had enjoyed a boozy dinner in a Hollywood restaurant, Dean invited Joan for a spin in his new red Porsche Spyder sports car. One of the group tried to discourage her, telling her that Jimmy drove like a maniac, especially after a few drinks, but she laughed, jumped into the car, and was duly terrified as Dean drove incredibly fast and recklessly through the Los Angeles traffic. Two months later, on 30 September 1955, he was to die at the wheel of the red Porsche when he smashed into another car up the coast at Cholame, near San Luis Obispo, two hours after being given a ticket for speeding. Miraculously the driver of the other car, Donald Turnupseed, survived.

Sydney arrived at last from Paris and lived openly with Joan in a small furnished apartment near the studio on Beverly Glen Boulevard – a daring move in those days when an actress could be fired for any hint of immorality, let alone adultery. No matter that the head of the studio himself, Darryl Zanuck, was a compulsive adulterer who propositioned every pretty actress who came his way. Soon after Joan joined the studio, she said, he cornered her in a corridor and pressed her up against the wall. 'You haven't had anyone till you've had me,' he leered. 'I've got the biggest and best and I can go all night.' She wriggled free and ran away. One of Zanuck's little egocentricities was to have on his desk a lifesize mould of his genitals in solid gold, which he liked to show to impressionable girls. He once made the mistake of showing it to the frightening Joan Crawford. 'Impressive, huh?' he said, grinning. She sneered. 'I've seen bigger things crawl out of cabbages,' she said.

Joan paid the rent for the apartment she shared with Sydney but was away all day working long hours while he could find no work and soon became bored with golf, watching television and playing poker all night with a few friends. Once the life and soul of every party, he was now often too tired and depressed to go anywhere. 'He had a very short attention span when it came to the ladies,' his wife Margaret told Kay Kendall's biographer Eve Golden. Inevitably Joan became fed up with him and started going out with one of his friends, Arthur Loew Jr – not the fat, pompous, grumpy Arthur Lowe who was to play Captain Mainwaring in the TV series *Dad's Army*, as Cosmo Landesman claimed hilariously in *The Sunday Times* in 2006, but the tall, thin, beaky, extremely rich, twenty-nine-year-old playboy son of the president of MGM and grandson of the founder of Paramount Pictures, Adolph Zukor. Loew was more reserved and less ebullient than Sydney had been at his best, but he was renowned for his wit and Joan found him funny and sensitive. Best of all, he listened to her woes. Loew was to specialise in listening to the woes of beautiful, distraught or disgruntled actresses and taking them under his wing. In 1948 he had consoled Janet Leigh after her divorce from her second husband, Stanley Reames, and in 1958 alone he was to console Elizabeth Taylor after the death of her husband Mike Todd; Debbie Power after the death of her husband Tyrone Power; and Debbie Reynolds after she was dumped by Eddie Fisher. Five years later he was to console Natalie Wood after she was dumped by Warren Beatty. 'He was a friend to all of us,' Debbie Reynolds told one biographer, 'and he loved women and he loved to be your boyfriend without taking you to bed. He really wanted to hold your hand and be the gentleman, take you out and teach you about all the good things in life. Arthur, who was a very, very rich man, was the sweetest.'

Loew did take Joan to bed and she gave Sydney the elbow. The end came when Sydney agreed to pick her up at Palm Springs airport one weekend, failed to show up, and she found him drunk with a bunch of cronies in a bar. 'Fuck you, Sydney!' she yelled. 'Fuck you! Fuck you! Fuck you! Fuck you!'

'And fuck you too,' he slurred.

'Well, that'll be the last time you'll *ever* fuck me,' she said.

He went on to make twenty-four more films, to appear on Broadway with Judy Holliday in *Bells Are Ringing* in 1956 – for which he was to win a Tony Award as Best Supporting Actor in a musical – and with Barbra Streisand in *Funny Girl* in 1964, to marry three times, and to open Chaplin's restaurant in Palm Springs. Joan, meanwhile, rented another small apartment on Olive Drive, near Sunset Strip. Encouraged by Loew, she started going to a psychoanalyst three times a week to Find Herself and discovered that the shrink was much more interested in hearing all the juicy details of her love life.

The reviews for *The Virgin Queen* were good but public response at the previews was not. Television was increasingly threatening the success of old-fashioned movies and the studio decided that the public would not really be interested in a big historical epic, even though it had been filmed in the latest wide-screen format, CinemaScope. They did send Joan to London to publicise the film but otherwise spent little to promote it and it lost money. Still, she had made such a good start in Hollywood that she was given immediately the lead in a film that had originally been meant for the studio's golden girl, Marilyn Monroe: *The Girl in the Red Velvet Swing*, which was based on a real American high-society murder case in 1906. Monroe turned the part down because she felt it was not serious enough for her, it was given to Joan instead, and the British Press went wild with stories that the Bad Girl had made it so big in Hollywood already that she was about to inherit Marilyn's crown, though none could quite match the inventiveness of the Italian magazine *Oggi*, which dubbed her 'The Pouting Panther'. She played Evelyn Nesbit, the beautiful, seventeen-year-old Broadway chorus girl whose jealous, bullying, millionaire husband (played by Farley Granger) had murdered her rich, married, forty-eight-year-old lover (Ray Milland) by shooting him dead in a theatre in 1906. Joan looked slim and gorgeous in the part – deliciously fresh, sweet and flirty, with beautiful eyes and lips, and very English, though the studio made her take lessons in how to speak with an American accent. It is easy to imagine a middle-aged man falling hopelessly in love with her. She seduces her lover after riding higher and higher on a romantic, red velvet swing – in real life it had had a glass-bottomed seat and Evelyn had ridden on it knickerless – but when her husband is charged with her lover's murder she gives reluctant evidence that saves him from the death penalty.

Before playing the part Joan met the real Evelyn Nesbit, who had gone on after the murder to be fêted as a great beauty for several years in New York but was later reduced to appearing in an undignified Atlantic City music hall act riding a red velvet swing. Her looks had long gone and she was now a heavy boozer in her seventies, hard up and addicted to gin, and Joan was depressed to see that a girl who had been as beautiful in her twenties as Joan was herself could end up like this. It was a terrible warning. She realised that a beautiful woman had to take good care of her looks, and for the rest of her life she used plenty of make-up – often far too much – as her shield against the elements, pollution and old age. Her make-up man on *The Girl in the Red Velvet Swing*, Whitey Snyder, taught her how to apply moisturiser and then a thin, delicate, subtly shaded base so that it looked just like her skin, and from then on she insisted on doing her make-up herself even for her films. Although she loved sunbathing she was always to keep her face out of the sun and wear baseball caps or hats with wide brims after her new Hollywood girlfriend Cappy Badrutt pointed to the darkly tanned women lying beside the swimming pool at the Beverly Hills Hotel and asked: 'Do you want to look like those lizards when you're forty?' She learned a lesson too from the director of *The Girl in the Red Velvet Swing*, Dick Fleischer, that she was to remember for the rest of her life: never go out in public looking scruffy. The fearsome, sixty-nine-year-old Hollywood gossip columnist Hedda Hopper once wrote that Joan obviously combed her hair with an egg-beater, and when Fleischer saw her lunching one day in the 20th Century commissary without any make-up and with her hair pulled back, he cried: 'My God! You look *hideous*! You can't go out like that. Never go out without make-up, and always be dressed properly. Never forget you're a star.'

The Girl in the Red Velvet Swing also introduced her to a Hollywood legend, 'OK Freddie', an ancient, wizened, lugubrious little extra who was blessed with such a huge penis that mischievous actors like Errol Flynn and David Niven would insist he displayed it to strangers. 'Come on, Freddie,' they would cry, 'show us your cock,' upon which Freddie would reply 'OK' and haul the monster out to general astonishment. There is no evidence that Joan ever inspected the massive organ herself but she liked to tell of the elegant garden party where Flynn and Niven were said to have persuaded Freddie to dress as a waiter and go round offering guests a silver salver held low and piled high with snacks neatly arranged around an enormous sort of sausage that turned out to be part of OK Freddie when one of the elderly lady guests prodded it fiercely with a fork.

The film took ten weeks to make, pictures of Joan and articles about her crammed the fan magazines, and *Life* put her on its cover in the autumn – a rare accolade for such a young, unknown actress. Her reviews were excellent. 'Joan Collins is startlingly beautiful and sexy as Evelyn,' said one. 'She's a torrid baggage,' said another. *Variety* called her 'a captivating bundle of sex-appeal' and the London *Daily Sketch* acclaimed her as 'a young woman of almost disturbing beauty, technically accomplished, perfectly poised, stylish from the top of her head to the turn of her ankle. She possesses the capacity to express an eager eroticism beneath the appearance of virginal innocence and gives a performance as sweet and intelligent as any we have reason to expect.' And Robert Ottaway wrote: 'Joan was the most mishandled actress that ever belonged to the Rank Organisation. Now she's set fair to join the ranks of top-grade international stars.' Once again the film lost money but it was hardly her fault. Joan was very, very good in the part, said her father.

20th Century was delighted with her too and rented her out immediately to MGM for *The Opposite Sex*, a lavish musical remake of a hugely successful comedy about a group of rich, gossipy, catty, society wives that had first been shot in 1939 with Norma Shearer, Rosalind Russell, Joan Crawford, Paulette Goddard and Joan Fontaine and titled *The Women*. Now, in 1956, Joan Collins was given the part of Crystal Allen, the role originally played by Joan Crawford, and the other parts in the new version went to June Allyson, Dolores Gray, Ann Sheridan and Joan Blondell. June Allyson is a perfect wife who discovers that her rich husband Stephen (played by Leslie Nielsen) is having an affair with a glamorous, bitchy, *femme fatale* chorus girl – Joan, of course, playing an early version of *Dynasty*'s Alexis Carrington – but battles to win him back and take revenge. Joan's face looked in the film strangely gawky but she was as sexy, vampish and naughty as ever, and in a cruel throwaway line of which Alexis would be proud, when Stephen's wife tells Crystal that he hates tarty clothes, she replies: 'When Stephen doesn't like what I wear I take it off.' She wallowed irresistibly in one of those fabulous Hollywood bubble baths, smoking a cigarette and chatting on the telephone, though during the three days that it took to shoot the scene so much detergent had to be added to the bathwater that by the end of it Joan's skin was raw. It turned out to be a delightful film, fun and funny, lighthearted, utterly over the top and glittering with 1950s style and elegance. Not surprisingly Joan was delighted about the way her career was flourishing, though she was disconcerted when an astrologer predicted that she would not be really famous until she was forty – eighteen long years away. The forecast was curiously accurate, though it was in fact not until she was forty-five that *The Stud* made her truly famous at last in 1978.

While Joan was filming *The Opposite Sex* at MGM one of the postboys, a dark-haired, blue-eyed, 'devilishly handsome' youth, always gave her a wolf whistle when she walked past the mail room – eighteen-year-old Jack Nicholson, who was soon to make his first, low-budget film. He asked her for a date. She turned him down, so he propositioned Elizabeth Taylor and Yvette Mimieux. They spurned him too. 'I was a brash kid,' he confessed years later.

Joe Collins flew in to Los Angeles to see how his daughter was doing and was delighted when the director of *The Opposite Sex*, David Miller, told him that she was the perfect actress: reliable, co-operative, always on time, and wonderfully untemperamental. Joe met Arthur Loew and liked him immediately, because he was smart, suave and courteous. Afterwards Joe begged Joan to settle down and moderate her glitzy nightclub lifestyle. 'Now you've met someone nice,' he said, 'instead of wanting to run around all the time, it would do you good to stay in occasionally and watch television.' She was appalled. 'Watch *television*?' she cried. 'I *hate* the horrid thing.' A few years later she was to tell the Hollywood gossip columnist Earl Wilson that TV was 'great for old people who can't go out, and for kids. But I'd sooner play cards, or *anything*.' Twenty-six years later it was to make her the richest actress in the world.

One ominous cloud darkened Joan's flourishing success: Max Reed refused to give up on their marriage. As her career began to soar his had stalled. By now she was making in modern terms the equivalent of £35,000 a month and in 1956 was to spend the equivalent of £74,000 on clothes, but since she had left him Reed had made only one film, was deeply in debt and desperate for money. He had for months been writing to tell Joan how much he loved her and wanted to get back together again, and now at the start of 1956 he turned up in Hollywood hoping to soften her heart. He telephoned and wrote but she refused to see him, so he took her to court, claimed that she had cruelly deserted him, and sued her for maintenance of £4,600 a month in modern terms. 'I still love Joan very much,' he told reporters, 'and I would take her back as my wife tomorrow if she would come.' He claimed that he had discovered, encouraged, and groomed her and made her a success. In March, to get rid of him and prevent him suing her years later when she would be earning much more, she agreed to pay him a lump sum of £33,700 in modern values plus £6,000 in legal costs, and on 29 May – after Jackie had flown in from England to give evidence – they were divorced in the Los Angeles Superior Court in Santa Monica, though she had to wait for another year before the decree became absolute. Strangely there was no mention in court of Reed's alleged violence or perverted sexual behaviour, evidence that would surely have destroyed his case all together, but 'he constantly made derogatory remarks about my appearance and my career', Joan told Judge Elmer Doyle. 'Generally he'd say I looked terrible. He said I had no talent as an actress and didn't see how I'd ever get a job. He said I'd better get all the work I could because by the time I was twenty-three I'd be too old.' They had been married for just over four years and the judge was baffled that she was prepared to pay so much to a thirty-seven-year-old man who seemed quite healthy enough to earn his own living.

'Uncle Max never talked about his marriage to Auntie Joan,' wrote Bebe Reed in the *People*. 'He wouldn't hear a bad word against her. He never remarried but had a permanent girlfriend. He would not criticise Joan – apart from saying that she was a dreadful actress. Even then he said it with affection. He used to try to teach her to act. But all her reactions were the same. He said she was useless. It was "like talking to a bar of soap" – he couldn't have known how fitting that remark was going to turn out to be!'

Jackie, now eighteen, decided to stay in Los Angeles and try her luck in Hollywood, where she attended 20th Century-Fox's charm school for hopeful starlets. Joan let her share her Olive Drive apartment and car and introduced her to most of her Hollywood acquaintances, including Marlon Brando, who had just made *The Teahouse of the August Moon* and with whom Jackie soon had an affair. 'He stared straight at my 39-inch chest – men often talk to my chest – and said: "That's a great looking body you have, little girl," she told Lester Middlehurst of the *Daily Mail* in 1995. 'I had a spectacular body – big boobs and a teeny 20-inch waist,' she told Pamela Coleman in 1984. Brando was spectacularly handsome too but Jackie was not quite the little girl she often claimed to have been. 'I was fifteen and he was in his thirties,' she told the *Express* untruthfully in 2001; she was in fact nearly nineteen and Brando thirty-two. She enjoyed several riotously sociable months in Los Angeles while Joan was away filming for much of the year and later claimed that it was then that she learned so much about Hollywood that she was later to use in her bestselling novels. But her first book was still many years away, and after eleven months in California Jackie was to return to England disillusioned, realising that she was never going to be as successful in films as her sister. To escape Joan's shadow she changed her name twice, calling herself Jackie Douglas and then Lee Curtis, but to no avail: everyone knew she was Joanie's little sister. She failed to get an American work permit and returned to London to live with her parents at Harley House. In England she was to struggle for recognition as an actress for three more years before giving up and marrying a rich man.

When Joe returned home he went down to Brighton to tell his mother about Joan's life in Hollywood. Hettie had followed her grand-daughter's career with pride, keeping cuttings of all the newspaper and magazine stories about her, and she read out with approval one of Joan's remarks in one of them: 'Men like to be kissed and I like kissing them. If people don't like me, that's just too bad!' Quite right, too, said Hettie: 'She's learning to stand up for herself. Speaking her mind.' She frowned. 'I wonder just how much kissing she's doing?' Well, enough to persuade Arthur Loew to let her move in with him at his ranch-style house up in the Hollywood Hills, in Miller Drive. Almost immediately she was pestering him to marry her. 'From the first, Joan set her sights on the most glittering prizes available,' wrote the glamorous, thirty-nine-year-old, Hungarian actress Zsa Zsa Gabor – who had already had three husbands and was to have six more – in her autobiography. 'Joan was always very beautiful, but no one wanted to marry her, and every time I would see Joan, she would wistfully ask me, "Zsa Zsa, how can I catch Arthur?" She and I were friendly and I knew that she was a strange mix of very tough and very insecure. She was always complaining to me, "I can never hold on to a man." I understood exactly why.

It seemed to me that Joan was like a man herself. You can't chase a man. He has to chase you. Let him chase you until you catch him. I always tell a man I want to marry him. But I only tell him when I'm sure he wants to marry me. Joan never understood my philosophy of love or marriage, but she definitely knew who and what she wanted.'

Joan's affair with Loew was not very passionate and she began to resent the fact that he had given her nothing except 'a few pieces of jewellery', a few gold pins and diamond rings, forgetting all the expensive dinners he had bought her, all the nightclub visits and the white mink stole he had given her for her birthday. She complained that although she was young, beautiful and highly desirable he gave her nothing – an astonishingly mercenary, gold-digger's complaint, since at twenty-two she was already earning the modern equivalent of £420,000 a year – and she told Loew that unless he married her she would feel free to have affairs with other men. She was about to leave Los Angeles for three months to make a film in Jamaica with Richard Burton, who was now thirty, *Sea-Wyf and Biscuit* – later to be renamed *Sea Wife* – and Loew assumed that she had her eye on Burton. Not at all, she said: he was married. Loew pointed out that she had sworn she would never marry again, yet now she wanted to become engaged less than a week after getting divorced. But Joan did not want logic, she wanted commitment. She flew off to London in June for two weeks of pre-production preparation and then joined Burton in Jamaica.

In *Sea Wife* – as in *Our Girl Friday* – Joan is shipwrecked with three men on a tropical island, but this time the film was one of her best and her acting excellent as one of a shipload of Second World War refugees who are evacuated from Singapore in 1942 but then sunk in the Indian Ocean by a Japanese submarine. Joan and the three men – Burton, Basil Sydney and Cy Grant – scramble into a dinghy and drift for several days before reaching an island. Joan is not only very beautiful but also manages to exude a luminous purity and innocence, and she and Burton fall in love, but she resists all his advances. Eventually they escape on a bamboo raft, are rescued by a passing ship, and go their separate ways, but Burton is haunted by the beauty and sweetness of his 'sea wife' and vows to track her down. He fails and never discovers why she resisted him for so long: she is a nun.

Many of the critics sneered at the film. Melvyn Bragg called it 'dreadful … a stinker' in his biography of Burton – but my wife and I both thought it was unexpectedly sweet and poignant, and the *News of the World* reviewer agreed that in it Joan conveyed 'an aura of loveliness and understanding'. Inevitably the British newspapers jeered and sniggered when the casting director, Roberto Rossellini, said that he had given her the role because she had 'a face of innocence'. Joan *Collins*? The Coffee-Bar Jezebel? Innocence? A *nun*? But she took the part seriously, studied some religious books, talked with a group of nuns in a small convent in London, and with little make-up and hair cut very short she was utterly convincing.

In Jamaica she rejected Burton's advances off-camera as well as onscreen, despite her adoration of him at RADA. His green eyes and glorious voice were still mesmeric but she recoiled to see at close quarters his pockmarked skin, blackheads and pimples, and his wife Sybil was with him, and Joan bridled at his arrogant assumption that he could ravish every one of his leading ladies. A few days after filming began he told her how lovely she was, kissed her, and started to undo her bikini top, but she laughed it off and resisted him for two months. They played Scrabble instead and, inspired by the romantic beauty of the Caribbean and her determination to punish Loew for refusing to get engaged, she had an affair with a twenty-six-year-old cameraman, a focus-puller, who she said was the most exciting lover she had had so far. Burton was seriously miffed that she preferred a humble member of the crew, tried to seduce her again, failed, and then dallied instead with several other women including, according to Joan, an elderly, almost toothless black maid.

'Richard,' Joan chuckled, 'I do believe you would screw a snake if you had the chance.'

'Only if it was wearing a skirt, darling,' he said.

The affair with the cameraman was halted briefly when Arthur Loew flew out to Jamaica during the last week of filming.

'Where's Joan?' asked the director.

'She's laying Loew,' said a wag.

She flew back to London for eight more weeks of filming and stayed with her parents at Harley House, rediscovering her childhood and her mother – who spoiled her rotten by giving her breakfast in bed – and her ten-year-old brother, Bill. She continued to cavort with the cameraman, who lived on a Thames houseboat, but away from the balmy warmth and heady luxury of Jamaica the affair cooled. So did her affection for Arthur Loew, though she returned to him for several weeks' holiday in Los Angeles, where she told the gossip columnist Earl Wilson that she wanted to wait a while longer before marrying Loew until she could be sure he was the right man. 'I'd hate to be one of those girls with four or five husbands,' she said, never dreaming that one day she would indeed marry her fifth. Then she flew off again to the Caribbean in November to make her next movie, a musical, *Island in the Sun.*

The film, produced by Darryl Zanuck, was supposed to be based on Evelyn Waugh's brother Alec's controversial bestselling novel of the same title about racism, black liberation and inter-racial sex on a British West Indian island. It was shot in Barbados and Grenada at the end of 1956 and early 1957 with Alec Waugh on hand and a cast that included James Mason, Joan Fontaine and Michael Rennie, while the black actors Dorothy Dandridge and Harry Belafonte provided the film's sexual titillation by having affairs with white lovers. Because it was the first American film to depict inter-racial love scenes, Zanuck and Fontaine were deluged with frightening death-threat poison-pen letters, many of them signed 'KKK' (the initials of the vicious, racist Ku Klux Klan), and the hatred increased when it was rumoured that twenty-nine-year-old Belafonte and thirty-eight-year-old Fontaine were having a real affair on location. Several American southern states swore to ban the film and eventually Zanuck and 20th Century-Fox took fright at all the racist threats and cut the Fontaine/Belafonte love scenes.

Joan looked delicious as James Mason's rich young sister, a white girl who becomes pregnant by the Governor's son (played by Stephen Boyd) and fears that she will not be able to marry him because her grandmother may have had some black blood. But apart from her and Dorothy Dandridge's excellent performances and the lush photography and scenery, the film is slow, stagey, melodramatic, and little more than a glorified travelogue. The script is thin, the direction leaden, the songs tuneless except for the title song, 'Island in the Sun'. Mason and Belafonte are astonishingly amateurish – Belafonte so wooden that *Time* magazine said he performed like a 'talking totem pole' – and Mason's bizarre, strangulated accent bears no resemblance at all to any known version of the English language. Waugh was appalled at the mess that Zanuck and the director, Robert Rossen, were making of his book and complained often but in vain.

Joan adored Barbados. The warm, happy ambience, like that of Jamaica, was wonderfully relaxed and romantic. The crew of more than a hundred men and women partied every night, drank heavily, played poker and Liar Dice, and fell in love. Joan went weak at the knees as soon as she saw the tall, lithe, handsome, smiley, caramel-coloured Belafonte, the 'King of the Calypso', the Caribbean's most famous singer and a renowned ladies' man, but he was married, she was wary of men with Don Juan reputations, she knew that the crew were watching them with amusement, and she dared not have an affair openly with a black man. They flirted and walked at night along the moonlit beach and promised to meet secretly when he was in Los Angeles a few weeks later.

According to Joan's first autobiography, in Barbados she was again pursued in vain by Darryl Zanuck, though her memory may have been flaky because her description of the attempt is identical to that in her second autobiography describing his previous attempt in Hollywood: 'I've got the biggest and the best. I can go all night and all day.' She claimed too that forty-seven-year-old Buddy Adler, who had just taken over from Zanuck as Executive Head of Production at Fox, also made a play for her that year. They were dancing together at his Beverly Hills mansion, she said, when he promised to offer her the best scripts and to make her the studio's biggest star if she was 'nice' to him. Joan told him icily to discuss the deal with her agent.

After an all-night party on the last evening in Barbados she went onto the beach at dawn for a final nostalgic swim and was so reluctant to come out of the sea that the production manager had to drag her out of the water to get to the airport in time. 'When they came and fished me out of the sea to catch a plane to New York I cried all the way because I thought I'd never be in another place that I loved so much,' she told David Wigg of the *Daily Express* in 1994. 'It was like leaving a lover.'

She left Arthur Loew a few days later. Back in Los Angeles they had a row at a New Year's Eve party. 'You're a fucking bore,' said Loew.

'And you're a boring fuck,' said Joan.

In search of less boring fucks she embarked at the age of twenty-three on nearly three years during which she was to have so many lovers that Hollywood gave her a truly memorable nickname. They called her The British Open.

CHAPTER FIVE

THE BRITISH OPEN

{ 1957–1959 }

As a young woman in Hollywood Joan 'went out with zillions and zillions of men', she told the comedienne Ruby Wax during a TV interview in 2003 – or as one famous English actress put it to me less elegantly 'Joan's had more hands up her than the Muppets'. Were you unfaithful? asked Ms Wax. 'Yes,' said Joan, 'but only on location. I used to say, "It doesn't count on location." Whatever I did on location, everybody was having a little fling. I don't suffer very much from guilt.' She added that at least she had never used the casting couch to further her career nor slept with a man who was older than forty-two. In fact, many of her lovers were to be younger than she. 'Joan really led a blazing trail,' Jackie told Melvyn Bragg in 1999, 'because when she came to Hollywood she was a very forceful, dynamic presence and – let me see how I can put this politely – I think she did her own thing sexually and I don't think women were doing that at that time.' As Joan pointed out herself in *Past Imperfect*, women in the 1950s were still expected at least to seem to be virtuous, so her promiscuous sex life made her the subject of crude jokes and she was widely considered to be a tramp by those she considered 'less indulgent folk'.

After Barbados she went off to Acapulco for a month's holiday but was saddened on her return to hear that her beloved grandmother, Hettie, had died of a heart attack in Hove on 10 March at the age of seventy-six. Back in LA her love life blossomed even though she was no longer on location. The New York *World Telegram* reported that she had dated fourteen men in a fortnight, among them Sydney's elder brother, thirty-year-old Charlie Chaplin Jr.; the actors Dennis Hopper, who was only eighteen and her first toyboy, Robert Quarry (twenty-eight), and RJ Wagner (twenty-four); the twenty-three-year-old composer Buddy Bregman; and the dissolute, thirty-year-old play-boy Nicky Hilton. Another date was with the English actor Michael Rennie, who had also been in Barbados filming *Island in the Sun*, but maybe they were just good friends because he was forty-four and Joan swore she had never slept with anyone who was over forty-two. For a while she was considered to be the most shocking girl in Hollywood, she confessed to the *People* in April, and twenty-eight years later she told Donald Zec of the *Sunday Mirror* that she was 'scorned, maligned, criticised and lied about for my fairly normal mode of living, which was considered scandalous and disgraceful. All of a sudden I found myself with the reputation of a swinger and a home wrecker. Beverly Hills wives were supposed to live in fear in case I cast my green orbs in the direction of their men. Ninety-nine per cent of this was total fabrication.'

But not all of it. One wife had very good reason to be suspicious of her: on 8 March Harry Belafonte married his girlfriend, Julie Robinson, who was four months' pregnant. Just a few weeks later, in April, he was singing in Los Angeles and consummating his flirtation with Joan. She must have known that he had recently married – he was one of the most famous singers in America – and she was still having an affair with Nicky Hilton, but when she went to Belafonte's opening show at the Coconut Grove she dressed as seductively as she knew how in a low-cut black dress with the white mink stole and acres of bare shoulder and cleavage. Two nights later they went to bed together in her apartment, and again the next night, and again the next night in his hotel. But they both knew that this could be no more than a three-night stand. Her affairs lasted either one night or six months, she confessed, and three days later she had to fly to Japan to make her next film and Belafonte to continue his singing tour.

Despite her busy love life Joan found time that spring to make a film with the buxom, 40–18–36, platinum blonde sex kitten Jayne Mansfield, *The Wayward Bus*, based on John Steinbeck's 1947 novel. It told the story of a ramshackle old bus rattling on a fifty-mile journey through the Sierra Mountains of southern California that becomes stranded between the towns of Rebel Corner and San Juan due to bad weather and a landslide, and of the passengers' reactions to the situation and to each other. Joan played the driver's boozy, slovenly, bad-tempered wife and Jayne a stripper who falls for a travelling salesman. Playing

Joan's husband was a tall, dark, saturnine thirty-year-old, Rick Jason, who looked remarkably like the young Maxwell Reed. Although Joan was always friendly, claimed Jason forty-three years later in his auto-biography, they barely spoke except on screen until the third week of shooting, when she suggested that they should lunch together in the studio commissary. After lunch, according to Jason, Joan pointed out that they were not needed back on set for some time and suggested: '"Let's go to my dressing room and fuck."'

'"What?"'

'"I said, 'Let's go to my dressing room and fuck.'"'

'"I'm married," I said.'

'"I know."'

'I sat looking at nothing in particular ...

'"Well?" she finally asked.'

'"I told you, I'm married."'

'"Is that your answer?"'

Jason nodded. Joan rose from the table, he said, left him to pay the bill, and never spoke to him again unless they were filming a scene. A few months later Jason was telling the story to some friends when one of them said: 'Don't you know that Collins is known around town as The British Open?'

Joan herself insists that this story is a total fabrication. Despite her naughty reputation, Joan did not succumb to every man who proposi-tioned her. One night in Las Vegas thirty-nine-year-old Dean Martin came banging insistently on her hotel door – crying 'hey, baby, you owe me one' – but she refused to let him in, though she admitted again a few years later in an interview with Steve Dunleavy of the *News of the World* that her promiscuity undoubtedly damaged her professionally. 'My reputation for being a bit of a swinger harmed my career and that upset me,' she said. 'They all thought I was more interested in dating than acting.'

So she was delighted to be given at last a meaty character part in *The Wayward Bus* that would require some real acting, but the reviews were poor and the film did badly in the cinemas. 'It simply doesn't jell,' said the *News of the World*, though Joan herself attracted some good reviews. Years later it still rankled that she was not fully credited for some of her better performances and she complained that many people thought she was a gormless starlet obsessed with parties, nightclubs and sex.

By now, in 1957, just two and a half years after coming to Los Angeles, she was earning the modern equivalent of £7,300 a week and had a beautiful apartment on Shoreham Drive, a pink Thunderbird car, and plenty of money to spend. Nicky Hilton lasted longer than most of her boyfriends: several months. As heir to the Hilton hotel chain he was immensely rich, tended to give his girlfriends chinchilla stoles and emerald bracelets, and like Joan he enjoyed fast sports cars, champagne, caviare and expensive nightclubs. His marriage to Elizabeth Taylor in 1950 – her first – had lasted just nine months, and he was a drug addict who also drank too much, a jaded wastrel who hated Jews and 'niggers', and the sort of crude 'sexual athlete' who boasted about the length of his penis, the number of his conquests and the duration of his sexual encounters. He even kept an orgasm scoreboard next to his bed – and a gun that he liked to fire in the middle of the night to frighten the neighbours. He was to die of a drugs overdose twelve years later, in 1969, at the age of forty-two. No wonder Joan told the *Sunday Dispatch* reporter in New York at the end of April that she was 'tired of falling in love' and added: 'I am not falling in love again until I feel I have to. It is so nice no longer being in love. When you are you always have to worry about what your man wants. When you aren't you can please yourself. I've got very tired of being told by men what to do and what to wear, how to look, when and where to come and go.'

A few days later she flew to Japan with RJ Wagner to make a very bad espionage thriller, *Stopover Tokyo*. Wagner was having an affair with the beautiful but highly unstable, one-time child actress Natalie Wood, who was now eighteen, had already made twenty-nine movies, and was furious that he would be away for two months with the noto-rious man-eating Joan Collins. To reassure her that he was not going to jump into bed with Joan, RJ took his parents with him and promised that they would be sharing his hotel suite in Tokyo. Every day for two months, sometimes several times a day, RJ telephoned Natalie from Japan, even though in those days it could take hours to connect a transpacific call and each was ferociously expensive. RJ was so faithful – and the men on the film crew all well over fifty – that Joan was bored, lonely and celibate, even after a visiting American actor took her to an amazingly explicit live sex show and begged her afterwards to sleep with him: in vain because she preferred straight heterosexual sex, hated anything kinky, and found the show a complete turn-off.

Natalie Wood was having much more fun back in Hollywood: she rewarded RJ's fidelity by having a fling with Nicky Hilton while their regular lovers were safely six thousand miles away, though she dumped Hilton as soon as RJ and Joan returned to LA on 2 July and Joan – whose divorce from Reed was finalised at last six days later – took up with Hilton again. Six months later RJ and Natalie married, Joan said she wished them all the luck in the world, and added undiplomatically: 'He'll need it with that dame!' She was right.

Stopover Tokyo, which Joan and RJ both despised and called *Stop Over-acting*, is a slow, stilted movie in which a very young, fresh-faced Wagner with a ludicrous Teddy boy quiff plays an American spy who saves the US ambassador to Japan from being assassinated. Joan is his beautiful girlfriend, allegedly Welsh but blessed with an excruciatingly tinkly, ultra-English accent. There is also a sickeningly treacly relationship with a little Japanese girl. Not surprisingly the film lost Fox about £7 million in modern terms.

Joan returned to Europe that summer and took up with a thirty-four-year-old English publisher, playboy and future Hanson Industries tycoon, Gordon White, later Lord White of Hull, whose list of girl-friends included Princess Margaret, Grace Kelly, Rita Hayworth and Ava Gardner. He escorted her around the South of France and London, where he took her to a party at Les Ambassadeurs for the arrogantly regal Joan Crawford, who looked Joan up and down with a sneer and then turned away when she was introduced to her as 'one of England's newest and brightest stars'.

Back in New York Joan quickly forgot 'Gordy' White when she fell heavily for a tall, good-looking, witty, always impeccably dressed, thirty-one-year-old married man with three small sons, the producer and director George Englund, Marlon Brando's closest friend. He had been married for four years to the actress Cloris Leachman, who was also thirty-one, had made three films, was to appear in many more, including *Butch Cassidy and the Sundance Kid*, and to become famous in the early 1970s on television as Phyllis Lindstrom in *The Mary Tyler Moore Show*. Joan and Sydney Chaplin had been friendly with the Englunds for two years and had made trips as a foursome to Palm Springs and Tijuana, so she considered George to be off-limits, but when they found themselves staying alone in the same hotel in New York, the Plaza, he took her to a romantic dinner at the Little Club and then went to bed with her. She was hopelessly smitten and over the next three days they spent every spare moment together. Englund told her that his marriage had been unhappy for years and that he and his wife had stayed together only for the sake of the children, and Joan wept when they had to return to Los Angeles.

It was the start of an ecstatic yet unhappy affair that was to last for nearly two years, though it did not prevent her having another fling in December with another toyboy, Peter ('Taki') Theodoracopulos, an immensely rich, twenty-year-old Greek playboy, who was four years younger than she and later to become the High Life society columnist for the *Spectator*. Taki spotted her one night with a very drunken Nicky Hilton at the El Morocco nightclub in New York, invited himself to their table, and asked her out. For night after night they dined, jazz-clubbed and slept together. 'She was the prettiest woman making the rounds that wonderfully festive season, and I felt rather proud,' wrote Taki in *The Sunday Times* in 2002. 'I was madly in love, she was amused by the whole thing. I had obviously lied about my age, making myself one year older.' Hilton became jealous and threatening and Taki's father, John Theodoracopulos, took a shine to Joan as well and gave her a diamond anchor brooch. When she returned to Hollywood Taki followed her but after a six-week affair she sent him back to New York with a dismissive quip: 'Surely you've been away from school much too long.' Taki believed that she dumped him because, despite her passion for George Englund, she had embarked on an affair with the producer and director Stanley Donen.

Joan's affair with Englund hit the tallest heights and the deepest lows. When they were together she was deliriously happy and insatiably sexy. They would often go out to dinner or a club as a threesome with Brando and she loved hearing two such intelligent men arguing in her little apartment on Shoreham Drive or sprawling with both of them on her bed watching television and eating chocolates. Brando warned her not to take acting seriously – 'It *means* nothing', he said, 'it's fundamentally a childish thing to do.' When she gave a party one night she found him by the fridge eating a third quart of ice-cream. Later he went to the lavatory, put a finger down his throat, and brought it all up. That was his way of dieting, he told her. The downside of her affair with Englund was that of most women who canoodle with married men. She would sit by the telephone anxiously waiting for him to call.

They would have to slink in and out of restaurants where they were unknown, though sometimes Brando would come along too to act as Englund's 'beard' by pretending that it was *he* who was Joan's lover. Englund was often late for dates, or would cancel at the last minute. He promised often to leave his wife and marry Joan, but he kept making excuses and it never happened. When he and Joan went on an idyllic, clandestine holiday to the island of Eleuthera in the Bahamas he spoiled it all by talking constantly and guiltily about his wife and children, and they flew back to LA after just three days. Eventually his wife found out about the affair and turned up one afternoon at Joan's flat, banging on the door, weeping and screaming. And if Joan went out on dates with other men Englund accused her furiously of being unfaithful to him and they had terrible rows. Even so she still believed that in any love affair 'a man should dominate the woman', she told the New York *World Telegram*. 'Not push her around, but he should wear the pants. American women are too aggressive and that's not feminine.' Yet despite the joys of their relationship and her attempts to be submissive and to understand Englund's problems and pressures, she was more often miserable and depressed, and in May told *Photoplay* magazine: 'I resent the freedom that men have ... They can go anywhere they want and do as they please ... Girls are forced to take subtle measures to get the right man to ask her for a date. I hate playing games and that's what it comes down to.' As Carl Clement wrote in the same magazine, 'while Joan has been establishing herself as a star, there is a question whether or not she has found herself as a person ... She is like a perky poodle, constantly tugging at a leash.' So although she was to refuse to play several parts that she felt were wrong for her that year – and was consequently put by the studio on suspension without pay – it was a relief when she was cast in a Gregory Peck western that was set in the 1880s, *The Bravados*, shot on location in Mexico for three months, even though once again she thought the film was wrong for her.

'Joan Collins was a sensational young girl, kind of a knockout,' remembered Peck, and she certainly looked stunning in the film and still very English, despite her attempt to speak with an American accent befitting the character she was playing, an aristocratic Spanish-American rancher looking for a husband. Peck himself was handsomely brooding as the cowpoke whose wife has been raped and murdered and who has come into town to see four men hanged for the crime, but they escape and he joins the posse that rides out after them. One by one he tracks them down and kills three of the four condemned men, but then he discovers to his horror that they were innocent. It is a pretty ordinary cowboy film and Joan's small part was completely unnecessary to the story. The riding terrified her: she was afraid of horses, petrified when she discovered in Mexico that she was expected to mount a huge, prancing, snorting, black stallion, insisted on a quieter ride, and once the film was over she never rode again. As for her love life on location, Peck was too old for her at forty-one, surprisingly shy, and in any case his wife was with him, but as usual on location Joan found another temporary bedmate until she returned to LA and George Englund.

Her affair with Englund screwed her up so much that five times a week she went to see her psychoanalyst, who told her that Englund was just another of her father figures, but she refused to believe it. Regularly she consulted an astrologer who told her that one day she would be very successful and always saved from physical or financial disaster at the eleventh hour, but that she would never be lucky or happy in love. She even forgave Englund when she discovered that he had another mistress, but she could not accept that he was still sleeping with his wife. One night, suspicious, Joan drove slowly past their house and was furious to see them undressing and going to bed together, even though he had promised her that they slept in separate rooms. And then he told her that his wife was pregnant again. Joan was incensed, hurled a bottle of vodka and an ashtray at him, and shrieked. 'That's my baby she's having. It should be mine! It's mine! It's mine!'

She took revenge in the best way she knew. Zsa Zsa Gabor had told her that Rafael Trujillo Jr, the incredibly rich twenty-four-year-old son of the vicious Caribbean dictator of the Dominican Republic, had been lusting after Joan for ages, and he was renowned for showering his girlfriends with lavish presents. He had given Zsa Zsa a red convertible Mercedes-Benz 220S and a full-length chinchilla coat worth £285,000 in modern terms, and he had given another Mercedes to another actress mistress, Kim Novak. 'It might be worth your while,' said the mercenary Zsa Zsa, whom so many men deluged with expensive gifts and jewels that she once confessed to being a marvellous housekeeper – 'every time I get a divorce I keep the house'. Zsa Zsa suggested an assignation with Trujillo, whom she called by his nickname, Ramfis. 'Joan's reply,' wrote Zsa Zsa in her autobiography, 'was "I only want to meet him if he gives me a beautiful present." Tactfully, I relayed the message to Ramfis, who shrugged and said, "Okay, if she wants something, call up Van Cleef and Arpels and order a diamond necklace for her." I obliged, ordering an item that today [1991] would cost in the region of $100,000 [£74,000 in 2007]. The date was duly arranged.'

Joan flew to New York and then Florida to meet Trujillo – more than three thousand miles for a one-night stand. He turned out to be a smooth, dark Latin, not especially handsome and married with six children. Moored off Palm Beach, they ate a magnificent dinner together on his 350ft yacht, the *Angelita*, eating off gold dishes with gold cutlery, and afterwards they danced, and although Joan did not pretend to any particular affection or even lust for him she went to bed with him. 'Afterward,' wrote Zsa Zsa, 'I asked Ramfis if he had had fun with Joan. "I picked her up in my yacht in Miami," he said tersely. "She was so boring that I put her ashore in Palm Beach." I said nothing, having quickly come to the conclusion that the clever Miss Collins had probably taken the diamond necklace and then proceeded to make herself appear to be so boring that she didn't have to do anything with Ramfis afterward.' Joan's own version of the story was that she did indeed sleep with Trujillo but did not receive the necklace until she returned to New York the next day. She claimed that she had wanted to return the bauble but was persuaded by Zsa Zsa and others that Trujillo would be insulted if she did, and that in any case a diamond necklace was nothing to a man as rich as he. According to her autobiography, George Englund's response to this action was to describe her as 'worse than a street corner tart.'

Joan and George Englund kissed and made up, he told her that his wife had had a miscarriage and that they were definitely getting a divorce, and he asked her to marry him. According to Englund's wife, Cloris Leachman, Joan was so convinced that she had got her man at last that she telephoned to tell her that she was in love with George. 'Well,' said Leachman, 'do you think you two can make a go of it?'

'Yes, I do,' said Joan frustratedly, 'but he loves you!'

Still, she was happy again and to make her happiness complete her burgeoning stardom was confirmed when she was asked to present the Best Cinematography Award at the annual Oscars ceremony and was then cast in a film with thirty-three-year-old Paul Newman, who had just made *Cat on a Hot Tin Roof*, and his new twenty-eight-year-old wife, Joanne Woodward, who had recently become Joan's friends. The film was *Rally 'Round the Flag, Boys!*, a lighthearted farce, which Joan said later was the best film she had made so far because she was able at last to use her talent for comedy. At first Fox wanted Jayne Mansfield to play the part, insisting that blondes are naturally funnier than brunettes, but Newman and Woodward persuaded them that Jayne would be too obvious and vulgar and that Joan would be better, and she played very well and amusingly the part of a gorgeous and irresistibly seductive but bored, frustrated, small-town man-eater who is looking for a lover and chooses to tempt a harassed neighbour (Newman) whose wife (Woodward) kicks him out when she suspects that he has been unfaithful. The film starts out as a jolly, frivolous jape but becomes laboured and frenetically silly, the reviews were lukewarm, and Newman and Woodward were both ashamed of their performances. Joan was rightly pleased with hers and enjoyed making the film with her friends, though it nearly ended in tragedy when she gave an end-of-movie dinner party, ate some shellfish, and developed a sudden frightening allergy that made it difficult to breathe and caused her face and throat to swell horrifically. Stanley Donen rushed her to hospital and her life was saved by an adrenaline injection.

More difficult to save was her affair with Englund. When he found out at a smart Hollywood party that Rafael Trujillo had given her a diamond necklace, and why, he was furious, called her a whore, 'a fucking little slut', and said 'you're worse than a street corner tart' before ripping the necklace from her throat and hurling it across the room, sending the diamonds flying, and storming out, leaving her on her hands and knees to pick up the pieces. Trujillo's generosity towards his women was soon to cause a huge scandal in Congress and the Press because the United States had recently given the Dominican Republic ten million dollars in aid and several Congressmen claimed that it was this American money that had paid for Trujillo's presents to his girlfriends. Zsa Zsa, Kim Novak and Joan were pilloried in the newspapers and Congressman Wayne Hays of Ohio went so far as to call Zsa Zsa 'the most expensive courtesan since Madame de Pompadour'. Once again Joan and Englund kissed and made up, and to mollify him she bought a similar but cheap, $125 fake diamond necklace, wore it when they had dinner one night at Malibu, and when they strolled romantically along the beach afterwards she threw it into the sea to show him how little it and Trujillo meant to her. Englund was astonished, impressed, and never mentioned Trujillo again – but a few days later she caught him in a car in flagrante with a married woman. And yet she forgave him, again and again. She was truly bewitched by the man. With a somewhat unfortunate choice of words she wrote in *Past Imperfect* that 'ups and downs seemed to be my destiny'.

In November Joan flew back to London to promote *Rally 'Round the Flag, Boys!* and stayed with her parents at Harley House, where her mother waited on her hand and foot as always. She was interviewed by the *Sunday Dispatch*'s showbiz columnist, to whom she complained that she was now having to pay sixty-five per cent of her income in tax. She fibbed outrageously by pretending that she had not been out with a man in six months and announced that she was ripe for marriage. 'We had that Arthur Loew chap staying here with us,' said Elsa wistfully. 'Nice chap, he was. We had great hopes of him. Oh, I would like to see her married, but that's her business.'

Another admirer was Spyros Skouras, the Greek president of 20th Century-Fox, but the fact that he was ugly and sixty-five years old counted against him. At the start of 1959 Fox was planning to make a lavish epic version of *Cleopatra* and for several months Joan was tested for the title role with numerous different costumes and three different Mark Antonys, coached in how to walk regally, and bullied into dieting, even though she weighed no more than 126lbs. She was so confident that she would land the part that she told friends that she had. Skouras promised her time and again that the part would be hers if she were 'nice' to him but she declined the offer, burst into tears, and rushed out of his office, and the part was to go eventually to Elizabeth Taylor – not that there is any suggestion that she succumbed to the randy old Greek to clinch it.

Joan was now so well established as a Hollywood star that she was asked to appear again at the Oscars ceremony in April, this time not as a presenter but as a performer, to sing a scurrilous song with Angela Lansbury and Dana Wynter poking fun at some of the actors present. She wore a stunning gold lamé dress but the lyrics were dreadfully unfunny, the victims offended, and the audience cringed with embarrassment. Otherwise she did very little acting in 1958 and 1959 except for some appearances on television as herself on Ed Sullivan's *Toast of the Town* show, *The Bob Hope Show*, and as a panellist on *What's My*

Line?. She turned two scripts down – *The Last Wagon* and *Madison Avenue* – because she did not consider them to be good enough and wanted to appear in another comedy, and Fox kept putting her on suspension so that she earned nothing, which dented her finances badly because by now she was earning £8,600 a week in modern values. Even her love life had become unexciting. Apart from Englund, who kept not leaving his wife and postponing his promised divorce, Joan was seen out and about on dates with only two other men: Stanley Donen and the actor Gardner McKay, of whom she said that their relationship was 'semi-platonic', whatever that may mean. She was still clingingly possessive about Englund, and Earl Wilson remembered a party at which George left her briefly to talk to someone else and she 'flounced off, and she can sure flounce'. Later, said Wilson, she was openly nuzzling Englund's ear.

One day in August she was in a restaurant with friends when she noticed a young man staring at her: Shirley MacLaine's little brother, twenty-two-year-old Warren Beatty, who was still unknown and would not make his first movie for another three years. It was the start of a seriously heavy affair that would last for two years.

CHAPTER SIX

THE FIRST SERIOUS TOYBOY

{ 1959–1961 }

Warren Beatty was eating with twenty-one-year-old Jane Fonda, who was in Hollywood to make her first film, when Joan spotted him in La Scala restaurant in August 1959. His face was spotted too, with adolescent acne. At twenty-six she was four years older but already susceptible to her lifelong taste for younger men. She thought he looked cute with his cheeky little nose, small short-sighted green eyes, sexy mouth, dimpled chin and curly hair. For his part he had fancied her hugely ever since seeing her photograph on a magazine cover and had persuaded his agent to invite her to La Scala when he would be there. 'I'd really been out of my mind trying to meet this girl,' he said later. 'She's got eyes that are big pools and she looks like a rain goddess in the rain.'

They did not speak but Beatty persuaded another agent to invite Joan to a Beverly Hills party given by her old flame Arthur Loew and Tyrone Power's widow Debbie to celebrate their engagement. Beatty was playing the piano brilliantly when Joan arrived and they smiled at each other, but he was so absorbed that once again they said nothing to each other. The next day, however, he left six messages with her telephone answering service and invited her out to dinner. They ate Mexican, drank a cascade of margaritas, and talked non-stop. She liked his intelligence and sense of humour and discovered that he was Aries – apparently a good match for her as a Gemini – and that he lived in New York, had been a construction worker and had made some TV programmes but wanted to break into movies. This was his first visit to Hollywood and 'he was just *desperate* to become famous', Joan reported later. When the joint closed well after midnight they returned to her flat in Shoreham Drive and went to bed together with none of that prissy nonsense about not screwing on your first date. From that first night they became an instant item and Beatty's friend Michael Pollard reckoned that Joan was 'the only girl he ever loved until he met Julie Christie'.

Beatty was a wizard in bed – 'Aries men are ruled by their cocks,' her astrologer told her – and Joan discovered that he could make love five times a day every day and would even conduct telephone conversations while he was ravishing her. Britt Ekland, who was to have an affair with him eleven years later, reported in her autobiography that he was 'the most divine lover of all. His libido was as lethal as high-octane gas. I had never known such pleasure and passion in my life. Warren could handle women as smoothly as operating an elevator. He knew exactly where to locate the top button. One flick and we were on the way.' Joan and Beatty became besotted with each other and spent every possible minute together. Her friends thought she was mad: he was poor, unknown, unemployed, and maybe using her to further his career, but for him she dumped George Englund, even though he begged her several times to change her mind and promised yet again to marry her. Her shrink persuaded her that Englund had made her suffer enough, would never make her truly happy, and that it was time to kiss Daddy goodbye, and he was right: the Englunds were not to divorce for another twenty years. Beatty moved in with Joan and she revelled in having at last a deep, stable, long-lasting love affair. 'I went through a short period, when I was very young, in which I experimented with several different partners,' she told the *Daily Mail* in 2002, 'and although it seemed exciting, I realised that it was a one-way ticket to disappointment. Because I was brought up by the generation that considered it "wrong" or "dirty" for women to enjoy lovemaking, in my own way I was attempting to prove that notion was a fallacy.'

Just before meeting Beatty she had started work on another film, *Seven Thieves*, with Edward G. Robinson, Rod Steiger and Eli Wallach, a silly but amusing, unexpectedly poignant little movie with a splendid twist at the end. She played a nightclub stripper who helps some gangsters carry out a clever raid to steal four million dollars from the Monte Carlo casino, and to prepare for it she had to spend days being coached exhaustingly by a bump-and-grind artist in how to dance and undress provocatively. Sadly the censor disapproved of the two erotic scenes and much of them had to be cut, but Joan looked as gorgeous as ever

– fresh, sexy, leggy, but surprisingly skinny and gawky – and she acted well enough although her accent was still remarkably English, despite five years in Hollywood.

In September the President of the Soviet Union, Nikita Khrushchev, and his fat wife Nina visited Hollywood and were given a tour of the Fox studio lot and then a lavish lunch attended by hundreds of Hollywood stars, among them Joan and Beatty. Shirley MacLaine, Juliet Prowse and Barrie Chase were in the middle of filming *Can-Can* and performed a risqué, high-kicking frilly-knicker dance to entertain the guests. Khrushchev grinned lecherously but Mrs K glared at them with stony disapproval, though she brightened up when Frank Sinatra sang. Later Mr K chatted for ages through an interpreter with Marilyn Monroe and could hardly keep his hands off her. Sensibly he was not introduced to Joan: who knows what global crisis might have occurred? At the end of the meal her elderly admirer Spyros Skouras made a speech in which he told Khrushchev that the USA was a land of great opportunity. 'Look at me,' he boasted. 'I was once a poor Greek shepherd and now I'm the boss of thirty-five thousand employees. That's America, Mr Khrushchev.' Khrushchev was not impressed. 'I was once a poor Ukrainian shepherd and today I'm the boss of two hundred million citizens,' he replied in his speech. 'That's the USSR, Mr Skouros!'

Sadly for Joan, Skouras and the other big cheeses at Fox decided at last that she was just not famous enough to carry *Cleopatra* and that to make a profit out of a movie that they reckoned would cost £10.5 million in modern values they needed a really big star to play the lead. They approached Sophia Loren, Gina Lollobrigida and Audrey Hepburn, but eventually gave the part in October to Elizabeth Taylor even though they had to pay her an unprecedented fee of a million dollars [£3.5 million] plus ten per cent of the gross profit. After months of dreaming about the role, waiting, being tested and coached, Joan wept. Fox tried to make up for her disappointment by offering her a seriously heavyweight part in D. H. Lawrence's gritty *Sons and Lovers* but she begged the studio to give her another comic role instead.

Beatty flew to New York to begin rehearsals for a Broadway play in which he had at last landed a part, *A Loss of Roses* by William Inge, who was said to be nurturing his embryonic career because he had a homosexual yearning for him. Beatty played appropriately a young petrol pump attendant in love with an older actress but also Oedipally attached to his mother and was absolutely right for the part, said Inge, because he was so sexually confident that 'he feels a wreath has been hung on his penis'. In November the play was given a pre-Broadway run in Washington and Joan joined him there as soon as she had finished filming *Seven Thieves*. Warren introduced her to his parents, whom she liked immediately, and their relationship became so intense that she decided she could not bear to leave him and fly to England to make *Sons and Lovers*, even though it would have been her first really challenging film and might have been the making of her as a serious actress since she would be acting with Trevor Howard and Wendy Hiller. But Beatty selfishly begged her not to do it. 'Don't go, Butterfly,' he wheedled. 'Don't leave your Bee.' When she told Fox that she would not play the part – her fifth refusal in five years – they put her on two months' suspension yet again, which cost her in modern values £67,000 in lost salary, and gave the role to Mary Ure, who played it so well that she was nominated for an Oscar. Rejecting the part was Joan's biggest professional mistake, yet nine months later she had the gall to complain to Roderick Mann of the *Sunday Express* that 'of course I'd like to make good films. Who wouldn't? But I always get stinkers ... I wish I'd had the breaks Warren's sister, Shirley MacLaine, has had.' More to the point was the remark of a Fox executive who told the New York *World Telegram*: 'When Joan is in love she simply takes off and to hell with her work, her career and her studio.' When eventually she saw the film she realised that it was a much better movie than she had expected and was always to regret turning the part down.

Joan and Warren went on to New York, where *A Loss of Roses* opened on 28 November and he won excellent reviews. 'Mr Beatty, sensual around the lips and pensive around the brow, is excellent,' wrote Ken Tynan in the *New Yorker*, and the *New York Herald Tribune*'s Walter Kerr agreed: 'Mr Beatty's performance is mercurial, sensitive, excellent.' But the play was still a flop and closed after only twenty-five performances. One of Beatty's friends, Lenn Harten, took an instant dislike to Joan, accusing her of being snobbish, but others thought they were great together. 'She was really right for him,' said Verne O'Hara. 'Sex *drives* Joan. She was besotted with him. And he was besotted with her.'

Joan had originally planned to spend that Christmas of 1959 in

England with Joe, Elsa, Jackie and Bill, whom she had not seen for a year, but now, short of money, she decided to stay on with Warren to party in New York, staying with friends for free and eating cheaply. Just four months after meeting they were already planning to marry, flew back to Los Angeles in January, rented a small apartment at the Chateau Marmont hotel, and narcissistically skimmed all the movie magazines to find pictures of themselves together.

Now that Joan was dizzily in love again she decided once more that a woman should be subservient to her man. 'I'm a completely old-fashioned girl,' she told Irene Thirer of the *New York Post* in February. 'I don't think females are equal to males. Man is superior, stronger physically, more intellectual, more logical. And I'm jolly glad! I don't want to be independent and make decisions.' A few days later, however, she did have to make a major decision. She discovered she was pregnant. Warren was appalled. She said she would like to keep the baby. He was horrified. They considered having the child adopted but Warren was immovable: a baby now could sabotage his entire career just as it was taking off. He persuaded her to have an abortion. This was illegal in 1960 but through one of his friends they found a doctor in Newark, New Jersey, who was prepared to do it. Joan was terrified but they flew to New York, drove to Newark and she went through with it. Three days later she lost something else: the Trujillo necklace was stolen from their hotel room.

Since Warren was about to make his first film, *Splendour in the Grass*, which was again written by his mentor William Inge and directed by Elia Kazan – who had previously directed *A Streetcar Named Desire, On the Waterfront* and *East of Eden* – he and Joan rented Paul Newman's and Joanne Woodward's apartment on Fifth Avenue and Warren went to work at the Filmway studios in New York. His co-star was Natalie Wood, now twenty-one and as gorgeous as ever, and they played a couple of 1920s Kansas teenagers who fall deeply in love but break up because she is a fragile, deeply moral girl who refuses to 'go the whole way' and consequently drives him into the arms of another girl. Joan, Warren, Natalie and RJ had become good friends in Los Angeles, often going for dinner and to nightclubs as a foursome, so Joan and RJ began to turn up on the set to watch and both were soon decidedly twitchy about the depth of passion that Natalie and Warren seemed to be putting into their love scenes. Joan and RJ became so suspicious and turned up so often on set that they were given canvas chairs with their names stencilled on the back, and the crew chuckled to see how closely they clung to their partners. 'RJ couldn't seem to keep his hands off Natalie,' one of the crew told their biographer Warren Harris. 'He was always kissing and hugging her, as if to show that he loved her so much that he'd punch the first guy that even winked at her.' Yet at first it seems that Natalie disliked Warren. He was arrogant and difficult to work with, she told friends, and she called him Mental Anguish. The crew had a cruder nickname for him – Donkey Dick – and the assistant director, Don Kranze, told Natalie's biographer Suzanne Finstad that 'Warren was a pain in the ass. He was very young, anyway, but his emotional maturity was about thirteen … we all sort of felt about Warren that he's an immature boy playing a man's game.'

Inevitably the gossips claimed that Natalie and Warren were having an affair. They 'are staying up nights rehearsing their next day's love scenes', sniggered the columnist Dorothy Kilgallen. Joan herself suspected that they might have had a brief fling during the filming of *Splendour in the Grass*, especially after she had to fly off to Rome in June to make another film, but most of Natalie's friends, including Robert Redford, insisted later that her affair with Beatty did not begin until a few months later. Her playwright friend Mart Crowley even told Gavin Lambert that at first Natalie hated playing love scenes with Warren because she suspected that he didn't wash enough, and sometimes he seemed so cold during their love scenes that Kazan urged him to pretend that Natalie was Joan.

In May Joan turned twenty-seven. It was the first of her birthdays to depress her because both her father and Max Reed had warned her that an actress was usually past it after her mid-twenties. To reassure her, or maybe out of guilt for making her have an abortion, Warren decided that they should become engaged. 'I feel like having some chopped liver,' he told her one afternoon and when she took the carton out of the fridge there, hidden in the meat, was a gold, diamond and pearl engagement ring. They told the Press that they planned to marry in January, and Joan flew off to Rome to film *Esther and the King*, an Italian co-production in which she was to have top billing, but it was a truly dreadful film, slow, dreary and quite ludicrous, yet another biblical epic set 2,500 years ago in which she played a Jewish girl who is kidnapped by a foreign king, falls in love with him, marries him even though she's engaged to a young Jewish man, and uses her womanly wiles to make him a nicer king and deliver the Hebrews from bondage. The main villain, the brutal Chief Minister, has a weirdly green face, all the men wear fetching little miniskirts, and the Chief Eunuch looks just like Bob Hope albeit in a pale blue frock and turban. Joan told Fox that the film would be rubbish and Warren urged her not to do it, but she could not afford to be put on suspension without pay again.

Rome was one of her favourite cities but she hated being away from Warren and they spent hours every day talking on the transatlantic telephone. On her second weekend away she flew on impulse the eight thousand miles to New York and back to see him for three days – and maybe to check up that he was not dallying with Natalie – and when she returned to Italy he bombarded her with passionate telegrams. To make matters worse only she and two other actors spoke their dialogue in English: the others all spouted Italian except for a Frenchman who delivered his lines in French and a Spaniard in Spanish. No wonder the film was a shambles. Bored and restless, Joan flew one weekend to London to order a beige chiffon wedding dress and a couple of weeks later to New York again, arriving on a Saturday night and returning to Rome on the Monday night. It was not a happy weekend. Warren accused her of having an affair in Rome, she suspected that *he* was having an affair, and they yelled at each other for two days. Back in Italy she took her revenge by embarking on a heavy flirtation with an Italian actor, Gabriele Tinti, and blatantly holding hands with him on set although she denied going to bed with him.

Elsa and Bill flew out to Rome to stay with her for a few days but the tabloids heard about Tinti, reported that Joan was having an affair with him, and Warren sent her at the end of July an angry telegram that reduced her to tears. She flew yet again to New York and simply failed to turn up for work without even telling the director of *Esther and the King*, Raoul Walsh, who was understandably furious. When she landed at Idlewild airport 'the runaway actress' was met by a barrage of reporters and photographers. 'I had toothache,' she told them, as though there were no dentists in Rome. 'I felt too ill to go on. I just had to get it fixed.' She and Warren spent an idyllic weekend together and were so 'lovey-dovey in the restaurant, kissing and holding', said one of their dinner companions, Donald Krantze, that 'I was a little bit uncomfortable, to tell you the truth'. When Joan returned to Italy the studio put a twenty-four-hour guard on the airport to stop her flying out again, and when Roderick Mann of the *Sunday Express* interviewed her over lunch a week later a studio executive told him: 'If you could manage to snatch her passport we'd be eternally grateful. Short of actually manacling her to the bed at the weekend there seems to be no other way of keeping her in Rome.' She admitted to Mann that she was jealous and possessive – 'it's the only kind of love that interests or means anything to me' – and swore that once she and Warren were married she would never allow them to be separated. 'That's the way most show-business marriages go on the rocks,' she said. 'He is the most magnificent man. I'm in love with him and I miss him dreadfully. I'll go back at every opportunity I can get. Of course, it costs me a lot of money, but what else is money for?' She added: 'My life and happiness must come before my career. That's why I have so many rows with my studio, 20th Century-Fox. I do what *I* like – not what *they* like.'

Both *Splendour in the Grass* and *Esther and the King* finished shooting in August and Joan and Warren flew back to Los Angeles and rented a house on Sunset Plaza Drive. Their love was slowly turning sour and they fought a great deal, although Joan still missed him so much when he had to report for three weeks' training as a national service reservist at the George air force base in Victorville, sixty miles north-east of LA, that she joined him there for one of his two weekends away. She was also beginning to tire of his incessant demands for sex and felt that she was becoming just a sex object. 'I'm an oyster in a slot machine,' she sighed to one of her women friends. Living together openly, as they did, they were increasingly accused in the Press of gross immorality even though they were engaged, and 20th Century-Fox reminded her that her contract included a morality clause under which she had undertaken not to embarrass the studio by behaving badly. Separate from Beatty, they said, or get married *now*, or we'll sack you, but Warren was going off the idea of marriage and Jackie beat Joan to the registery office when she married the rich managing director of a dressmaking company, Wallace Austin, in London on 13 December 1960.

Jackie was twenty-three, still living with her parents at Harley House and still calling herself an actress, although she had not made a film for two years and was not to make another. She was married at Marylebone register office but wore a traditional white satin bridal gown. Austin, who was ten years older, had been born Wallace Ornstein but had changed his name by deed poll. Joan thought he was 'a jerk' and tried to dissuade Jackie from marrying him, but Joe Collins liked him a lot and was happy to pay for the reception at the Grosvenor House hotel and hire a decent band until Austin's mother announced that she wanted to invite six hundred guests. Joe blenched and eventually they agreed that he would pay for a third of the cost and Mrs Ornstein would pay two-thirds. In later years Jackie was to lop five years off her age and tell interviewers untruthfully that she was only eighteen when she married. After a honeymoon in Mexico the newlyweds moved into an expensive new house with all mod cons on a smart estate near Hampstead Heath, where Jackie was to employ a maid and enjoy for several years a genteel life of suburban luxury.

Joan and Warren flew to London for Jackie's wedding and Elsa was easily charmed by Warren, but Joe had his doubts even though Beatty was polite, because Joe sensed that he would never marry Joan and was too restless to settle down yet. He was right. In January, when Joan and Warren had planned to marry, the wedding was postponed until March. They flew back to Hollywood but at the end of February, the day before her twenty-ninth birthday, Liz Taylor was suddenly taken seriously ill in London, where she was about to start filming *Cleopatra*, was rushed to the London Clinic with a fever and lobar pneumonia, and within forty-eight hours was rumoured to be dying. She had terrible trouble breathing so the doctors performed an emergency tracheotomy, cutting a hole in her throat, and inserted a tube into her lungs. 'She had almost stopped breathing completely,' one of her doctors, Dr Middleton Price, told her biographer Donald Spoto. 'She might have survived fifteen minutes longer, but no more.' She developed phlebitis, her temperature reached 108, and she drifted in and out of consciousness. The chances of surviving her type of pneumonia were about 50–1 and 20th Century-Fox flew into a panic. If their star died they would lose millions. In desperation they ordered Joan to stand by to fly to London and take over Liz's role at short notice. Joan was appalled by their callousness, but Warren urged her not to be so sentimental and to think of her career: if she played Cleopatra after all she would be confirmed at last as a major star. For four days Liz Taylor's life teetered on the brink of oblivion, but by the fifth day it became apparent that she was going to live. 'On four occasions Miss Taylor was as near to death as she could be,' her specialist, Dr Carl Goldman, told the Press. 'Her courage and will power pulled her through.' Even so she was to stay in the clinic for a month and not leave it until the end of March.

By then Joan's marriage had been postponed again and Fox, no longer needing her to rescue them from disaster, terminated her contract. She had been with them for more than five years and was happy to go, though the loss of her salary of £17,000 a week in modern values was a huge financial blow. But she was fed up with appearing in third-rate films and being considered a permanent member of the 2nd XI. Not only was she the poor man's Liz Taylor, she was 'the poor man's everything', she told Donald Zec of the *Sunday Mirror* in 1985. 'I was the poor man's Hedy Lamarr, the poor man's Ava Gardner, the poor man's Brigitte Bardot. I was a kind of utility infielder. If they couldn't get Susan Hayward or Gene Tierney, they'd use me.'

Soon after Liz Taylor's crisis Joan and Warren flew to London for him to start work on his second film, *The Roman Spring of Mrs Stone*, and were interviewed again by Roderick Mann. 'I've finally left 20th Century-Fox,' Joan told him, 'and I intend to do nothing now until I'm offered a worthwhile film. I don't care how long I wait. There'll be no more junk. Fortunately I'm financially secure. In fact, I'm quite rich. I've been earning good money since I was seventeen and if I didn't work for another five years I could live quite well. I'm part-owner of a New York apartment house and I own a lot of shares, so there's no panic.' This was untrue: she had in fact lost money on her shares and a couple of investments, was in debt and owned nothing. 'I've really appeared in some rubbish, haven't I?' she asked Mann. 'In most of them I didn't even try. I reasoned that, as my notices were bound to be bad, I could always console myself that it was because I'd made no effort. If I'd really tried and then got bad notices, I don't know what I'd have done.'

'Joan's underrated,' said Warren loyally, and then made the mistake of asking, 'Why have all those English actresses who come to America got such big busts?'

'Who are you talking about?' said Joan frostily.

'Oh, Diana Dors and all those others.'

'Dors?' shrieked Joan. 'She's got nothing to brag about.'

'Oh, really?' said Beatty.

'An attractive couple,' wrote Mann. 'I hope Miss Collins gets the films she deserves. I hope she gets Mr Beatty too, though I wouldn't bet on it.'

In *The Roman Spring of Mrs Stone*, which was based on a Tennessee Williams story, Warren was to co-star with forty-seven-year-old Vivien Leigh, the legendary but neurotic star of *Gone With the Wind*, *Anna Karenina* and *A Streetcar Named Desire*. She was near the end of her career and this was to be her penultimate film. Her divorce from Laurence Olivier was about to become absolute and she felt particularly vulnerable because she still hoped to win him back, even though she had a lover, Jack Merivale, of whom she was very fond. 'Poor Vivien is, I am afraid, on her way round the bend again,' wrote Noël Coward in his diary. 'She looks ghastly. What has driven her round the bend is the demon alcohol; this is what it has always been. She arrived ... almost inarticulate with drink and spitting vitriol about everyone and everything. But however upset she may be about Larry she should control herself and behave better.' She was crushed when Olivier married his third wife, thirty-one-year-old Joan Plowright, in Connecticut on 17 March while she was filming in London. Charles Castle, who was personal assistant to the film's director, José Quintero, told Vivien's biographer Alexander Walker that when she arrived on the set that day 'she had obviously been crying her eyes out. She looked awful – woebegone and bloated. She was in the middle of doing her big love scene with Warren Beatty, too, where she had to act tenderly and affectionately.'

It was not a happy film to make. The character Vivien played, Karen Stone, was rather too close for comfort to her own: a lonely actress in her late forties whose looks are fading, whose career is on the skids, and who has just lost her husband – not by divorce but to a heart attack on the plane as they are flying to Rome. She decides to stay on for a while and has an affair with a handsome Italian gigolo, played by Warren, a cunning, narcissistic young whore who uses her to advance his hopes of a career in film – just as many felt that the narcissistic Beatty himself was using Joan. At first Vivien took to Warren. 'She felt she needed a light flirtatious relationship with him in order to make their love scenes work in the film,' said Castle. But she took an instant dislike to Joan. 'Why do you spend so much money on clothes?' she demanded over lunch in the Elstree Studios' restaurant one day. 'It's an absolute waste of good money. Why, I've never seen you twice in the same outfit.' Several witnesses said that Vivien started to go off Warren too when she realised how arrogant he was and not a perfectionist, as she was. When he kept failing to get one scene right she snapped: 'If he doesn't do it next fucking time, I'm going home.' Work on the film was painfully slow. 'All Vivien does is listen, all Warren does is talk,' said Lotte Lenya, the German actress who was playing Mrs Stone's procuress. 'Neither really liked the other off set,' wrote Walker. 'The camera showed it, so the movie had a colder heart than even Tennessee Williams's novella.' Warren's final gaucherie was when he stood up at the black-tie end-of-shooting party and said: 'I want you all to know how much I've enjoyed being in England, even if the film turns out to be a bomb.' The rest of the cast and crew were not amused. 'Altogether it was a tense production,' the film's assistant director, Peter Yates, told Walker.

Yet some believed that Vivien and Warren had had a real affair. Joan was suspicious herself but uncertain whether they actually became lovers until one of his later girlfriends, the singer Madonna, reported years later that he had admitted it. Joan and Warren were still not getting on at all well and when they returned to London he rented a house near Harrods and she moved back for a while into her old bedroom at Harley House to be with her mother, who had recently had an operation for breast cancer. Joan admitted that part of her problem with Warren was that she was no longer prepared to be subservient to any man and was sometimes too aggressive towards him, and that he, being insecure, would become belligerent in return. Another problem was that his star was rising rapidly whereas Joan's was fading. Already he was being offered scripts at more than a million pounds per movie in modern terms while Joan, with no Fox contract, fat salary or even the glimpse of another film on the horizon, was suddenly assailed by an unaccustomed feeling of worthlessness and failure. Now that she was living at Harley House again she took refuge in comforting memories of her childhood and let her mother wait on her and bring her breakfast in bed, even though Elsa had just had an exhausting and depressing operation. Meanwhile in Rome Warren was happily pursuing three young American actresses: Julie Newmar, Jeanne Rejaunier and Susan Strasberg. He actually moved into Strasberg's apartment for two weeks and on one occasion ravished her during a fifteen-minute visit to the bathroom in the middle of a party at the director Luchino Visconti's villa.

Joan and Warren did share one more happy weekend when they visited Paul Newman and Joanne Woodward in Paris, where they were filming *Paris Blues*, and the four of them spent an hilarious drunken evening in a homosexual nightclub where the dancing 'girls' came over to their table and drooled over Newman and Beatty. But Warren also went to the Cannes Film Festival to promote *Splendour in the Grass* with Natalie Wood, and that alone should have rung Joan's alarm bells. Back in Los Angeles and the house in Sunset Plaza Drive he even complained when she invited Elsa and Bill, now fifteen, to stay so that her mother could recuperate from her operation. Warren telephoned Natalie, who was now filming *West Side Story*, to say that he was back in town, and listened sympathetically to the problems she was having with the director as well as RJ. The result was inevitable: they began a passionate affair.

When Joan and RJ found out about it, in June 1961, the Wagners separated and put their luxurious Beverly Hills mansion up for sale. Hollywood was stunned – this was the golden young couple whose marriage had seemed so perfect – and it was reported that Liz Taylor, no stranger herself to divorce and married to her fourth husband, Eddie Fisher, was so upset that she took a couple of tranquillisers and went to bed. The gossip columnist Louella Parsons reckoned it was the most depressing news that Hollywood had had to face since its sweethearts Douglas Fairbanks and Mary Pickford had divorced in 1936. 'RJ didn't stand a chance of getting his wife back while Warren was on the scene,' one of their friends told the Wagners' biographer Warren Harris. 'RJ was too conservative, a square, really. Natalie got bored with him. A woman who's an actress usually craves excitement and conflict, even brutality, in her relationships. Warren gave her that. He was the exact opposite of RJ: dominating, ruthless, greedy to have it all.'

Joan stayed on with Warren as long as possible, terrified of losing him. Now that she had no studio or income, who would she be if she lost him as well? But when Natalie rented a house up in the hills at Bel Air and everyone knew that Warren was visiting her there regularly, even Joan realised that it was time to end the affair. Was it her fault? she asked herself. Was she doomed always to get it wrong with men? Was she maybe too masculine, too pushy? Had she driven him away? Or was it that she was still trying to prove herself to Daddy by loving only difficult men who were themselves incapable of love? Natalie always

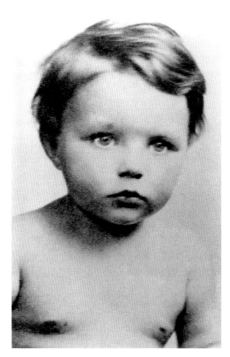

THE PROMISE OF A LEGENDARY
BEAUTY: Joan in 1934
(Archibald Gilmour/Camera Press)

...and as a sultry teenager at Francis Holland School and
still in plaits at the age of 14 in 1947. (Francis Holland)

THE MOTHER WHOM JOAN AND JACKIE BOTH ADORED: Elsa Collins at home with the girls in London in the 1950s . . .
(Starstock/Photoshot)

. . . and with 24-year-old Joan (*above*), 19-year-old Jackie and 11-year-old brother Bill (*left*) on the French Riviera at the Hôtel du Cap, Antibes, for the Cannes Film Festival in 1957. Jackie had recently returned from Hollywood, where she claimed she had an affair with 32-year-old Marlon Brando.
(Edward Quinn/Camera Press)

Joan's first wedding, on the day after her nineteenth birthday, in London in 1952. Her husband was a 33-year-old Anglo-Irish actor, Maxwell Reed, whom the Press called 'The Beautiful Beast.' The marriage lasted only eighteen months but decades years later Joan admitted that 'he was the most devastatingly beautiful man I'd ever met. And those gorgeous eyes just melted my heart.' (PA/PA/Empics)

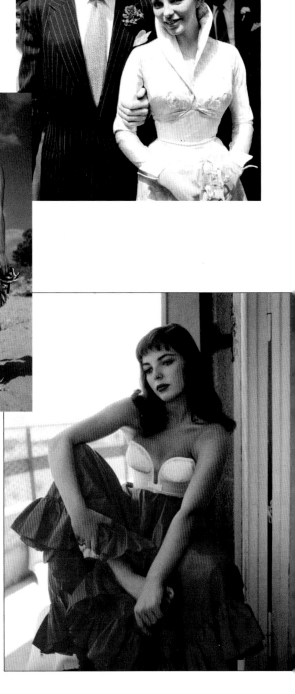

Joan in Majorca in 1953 in the first film that had her name blazoned above the title, *Our Girl Friday*. She played a spoiled, bossy girl who is shipwrecked on a tropical island with three lecherous men: Kenneth More, George Cole, and Robertson Hare (*above*) as a fussy, pompous but besotted old professor.
(Renown/Fox/The Kobal Collection)

Joan aged 21 and languidly sexy in Rome in 1954 while filming *Land of the Pharaohs*.
(David Seymour/Magnum Photos)

Joan with her 28-year-old lover Sydney Chaplin, son of Charlie, in *Land of the Pharaohs*, a huge, lavish, hilariously ludicrous pyramids-and-camels epic about Ancient Egypt that starred Jack Hawkins as a pharaoh and James Robertson Justice as a fat slave architect. Chaplin played the captain of the palace guard, Joan a dark, sultry villainess. (Warner Bros/The Kobal Collection)

With Bette Davis, who played Elizabeth I in Joan's first Hollywood film, *The Virgin Queen*, in 1955. 'She terrified me,' said Joan. 'She terrified *every*one ... I and the five other girls playing her ladies-in-waiting, all of us between the ages of 19 and 21, would cower in a corner giggling nervously and chewing gum and terrified that she might *pick* on us.' (The Kobal Collection)

With 30-year-old Richard Burton in Jamaica in 1955 in *Sea Wife*, in which Joan again played a girl who is ship-wrecked with three men on a tropical island but this time (unknown to them) turns out to be a nun. Burton tried to seduce her both on-screen and off but Joan and her character resisted his charms. (Sumar Productions/The Kobal Collection)

After Loew came George Englund (*above*), a film producer who was married to the actress Cloris Leachman and was Marlon Brando's closest friend. For two ecstatic yet tormented years Joan pestered him to marry her, too, but when he kept making excuses she dumped him for the baby-faced, twenty-two-year-old Warren Beatty (*below*), who had yet to make his first film. She and Beatty lived together for two years and became engaged but he too kept postponing the marriage and they split up when he embarked on a fling with Natalie Wood. (Hulton Archive/Getty Images)

Joan in 1957 with her rich Hollywood lover Arthur Loew Jr, the playboy son of the president of MGM and grandson of the founder of Paramount Pictures. She pestered him to marry her but after more than a year the affair ended at a New Year's Eve party when he sighed 'Joan, you're a fucking bore' and she snapped back 'and you're a boring fuck.' (Bettmann/Corbis)

Joan with two other cinema icons, Marlon Brando and Cary Grant, in the Huntington-Hartford theatre in Hollywood in 1959. (Bettmann/Corbis)

Joan with her second husband, Anthony Newley, and Sammy Davis Jr at the first night of the Broadway performance of Newley's musical *The Roar of the Greasepaint – The Smell of the Crowd* at the Schubert Theatre, New York, in 1965. (Bettmann/Corbis)

'Does my bum look big in this? Are my legs as nice as Mummy's?' Joan's first child, 5-year-old Tara Newley, dressed as a mouse for a charity performance of *Airs and Graces* at the Scala Theatre in 1968. (Keystone/Getty Images)

Joan and Newley with their daughter Tara in 1964 ... (Rex Features)

... and filming Newley's weird movie *Can Heironymus Merkin Ever Forget Mercy Humppe and Find True Happiness?*, in which all four members of the family had parts, in 1968. Joan wept when eventually she saw the film because she realised at last that Newley no longer loved her. (Scope Features)

denied that it was Warren who broke up her marriage and insisted that they had not begun an affair until after she and RJ separated, but for Joan the end came in July when she accepted the offer of a part in a new Bing Crosby/Bob Hope comedy that was to be filmed in London, *The Road to Hong Kong*. Despite the fact that Beatty thought it was rubbish, Joan told him that she wanted to get away from him and that there was good money to be earned.

And then she spoiled it all by crying. They hugged each other tight but it was finally over. Beatty was to go on to have affairs with dozens of beautiful women including allegedly Isabelle Adjani, Brigitte Bardot, Candice Bergen, Claudia Cardinale, Judy Carne, Leslie Caron, Cher, Julie Christie, Faye Dunaway, Goldie Hawn, Diane Keaton, Elle Macpherson, Madonna, Carly Simon, Twiggy, Kathleen Tynan and Liv Ullman, and was eventually in 1992 to marry Annette Bening, by whom he was to have four children. But during his younger days 'Warren was incapable of lasting love', wrote Britt Ekland. 'When he picked a bloom it was only for a season.' Years later Britt met him again and wrote: 'Alas, his college boy looks were becoming slightly crumpled. The eyelids were heavy, the cheekbones mottled. Much of the charm was still there, but the old magic was missing. It looked like Warren had made himself too available: it seemed to me that practically anyone could have him.' Even so, his friend Michael Pollard reckoned that of all his many mistresses Warren's greatest love was Julie Christie, with Joan a close second.

CHAPTER SEVEN

A TOTAL BLOODY IDIOT

{ 1961–1963 }

Joan was never without a man for long. They seemed to queue up like cabs on a taxi rank waiting for her to hail them. When she flew to London at the end of July 1961, and Warren moved into Natalie's house in Los Angeles, she must surely have considered taking revenge in her usual way by having an affair – and what would be better than to have an affair with Natalie's husband, RJ, who just happened to be in London too filming *The Longest Day*? But RJ still adored Natalie and was devastated to have lost her, so although he and Joan consoled each other in London by going out together to dinner, clubs and the theatre, Joan denied that they ever became lovers, mainly because he was just too nice and gentle, not nearly difficult or complicated enough for her.

Her immediate revenge was to denigrate Beatty, and she told Natalie's biographer Suzanne Finstad that his affair with Natalie was just a typically cynical ploy to promote his career. Natalie had just been nominated for the Best Actress Oscar for her performance in *Splendour in the Grass* and 'knowing Warren was the most ambitious person I'd ever met', said Joan, 'a sizzling romance with the hottest film star helped him *enormously*. Don't forget he dumped Jane Fonda for me and I introduced him to everyone I knew in Hollywood.' Many believed that Beatty had indeed used Joan to further his career and suspected that he was now using Natalie too. 'He had probably been in love with Joan Collins once but the publicity of the relationship opened more doors for him than it did for her,' wrote Beatty's biographer John Parker. When Warren's sister, Shirley MacLaine, asked Joan 'how was my brother?' she sneered 'overrated', and being dumped by him still rankled forty-five years later: when Cosmo Landesman of *The Sunday Times* asked her in 2006 if it was really true that she and Beatty had made love seven times a day she raised an eyebrow and purred: 'Maybe he did, but I just lay there.' Even so, when she and Natalie became friends again years later and discussed over lunch how good Warren had been in bed it was Joan who gave him ten out of ten and Natalie who gave him only five. Warren later returned the compliment by rating Joan the best of all his lovers.

In London she moved back in with her parents at Harley House, and filming of *The Road to Hong Kong*, the seventh of the light-hearted *Road* movies starring Bing Crosby and Bob Hope, began on 2 August at Shepperton Studios. It was a dreadfully silly, utterly unfunny 'comedy' with a ridiculous knockabout plot, absurd dialogue, feeble jokes, corny songs and appalling acting. Hope and Crosby played a pair of crooks selling fraudulent tickets for a journey into space, Joan a gun-toting secret agent in pursuit of a secret Russian formula for rocket fuel. After glimpses of Peters Sellers (as a doggedly unamusing Indian doctor), Zsa Zsa Gabor (as a nurse) and David Niven (chuckling wickedly over *Lady Chatterley's Lover*) Hope, Crosby and Joan fly to Hong Kong to meet Joan's boss, Robert Morley, who plays a brutal 'Goldfinger' character straight out of a James Bond spoof, the leader of a sinister group that blackmails the United Nations by threatening to destroy the world's great cities. Morley has Hope and Crosby blasted into outer space instead of apes, planning to dissect them on their return, but Joan feels so guilty about leading them into this trap that she helps them to escape. Finally, all three are launched into space and land on another planet, where they are greeted by Frank Sinatra and Dean Martin and all five of them burst into song. It must be the only 'comedy' I have ever watched where I smiled only once, when Crosby and Hope hopelessly try on the apes' bulky spacesuits.

Joan did not have much fun making the film, either. In her autobiography she claimed that she liked Bob Hope a lot but not Bing Crosby, who she said was detested by the crew as well. She found him grumpy and off-hand and loathed his pipe-smoker's habit of clearing his throat and spitting globules of phlegm onto the studio floor. Worst of all, she said, his breath was rancid and in two scenes she had to kiss him with enthusiasm. In one scene he sings a song so closely into her face that you can see her backing away, and then kisses her languorously. In the final scene their kiss seems to last for ever. Joan said she hated it. 'How would you like to have to kiss him?' she asked one of the cockney crew who particularly loathed Crosby. 'I'd rather go down on 'itler!' he said. Yet twenty-seven years later the *Daily Mirror* alleged that in fact Joan and Crosby had had an affair when the film was made. 'It was well known that they were having an affair,' the paper reported. However, Joan has always denied that any affair took place, saying that their relationship while filming was not good. One of the cast with whom she would love to have had a fling was Sinatra, whom she now found irresistibly sexy and decided to seduce only to be mortified to discover that her stand-in had beaten her to it.

In all the previous *Road* films, over twenty-two years, Dorothy Lamour had co-starred with Hope and Crosby – always wearing a sexy sarong – but this time she had been dumped because Crosby reckoned that at forty-seven she was too old and not sufficiently glamorous, even though he and Hope were both fifty-eight. Hope fought to keep her in the cast but was overruled. 'I felt bad at first, but then just took it in my stride,' Joan told Hope's biographer Charles Thompson. Dorothy felt deeply upset, insulted and humiliated to lose the role of leading lady but eventually agreed to play a tiny part in the film, as herself, and to sing a song. When she arrived in England she was met by crowds of fans and scores of photographers and journalists who reported that she had been treated disgracefully. 'It was terribly exciting and gratifying,' she wrote in her autobiography. 'The next day I went out to the studio to lunch with Bing, Bob, Norm and Mel [the film's producers, Norman Panama and Melvin Frank], and to meet Joan Collins. I knew our first meeting would be strained, especially since one of London's top newspapers had called just before I left New York: Miss Collins had stated that because I was jealous of her getting the larger role in *Hong Kong*, I was looking to start a feud. What was my reaction? I had to laugh. In all my years in the business I had never been jealous of anyone. My reply was short but sweet: "There is no feud. I have never had a feud with anyone, but *if* I even considered having a feud, it would be with the *stars* of a film."

When the movie was eventually released in 1962 Dorothy was delighted to see that the American reviews had headlines such as BING, BOB AND DOTTIE BACK ON THE ROAD and BOB, DOTTIE AND BING TOGETHER AGAIN.

'How about that?' said Hope. 'They don't even mention Joan, do they?'

Dottie smiled sweetly. 'I now know,' she said, 'how it feels for the cat to swallow the canary.'

The reviews were almost all terrible but *Films and Filming* listed it as the fifth most successful movie of 1962, Crosby and Hope were said to have earned £6.5 million each from it in modern values.

In the middle of August, just a couple of weeks after she had arrived in London to work on *The Road to Hong Kong*, RJ took her to the Queen's Theatre to see a new stage show, *Stop the World – I Want to Get Off*, a one-man musical in which a short, pale, skinny, thirty-year-old cockney singer, Anthony Newley, dressed as a white-faced clown, enacted the life story of an ordinary little Everyman called Littlechap, a teaboy who rises to become a Lord but discovers that all his success is worthless and empty. Newley sang sixteen songs in the show, including the hit 'What Kind of Fool Am I?', but many of the critics, among them Kenneth Tynan, thought that he was a pretentious weirdo and rubbished the show as a 'giant ego trip'. Even so the public loved it, it became a huge hit, and Joan decided that Newley was magical and brilliantly original and creative. She and RJ were so impressed that afterwards they went backstage to Newley's dressing room.

His dressing room was guarded by a burly, suspicious, middle-aged minder, Terry Cooke, an ex-policeman who growled brusquely that they would have to wait while 'The Young Master' removed his make-up. Taken aback by this grandiose title, Joan and RJ became increasingly irritated as they waited and waited in a scruffy room that was divided by a tired old green velvet curtain behind which The Young Master was cleaning his face. After twenty minutes Joan decided that she had had quite enough of this rudeness. 'We're going,' she announced sharply.

'Oh, hang on a minute, love,' came Newley's cheeky cockney voice from behind the curtain. 'I'm just putting on me drawers.'

He emerged: short, painfully thin, deathly pale, but in Joan's eyes surprisingly sexy. He apologised for keeping them waiting – 'this muck takes forever to scrubb off' – and they forgave him and told him how brilliant he was and how much they had loved the show and his performance, and despite the minder's openly curmudgeonly disapproval Newley suggested that they join him for dinner. He took them to his favourite nearby Itakian restaurant, the packed, rowdy Trattoria Terrazza, and right from the start he made her laugh and called her Pretty Lady and Flower. She loved his sense of humour, and when she learned that the lyrics of 'What Kind of Fool Am I?' were autobiographical they seemed to be a challenge as well as a warning, for in the song he claimed to be a selfish, empty, lonely man who was incapable of falling in love and never had. It was a challenge that Joan could not resist. Here was another screwed-up, impossible man for her to take on and prove herself to Daddy. Daddy, however, found Newley morose, dull and unfriendly. It was a huge task that she set herself because Tony Newley was to turn out to be utterly neurotic, insecure, depressive, egocentric, selfish, callous, anti-social and compulsively unfaithful. 'With my background,' he once said, 'I should have ended up as a small-time criminal.' He had been born a failed abortion in a Hackney slum workhouse, the illegitimate son of a married second-hand clothes salesman and a poor Salvation Army spinster. He had been abandoned by his father, spoiled and then abandoned by his mother, and evacuated at the age of eight to a country village during the war where he had to live with a couple he hated. Later he had been raised by an aunt and uncle, semi-educated, leaving the local council school at thirteen to work in a piano factory, a gasworks, and then as an office boy before he spotted a newspaper advertisement for the Italia Conti Stage School. The school gave him a free place and lessons in acting, elocution and singing, and as a child actor he had landed parts in eight films, notably at the age of sixteen as the Artful Dodger in David Lean's *Oliver Twist* with Alec Guinness and Robert Newton. This led to a seven-year contract with the Rank Organisation and a teenage affair with Diana Dors, though Rank soon sacked him when the couple were found entwined under a grand piano during a Rank cocktail party.

Despite all his early success Newley wallowed in melancholy and had written moodily in his diary at the age of eighteen to bemoan what he saw as the farcical, nightmarish misery of human life. He called it 'this waiting room of death' and despaired of humanity's ignorant stupidity, buzzing aggressively and pointlessly around each other like vicious bees and feebly struggling to survive, watched with grinning amusement by Death and its certainty of eventual victory. As for the possibilty of an afterlife, wrote the horrified boy, it was surely inconceivable that any god would torture humanity even further with yet another life. Such was the man who was to become Joan's second husband.

As a teenager Newley had been called up to serve two miserable years of compulsory national service in the army but cunningly managed to behave so badly that after six weeks he was discharged as being mentally unstable. An older, homosexual friend set him up in a flat in South Kensington and gave him an allowance but he became depressed, started drinking too much, and was dumped by the homosexual friend before joining a repertory company and beginning to make films again. By the time he met Joan he had married a young actress, Ann Lynn; served a twenty-eight-day sentence in Brixton Prison for driving a car while disqualified; and had had a son born tragically with spina bifida, brain damage and encephalitis whom coldly he rejected but who died after six weeks. He had had several affairs; made several more films; separated from his wife; forced his eighteen-year-old live-in mistress, Anneke Wills, who had been in the TV series *The Railway Children*, to have an abortion; and was now having an affair with a sixteen-year-old, Susan Baker, one of a pair of delectable twins, blonde, blue-eyed actresses who were playing his daughters in *Stop the World*. The year before he met Joan he had had two number-one hits in the pop charts, 'Why?' and 'Do You Mind?', both written by Lionel Bart. And he was a Libra – apparently disastrous for Gemini Joan.

Despite Newley's seriously damaged character he was deeply loved and admired by those who knew him well. 'He was the brother I never had,' wrote his *Stop the World* co-author Leslie Bricusse after Newley's death in a foreword to Garth Bardsley's biography of Newley. 'Writing together, we became the two halves of one person.' Whenever they worked together they howled with laughter, although Bricusse admitted that Newley had some very weird traits: even when he was young he seemed old, cosseting himself with geriatric eye masks and blankets, so much so that Joan called him Old Crusty. Newley and Bricusse so admired the Swedish director Ingmar Bergman that they adopted nicknames adapted from his surname: Newley became 'Newberg' and Bricusse was 'Brickman'. 'You were a shining light in my life,' wrote Bricusse, 'a total joy, a talent supreme, a friend beyond compare, and a total bloody idiot in the way you handled your life and your career.'

Joan claimed that it was three weeks before she and Newley became lovers. She said that he turned up one afternoon at Harley House, where she was in bed with flu, jumped under the sheets with her, and ravished her despite her runny nose, red eyes, sore throat, feeble protests that her parents would hear, and the fact that he had come to her straight from the actress Linda Christian's bed. What a man! In fact she said later that he was never much good as a lover. Bricusse remembered the start of their affair quite differently and reported in his autobiography that it was only two days after they met that she invited Newley and the Bricusses to dinner at the White Elephant, went home with Newley that night, and immediately moved in with him. 'I don't think poor old Newberg ever knew what hit him,' wrote Bricusse. 'A truck could not have done a better job, but then very few trucks look as good or move as fast as Joan Collins when she has her foot on the pedal.' Just three weeks after leaving Warren Beatty she was tucked up in London with Tony Newley.

He told her that despite 'What Kind of Fool Am I?' he *could* fall in love and had – with her – and she believed him. Jackie was about to have her first baby and Joan decided that it was time she had a baby too and that Tony was just the right man to be the father. He threw his young mistress, Anneke, out – when she threatened to kill herself with a kitchen knife he said 'don't be silly, darling. I'll call you a taxi' – and his mother, Grace, took over all the household and laundry chores and brought him breakfast in bed, ignoring Joan even though she was lying beside him. Officially she was still living at Harley House, where the family watched helplessly as Elsa began to die. Her operation had not been a success and although she was only fifty-six the cancer had spread all over her body and the family had been told that she had no more than six months to live.

It was dreadful to watch her in so much pain and rapidly losing weight, although she was granted a few moments of happiness when Jackie's daughter Tracy was born in October and for the next few months Jackie brought the baby regularly to see her.

As soon as the filming of *The Road to Hong Kong* ended on 3 November Joan and Newley became inseparable and she chose one of his songs, 'I Was Never Kissed Before', as one of her eight favourites when she was asked to appear on radio's *Desert Island Discs*. She also chose another of her lovers, Harry Belafonte, singing 'Hava Nagila'; Frank Sinatra's 'Come Fly With Me'; Peggy Lee's 'Lover'; Sarah Vaughan singing 'Serenata'; Rene Touzet and his orchestra playing 'Mambo Inn'; Toni Harper singing Gershwin's 'My Ship'; and Edith Piaf's 'Milord'. Her choice of book to read on her desert island was a teach-yourself course of 'all the main languages' and her luxury was a television set – a surprising choice since she had always sworn that she hated TV, though of course she would not have been able to watch it on a desert island without electricity.

Joan quickly became friendly with Bricusse, who was thirty, and his beautiful, twenty-three-year-old wife Evie, the actress Yvonne Romain, who were to remain lifelong friends. With Newley they went everywhere together. Bricusse and the comedian May Bygraves owned a restaurant, Maxim's, near the Bricusses' flat in Stanmore, on the edge of London, and they would often eat there with another Stanmore resident, thirty-five-year-old Roger Moore, who had just begun to star in the TV series *The Saint*, and his girlfriend Luisa Mattioli. In *Past Imperfect* Joan said that she refused to leave England while her mother was so ill. In fact in December she, Newley and the Bricusses flew to Paris to spend a weekend there together, and she spent Elsa's last Christmas with Newley and the Bricusses in Stanmore, where they exchanged a hundred and thirty presents. On 3 January she flew to Switzerland and then to Los Angeles, where Newley and the Bricusses joined her for a twelve-day holiday and 'the four of us embarked upon the best voyage through the Swinging Sixties that any four people on the planet ... could possibly have enjoyed', wrote Bricusse in his foreword to Bardsley's book. 'The Famous Four, as we modestly called ourselves, lived the high life ... We were together all day, every day, and never tired of the extraordinary energy we created together.' In Los Angeles they rubbernecked through the city. They photographed each other at Disneyland with Mickey Mouse and Donald Duck, fooled about for four days in Palm Springs, and partied for three days in Las Vegas with Sammy Davis Jr, whose cabaret act included 'What Kind of Fool Am I?' and who was urging everyone to see *Stop the World*.

Back in London, Newley and Bricusse learned that they had won three Ivor Novello Awards for *Stop the World*, Newley rejoined the London cast for a few months, made a film, *The Small World of Sammy Lee*, worked on two more shows with Bricusse, recorded a couple of records, and appeared on several television programmes. During the filming of *The Small World of Sammy Lee*, a black-and-white portrait of the seedy underworld of London's Soho, Joan ensured that she was with him almost every day, probably because his innocent, fresh-faced girlfriend in the film was nineteen-year-old Julia Foster, there were nude love scenes, and she didn't trust him. She frightened him by telling him firmly that she wanted to marry and have his children. 'What can a rich, young, single film star see in a married Cockney, half-Jewish git?' he asked her mournfully. He was simply not ready to marry again and after the tragedy of his doomed son's birth he was not at all keen on having more children, either. He also seemed to be carrying some heavy psychological burden despite all his fame, new wealth and success. 'There must be a hole in a man who gets up on a stage and cries "Look at me! Look at me!"' he told the songwriter Herbert Kretzmer, a reporter for the *Daily Express*. 'I am still a paramount egotist forever watching myself. I am always aware of myself and the impression I make crossing a road, entering a room, leaving it, being recognised, being admired. I am also searingly aware of being disliked and rejected. Why? Why do I find life so ugly at times?' He blamed his fatherlessness and having had a working-class mother who had never given him enough attention. Referring to himself in the third person, he told Kretzmer: 'He was born with an engaging little face and nothing more. So he uses his cuteness to get love. It is a device. The process continues throughout his life, into maturity. He sharpens and hones that ability until it is an art. He uses it as the key to something he never had. It is a craving. Acting, when you boil it down, is just a plea for approval, for love.' And yet when a beautiful woman like Joan offered him both approval and love he kept resisting and betraying her. This was going to be a strange, difficult romance.

Newley told Joan that he loved her and was going to divorce Ann, but secretly he continued his affairs with Anneke Wills, slipping into her bed on his way home after the show, and with Susan Baker. Yet he seemed genuinely besotted by Joan. When she flew to Switzerland from London Airport he flouted the airport's regulations by walking out onto the runway to see her off. Three weeks later, when she flew to Los Angeles, he committed another offence by using without permission a private lounge, and the following month he persuaded airport officials to let him say goodbye to her at the door of the plane. His behaviour irritated the Member of Parliament for Gillingham, Squadron-Leader Frederick Burden, who raised the matter in the House of Commons and complained that 'this sort of thing creates resentment among ordinary air travellers'.

Early on the morning of 8 May Elsa died in her bed at Harley House.

She was only fifty-six and she and Joe had been married for thirty happy years. 'My father was absolutely devastated when the end came,' Jackie told the *News of the World* in 1984. 'Whenever I needed her, she was always there, always ready to listen. Looking back, I couldn't have had a more perfect mother.' Joan agreed. 'She was the kindest, gentlest, sweetest woman,' she told Ian MacGregor of the *Daily Express* in 1992, 'and I didn't appreciate it. I was too young.' She blamed Joe for her mother's death and was convinced that she had died so young because he had been so dominant. 'I truly believe it was because she was never allowed to speak her mind,' she told Lynda Lee-Potter in 1999. 'I feel that if my mother had asserted herself more, then maybe she wouldn't have contracted cancer. I believe that a lot of disease is caused by inner conflict and pain that's coming from the inside and which you can't express. He was incredibly upset when she died, but if he did feel guilty he never showed it.' Joe was in fact so distraught that he wrote mistakenly on Elsa's death certificate that she was only fifty-four. She left £2,473–8s–8d, which would be worth £37,400 in 2007. They buried her in Hampstead cemetery and Joe returned to Harley House with Bill, who decided to leave school now that he was sixteen and to work for Joe's agency.

In August Joan went to Italy for a beach holiday in Portofino and wept when she heard that Marilyn Monroe had also just died at the age of thirty-six. In September Tony went to New York to rehearse for the Broadway production of *Stop the World* and to canoodle with Susan Baker, leaving Joan to have fun on her own with the Bricusses. In the same month Joan's father, who was almost sixty, met Irene Korff, the dainty, blonde German woman who was to become his second wife. She was only twenty-six – three years younger than Joan and thirty-three years younger than Joe. Joan and the Bricusses went to Jamaica for a ten-day holiday and then to Philadelphia for the first American production of *Stop the World*. There Tony gave Joan a French poodle called Ladybird and confessed not only that he had been having a fling with Susan Baker but also that he had always had a helpless, legally dangerous sexual obsession with under-age nymphets, especially those of fourteen or fifteen. Joan was devastated and flew miserably back to Los Angeles but she returned to New York for the first night on Broadway on 3 October and attended it with the Bricusses and the Paul Newmans. Three of the first New York reviews were dreadful and again slammed the show as pretentious, self-indulgent and egotistical, yet four others were positive, once again the public loved it, and it became a huge hit, partly because many of the songs had been released and were already popular.

Joan took revenge on Newley for his infidelity in her usual way by having a fling with her third toyboy, the pretty, twenty-three-year-old English cockney actor Terence Stamp, who was six years younger than she and had just made his second film, *Billy Budd*. The romance did not last very long. 'He was the only man I knew who got to the mirror in the morning quicker than I did,' she said, but the fling served its purpose: it made Newley so jealous that he begged her to take him back, agreed to marry her, promised to dump Susan and to try to cure his lust for jailbait girls. He admitted hopelessly that he still had no idea what love was but that he was miserable without her.

Bravely and foolishly she decided to take a chance. They moved into a big, expensive, unfurnished apartment on 69th Street and Lexington Avenue, and six weeks later she became pregnant just as Anneke Wills gave birth to Newley's daughter Polly in London. Anneke asked him for nothing, not even a small amount of money, but she did send him two ecstatic letters describing his baby daughter. He never bothered to reply. Joan should have been alerted by this callous, selfish behaviour – and her father warned her that she would be making another big mistake if she married Newley – but it was in fact the start of three of the happiest years of her life, and reminded her of how lucky she had been to escape Warren Beatty. His affair with Natalie Wood ended early in 1963 in a disgracefully shameless fashion. He took Natalie to dinner at Chasen's in Beverly Hills, where the other guests that night included the Alfred Hitchcocks, the Gregory Pecks and the James Stewarts. Towards the end of the meal he went to the gents' lavatory and simply disappeared. He had taken a fancy to the sexy blonde cloakroom attendant and whisked her off through the back door into the night for three days of passion, leaving Natalie to pay the bill. She was deeply humiliated and hovered on the verge of a nervous breakdown. When he turned up at her house a few days later to collect his clothes and possessions he discovered that she had burned everything in the incinerator. 'Warren's a terrible user of people,' another of his mistresses told Warren Harris. 'He'd gotten all the publicity mileage he could from the relationship. When it started, nobody had ever heard of

Warren Beatty. By the time he left Natalie they were calling him the hottest star since Brando.'

On 22 May 1963 Tony and Ann Lynn were divorced at last and five days later he and Joan were married by a Justice of the Peace, Michael Strepkowski, at Sardi's restaurant in Norwalk, Connecticut, thirty miles outside New York. She was thirty, he thirty-one. The only guests were Tony's best man, the actor Michael Lipton, and Joan's matron of honour, her old Los Angeles friend Cappy Badrutt, and it seems entirely appropriate that the Justice of the Peace's flies gaped unashamedly open throughout the ceremony.

CHAPTER EIGHT

WIFE AND MOTHER

{ 1963–1969 }

For the first three years of Joan and Tony Newley's marriage she was so content to be just a wife and mother that she made only one film and a flicker of brief appearances on television. Even when she was offered the part of the Jean Harlow-esque character in Harold Robbins's *The Carpetbaggers* she turned it down and it went to Carroll Baker. In August, however, she did join Newley, Bricusse, Peter Sellers and Daniel Massey in making a satirical LP record, *Fool Britannia*, which was written by Newley and Bricusse while the Famous Four were holidaying together on Long Island. It poked fun at the British Establishment's tizzy over the Profumo Affair, when the Conservative government's Minister for War, John Profumo, had been forced to resign on 5 June after lying to the House of Commons about his relationship with a call girl, Christine Keeler, and her friend Mandy Rice-Davies. Newley and Bricusse cobbled together thirteen short, thin, pretty juvenile cabaret sketches and recorded them in New York in front of a chortling midnight celebrity audience. The LP covered several aspects of the scandal: Sellers mimicking the British Prime Minister, Harold Macmillan, bumbling away in the House of Commons; Fleet Street editors debating whether to buy a prostitute's salacious memoirs; a sleazy Italian producer planning a movie entitled *Last Year in Mandy's Bed*. Joan's contribution was small: she appeared briefly in four sketches, in one of which she mocked Christine Keeler's frenetic attempts to satisfy both Profumo and the Russian spy Yevgeny Ivanov. The major British record labels refused to distribute the LP, possibly because in one sketch, *We Are Not Amused*, Sellers and Massey portrayed the Queen and Prince Philip at the breakfast table with Her Majesty humming 'God Save the Queen' ('it's our tune') and the Duke telling her, 'Darling, we're at home now. You don't have to keep smiling and waving.' A spokesman for Decca sniffed that the LP was in bad taste and the *Daily Herald* reviewer Anthony Carthew said unconvincingly that it was 'nasty, smutty and offensive'. Even so, or maybe because of that, the LP reached the British top ten and stayed in the charts for ten weeks.

Joan took her pregnancy extremely seriously. She rested a great deal, gave up smoking, swallowed plenty of vitamins, vegetables, milk and eggs, and went to natural childbirth classes. She read Dr Spock's fashionable child-rearing manual. She claimed later that she even did the shopping and housework and learned to cook a bit at last – sausage and mash, shepherd's pie, toad-in-the-hole – but nearly thirty years later Tony was chuckling that she was still as hopeless as ever in the kitchen. Her passion for him is puzzling. He was obviously talented, and at twenty-nine she had started to look urgently for a man to father her children, and because he was rich and successful she felt he would be a good provider, but she knew how callously he had treated his previous women and was fully aware of how selfish, difficult and unfaithful he could be. He was not particularly good in bed, she said, and judging by a home movie that shows them dancing together in October, two days before she was due to give birth, he was not good-looking, either: jigging up and down, almost naked, he looked like an ugly, skinny, gawky teenager with scrawny legs. 'I didn't fall in love with Tony because he was the best looking guy in London, or the biggest star,' she admitted to Roderick Mann in 1970. 'I fell in love with him because he could make me laugh. A sense of humour, that's what a girl should look for in a man.'

Tony was present when their daughter was born on 12 October 1963 in a private room at the Mount Sinai hospital in New York. They gave her the rhyming names Tara Cynara. Cynara, the Latin for artichoke, was maybe Newley's little joke about his compulsive infidelity because Cynara is the subject of a famous love poem by the nineteenth-century English poet Ernest Dowson in which he admits that whenever he sleeps with other women he is haunted by Cynara's memory, and each verse ends with the line 'I have been faithful to thee, Cynara! In my fashion.'

To the horror of many of Joan's figure-conscious friends she breast-fed the baby, urged to do so by Joanne Woodward, and refused to hire a nanny, preferring to change the nappies and push the pram herself. Even so she put on nearly thirty pounds after the birth, hated being overweight, and swore never to let herself become fat again. Becoming a mother changed her, she said. 'I'm different now,' she told Barry Norman of the *Daily Mail* six months after the birth. 'Somebody told me the other day that I'm more tranquil, and I think that's it. Happier, more contented. Marriage and a baby do that to a girl. It wouldn't make me sad if I never did another film. I find the thought of making movies a terrible drag these days. All that getting up early and sitting around a set all day. There's no glamour in it, no great joy. I like acting but not just for acting's sake. I'm not so ambitious that I want to get out there and make something of any old cheesy part that comes along. No, I'm not exactly dedicated. Except to my husband and baby and our home. They come first for me, definitely and always. I've got much less interest in myself and my career. Looking after Tara is so much more satisfying. I can't imagine going away and leaving her. I did it once for a week and when I came back I thought she hated me, so I won't do it again.' In 1999 Jackie told Melvyn Bragg that at first Joan and Newley were wonderfully contented together and Joan happier than at any time in her entire life.

Newley too had every intention of being a wonderful father. 'I shall take my little girl into the country,' he told Tony Wells of *Today* when Tara was six weeks old, adding bizarrely that he would give her pets 'so that she can see the pets have children and watch them die. And I shall say to my little girl, "This is real, this is what you build your life on – not on the telly and money and polythene and beautiful girls in advertisement."' He resented not having had a rural childhood himself. 'A child should spend the first few years of its life seeing the daisies grow and animals being born and dying,' he said. 'What I find so dreadfully sad about being brought up in a city is that you get all the wrong values. You finish up with your values based on things like money, good looks and how much time you can nick off work.' He said he would also teach Tara all about sex when she was eight or nine.

At first, despite all this domesticity, the Newleys never settled anywhere for long enough to put down roots because as Tony built his career they found themselves flying constantly across North America, the Atlantic, and the English Channel. Their first move was inspired by the assassination of President Kennedy in Dallas on 22 November.

Tony was so appalled by this evidence of a vicious sickness deep in American society that he vowed to escape it as soon as the show closed, and he sent out homemade Christmas cards made up of scraps of newspaper headlines reporting violent atrocities in New York.

During the Christmas holiday Anneke Wills turned up in New York with her husband, the English actor Michael Gough, and met Tony secretly for dinner to show him photographs of his and her daughter, Polly, who never did learn that he was her father, but he was to take so little interest in the child that Anneke did not bother to tell him even when she was killed in a car crash at the age of nineteen since she knew he wouldn't give a damn. Anneke was to go on to appear in nine episodes of the science-fiction TV series *Doctor Who* in 1966 and 1967 as Patrick Troughton's sidekick Polly Wright before abandoning acting to run a craft shop in Norfolk.

The Broadway run of *Stop the World – I Want To Get Off* ended in February 1964 after five hundred and fifty-six performances, and the Newleys flew immediately back to Europe – not to England, where they would have to pay punitive British taxes if they arrived before the end of the tax year on 5 April, but to Paris, where they checked in to a suite on the Champs-Elysées at the Grand Point Hotel. At first Joan had terrible trouble persuading three-month-old Tara to sleep, and in desperation telephoned a nanny she had met in New York. 'Put the baby down in the cot, see that she's had enough to drink, is warm and comfortable, and tell her very firmly that you have to go to sleep now,' said the nanny, who advised Joan that after that she should not go in to see the child again, no matter how much she screamed. 'It wasn't easy,' Joan told the *Daily Mail* in 2006. 'I stood outside the door for two nights crying to myself as Tara screamed for ten or fifteen minutes. But on the third day she just drifted off to sleep. From then on she was a good sleeper. That's what's called tough love.'

The Newleys had intended to stay in Paris for two months but one night early in March they awoke to find that their hotel was on fire. There was thick smoke in the corridor, living room and second bedroom, where the baby was asleep. Joan grabbed Tara, her jewellery and mink coat, and retreated onto the small, seventh-floor balcony. Above them, where the fire was fiercest, hotel guests were screaming in panic; below, in the street, a small crowd assembled to enjoy the spectacle. Tony tried to find an escape route by edging along a narrow ledge but returned defeated. They were terrified, trapped for what seemed like an eternity, but eventually two firemen burst into the suite and yelled at them to cover their heads with wet towels, crawl along the hot floor of the corridor, and escape down a staircase.

Traumatised by the experience, they flew the next day to the jet-set Swiss ski resort of St Moritz to seek refuge with Cappy Badrutt, whose husband owned the luxurious Palace Hotel. There they stayed until 7 April – Tony writing, Joan revelling in motherhood and getting pregnant again – until it was financially safe to return to London. The elegant ladies wintering in the village were so appalled to see her caring for her baby without a nanny, even changing and washing nappies herself, that the New York *Herald Tribune* carried an amusing, tongue-in-cheek article about her by John Crosby that was headlined A MOST PECULIAR MOTHER and reported that 'in this citadel of the rich, this is a throwback to primitive behavior patterns almost unknown in these parts since they introduced the Roman alphabet'.

When they returned to London they rented the actor Keith Michell's house in Hampstead. 'Joan Collins moving into a house is like relocating Harrods,' said Bricusse, and he and Newley set to work writing their next show, *The Roar of the Greasepaint – The Smell of the Crowd*, as well as the title song for the third James Bond film, *Goldfinger*. Joan was delighted to be reunited with Evie, who had just had her own first child, Adam, and she started looking for a house to buy, eventually finding a run-down, three-storey, six-bedroom Edwardian mansion with extensive grounds and outbuildings in Hertfordshire: Friars Mead, near the Elstree film studios. Newley baulked at the price, £20,000 [£287,000], especially since the house needed a lot of expensive renovations, but Joan persuaded him that they had to settle somewhere and put down roots, especially now that she was pregnant again, though sadly she was soon to have a miscarriage. She hired a fashionable Hampstead interior designer, Robin Gild, to undertake major renovations and create a Spanish dining room, a green-and-white-lace Victorian master bedroom, and a private cinema. To help pay for it all Tony persuaded her to accept a part in one episode of the TV series *The Human Jungle*, in which Herbert Lom played a psychiatrist and Joan a patient who tries to take her clothes off at a London Underground station. She also accepted a part in an Italian film, *La Congiuntura (The Combination)*, which was to be filmed in Rome, Portofino and Lugano in October.

But the Newleys were never to live at Friars Mead, at first because that was impossible during all the renovations and later because Tony's career and the exorbitant demands of the British taxman were to drive them back to America within a few months.

Joan and one-year-old Tara flew out to Rome in October to make the Italian film, which Joan particularly enjoyed because it was a comedy and she always reckoned that she was born for comedy rather than drama. In *La Congiuntura* she played an English girl who cons a randy Roman prince into helping her smuggle a million dollars from Italy into Switzerland. It was one of the top ten most popular films in Italy that year but was never released in Britain or the USA, much to her chagrin, and to add to the Newleys' bad luck that year the British critics were brutally dismissive about *The Roar of the Greasepaint – The Smell of the Crowd* when it opened with Norman Wisdom playing one of the two leads, Cocky. Some of the audiences in Nottingham, Liverpool and Manchester walked out and the show closed after six weeks on tour without reaching the West End. But the Broadway producer David Merrick saw it and offered to stage it in New York if Tony rather than Wisdom would play the lead. Tony, faced with a British tax demand for ninety per cent of his earnings over the next year if he stayed in Britain, had little choice but to accept. Under the tax regulations neither he nor Joan could own a house in Britain, so with heavy hearts they sold Friars Mead, which Joan believed that she and Gild had now made truly beautiful, before they had had a chance to move in. She was nearly thirty-two and suddenly nervous and vulnerable, increasingly conscious that she still owned nothing solid except a lot of expensive clothes and jewellery. But the year did end on a happy note: she became pregnant yet again.

In January 1965 they flew to New York, taking Tony's mother, Grace, and her husband Ron Gardiner as their paid housekeeper/nanny and gofer/handyman, and rented yet another furnished apartment, this time on 72nd Street. *The Roar of the Greasepaint – The Smell of the Crowd* opened in Delaware on 4 February and Joan and Tara followed Tony on tour as it moved on to Washington, Philadelphia, New Haven, Boston and Toronto and broke box office records in most places before reaching New York. Tony had been working so hard for so long that he told the London *Evening Standard* that after eighteen months of marriage he and Joan had been out together only six times.

'She's a great social girl,' he said, 'and she went and married a monk,' and he told Joe Collins that he was such a reclusive workaholic that sometimes he and Joan had rows, though usually she was wonderfully patient and tolerant. The show opened on Broadway in May to wildly mixed reviews. Some American critics hated both Tony and the show ('banal, pretentious, corny, third rate') but others loved them ('superb, endlessly funny') and they became hits at the box office. Meanwhile the Newleys rented a house on Long Island for the summer at Sands Point, where Joan lounged around all day with Tara, swam, sunbathed and revelled in her pregnancy.

Back in England Jackie divorced Wallace Austin after four and a half years of marriage, claiming that he was a manic depressive drug addict who was in and out of psychiatric hospitals and had spent all their money. 'When he was well he was wonderful,' she told Lester Middlehurst of the *Daily Mail* in 1995. 'He was a very exciting man. He would tell me we were going out to dinner, we would get into his Aston Martin and then we would drive to the airport, fly to the South of France, gamble all night and then fly back the next morning. But his drug addiction became worse and worse [*and*] I couldn't cope any more. I had to send him to the hospital ten times to have his stomach pumped. You can only take that for so many years.'

After just two years of marriage Joan was beginning to have her own marital problems and suspected that Tony was enjoying fresh young meat again. When she had been filming *La Congiuntura* in Italy word had reached her that back in London an oriental pimp had been providing Tony with young girls who telephoned him brazenly at Harley House, where he was staying with Joe, and in August she surprised him in his dressing room one day enmeshed with a pretty girl who was in the show. She suspected that he was also having an affair with a proper, grown-up woman: Elliott Gould's twenty-three-year-old wife, Barbra Streisand. Tony's infidelities began seriously to tarnish the marriage, which was damaged increasingly by rows, sulks, long silences and his workaholic hermit nature. Joan, of course, blamed her marriage problems and her inability to find a man who truly loved her on Daddy: poor old Joe, who was now courting his young German girlfriend, Irene Korff, who was also a theatrical agent. Joe admitted that Tony was hugely talented and that Joan seemed on the surface to be happy and contented at last but confessed that he was never able to like the fellow. Newley was a very peculiar person: weird, moody, morose, introverted, irritatingly untidy and downright rude, said Joe in his autobiography. When he came to stay at Harley House on his own he complained about the room he was given, even though it was Joan's perfectly nice old bedroom, and left his wet towels all over the apartment. He would stay in his room during daylight hours with the curtains drawn, said Joe, and 'when I had party guests ... Newley would retire to a corner and stay there, not talking to anyone ... There was not a bit of fun in him.'

In public, however, the Newleys seemed to be a loving couple and on 8 September 1965, in the same Mount Sinai hospital room in which Tara had been born, Joan gave birth to their son Alexander Anthony, who would always be known by the Russian diminutive of his name, Sacha. This time she did hire an efficient English nanny, Rosie Riggs, to help her cope with her two small children after she fell dangerously ill with the sometimes fatal genital infection puerperal fever.

By the time that *The Roar of the Greasepaint – The Smell of the Crowd* closed on 4 December after two hundred and thirty-two performances Tony had accepted a part in 20th Century-Fox's lavish musical movie *Doctor Dolittle*, written by Leslie Bricusse and the most expensive ever made. Rex Harrison had already agreed to play Dolittle, Tony had signed as his Irish friend Matthew Mugg, and he and Joan moved back to Hollywood to be close to the action, taking Grace, Ron Gardiner, and the nanny with them. They rented yet another house, this time at Bel Air, and since Tony was not due to start filming *Doctor Dolittle* for several months Joan, who loved parties, restaurants, discos and late nightclubs, tried to involve him in more of a social life and for a while they were Hollywood's new flavour of the month. She soon built up a wide circle of friends and playmates – Herb Alpert, Bobby Darin, Sammy Davis Jr, Sean Connery, Diana Dors, Samantha Eggar, Mia Farrow, David Hemmings, Peter Lawford, Roger Moore, Peter Sellers – and filled the house with fun, laughter and famous faces. One night Sammy Davis Jr tried to persuade her to snort some cocaine, which she abhorred, and was furious when he offered her a handful of the white powder and she blew it all over his smart dark velvet jacket. But Tony soon tired of all the frenetic fun, noise and exhausting company and crept back increasingly into his study, infuriating Joan when he would suddenly decide at the last minute not to accept an invitation after all and she had to find someone else to take her. Even when she threw a dinner party at home he would cry off at the last minute and hide in his study, working, and on the rare occasions that they made love he drove her mad by saying 'thank you' afterwards. Joan wished she could find some work herself and lobbied hard to win the part of the female lead, Emma Fairfax, in *Doctor Dolittle*, but Darryl Zanuck was back in charge at Fox, doubtless remembered her refusal to sleep with him, and gave the part instead to the twenty-seven-year-old English actress Samantha Eggar without managing to have his wicked way with her, either.

Tony was fully aware of his own failings and difficult nature. When he returned to England in May 1966 to film the location scenes for *Doctor Dolittle* he told Peter Evans of the *Daily Express*: 'The real ambition now is, like can I find success as a father, a husband? I mean, that is the basis of what I have to live with for the rest of my life. I think anything else, any other success, must follow that.' He knew it would not be easy. 'I only wish I wasn't cursed with the old problem all actors have of continually watching themselves come into a room,' he said. 'I'm still that self-centred and the art of giving a piece of yourself is still tough for me. I'm still as unstable as the next ego-maniac actor. It would be easy if I drank. I know a lot of actors who find the world comfortable when they're stoned. But me, now I find my contentment in ... other ways.' Indeed he did, and while he was away in New York preparing for *Doctor Dolittle* Joan treated herself to a bit of adultery too. She had finally had enough of Tony's boring way of life, sullenness and infidelities, and decided to have some fun with yet another toyboy: the tall, blond, twenty-five-year-old actor Ryan O'Neal, who was eight years younger than she and had recently become famous in the TV soap opera *Peyton Place*. She met him one night at the fashionable Daisy discotheque, thought him good-looking, charming, funny, and a great dancer. For several weeks he pursued her, even though they were both married, and eventually, on her thirty-third birthday, she succumbed, giving him to herself as a birthday present.

Jackie, now twenty-nine, had found herself a new man too, though she preferred much older men. He was forty, Oscar Lerman, the rich American owner of the Ad Lib nightclub in London, whom she married in the Newleys' house in June without bothering to tell her father until the night before the wedding. Joe came to like and respect Lerman, Jackie gave birth a few months later to her second daughter, Tiffany, and the marriage was to last twenty-six years, twice as long as even the longest of Joan's relationships. A month later Jackie's ex-husband Wallace Austin drove from London to Cadnam in the New Forest in Hampshire and took an overdose, possibly of Tuinal, a highly danger-ous combination of two powerful barbiturates. He was thirty-nine. He died intestate but left £22,528–9s–0d [£296,000] net, which was to be inherited in due course by his and Jackie's five-year-old daughter Tracy when she was twenty-one.

Joan was desperate to relieve her boredom and frustration by getting back to acting but she had been out of Hollywood and films for so long that she was all but forgotten. She did land a few jobs on television, one of them in a *Bob Hope Show* comedy special in which she joined seventeen of his other leading ladies in apparent auditions for a remake of *Gone With the Wind*. Another was an episode of her RADA friend David McCallum's thriller series *The Man From U.N.C.L.E.* and she accepted an offer from Paramount of a tiny, two-scene part in a truly dreadful Los Angeles detective drama, *Warning Shot*, which starred a wooden, emotionless David Janssen, in which she played Janssen's estranged wife, wore a terrible wig, absurdly long false eyelashes, sur-prisingly pockmarked skin, and seemed to have forgotten all together how to act.

In May Tony flew to London for three months to work on *Doctor Dolittle* with Rex Harrison and Samantha Eggar, who had become a close friend even though she was a dozen years too old for him, and when he made it plain to Joan that he did not particularly want her with him on location she continued to revel blatantly in her fling with young Ryan O'Neal. He was an excitingly inventive lover, she said, and O'Neal's first wife, Joanna Moore, concurred: 'He is an incredible lover, totally devoted to giving a woman pleasure.' Joan and O'Neal were so fond of each other that they became carelessly indiscreet. He would even bring his children, Tatum and Griffin, to her house to play with her children, and when they were almost exposed in a gossip column and Tony heard the rumours Joan decided that if she had any hope of saving her marriage the affair had to end. Reluctantly she gave O'Neal the push and flew with the children to join Tony in England, where she found to her delight that her adultery had made Tony so afraid of losing her that for several months he became almost human and paid her much more attention.

In the autumn of 1966 the filming of *Doctor Dolittle* moved for several months from England to the Caribbean island of St Lucia, where Tony gave the *Daily Mail*'s David Lewin an interview that was so astonishingly naïve you would never believe that he was thirty-six. 'What I want to become now is a film star,' he said ingenuously, 'a great big film star. I like the idea of people recognising me and stopping me in the street. It is time at my age that I started to leave some footprints behind in the concrete.' He boasted that he had just signed a $1 million contract to appear at Las Vegas but still had huge psychological problems. 'With everything I've got I hate myself more and more,' he said, 'and I'm more scared than ever I've been. There is a disjointedness and a sad sort of decadence. I am still trying to find out why I have no faith in me and why I don't believe in God and what I can do to replace that and find some faith in anything.' He added pathetically: 'Any amateur Freudian can tell you that the reason for acting is an emotional inadequacy in early life. As you grow older you can look at this fairly logically but there is nothing normal about putting on make-up and saying "look at me – I can sing and dance".' As for the future, he said, 'my aim now is to stay one step ahead of what is hurting me. I'm still trying to find the answer to the question about life – *IS IT ALL THE JOKE THEY SAY IT IS?*' Joan sure had her hands full with this melancholy husband.

To be fair to Newley, making *Doctor Dolittle* was not a happy experience. Rex Harrison, a fifty-nine-year-old monster who was widely considered to be the meanest, most arrogant, snobbish, unpleasant person in the entire world of acting, decided to loathe Tony, denigrated him constantly behind his back, and yelled that he and Bricusse were 'sewer rats' who were conspiring against him. They in turn were delighted when Harrison was bitten by every one of the film's two thousand animals that came anywhere near him. When Joan told Harrison that Tony and Samantha Eggar looked so good together onscreen that the script should be rewritten so that their two characters had an affair, Harrison was stunned: 'Are you saying that she would prefer *him* to *me?*' Joan smiled sweetly. 'Well,' she said, 'they *are* so much closer in age.' When *Doctor Dolittle* reached the cinemas in December, Tony boasted to Weston Taylor of the *News of the World* that it would make him a household name 'and give me a passport to all kinds of exciting things in Hollywood'. The movie did win him another film part – in

Sweet November with Sandy Dennis – and Bricusse an Oscar for the best original song, 'Talk to the Animals', but it lost a fortune and almost brought 20th Century-Fox to its knees.

When the Newleys went to the New York première Joan wore an astonishingly low-cut dress that barely concealed her nipples, much to the lofty disapproval of *Time* magazine, which accused her of being an exhibitionist. She and Jackie were shocked themselves in January 1967 to learn from their father that he had just married Irene Korff at the Marylebone register office in London. He was sixty-four, she just thirty. Bill, who was now a quiet, level-headed twenty-year-old, unimpressed by showbiz and working for his uncle Mark Godfrey's property company, approved of the match and signed the marriage certificate as a witness, but Joe had been nervous about telling his daughters and wrote in his autobiography that Joan and Jackie were both deeply upset that he had remarried and that they seemed to feel that he was somehow betraying their mother by loving another woman. Their disapproval was decidedly hypocritical considering they had both been divorced and that it was now nearly five years since Elsa had died, but gradually they came to realise that Irene was a good woman who made their father very happy.

By now three-and-a-half-year-old Tara had endured a childhood of rented apartments and hotel rooms that was almost as restlessly gypsy as her mother's had been, and Joan was determined to buy a house to give the family roots and a sense of security. She found it in Beverly Hills at 1151 Summit Drive, a beautiful, elegant, colonial-style house with a swimming pool and two acres of land that had once been owned by Tony Curtis and Janet Leigh. She hired a Portuguese couple, Alice and Umberto Ferreira, to run it and installed a jukebox in the big entrance hall. Tony spent much more time with the children than before, was much more sociable, and helped to entertain Joan's showbiz friends. He even joined her, Sammy Davis Jr, Peter Lawford and Paul Newman to open a gassy, exclusive discotheque that quickly became the trendiest place in town. They called it The Factory – it was on the huge top floor of a derelict Second World War bomb factory in the industrial area of Beverly Hills – and had it decorated in what the *New York Times* called 'turn-of-the-century bawdy-house-elegant style'. Within a few weeks its members included the Beatles, Tony Curtis, Henry Fonda, George Hamilton, Laurence Harvey, Robert Kennedy, Steve

McQueen, Liza Minelli, Ronald Reagan, Frank Sinatra, the Rolling Stones, Barbra Streisand and Andy Williams. The notoriously randy Bobby Kennedy soon propositioned Joan, who was hugely tempted by his looks, twinkly blue eyes, charm and charisma, but he was a famous politician, possibly a future president, and married with ten children. Reluctantly she smelled danger and turned him down. Like so much in Hollywood, The Factory quickly went out of fashion, lasting for less than a year – about as long as what was left of the Newleys' marriage.

By now Tara was going to nursery school and Joan's growing boredom, frustration and restlessness in 1967 led her to accept several parts in television series at the going rate of $2,500 an episode [£7,500]. In April she appeared – stiffly, with a pout, an unbelievably English accent and a soft-focus, Vaseline lens – in an amateurish episode of *Star Trek* that is nevertheless considered by Trekkies to be a classic. Entitled *City on the Edge of Forever*, it was a tale in which Captain Kirk, Mr Spock and Dr McCoy travel back to New York in 1930, where Kirk falls in love with a pacifist social worker, Edith Keeler, who is destined – unless she dies first – to persuade President Roosevelt not to join the war against Hitler. Spock persuades the besotted Kirk that she must be killed if the world is to be saved from Nazi tyranny. The actor who played Kirk, thirty-six-year-old William Shatner, an unhappily married philanderer, took such a fancy to Joan that the camera crew laid bets as to whether they were having an affair. Joan denied it after surprising Shatner wigless in his dressing room and discovering that he was bald. This could well have been a lucky escape because Shatner was a firm believer in flying saucers and soon after shooting the episode 'observed a UFO in the Mojave Desert north-east of Palmdale, California', reported his biographer Dennis Hauck. 'During the encounter he seemed to have engaged in psychic contact with extraterrestrials, and some evidence suggests that he may even have been abducted' – no doubt by aliens with pointy ears like Mr Spock.

In August Warren Beatty demonstrated his abiding affection for his old girlfriends by inviting both Joan and Natalie Wood to a select early screening of his latest film, *Bonnie and Clyde*, and in September Joan surfaced in two episodes of *Batman* as The Siren, a temptress who mesmerises men with her high-pitched singing, and in one episode of the 1890s Western series *The Virginian*, and in October she popped up with Bing Crosby on NBC's *Danny Thomas Hour* drama *The Demon*

Under the Bed. Appearing in *Batman* was not a happy experience. Its star, Adam West, told Joan's early American biographer Jeff Rovin that although she was 'very sweet and co-operative ... the director made things terrible for her, and she became very sad, very frustrated and intimidated ... He really gave her a rough time, bringing her almost to tears.' Unfairly, said West, many people in films thought she was a selfish hedonist who did not take acting seriously.

At the end of the year she was offered a part in only her second film in four years, *Subterfuge*, with Gene Barry, Richard Todd, Suzanna Leigh and Michael Rennie, but it was a very poor 'thriller' without thrills in which she played the wife of a British double agent who becomes involved with an American spy who is kidnapped and tortured for information. Yet again she seemed to have forgotten everything she had ever learned about acting, for she was wooden, her melodramatic pouting was embarrassing, and she managed to look ridiculous with far too much make-up, mysteriously vast tombstone teeth, tiny miniskirts and huge wigs, one as big as a British guardsman's bearskin. Her dialogue was dreadful – 'is there any kindness left anywhere in the world?' – the 'music' was raucously tuneless and the hokum plot incomprehensible. Still, it got her out of the house and in January she flew to London to shoot it. Unfortunately she missed.

The Newleys planned to spend most of 1968 in Europe and to be based in London, though they did take a trip to St Tropez where Joan was persuaded at a party to take her one and only snort of cocaine. 'It was horrible,' she told TV-am's presenter Anne Diamond in 1986. 'I didn't sleep for forty-eight hours. I'd never try it again. Once you start sticking it in your veins you might as well throw yourself in an open grave. I think it's the most terrifying thing that our culture has to deal with.' They let the Los Angeles house in Summit Drive to Elliott Gould and Barbra Streisand and in London they stayed for several weeks at Jackie's flat in Hampstead, though Joan was also discovered embarrassingly one day in Suzanna Leigh's mews house in Belgravia. Suzanna, who was twenty-two, was having an affair with her twenty-year-old hairdresser, Leslie Cavendish, who worked in Vidal Sassoon's salon and barbered the Beatles. 'Suzanna was very friendly with Joan,' Cavendish told me. 'I was pretty immature, getting possessive, and suspected that Suzanna was having an affair with someone else, so I went round to her house in Belgrave Mews South, looked through the letterbox, and heard moaning and groaning coming from upstairs. I started banging on the door and kept on banging until eventually a top window opened and out came Joan's angry face.

'"Is Suzanna there, please?" I said.

'"No, she's not," said Joan furiously, and I discovered that she was in there with one of the *Subterfuge* cameramen and that they were having an affair.'

Tony had been signed up by Universal Pictures to make a million-dollar autobiographical musical movie in which he was to be its subject, writer, composer, producer, director and star. It was not quite a one-man show – Herman Roucher rewrote much of his screenplay, Herbert Kretzmer collaborated with the lyrics, and there were thirty-six other actors in the film, including several beautiful young girls and Joan, Tara and Sacha, who played his wife and children – but it was an enormously self-indulgent, narcissistic, avant-garde representation of Newley's own life. 'I'm beginning to feel more and more that the only things I really enjoy are things that emanate directly from inside my small cockney head,' he said big-headedly. The film's title alone indicates how facetiously pretentious it was: *Can Heironymus Merkin Ever Forget Mercy Humppe and Find True Happiness?* The name Heironymus may be a clue to Newley's intention: the only previously famous Heironymus, Hieronymus Bosch, was a fifteenth/sixteenth-century Dutch artist whose obscure, symbolic paintings revealed an obsession with Hell, sin, evil and immorality – an obsession mirrored by Newley in this obscure, symbolic film about his own sins and immorality. As for the characters' names, they were sniggeringly adolescent. A merkin is a pubic toupée. Hump means fornicate. Joan's character is Polyester Poontang, and poontang is American slang for fucking. Judy Cornwell played Filigree Fondle. Another character was called Trampolena Whambang. Another was Maidenhead Fern. Another was Hope Climax. It was all very childish but the film was so blatantly exhibitionist that it was finally to destroy the Newleys' marriage, for when Joan saw it eventually she realised fully just how faithless he had been to her both physically and mentally.

'I looked at the script,' Judy Cornwell told me, 'and thought, "Does Joan Collins *know* that he's going to leave her as soon as we've finished this film?" Because that's what he'd put in it. Obviously she didn't realise until the very last page.' Tony even went as far as to admit openly his erotic obsession with very young girls, included a song describing himself and Joan as being 'as different as chalk and cheese', and described her in the film as 'one of those women who wanna make marriage work no matter what havoc you wreak on your husband'. Leslie Bricusse realised right from the start exactly what was going on and how much Joan was going to be wounded by the film. He was now so successful that he was being offered a great deal of work on his own and when Tony asked him to collaborate with the lyrics he refused. 'By then I knew him so well I could see what he was doing,' Bricusse told Garth Bardsley. 'I didn't want to be part of it. I would have enjoyed writing the songs but I didn't like the implication of what the film was going to do.' He was right to be wary. Towards the end of the film Heironymus/Newley says: 'I can honestly say there's never been a woman who commanded even a moment of my regard once I'd made love to her. The flowers, the poems, the love songs, have all been – bribes. And I suddenly realise that, not only do I have no respect for women but – I may very well hate them. And it's really – I have really been committing a kind of – sexual murder. The ritual homicide of the female sex; forever reopening and stabbing the divine wound.' When Joan read those lines she must surely have known that she could no longer keep this marriage alive.

In March they flew to Malta to begin three months of filming, all on a beach, with a cast that included Milton Berle, Patricia Hayes, Victor Spinetti and Bruce Forsyth. It was a difficult shoot. The weather was so foul and windy that it frequently brought filming to a halt. The naked episodes had to be hidden from the sternly moralistic Roman Catholic government and smuggled off the island, and when the local church found out about the nudity they threatened to send Tony to prison. They forbade one bed scene involving Joan, calling it 'a disgrace', and it had to be shot months later in England. But Judy Cornwell, who was later to play fat Onslow's equally fat wife Daisy in Patricia Routledge's 1990s TV series *Keeping Up Appearances*, greatly enjoyed making the film. 'Tony Newley was an actor's director,' she wrote in her autobiography. 'He knew the key words to give you so that you could give him the performance he wanted.' But 'respectable Maltese society was very put out by our miniskirts. We were not allowed to enter any churches and some of the older peasant women would spit at us. Often, while filming on the beach, we would see above the sand dunes, like stalking Red Indians, the tufts of hair belonging to young Maltese males trying to catch a glimpse of the girls. Joan Collins spent most of her time with her secretary and children on the beach and posing for photographs ... I wondered whether she had read the script properly as she laughed and cavorted with some of her friends.'

Not everyone was as enamoured of Tony as Judy Cornwell. He worked the crew so late that in May seven went on strike at 2.30 a.m. and were sacked. Five-year-old Tara got badly sunburned, and Judy Cornwell, who was twenty-eight, thought Joan was ignoring her because she was younger and very pretty, but Joan escaped often with her friend Judy Seal to go shopping and clubbing in Rome. She was also delighted when her stepmother, Irene, gave birth to a little girl, Natasha Jane, on 4 May, even though her new half-sister was thirty-five years younger than she. But a month later Joan was devastated when her handsome, forty-two-year-old admirer Bobby Kennedy was assassinated in Los Angeles on 5 June.

Throughout filming in Malta she tried to ignore the truth about the movie and when in April the *Sun* sent David Nathan out to Malta to write about it Joan told him bravely: 'If Tony was as much of a so-and-so as Merkin is in this movie I wouldn't be married to him. Merkin is a black rotter and Tony isn't. Tony's just a bit of a rotter sometimes. But then he wouldn't be interesting if he wasn't.' But when she finally saw the film alone in a little screening room in Soho she realised that it was all true, that Newley was indeed a black rotter, that maybe he did indeed hate her, and she sobbed her heart out. Their marriage was over.

When the film was finished someone asked a bewildered Milton Berle what it was about. 'It's about two hours,' he said, and eventually most of the critics savaged it. 'For pretentiousness and vulgarity, not to say tedium, *Can Heironymus Merkin Ever Forget Mercy Humppe and Find True Happiness?* would be hard to equal,' said the *Daily Telegraph*, and the *Illustrated London News* reckoned that 'the kindest thing for all concerned would be that every available copy should be quietly and decently buried'. In America the New York *Morning Telegraph* dismissed it as a 'pointless, witless, sniggering obscenity' and the *New York Times* said that 'Newley so overextends and overexposes himself that the movie comes to look like an act of professional suicide'. Inevitably it was a box office flop and made a loss.

Joan and Tony stayed together for another year for the sake of the children, leading mostly separate lives while Tony battled in Los Angeles with his demons and disappointment and Joan in London rented a large Mayfair maisonette at 12 Park Street and struggled to kick-start her dormant career – with some success, landing parts over the next six months in three films and two episodes of two TV series, *Mission: Impossible* with Peter Graves and Martin Landau and *The Persuaders!* with Roger Moore and Tony Curtis. Shooting the latter in the South of France in April 1969, Joan and Curtis did not take to each other at all and while filming one scene he made the mistake of calling her a cunt. 'I have never said that word before, never to anyone,' Curtis told Moore's biographer Roy Moseley. 'She leaned out of the window of this little van and said, "Do you know what he called me?" The crew was there, Roger was standing there, and [*the producer*] Bob Baker, and she's screaming, "He called me a cunt!" Roger almost fell out of his suit. Joan leaped out of the van and went to her dressing room. I said to Roger, "I'm sorry, Roger, but I couldn't stand it, I mean, she was just such a pain in the ass."' Eventually Curtis bought her two dozen roses, apologised and she forgave him.

The first movie was much better than most of her recent films. It was a jolly little comedy about a coachload of American tourists 'doing Europe' by visiting nine countries in eighteen days, *If It's Tuesday This Must Be Belgium*. Unfortunately Joan had nothing to do with its success because although she was given a big 'Guest Star' credit for her appearance as a London Sixties dolly-bird 'Girl on Sidewalk' it consisted of just one ten-second scene in which she wore a miniskirt, tripped across the swinging King's Road, and said nothing at all. The second movie was an Italian 'art' film about a love affair between an unhappy young widow and a seventeen-year-old boy, *L'Amore Breve* (The Brief Love Affair), which was for some reason entitled *Besieged* in the English version. For this performance Joan was paid much less than usual, flew to Trieste, and appeared in bed with a twenty-year-old French actor, Mathieu Carrière, in her first nude film scene, though she was naked only above the waist. The third film, *The Executioner*, which was shot in Greece in May with George Peppard and Keith Michell, was yet another dreary, derivative, sub-le Carré spy 'thriller' about a double-agent 'mole' in British Intelligence. Joan's part, as the double agent's unfaithful *femme fatale* wife, was very small – a blessing for the audience since once again she managed to appear surprisingly unattractive, with an ugly profile, a huge nose, and a thin, squeaky voice. In her years away from films she seemed to have lost all her old screen presence and charisma, but to be fair it was not a happy film to make since Peppard refused to speak to her except on camera after she declined to go to bed with him.

It was not long before Joan found yet another youthful lover, this time a man just two years younger who was to become her third husband: thirty-three-year-old Ron Kass, the tall, green-eyed American boss of the Beatles' Apple Records, whom she and Newley met when they were briefly together in London and invited to dinner by their tailor, Doug Hayward, at the King's Road Italian discotheque Club dell Aretusa. Kass, the son of a Russian immigrant and an Englishwoman, whose real name was Kaschenoff, was separated from his wife and three children, who lived in Switzerland, and Joan was immediately smitten. Not only was he handsome, warm, vibrant, funny, party-loving and outgoing, unlike Tony, he had been born under the sign of Aries on 30 March, the same date as Syd Chaplin and Warren Beatty, which for some reason Joan considered to be a good omen despite the fact that her affairs with Chaplin and Beatty had both ended in tears. Tony left the restaurant after dinner to return home to work, leaving Joan and Kass to dance together all night. Soon they became lovers, after dinner at another trendy London disco, Annabel's, where Joan wore a blonde wig with a fringe to disguise who she was. Tony was furious when she told him. She pointed out that she was doing only what he had for years. 'It's different for men!' he yelled, but eventually accepted that as they were drifting apart she was entitled to do what she wanted.

The Newleys returned temporarily to Los Angeles: Joan and the children to the house in Summit Drive, Tony to live in his office in Doheny Drive. For months they fought and argued while he openly romanced a much older woman than usual, Stavros Niarchos's twenty-seven-year-old ex-wife Charlotte, and Joan pined for Kass and London and agonised over the damage that divorce might inflict on the children, who were now five and three. The stress she was suffering is obvious from the way she looked in a film that she made in New Mexico at the time, towards the end of 1969, *Three in the Cellar*, in which she is drawn, haggard, decidedly middle-aged, and speaks in a strained, strident, squeaky voice. Yet another movie that is best forgotten, it starred her old friend Larry Hagman as an American university president and Joan as his wife – a silly, crass little film in which Joan's character, an astrology freak, shrieks the names of the planets when she has an orgasm. Not surprisingly Hagman has her committed to an asylum. She also made a movie for NBC TV, *Drive Hard, Drive Fast*, about a racing driver trying to deal with an eternal triangle love affair as well as a stranger who wants to murder him. The film was so bad that NBC sat on it for four years before releasing it.

Joan's decision to get a divorce was made especially difficult because both children adored both parents. 'They loved us both very much and were never afraid to express that love,' Tara told Debbie Pogue of the *Daily Star* in 2001. 'We never felt neglected by them – it was just their jobs – and we knew they were always there for us.' Little Tara loved watching her mother dress and put on her make-up before going out in the evening and would bury her face in the textures and scents of Joan's gorgeous gowns. Joan had already given her a white rabbit fur coat, matching hat and a wicker basket full of clothes and shoes for dressing up, but Tara loved her father too and felt even closer to him than she did to Joan. Later Tony would say that he had been a remote, absentee Dad, just a 'telephone father', but Tara loved the way he used to sing her to sleep with a lullaby that he had composed just for her – 'Old Father Moon Has Got His Eye On You' – and she was already following him by composing, singing and recording her own songs. 'We were tremendously close,' Tara told John Walsh of the *Independent* in 2001. 'We were both Librans, so we had a natural affinity and could talk about anything. He dressed up as Santa at Christmas. He got us new Disney movies on the black market.' Sacha too had fond memories of his father. 'Daddy spoilt us horribly with toys,' he told David Wigg of the *Daily Mail Weekend* magazine in 2001, when he was thirty-six. 'He would buy me the biggest toy from this toy store in Beverly Hills. Then we'd get down on the carpet where we'd spend hours putting the toys together because he had always thrown away the instructions.' It was Joan rather than Tony who disciplined the children and insisted on good manners. 'She was quite strict, in a very good way,' Sacha told Wigg. 'Daddy was a little too lenient. I think discipline is important. Mummy's a very disciplined person. Her drive is extraordinary. Daddy would be the first to admit that he didn't have that.'

But despite the children's love for their father Joan decided that she could no longer live a lie, especially now that she was convinced she was deeply in love with Ron Kass. She and Tony sat the children down in the living room at Summit Drive and explained that Mummy and Daddy were no longer happy living together: 'We still love you very much but we think it's better for us to live apart,' they said. The children were stunned. 'Can I go back and play now?' said Sacha. For many years the little boy was to be deeply affected by his father's departure, which left a hole in his life that he could not understand. Tara was also devastated when their parents separated for good on 3 October 1969. Joan returned to London with the children and a month later filed for divorce in California. Eight years of unlikely domesticity were over.

CHAPTER NINE

KASS AND KATY

{ 1970–1975 }

Sammy Davis Jr bought the Newleys' house in Summit Drive, Los Angeles. They had owned it for little more than two years and enjoyed it for not much more than one. Joan took most of the proceeds of the sale and Tony agreed to pay a generous amount of maintenance to support Tara and Sacha, the equivalent of £70,000 a year in 2007. In London Joan moved with the children and nanny into a rented house at Regent's Park and at first the separation seemed almost affectionate. More than twenty years later Tony told *You* magazine that Joan had given 'the best shot she could at being a wife and a mother during our years together and I am the one who felt guilty afterwards because of the children'. But soon after they split up he became deeply depressed, missed the children dreadfully, consulted his psychoanalyst as often as three times a day, and seethed with bitterness and resentment at Joan's regular demands for even more money. 'I work for an organisation that supports Joan Collins,' he said sourly during a television interview. 'I keep Joan Collins in the style to which she became accustomed during her marriage to me.' He even claimed that 'women who get money from men after they divorce are worse than whores', but how was Joan to raise his children without his financial help? She had sacrificed her career to look after them and his complaint was ungenerous considering he was now earning more than £5 million a year in modern terms to perform his cabaret act for just three months each year at Caesar's Palace in Las Vegas, on tour across the USA and on television – an act that earned rave reviews and for which he was compared favourably with Noël Coward, Frank Sinatra, Sammy Davis and Andy Williams. Yet he saw fit to jeer at Joan onstage and repeat the old joke about her nickname, 'The British Open'. As long as seventeen years later, when she was at the peak of her fame in *Dynasty*, he was still being poisonous about her. 'To the unwashed public that woman is a star,' he told an American interviewer in 1986, 'but to those who know her she's a commodity who would sell her own bowel movement. I was tremendously hurt by her. She stuck the knife in and twisted the handle.'

Joan celebrated her freedom and the end of the Sixties with a slick of Arab oil sheiks at the billionaire Saudi Arabian arms-dealer Adnan Khashoggi's New Year's Eve party, where she introduced Kass to Natalie Wood and her new husband, the agent Richard Gregson, and made a New Year resolution, telling the *Daily Sketch* that she would never marry again because 'the whole institution is obsolete and archaic' – never dreaming that she would in fact marry three more times. Her pleasure at being in London again with Ron was enhanced by the fact that she could now see more of Jackie, who welcomed her back with a party at her husband Oscar's fashionable new nightclub, Tramp. Jackie had by now given birth to her third daughter, Rory, and had published the first of her raunchy bestselling novels, *The World is Full of Married Men*, a copy of which she gave to her father. He stopped reading it after just a few pages. 'Jackie's racy style was altogether too much for me,' he wrote in his autobiography, and for the rest of his life he was never to read more than the first few pages of what he called her 'potboilers', even though she always sent him a signed copy with an affectionate inscription. 'I am not a prude,' he wrote. 'I'm thick-skinned and broad-minded and hard to shock [*but it is*] distasteful for a father to read his daughter's descriptions of sex.' His dislike of Jackie's books was eventually to ruin their relationship.

By contrast he approved of Joan's latest lover. He liked Kass's clean-cut American looks and easygoing manner, decided that he was re-assuringly reliable, and admired his success as the boss of Apple Records and impressive academic qualifications: a business studies degree from the University of California, another degree in music, a diploma as a certified public accountant. Kass had even once played the trombone professionally as a member of Herb Alpert's Tijuana Brass band, which was alone enough to endear him to an old vaudeville agent like Joe Collins. He also proved himself to be confident and resourceful when he was sacked by Apple, despite having done an excellent job for the company, and swiftly found himself two even better jobs as president of MGM Records and a music publishing company, with offices in New York as well as London. Six-year-old Tara and four-year-old Sacha, too, soon became fond of Kass. 'Ron was a lovely, gentle man,' Tara told Corinna Honan of the *Daily Mail* in 1994 and Sacha agreed: 'He was a wonderful man, very gentle, very humorous.'

To make it easier for the children to come to terms with their mother's new man, Ron and Joan did not live together in his Mayfair house for several months. She rented a small furnished flat, found new schools for the children, and embarked on what she later said were the five happiest years of her life. She loved being back in England – 'the last civilised place left' – and loved London and Ron. The children also preferred England to California, she began once more to land parts in films, and within a year she was pregnant again. 'They were almost perfect years,' she told Sue Lawley on *Desert Island Discs* in 1989. 'I had done the career. I don't really consider that I was ever really a star, but I was quite well known and had acted opposite some of the most illustrious people in Hollywood, and I had decided that by that time, although I liked being a star, it wasn't the be-all and end-all of my life. I really wanted to concentrate on having my children, bringing them up and doing a bit of acting if it came along ... and I really couldn't have cared less whether I was a star or not.'

Even so, she agreed to appear in a second episode of *The Persuaders* with Roger Moore and Tony Curtis and was planning to star in a movie version of Jackie's latest novel, *The Stud*, but 'my private life will always come first', she told Roderick Mann at the end of May. 'Always. I'm enjoying myself more in my thirties than I ever did in my twenties. I even feel more attractive. And I know I'm more confident. For a long time I'd be whatever a man wanted me to be. It was a throw-back to wanting to please Daddy as a little girl, I suppose [*but*] now I've got sufficient respect for my opinions to say to a man: "Look, this is the way I am and if you don't like it, well, I'm sorry."' Five months later she was to be even more vociferous. 'It's because I've discovered who I am at last,' she told Angela Lambert of the *Sun*. 'I feel free to be Joan, and don't bother any more with trying to live up to some false image of myself. This is me: Joan Collins. And people can either like it or lump it.'

In June Newley was in London too to work with Bricusse on the musical score of a film version of Roald Dahl's children's novel *Charlie and the Chocolate Factory.* 'I like the freedom of being a bachelor,' he told Barry Norman of the *Daily Mail.* 'A married man is like a snail with a shell on his back – wherever he goes he has to hump wife and family and nannies around with him.' For Sacha, who was almost five, his father's absence felt 'like an eternity', he told David Wigg of the *Daily Mail* in 2001. 'I have a vivid memory of him picking me up at Hill House School, in Chelsea. That was wonderful. Then he would go again.' By now Joan and Tony were refusing to communicate with each other except through their solicitors or the nanny and Joan's doctor urged him to see Sacha again as often as possible because the little boy was pining for him.

Now that Joan was back on the London scene she began to make numerous public guest appearances. In November she joined Princess Margaret, Lord Snowdon and a celebrity audience at the première of the film *Catch-22*, and in December she was one of nine judges of the 1970 Miss World contest at the Royal Albert Hall, among them Glen Campbell, the Danish singer Nina Møller (of the Nina and Frederik duo), and the Prime Minister of Grenada, Eric Gairy. While the MC, Bob Hope, was cracking a string of jokes on the stage and the judges were deciding which girl should be the winner, a couple of dozen screaming Women's Liberation Movement activists suddenly staged a noisy protest, surging down the aisles, exploding fire-crackers, blowing whistles, waving football rattles, hurling ink bombs, smoke bombs, paint bombs and rotten tomatoes at Hope, dropping bags of flour from the balconies, hoisting placards that read YOU ARE SELLING WOMEN'S BODIES and MISS WORLD IS A SYMPTOM OF A SICK SOCIETY, and yelling: 'Bar this disgraceful cattle market!' There was pandemonium. 'They started to throw these stink bombs on the stage and they exploded,' Joan told Hope's biographer Charles Thompson. 'But one didn't know they were stink bombs! It was quite frightening really.' Hope made a brisk exit off the stage and was later accused of cowardice by the British Press. The situation deteriorated further when the judges announced that the winner was Miss Grenada, twenty-two-year-old Jennifer Hosten – an unwise choice considering that one of the judges was the prime minister of Grenada. Some of the audience booed, some of the contestants were convinced that the result had been rigged, and Miss Sweden, Maj Johansson, insisted that she should have won because four of the nine judges had placed her first and only two had put

Miss Hosten first. Hope was furious about the demonstration. 'Is there anything immoral about beauty?' he asked reporters afterwards. 'All it is is that a pretty girl wins a competition; travels around a lot; goes on television; makes a lot of money. There's nothing immoral about that.'

In January 1971 Ron finally moved in with Joan, Tara and Sacha. They kept his house and waterbed in Mayfair but also bought for £40,000 [£400,000] a simple, red-brick, semi-detached, 1930s house in North London opposite Highgate golf course, 42 Sheldon Avenue – not at all the sort of place you would ever expect to find a Hollywood star but the whole family loved its cosy homeliness. It had four bedrooms, a formal drawing room with walls that Joan had painted silver, a family sitting room, a TV room and a playroom. 'I have such happy memories of living there,' Tara told Jane Slade of the *Mail on Sunday* in 2003. 'My brother and I used to ride our bicycles down the lane to Kenwood House, which had enormous grounds. We had a trampoline in the garden and lots of lovely trees to climb. And when my little sister Katy came along, Mum built me my own bedroom above the garage, which was heaven.' They also had a beloved nanny, Sue Le Long, who sometimes took Tara and Sacha to visit her sister in the Somerset seaside town of Weston-super-Mare, where they met Sue's nephew, Richard, who was to father Tara's second child thirty-two years later. 'I spent much of my time with nannies,' Tara told the *Daily Mail* in 2006. 'When my mother was away working I really missed her. She would send me fabulous photos of her on the set of strange horror movies ... with lovely notes, but I wanted her to be at home.' Joan's children had emotional problems and feelings of insecurity at the time and her frequent absences cannot have helped.

Joan's old employer, Rank, signed her up to make her first movie of the 1970s with Tom Bell and Denholm Elliott: an unusual, romantic science-fiction film, *Quest For Love*, based on a story by John Wyndham, in which an English scientist (played by Bell) finds himself in a parallel universe where neither the Vietnam nor Second World Wars have happened and President Kennedy has not been assassinated. To make matters worse, Bell is now married to a woman (Joan) who hates him. He persuades her that he is not the man she thinks he is and they fall in love, but when she dies of heart disease he returns grief-stricken to his original world to try to save her alter-ego from a similar fate and recreate their happiness. Despite several silly moments when he sets out to find the alter-ego of the woman he loves, it is a surprisingly touching film and much better than most of Joan's. She is as beautiful, elegant and stylish as ever but also unusually sweet, vulnerable and convincing, and for once understated and not as grotesquely over-made-up and over-the-top as she had so often been. The *Sunday Telegraph* thought that the film was 'great fun' and *Variety*'s critic wrote that 'Joan Collins has rarely been better' and added that 'beautifully gowned throughout and looking gorgeous, she acts with warmth'.

She was to make two more movies in 1971, both horror films: *Revenge* and *Fear in the Night*. Her parts in both were small but *Revenge* was a tense, gripping thriller with an excellent cast and again much better than most of her films. Unusually she played the demure little second wife of a pub landlord (played by James Booth) whose ten-year-old daughter by his first marriage has been murdered by a paedophile. The police suspect that the killer is a weird recluse (played excellently by Kenneth Griffith) but cannot prove it and are forced to release him, whereupon the enraged father, his son and the father of another murdered child take the law into their own hands, kidnap the recluse, and torture him to the brink of death. The second movie, a Hammer horror chiller, *Fear in the Night*, was shot at Elstree Studios in November and December. The female lead, the soppy, neurotic young wife of an English prep school teacher, went to twenty-three-year-old Judy Geeson, who had just made *10 Rillington Place* with Richard Attenborough and John Hurt. Joan was the vicious, adulterous wife of the creepy headmaster (played by Peter Cushing) and the film was genuinely spooky.

Now that Joan was earning again she was able to send Sacha to a remarkably liberal, arty new school nearby in Hampstead, the King Alfred. 'They weren't bothered with English and maths,' he reported later. 'I couldn't read until I was ten,' but eventually, thanks to a devoted art teacher called Dawn, it was there that he was first encouraged to become a portrait painter.

In August Joan's divorce became final at last on the ground of 'irreconcilable differences', two years after she and Tony had separated, but the Californian court reduced the amount of his maintenance order so that now he had to pay her only £59,000 a year after tax in 2007 values. Later she complained that this was 'far from generous', 'a small basic sum' and 'not a fair settlement' even though it was more than three times my own salary then as literary editor of the London *Sunday Express*, which was quite enough for me comfortably to support a wife, two children, a mortgage and the taxman. The judgement was in fact extremely reasonable since Newley had already given Joan the proceeds of the Los Angeles house; had had to buy himself another house in LA, at Lloyd Crest, where he was now living with a beautiful, twenty-three-year-old American air hostess, Dareth Rich; was still supporting his mother and newly discovered father and about to buy them a house in California; and Ron was earning a great deal of money and Joan was making films again.

At the end of 1971 she shot another nicely spooky horror film, *Tales From the Crypt*, with Ralph Richardson, Peter Cushing, Ian Hendry, Richard Greene and Nigel Patrick. She played one of five tourists who lose their way in a sinister maze of ancient English catacombs and find themselves in a sealed chamber and being lectured by a stern, hypnotic old monk (Richardson) who shows each of them graphically the evil that each will soon commit and what will happen to them afterwards.

Understandably Joan was wary of marrying yet again but in September she discovered that she was pregnant, decided that a child should not be born out of wedlock, and she and Ron agreed to marry. She felt that he was a good man who loved her truly, and it helped that their sex life was apparently wonderful. 'Every time we made love it was like the first time,' he told the *Sunday People* in 1983. 'Joan and I were very much on the same wavelength sexually. We were so tuned in to each other we had our own body language and expressions. I always made a point of buying her expensive sensual nighties. No woman on earth can look as devastating as Joan in a chic black see-through nightgown slit to the thigh. If she came into the bedroom wearing that I knew we were going to have a great night ... She's every bit the raving sexy lady that people think she is ... She is a *very* sensual woman. Just watching the way she dressed and undressed always aroused me.'

They were married on 11 March 1972 while on holiday in Jamaica. 'Joan Collins is quite the businesswoman,' *Women's Wear Daily*'s London correspondent Steffi Fields told Paul Callan of the *Express* in 2003. 'I remember Ron Kass, who was a really nice guy, being told to call me so that I could ask the designer Zandra Rhodes to let Joan have her wedding dress wholesale. Zandra agreed and Joan got the price she wanted. I guess there's nothing like asking, and Joan is no shrinking violet in that area.' Joan's capacity for blatant freeloading had also been mentioned by the *Sunday Express* writer Clive Hirschhorn when he interviewed her at the end of December.

Joan's third baby, a daughter, was born on 20 June 1972 in the Welbeck Clinic in London. They gave her a Russian name in honour of Ron's Russian ancestry and called her Katyana Kennedy Kass – the middle name in honour of Joan's idol and admirer Bobby Kennedy – forgetting that for most people in the United States the initials KKK referred to a secret, murderous, racist gang, the Ku Klux Klan. Like Joan the baby was born a Gemini so that she believed for the rest of her life that they understood each other better than anyone else. Tara and Sacha were delighted to have a little sister and when Katyana – or Katy as she soon became – was christened Joan chose as one of the godmothers Tony's secretary, Judy Bryer, who was to remain one of her lifelong friends.

July and August brought more happiness: Natalie Wood had divorced Richard Gregson for adultery after two years of marriage and she remarried RJ Wagner, with whom she was to have a daughter, Courtney, two years later. And in August Joan and Ron took their six children, including his three young sons by his first marriage – Robert, David and Jonathan – to southern Spain, where they bought a holiday villa in Marbella. A month later the *Sunday Mirror* sent reporter Peter Evans and photographer Eddie Sanderson to Marbella to interview Joan, who admitted that she was '*very* materialistic' and told them: 'Ron has made me more aware of myself. He has helped me smooth out all those actressy kinks in my personality. My life was very ... *unreal*, you know.' Sanderson was to photograph her hundreds of times in future and to become her favourite snapper and one of her closest friends because she respected and trusted him completely.

By now she had made so many low-budget, downmarket chillers that newspapers were calling her 'The Queen of the Horror Flicks', so she was delighted to be offered at last a part in a famously hilarious comedy starring one of Hollywood's greatest icons, Orson Welles. It was a two-hour NBC TV film version of the Moss Hart/George Kaufman play *The Man Who Came to Dinner*, which had been a huge success on Broadway in 1939 and in theatres all over the world for more than thirty years. Joan's part as the larger-than-life Lorraine

Sheldon was based on the real Gertrude Lawrence and would give her a chance to show how well she could play comedy, and she was overawed by the legendary Welles, but during three weeks of rehearsals and five days of filming she became swiftly disillusioned. He threw his vast weight around, refused to learn his lines, insisted on reading them from huge three-foot-square prompt cards, constantly upstaged the rest of the cast, bullied anyone who looked vulnerable, and drank red wine all day, which did not improve his temper. As a result the production was notoriously unfunny, but Joan was delighted when Moss Hart's wife told her that she was the best Lorraine Sheldon she had ever seen.

In November – after launching Katy's own film career as 'The Ellis Baby' in Peter Sellers' heart-warming musical *The Optimists*, which Ron produced – Joan made yet another horror film at Shepperton Studios, *Tales That Witness Madness*, an anthology of four separate stories that examined the warped minds of the inmates of a psychiatric hospital run by Donald Pleasence. In Joan's bizarre but amusing episode she is married to Michael Jayston, who brings home one day a dead tree trunk that looks weirdly human. When he displays it in their living room as a work of art and strokes it erotically Joan becomes jealous, attacks it with a cleaver (while wearing a sexy baby-doll nightie) and the trunk fights back, kills her and climbs into the marital bed with her husband. Kinky. During one of their bed scenes Jayston was amused to see that Joan was wearing knickers embroidered with the question 'Do you come here often?' Until then, he said, he had been a little scared of her.

'We don't call them horror films any more,' she reprimanded Roderick Mann. 'We call them psychological thrillers. Sometimes when I'm there on the set I do think, "What am I doing here? Why aren't I home with my baby?" But I think it's important to keep a career going.' As for Ron, 'I've made him enjoy having breakfast in bed,' she reported. 'I've always loved having breakfast in bed. Now he does too. Even when I have to make it myself I get back into bed to eat it.' Their bed was her haven, specially made and 7ft wide. 'Sometimes I stay in it all day,' she told Mann. 'It's so good for the legs. And one of my chief pleasures at night is going to bed early. I turn on the TV and get in and surround myself with cigarettes and papers and chocolates and the baby. Oh yes, and Ron.' TV? After all she had said in the past about television, that it was fit only for children and old fogies? Middle age was obviously creeping up on her.

She was still a convinced believer in astrology and just before Christmas explained to the *Daily Express* why she took it so seriously, why she thought she was a typical Gemini – moody, fickle, restless, dilettante – why her lovers tended to be Arians or Librans, and why she disliked Scorpios and Sagittarians and would never employ one. She said that she had had her birth chart drawn four times and that each time the astrologer had correctly forecast a happy, successful, restless life with no money problems and that she would marry three times, so she knew that Ron would be her last husband. Sadly the stars were wrong.

That freezing English winter of 1972–3 she made yet another 'psychological thriller' set in a mental hospital, *Dark Places* with Christopher Lee, who had just finished filming the brilliant, classic horror movie *The Wicker Man*. Also in the cast were Robert Hardy, Herbert Lom, Jane Birkin and Jean Marsh. The hospital's administrator (Hardy) has inherited an old house and one of the psychiatrists (Lee) and his over-sexed sister (Joan) plan to steal a secret cache of money that they are sure must be hidden there. But Lee becomes furious when he discovers that Joan has slept with Hardy. 'You dirty, filthy little slut!' he yells, which allows her to stroke his cheek incestuously and purr: 'Poor Ian, don't you sometimes wish that I wasn't your sister?' In the end Joan is strangled, Lee hacked to death with a pick-axe, and the screen littered with more corpses than the last scene of *Hamlet*. It was 'a fascinating, very clever story, a fantasy', Lee told his movie biographer Robert Pohle. 'It was shot in a house not far from Pinewood Studios: a house empty and abandoned, water dripping down the walls, no proper plumbing, no heating. Thoroughly uncomfortable film to make.'

Joan made only one more film and one television play that year of 1973. The TV drama, in which she appeared with Anton Rodgers, was *The Dinner Party*, one of a series of *Orson Welles' Great Mysteries* that was fronted by the great man himself, though to Joan's relief he did not appear in any of the plays himself and she did not have to act with him again. The film was another Italian movie, *L'Arbitro* (*The Referee*), a comedy for which she flew out to Rome with Katy at the end of October. It was based on the story of a famous, forty-nine-year-old Italian soccer referee, Concetto Lo Bello, who had run the 1966 World Cup semi-final between West Germany and the Soviet Union at Goodison Park and was about to retire after thirty record-breaking years as an international referee. The film was retitled in the USA *Football Crazy* and *Playing the Field* – a much more promising title since Joan was playing a seductive journalist, but it was a misleading one. 'The script could just as well have been used for ground fertiliser,' wrote Hal Erickson in the *All Movie Guide.*

Otherwise Joan revelled that year in the happiness of her family life rather than her career. At the end of March, a week after Tony and Dareth Rich's daughter Shelby was born in London, Joan and Ron flew with the children to Los Angeles to see his parents. In May she tried to forget that she had just turned forty, at the end of July they flew off to the villa in Marbella for a week, and throughout the summer they enjoyed inviting friends to lunch parties in the garden at Sheldon Avenue. 'Life is more tranquil,' she told Roderick Mann in June. 'I don't have to go rushing around any more. When I was married to Tony we had so little to say to each other that I collected lots of friends around me. Now I don't need them. Ron is my friend.' Even so, she confessed that she and Ron sometimes had 'the most tremendous fights. I go red with rage [*but*] I get over it quickly, so it isn't too bad. The children have just had to come to terms with the fact that Mummy's got a bad temper.' Naughtily Mann began his article by writing: 'The interesting thing about Miss Joan Collins is that everybody knows who she is but hardly anyone seems to have seen any of her films.'

One friend who did drop in one quiet Sunday afternoon was Joan's old pal Peter Sellers, who caused consternation in Sheldon Avenue – where many of the residents were Jewish – by turning up dressed as a Nazi SS officer, complete with steel helmet, swastika armband, and black Mercedes-Benz with darkened windows. He was in disguise, he explained, because he was in the midst of a divorce from his third wife, Miranda Quarry, and pursued by reporters who had learned that he was having a romance with Liza Minnelli. Two hours later he emerged from the house, gave a Nazi salute, cried 'Heil Hitler!' and returned to the Dorchester Hotel.

In September Tara, who was now almost ten, joined a Roman Catholic convent school in Hampstead, St Margaret's, and although she was a bright girl who achieved excellent academic results she began to exhibit an increasingly rebellious nature that was to flourish spectacularly in her teens. St Margaret's 'made St Trinian's look like Sunday school', she told the *Daily Mail* in 2002. 'Any teacher who showed the slightest weakness was subjected to loud hissing from the classroom whenever their backs were turned, porn glued to their table tops and obscenities on the blackboard. A box of chalk dust could be balanced over the classroom door so the teacher would receive a good dusting at their arrival. One of my favourite tricks was removing the seat of the teacher's chair and putting their coat over the aperture. When they sat down they got lodged in the gaping hole. Banging on the staff-room door and then running for your life was called "Knockout Ginger" or "Cherry Knocking" although the meaning is lost in the mists of schooldays. Playing truant was the natural next move. With a bottle of wine tucked under my blazer, my friends and I would make for a nearby wood. We would drink the contents up a tree and nearly fall out of the branches. Then we would saunter back to take our punishment. Not even the threat of hell fire could make us change our ways.'

Sacha's best friend at the time (1974) was Leslie Bricusse's son, Adam. 'We were Sacha's adopted family,' wrote Bricusse in his auto-biography. 'He was a rather sad little boy at this time, missing his father … and not too ecstatic about his mother's new marriage … So Sacha was happy to escape to us whenever he could.' He was perhaps a little jealous of the new baby, and not only did he look just like Newley, he had also inherited some of his father's melancholy. When Evie Bricusse asked Sacha why he was looking miserable, the boy replied, 'That's all right, Auntie Evie. I *like* being miserable!'

In 1974 Joan worked more than she had in 1973 and made three movies and two TV plays, but she always tried to avoid the worst of the European winter so first, in January, the Kasses flew off to one of her favourite sunspots, Acapulco in southern Mexico, for a holiday. 'If Ron were a millionaire and asked me to give up movies completely I'd do so like a shot,' she told Clive Hirschhorn of the *Sunday Express*, which was now interviewing her so often that it had almost become *The Joan Collins Fan Club Weekly* and blindly believed her regular claims that she was younger than she was. This time she fibbed that she had first gone to Hollywood when she was eighteen when she had in fact been twenty-one. 'The secret is to marry someone who's stinking rich, and to hell with work,' she told Hirschhorn. 'When I look around me and see all the neurotics in this business, I often ask myself why I bother to stick it out. Take all the people who want to be superstars but aren't and never will be. People such as Tony. There's something rather sad and bitter about Tony today because he hasn't made it as big as he would have liked. And that's a pity, because he's a great guy. Believe me, there are dozens of people like him – all trying to be superstars. And even some of the superstars go to pieces – for it's just as hard to remain at the top as it is to get there. But in spite of everything I still enjoy the glamorous side of the business and I enjoy living like a film star.' Even so, in June she changed her mind about playing Marilyn Monroe in a West End stage play, *Legend*, that she had already agreed to do. Ron announced that she had changed her mind because she preferred to be in London with the family than to spend six or seven weeks taking the play on a provincial tour before bringing it into the West End, but the real reason was that she felt that the script besmirched her one-time admirer Robert Kennedy over his affair with Marilyn. 'Bobby Kennedy was one of the finest men I ever met,' she told Noreen Taylor of the *People* in 1977. 'I hero-worshipped him [*and*] there's no way I'd have the memory of that man denigrated.'

Her careless neglect of her career began to worry her father when he overheard a girl in a restaurant saying to her companion: 'Joan Collins? Isn't she the one who used to be married to Tony Newley?' Joan brushed him off when he told her. 'We've got to admit it, Daddy,' she said breezily, 'Joan Collins is not the name she used to be.' She and Ron did, however, buy the TV rights to several Noël Coward plays – though sadly not her favourite, *Private Lives* – and in August Ron produced and she starred in two of them for Anglia TV, fulfilling at last her old ambition to play the lead in a Coward comedy. She particularly enjoyed making *Fallen Angels*, the tale of two young wives who get rid of their husbands for a weekend so that they can meet the sexy Frenchman who had once been their lover. Joan's co-stars were Susannah York and Sacha Distel and she believed it to be one of the best performances of her life so far. Susannah, who was to become a good friend, agreed. 'What a superb light comedienne Joan Collins is,' she said when the play was finally broadcast just before Christmas. 'It's a great pity most producers still tend to think of her as just a sultry sex symbol.'

Well, she hardly discouraged them. Her father was so worried about her faltering career that he urged her to try to build a solid reputation on stage, but she told him that she would never earn enough in the theatre to pay for her expensive lifestyle and she was not prepared to cut down on that; the only way she could earn serious money was in the cinema. In that case, he told her, she should cause a real stir and boost her career dramatically by stripping onscreen, and she duly did so in the only movie she made in 1974, *Alfie Darling*, in which she was shown topless in bed with the pop singer Alan Price. 'I've got no hang-ups about nudity,' she told Don Short of the *Daily Mirror*. 'Ninety per cent of films nowadays contain nude scenes or simulated sex, so it would have been hypocritical to have turned the role down. In any case, *Alfie Darling* is much more of a comedy than something lewd.' When Short asked what her children would think of her naked on the screen she grinned: 'They often see me walking around the house with no clothes on,' which is not quite the same thing.

Alfie Darling, which was retitled *Oh, Alfie!* in America, was a sequel to the hugely successful 1966 Michael Caine film *Alfie* and recounted the adventures of a randy Cockney long-distance lorry driver who seduces girls all over Europe, among them Rula Lenska as a French waitress and Joan as the posh, horny wife of an English businessman. Price was depicted as a crude yob with a one-track mind but Joan looks delicious even when Alfie is ravishing her as she talks on the telephone to her husband. There are a couple of nice lines. 'You dirty, filthy swine!' she moans as he pleasures her, and 'mind my hair,' she says as he runs his fingers through it. 'Mind my hair?' he says. 'It's a wig!' But otherwise it was thin stuff, not a patch on the original Michael Caine film.

While Joan was making *Alfie Darling* at Elstree Studios Max Reed died of cancer on 31 October. She was unmoved and unforgiving when she heard the news.

The two other movies that she made that year were both quite dreadful. The first, *I Don't Want To Be Born*, which she filmed at Pinewood Studios for Rank, was a truly ludicrous, embarrassingly derivative, quite unfrightening 'horror' flick that plagiarised scenes from *Rosemary's Baby* (made six years earlier) and *The Exorcist* (released the previous year), in which she played a young stripper who spurns the advances of an evil dwarf who then curses her to give birth to a child of the Devil. The film was so bad that in a desperate attempt to make it more attractive it was released on film and video under six other titles as well: *The Devil Within Her, It's Growing Inside Her, It Lives Within*

Her, The Monster, The Baby, and *Sharon's Baby* (even though Joan's name in the film is Lucy). The ploy was in vain. The film was without any tension at all and the sight of Joan giving melodramatic birth to Satan's vicious son – writhing, gasping, squealing, shrieking yet looking immaculate – could be rated as one of her great comedy performances were it not meant to be taken seriously. When the child is born it looks at least six months old and even the usually sinister Donald Pleasence is about as threatening as a teddy bear. Five people who come close to the baby die horribly but their deaths are so absurd that it is difficult not to laugh each time another is knocked off.

Even worse was to come. Joan flew off to Spain to make what is possibly the worst movie of her entire career, maybe one of the worst ever made, another hilariously awful Italian film, *Il Richiamo del Lupo*, which was titled *Call of the Wolf* in Britain, *The Great Adventure* in the USA, and *La Llamadad del Lobo* in Spain. Based on a book by Jack London and co-starring Jack Palance, it was set in the icy wilds of Alaska during the Yukon gold rush of 1897 and told of a poor, abandoned orphan boy who is befriended by a wild dog and cleans up the corruption and brutality of Dawson City. Joan played a singer/dancer in Palance's Last Chance Saloon but looked much older than usual, haggard, with dead eyes – not surprisingly, perhaps, because she must have been truly desperate for money to take on this part for which she was paid much less than her usual fee, just £20,000 in modern values. The acting was abysmal, the 'music' terrible, the plot crass and quite unbelievable; even the dog looked as if it was thinking of sacking its agent.

After that matters could only improve and early in the new year Joan joined a distinguished cast in another sexy romp, *The Bawdy Adventures of Tom Jones*, but this time kept her kit on. Based on a Las Vegas stage adaptation of Henry Fielding's eighteenth-century novel, it was a rollicking, over-the-top musical about the sexual adventures of an engaging young rogue, a bastard who was found abandoned as a baby in a country gentleman's bed. Nicky Henson was young Tom, Trevor Howard played randy, seedy Squire Western with wild, fruity panache, and Arthur Lowe and Terry-Thomas were excellent as harrumphing tutors. Georgia Brown was ebulliently lusty as the nymphomaniac village hoyden and Joan excellent as Black Bess, an irresistibly luscious highwaywoman who rides up on horseback wearing a black eye-mask and wielding two pistols to hold up a stagecoach and actually cry 'stand and deliver! Your money or your life!' At forty-one she was in her prime: beautiful, delicious, self-assured, and looking much more attractive than she had ever done when she was younger. During the film she thrashes two swordsmen in a swashbuckling fight, gatecrashes a fancy dress party to rob the guests, forces poor Tom into a bedroom where she makes him undress at gunpoint and starts to rape him before they are disturbed, and is finally arrested and condemned to hang before she and Tom escape prison. It is a lavishly costumed and lushly filmed piece of hokum, though the songs are a tuneless racket and the critics gave it a bashing, comparing it inevitably unfavourably with Tony Richardson's and John Osborne's *Tom Jones* of twelve years earlier in which the splendid Albert Finney had played the lead. Trevor Howard responded by calling the critics 'pretentious bastards, completely off their heads', and told his biographer Michael Munn: 'It was obvious going in that the film was going to be knocked, but you can't keep making films to please the critics. I knew it would be commercial, especially with all the randy goings-on that could be portrayed more freely than when Tony Richardson made *Tom Jones*. And the squire was a fun part. Those don't come along often. It's fun to be outrageous every now and then. And these little English films that you know are never going to be taken seriously are almost without exception fun to make.'

Less fun for Joan was the news that Ron, who was by now feeling insecure and threatened as the head of Warner Brothers Records in London, had been offered a job in Los Angeles as the boss of the American billionaire Edgar Bronfman's film company Sagittarius Productions and that he had accepted it. Joan had always mistrusted the sign of Sagittarius and this time she was right to do so. She loved London and their life there, and by now she was all but forgotten in Hollywood, whereas in England she was slowly rebuilding her career. She pleaded with Ron not to take the job. 'I begged him on my knees,' she told David Thomas of *You* magazine in 1987. 'I said we cannot go, it will ruin everything. I've never been so vehement about anything. But the little woman had to do what he said. So we went to Los Angeles and that's what destroyed him. It killed him eventually.'

They quickly sold the house in Sheldon Avenue that she loved so much, and she wept when Ron gave her the papers to sign. They flew to Los Angeles to look for a home there, and spent an evening trying to cheer up Britt Ekland, who had just broken up with her long-time lover Lou Adler, by taking her to see a Rod Stewart concert at the Forum. Stewart joined them afterwards for dinner and they went on to a party at Cher's house, where Britt and Rod Stewart began a romance that was to become a passionate, two-and-a-half-year love affair. 'Out of the corner of my eye,' wrote Britt in her autobiography, 'I caught a glimpse of Ron and Joan smiling towards us, obviously feeling that their matchmaking efforts had succeeded.' The Kasses took out a mortgage to buy a big house in Chalette Drive and flew back to London, where they held a farewell party to which they invited Joe and Irene. 'Irene and I are very close friends. We got a bit weepy,' she told the *Sun* and 'I shall miss Joan terribly,' said Irene. Joan, Ron and the children left for California on 1 May 1975. Her five blissful years of domesticated contentment with Ron had come to an end, and it was also the beginning of the end of their marriage.

CHAPTER TEN

DESPERATION AND THE DOLE

{ 1975–1977 }

Joan tried as always to make the best of the situation. She loathed having to start all over again in Los Angeles but 'the children will be put into local schools', she told the *Sunday Express*. 'They don't mind the change. They are adaptable.' She was wrong. They minded very much indeed.

Tara, who was eleven, was sent to Beverly Hills High School and stunned by the culture shock. 'I'd been at an all-girls Catholic school in London and was still at the stage of playing with dolls,' she told Corinna Honan of the *Daily Mail* in 1994, 'and I moved straight into a co-ed school, which was all drugs, sex and rock 'n' roll. The girls were already all waxing their legs, but what really shocked me was all the necking that went on. For the whole of that first year I used to eat my lunch on my own in the library and hide away. I was a stranger in a strange land. The American kids would say "say something, your accent's so cute" and I'd say "get stuffed". I was picked on for being English and the boys used to push me into the bushes.' Sacha, now nine, was unhappy too and deeply bewildered by the family's rootlessness. 'There was the strangeness of so many schools, so many houses, being parachuted into new situations, having to learn the lingo and who the school bullies were,' he told David Wigg in 2001. 'I've always been envious of any artist who knows his roots and has a sense of belonging. That transatlantic flight from LA to London – that's my roots!' A few years later Joan confessed that Tara and Sacha 'had a terrible life. I felt awful about it at the time'.

Joan began to supervise a major programme of rebuilding and decorating the house in Chalette Drive. It was a sprawling, four-bedroom, five-bathroom, modern, motel-like bungalow that stood high up

138

in the Hollywood Hills at Trousdale with stunning views over Los Angeles on the few days a year that the city was not blanketed by smog. It had a swimming pool, tennis court, servants' quarters, and Joan set about converting it into a glittering glass, silver and marble monstrosity. Over several months she furnished the living room with a white marble fireplace and floors, black marble bar with white leather stools, glass tables, silver curtains, sofas and statues. There were mirrors everywhere, ornate gilt chairs and tables in the hallway, and the dining room was blue, white and silver with a white marble floor, blue carpet, crystal and gold chandelier, mirrored wall and glass table and chairs. 'It's all a bit flash, isn't it?' she admitted when it was finished eighteen months later.

She was determined to rebuild her career, even though she was hardly remembered in Hollywood, and started by accepting every TV offer that came her way, often appearing for just $2,500 a time [£4,500], half her usual rate. She did *The Bing Crosby Show* and a *Bob Hope Special*, the game show *Match Game*, and episodes of the detective series *Ellery Queen*, *Switch* and *Baretta*. She did *Space: 1999* and two episodes of *Police Woman* with Angie Dickinson. And then, in May 1976, Edgar Bronfman sacked Kass. Ron and Joan were suddenly broke. Ron was deeply hurt but Joan was incandescent with rage. They had been close friends. They had made up foursomes for dinner and nightclubs. They had holidayed together at Bronfman's villa in Acapulco. He was Katy's godfather, and on the day before he fired Ron – by letter – the Kasses had thrown a lavish twenty-first birthday party for Bronfman's son, Edgar Jr, which had taken them weeks to organise and had cost them more than £14,000 in modern terms. What's more, Bronfman was a Gemini: how *dare* he do this to another? The probable answer was that Ron had started seriously taking drugs and was no longer doing his job properly. Being fired was to make him worse and destroy their marriage.

Suddenly they were both unemployed. How were they to settle all their huge bills? Their only income was Newley's maintenance payments and they were not nearly enough to pay for Ron's drugs, his ex-wife's alimony, and Joan's extravagant lifestyle. She tried and failed to find parts in films. Joan *Who*? they asked, and with typically feisty bravado she bought a numberplate for her gold Mercedes that read JOANWHO.

They sold the glass palace in Chalette Drive and bought a smaller but still modern, glass and chrome house in the cheaper outskirts of Beverly Hills, in Carolyn Way, off Coldwater Canyon. Joan was too proud to admit that they were moving because they were broke and fibbed to Lesley Salisbury of *TV Times* that it was because 'I love moving, love stripping a house from top to bottom, choosing new decorations, new furniture. I get terribly frustrated when a house is finished and there's not a single thing more I can do to it.' With un-conscious irony Ms Salisbury wrote: 'It's a good job she never runs out of money.' Then Ron's ex-wife, Anita, demanded a share of the proceeds from the sale of the house, claiming that her alimony and child support were not enough. In desperation Joan flew to Rome to make yet another downmarket Italian movie, *Il Pomicione* (*The Necking Boyfriend*). She made a 'guest appearance' in an episode of the TV detec-tive series *Starsky and Hutch*, 'Murder on Playboy Island', and even though she had to go to beautiful Hawaii for eight days with David Soul, Paul Michael Glaser and Samantha Eggar, and had always wanted to see the island, she hated every minute. She hated being treated no longer as a star and having to share a tiny dressing room with a bit player. She hated the weak script. She hated it when Glaser crashed their car into a ditch. She hated having to spend three hours in a boat soaked to the skin but also baked so hot that she was badly sunburned. When she returned to Los Angeles she hated having to crawl to NBC and lie that she was only thirty-three instead of forty-three so that they would pay her a measly $5,000 [£8,800] to play an expensive hooker in their new Arthur Hailey TV mini-series about life in a big bank, *The Moneychangers*. For that measly $5,000 she even had to appear naked, but as fast as she earned some money it evaporated.

Her agent, Sue Mengers, took her out to lunch one day and sug-gested gently that now that she was over forty her career as an actress was probably over. 'Go home and concentrate on real life,' she said. Joan cried a little, but then said: 'Never!' She remembered Jackie's old novel about a randy London discotheque manager, *The Stud*, which they had thought of filming several years earlier, and persuaded Jackie to let her have the film rights for free. Jackie agreed, feeling that she owed Joan something for letting her live in her Hollywood apartment free for a year when she was eighteen. She also agreed to write a sexy, explicit screenplay, and in July Joan flew to London to try to persuade the lusty Welsh singer Tom Jones to play the part of the stud and to find financial backing for the film. Jones declined, deciding to keep his skin-tight trousers firmly zipped because he reckoned that the part was too raunchy even for him, and it was to take Joan ten months to find the finance. Even her father's old partner Lew Grade turned her down. In the meantime, back in LA, Samantha Eggar and Judy Bryer persuaded her that she was entitled to apply for the dole – which was then £212 a week in modern values – even though she still had a house, the villa in Marbella, children at expensive schools, a gold Mercedes, and cupboards full of expensive clothes and jewellery. One afternoon she slipped nervously down to the unemployment benefits office on Santa Monica Boulevard – foolishly in the Mercedes and wearing a $400 chiffon dress and Charles Jourdan shoes because she had just opened a glamorous new boutique. She wore a raincoat, scarf and dark glasses, and at first nobody recognised her in the slow queue of hopeless, down-and-out blacks, Hispanics, derelicts and drunks shuffling towards the desk, but as soon as she reached the clerk the woman asked whether she wasn't Joan Collins.

'I still am,' she muttered.

'What are you doing down *here*?'

'I'm not working at the moment,' mumbled Joan, cursing Samantha and Judy for getting her into this situation. 'I'm resting.'

Very soon the entire room was agog. Joan *Collins*? *Here*? On the *dole*? The clerk was brisk. Had she been trying seriously to get a job? Had she tried anything other than acting? Waitressing, perhaps? Working in an office? Typing? Eventually Joan was given an IOU to say that she would be paid in a couple of weeks, once the bureaucrats had investigated her case, but as she drove off red-faced in the gold Mercedes she felt so humiliated that she never returned to collect the money and swore that she would never ask for a handout again from anyone. If she could no longer make a living as an actress she would become an interior decorator or a writer. But first she would act in anything at all, and the first movie offer that came her way was *Empire of the Ants*, another ridiculous 'horror' flick that was based on an H. G. Wells short story about a colony of giant ants that prey on humans. Later she admitted that it was a 'dreadful' movie but it would earn her $35,000, the equivalent of £62,000 today. How could she turn that down? In November she flew to Florida for six weeks to take on the giant, plastic insects.

The film was utterly absurd. She played a bossy Florida property developer showing prospective buyers around a beachside development without realising that a colony of local ants has eaten radioactive waste material that has washed up on the beach and turned them into six-foot monsters. The gigantic insects attack the group and kill six of them, the survivors flee through the everglades swamp, and realise to their horror that the ants are herding them like cattle towards a huge sugar refinery where the queen ant brainwashes her human slave-workers by breathing pheromones over them and Joan is last seen as a mesmerised robot. The movie squawks constantly with shrieks of terror, Joan's piercingly shrill voice, and some *Jaws*-type music that is meant to be sinister, but the film is never remotely frightening.

Still, she earned her $35,000, and how. The filthy Florida swamp where the film was shot crawled with crocodiles, snakes, rats and huge, slimy plants, and in one scene she had to fall into the fetid water and swim for her life, swallowing some of the disgusting muck as she did so. She developed festering cuts all over her legs so that she had to act with them wrapped in hidden bandages. During a gale she gashed her eyebrow on the door of a station wagon, and in the refinery scenes the powerful stench of melting sugar cane was so nauseating that the cast had to wear masks. And she had to miss both Thanksgiving and Christmas at home with the family.

The children increasingly resented her absences. Tara became a recluse at school and would hide in her bedroom writing songs and playing her new guitar. 'My mother hadn't much time to devote to me,' she told Linda Duff of the *Daily Star* in 1991, 'and I think I missed out on a lot of family life.' When she was thirty-one, in 1994, she told Corinna Honan that she had wanted her mother at home, not a nanny, but Joan had wanted to get back to her career: 'I resented that.' When she was thirty-seven she told Judith Woods of the *Daily Telegraph* that 'having a famous mum has been a real handicap. Sometimes it felt like having a "Kick Me" sign around my neck. Many times I really wished for a mum who was there to cook me dinner and help with my homework. But that was not the way it was.' Joan, however, saw it in a different way. 'I'd say for a working mother I did pretty well,' she told Lynda Lee-Potter defiantly in 1993. By 1977 'I was basically the breadwinner', she said. 'I was not able to be with my children twelve hours a day, but I was forever giving a list to the nanny saying "she's got to do her homework, he's got to go to football practice, the baby's going out to tea," and at the same time I had to think of the part I was playing. Of course children want their mother there all the time, but it was impossible. I'm basically a gypsy. I create my nest wherever I am.' Good mother or not, it was probably not the best idea when Joan offered Tara an unusual fourteenth birthday present that year: she offered to pay for her to have plastic surgery on her nose. 'It was very upsetting and it still hurts,' Tara told Corinna Honan. 'I don't like my nose: it's too big and not the nose I would have given myself, but it's *my* nose.' She declined the offer. Later she rebelled by becoming a surly punk; she wore her hair in spikes, dyed it black, blonde and pink, went to school in torn clothes fastened with safety pins, began to drink alcohol, and had the word MOTHER tattooed on her arm.

At the end of 1976 the legendary Hollywood agent Irving 'Swifty' Lazar came to Joan's rescue by suggesting that she should write a kiss-and-tell-all autobiography. Why not? She had been good at English at school and had always enjoyed writing, and a bestseller could solve her immediate financial problems. In January she started writing it at the Bricusses' house in Acapulco, calling it first *I Was a Stranger* but later *Past Imperfect*. She hoped to emulate David Niven's hugely successful autobiography but to add a touch of a sexy historical novel by Kathleen Winsor. 'What I'm aiming for is a mix between *The Moon's a Balloon* and *Forever Amber*,' she told Roderick Mann. She knew that if the book was to make much money it would have to be as spicy as possible, so she included explicit descriptions of even the most reprehensible, embarrassing and tasteless episodes of her life, including the sadistic assaults by her homosexual boyfriend when she was at RADA, her alleged rape by Maxwell Reed, her abortion of Beatty's baby, and her startling promiscuity. She named most of her lovers – though for some reason neither Harry Belafonte nor George Englund – and wrote much more about her sex life than her acting. The book's only virtue was her unashamed honesty, though she could not bring herself to admit that she and Warren Beatty had split up because he had been having an affair with Natalie Wood. But otherwise it was a shallow book written in a gauche, pedestrian style and her memory was so unreliable that often her dates and chronology were completely wrong, sometimes by several years.

Soon after starting the book she flew to Rome to make yet another abysmal Italian movie, *Poliziotto senza paura* (*Detective Without Fear*), which was once again released in English under several titles: *Fearless*, *Magnum Cop*, *Fatal Charms*, *The Day of the Fox*. She played a nightclub stripper who becomes a villainous brothel madam in an unintelligible story about the kidnapping of girls for prostitution. This allowed her to perform an ungainly dance and expose her surprisingly scrawny breasts, over which the hero later drags his pistol roughly, molesting her nipples before shooting her dead. There was an air of desperation about her performance: she looked strained, worried and unusually old and ugly with a strangely shaped nose, profile and wrinkled arms and hands. Her acting was embarrassingly amateurish and the script so ridiculous that she must have been truly at her wits' end to accept the part.

She was indeed under so much pressure that she joined a fashionable 'Actualizations' group at the Biltmore Hotel, which held workshops 'for the exploitation of human potential' where deeply unhappy people would try to 'find themselves' and told each other how deeply unhappy they were. Bravely Joan went along with Frank Sinatra's disgruntled wife Tina and stood up in front of dozens of strangers – who must surely have known who she was – to say how awful her marriage was, and she was taken aback when the group's leader told her that she should be nicer to Ron and more understanding of his problems. She threw herself into work and made two quick TV episodes, one for the science-fiction series *The Fantastic Journey* and one for *Future Cop*, and a TV game show, *Tattletales*. She also agreed to go to the Cannes Film Festival in May to promote *Empire of the Ants* even though she hated the film. It was a wonderfully lucky decision. At a lunch at the Carlton Hotel she found herself sitting next to the brother of the heavyweight boxer Billy Walker, George Walker, who was now the boss of a small movie distribution company, Brent-Walker, and keen to become a producer. She told him about *The Stud*, he read Jackie's screenplay, liked it, and within a week had signed a deal to finance the film so long as Joan would appear in it naked. Five years previously she had told Clive Hirschhorn: 'I won't ever strip in a movie. I think a woman (and a man for that matter) is more exciting with her clothes on. Garbo never stripped. Dietrich kept her clothes on, and so did Vivien Leigh. And who is more glamorous than them? What people do in their private lives is one thing. Making exhibitionists of themselves is quite another. Don't think I'm a prig because you know I'm not. My own private life has been anything but virginal. But I honestly believe that actresses have a certain responsibility to their audiences – a responsibility never to offend them.' But times had changed: now she was desperate for money. If she had to get her kit off to make some money, even though she was forty-four, so be it. She had already appeared nude more than once in her Italian films, hoping they would never be seen in England or America, so she told Walker that she would do it, and he agreed that Ron and Jackie's husband Oscar should produce the film and that shooting would begin as soon as possible.

While Ron and Oscar were setting up *The Stud* Joan flew to England in August to make an excellent movie for a change, *The Big Sleep*, with a distinguished cast that included Robert Mitchum, Sarah Miles, James Stewart, Sir John Mills, Oliver Reed, Edward Fox and Richard Boone. Based on Raymond Chandler's novel about his fictional Los Angeles private eye Philip Marlowe, it was written, produced and directed by Michael Winner, who realised that there was no point in simply remaking Howard Hawks' acclaimed 1946 version – with Humphrey Bogart and Lauren Bacall – so he set it instead in England, mainly in London, although Marlowe himself, played by Mitchum, remained American. Old Jimmy Stewart played a rich, touchingly frail general with two sexy, predatory daughters who asks the laconic, world-weary Marlowe to investigate an attempt to blackmail him, and in the process Marlowe discovers a festering nest of drugs, gambling, gun-running, pornographic photographs and murder. Joan played one of the baddies, a bookseller's assistant, with cool elegance – and 'enough sex appeal to stampede a businessman's lunch,' drawls Marlowe – and was un-recognisable by comparison with her two poor previous performances. There are guns and violence aplenty, six bodies hit the dust, and in one scene Joan wrestles with Mitchum and bites his leg, yet the film is not just another thud-and-blunder potboiler. The atmosphere is slick but tense throughout, with long, effective silences, discreetly moody music, beautifully filmed locations, and memorable performances by Sarah Miles and Candy Clark as the general's flirty but dangerous daughters and by Oliver Reed as the smooth, menacing owner of a gambling club.

It was a wild film to make. Mitchum, a champion drinker and womaniser, kept his hands off Joan, who admired him hugely and loved acting with him even though he told her that the film was 'crap' and was rumoured to have accepted the part only because Winner had promised him he could keep the twelve Savile Row suits he wore in the movie. He would sit up until 3 a.m. boozing with his cronies but still managed to seduce two of the young cockney girls in the film, tried in vain to pull another, and demanded that Winner should tell him where to find prostitutes. He became so drunk one day that when a German TV crew turned up to interview him he yelled that they were all Nazis, gave them a Hitler salute, and sent them packing. Richard Boone had an impressive thirst, too, and would get through a bottle of whisky a day on the set, and the ebullient Oliver Reed, just as heavy a drinker as Mitchum and Boone, would often arrive on the set seriously overhung. Reed announced one day that on the previous night he had been playing a fighting game in which the contestants had to sit astride a pole and batter each other, and 'it competely did in my balls,' he said. 'Would you like to see them?' Mitchum declined the offer too late: Reed dropped his trousers and thrust his badly bruised genitals under Mitchum's nose. Reed, like Joan, was also writing his autobiography and claimed that he was going to call it *I'm The Only Man Who Didn't Go To Bed With Joan Collins*. Sarah Miles was notoriously difficult and demanding, insisted that her room should be repainted white, and then shrieked because it still had a red cushion in it. As for Joan, Winner begged her not to wear her beloved wigs and on the first day of filming tugged her hair to check whether it was real. But as she left the set on the last day of shooting she trilled '*Michael!*', pulled her wig off triumphantly and waved it at him.

As soon as she finished *The Big Sleep* she resumed her search for a hunky, virile actor in his late twenties to co-star with her in *The Stud*. She approached Paul Michael Glaser but he was too busy with *Starsky and Hutch*. She considered the black boxer John Conteh and the soccer player George Best, and at the end of September flew off to Rome 'to look at a couple of Italians'. In vain. She flew again to Los Angeles and eventually chose a sultry, Swiss-born, thirty-year-old, Oliver Tobias, the star of an Australian outback TV series, *Luke's Kingdom*, who had also played the ancient Celtic King Arthur both in a television series and a movie. 'He has this burning quality,' said Charlotte Rampling, who had acted with him six years previously as incestuous brother and sister in the film *'Tis Pity She's a Whore*. 'I can understand why women go for him.' The black model Mynah Bird, an old friend of

Tobias who was to play one of his lovers in the film, said: 'Wow. I can hardly wait. We were great buddies. Oliver has got the lot. It will be just like old times. He's one hell of a man.' An Australian friend, Jack Thompson, recalled the time he had spent with Tobias filming at a remote farm in the outback. 'I'd class him among the top-ten studs I've ever met,' he said. 'Every night was an orgy. We had girls, girls, girls. It was nude beach parties and naked trips through the forest and nude swims in country streams.'

Tobias sounded absolutely right for the film, for which shooting began in November and in which George Walker's brother Billy made a cameo appearance. It was a vulgar, raucous soft-porn movie in which Tobias, playing a trendy London discotheque's young working-class greeter, was used and abused by one tacky woman after another – including a sixteen-year-old virgin played by the broadcaster David Jacobs's nineteen-year-old daughter Emma – but mainly by Joan, who played Fontaine Khaled, the predatory, nymphomaniac wife of the disco's rich owner. She and Tobias are shown screwing in a lift while being recorded on video tape, screwing in the back seat of a limousine, screwing in a swimming pool during a wife-swapping orgy, and screwing on a swing-chair decorated with flowers. There are numerous shots of Joan and other women naked and one slow close-up of languid, erect nipple-licking. There is even a homosexual grope in the swimming pool and a lingering close-up of Tobias's trousered crotch. It was all obviously meant to be erotic but watching it nearly thirty years later the movie is strangely sexless and simply dull. None of the nudes looks at all desirable, not even Joan, who pouts and simpers with the best of them, and the whole enterprise is fatally humourless except for one line when the unquenchably randy Tobias is dubbed sarcastically 'Warren Beatty'. Otherwise the standard of dialogue was hopelessly crass. Referring to her boring husband, Joan remarks dismissively that 'Ben gets his cock sucked once a month and always in the dark'. Referring to the stud, she sneers that until she took him in hand and educated him sexually 'he thought 69 was a whisky', and she tells him at the end: 'Fuck yourself, darling. You could do with a little practice.' Finally, when she sacks him, he yells at his rival: 'You bastard! You cock-sucking bastard!' When Melvyn Bragg interviewed Jackie in 1999 she claimed that she and Joan had not tried to make a 'cheesy' movie, even though that might make them a fortune, but wanted it to have 'a little style and a little class'. If Jackie thought that *The Stud* was stylish, classy and not cheesy it would be interesting to see what she could get up to with a slab of Gorgonzola.

The film was equally cheap to make, took less than four weeks, and cost just over a million pounds in modern terms because Soraya Khashoggi let them use her luxurious house as a set and they shot the disco scenes for free at Tramp. Jackie told the *Evening News* that Joan was 'totally right for this part of a jet-set nymphomaniac lady. She seems to have grown into the part. It goes perfectly with her.' Then, realising that it sounded as if she was saying that Joan was a nympho-maniac, she added hastily: 'I don't mean she is like that, but she has spent a lot of time studying people like that.' Joan was not nearly so coy. 'When I'm working with a man in a love scene it's important that I fancy him,' she admitted, 'even if he's got bloodshot eyes and bad breath. I've still got to try and turn myself on.' She claimed often that Ron was never jealous and did not mind her playing heavy love scenes, but in fact he minded very much when an actor in the swimming-pool scene, Mark Burns, was filmed fondling her breast rather too enthusi-astically. Ron claimed that the director, Quentin Masters, had ensured that Joan would lose her inhibitions by giving her and Burns a lot to drink.

When *The Stud* was released in April 1978 Joan said that she was proud of it and claimed that it was a morality tale, which showed that 'the people who are written about in the gossip columns and who are considered by the average reader to have everything – to have money, fame, success, looks, all of those rather materialistic things – are basically very sad, very lonely and very lacking in a lot of the human qualities.' It was a spurious justification because the only character to emerge triumphant is the most successful, predatory and nastiest of them all, Fontaine herself. The people she has used and abused all end up losers. When the film opened in America a year later the critics were just as caustic as the British. '*The Stud* is an ugly soft-core pornographic account of the rise and fall of a fancy man,' said the *New York Times*. 'It is illiterate and anti-erotic. The performances, Quentin Masters' direction and cinematography and editing are all amateurish.' *People* magazine was even more savage. 'If you miss one movie this year,' it suggested, 'make sure this is it. Joan Collins, debasing herself as few actresses of substance have done ... still has an attractive body, but displays it with such insistent regularity that she seems more ludicrous than sensuous. The script is, to be generous, slimy, vulgar and stupid.'

Eight years later Joan admitted that she regretted making the movie. 'Looking back in embarrassment I cringe and say, "Oh my God, did I do that?" she confessed to TV-am's presenter Anne Diamond in 1986. 'But you see, I was hungry then, and when you're hungry you often do things that go against the grain. The nudity went against my grain quite a bit, but I was talked and conned into it. There's no way I would do a film like that today.' Tobias, however, told Melvyn Bragg that when she stripped off for the film she was not at all reluctant – 'she got right into it, loved it' – and Ron denied that she had been forced to shoot scenes against her will. 'Joan has often blamed me for forcing her to do things like nudity and sex sequences,' he told the *Sunday People* in 1983. 'It's not true. The sex scenes I designed for her were always tasteful – erotic, not pornographic. During filming of *The Stud* we choreographed the love scenes the night before. We ended up making love because she always roused me – she *always* could.'

Tobias also came to regret appearing in the film. Soon after it was released in April he complained publicly that the script had been irretrievably shallow and that he had been paid 'peanuts'. Joan and Jackie retaliated by saying that they had never wanted him for the part in the first place and that he was being appallingly ungrateful – 'you take a guy from nowhere and make somebody out of him and he starts complaining' – and Joan sneered that she hadn't fancied him at all, that he took himself too seriously and was insecure and humourless. The first time she met him, she said, 'he was unshaven, wearing the worst set of clothes I've ever seen, smelling of garlic', she told the *Daily Mail*. 'He isn't sexy. I saw him luck out three times on the set. He tried to pull three of the girls including Emma Jacobs and failed.' Eleven years later Tobias told Jim Taylor of the *Sun* that 'making love to Joan Collins was the worst thing I ever did' and 'it was all pretty dull'. Quentin Masters, the director, was also unhappy about the film and had such doubts about the 'integrity' of the finished product that he refused to go to the première. 'Integrity?' bellowed George Walker. 'If it costs more money I don't want it!'

Jackie denied all responsibility for the sleazy scenes. 'The sex in it was meant to be subliminal like *The Graduate*,' she told Lester Middlehurst in 1995, 'but when I saw it, there was Joan totally naked on a swing, going back and forth. She did the same thing in *The Bitch* [*a year later*]. I don't know why she did it because I never wrote those scenes. She rubbishes them now but I can't help thinking to myself, "Well, nobody had a gun at your head, baby!"' Joan's eighteen-year-old English assistant and fan club organiser, Barry Langford, claimed five years later that it was indeed Ron who persuaded her to do the naked scenes. 'He begged and pleaded with his wife to do nude scenes for the cameras,' Langford told the *Sun* in 1983. 'He promised to boost her flagging career if only she would strip.' Langford reported that Ron loved showing nude photographs of Joan to his cronies and boasting how good she was in bed: 'I was disgusted once when he told a male visitor to the house in Beverly Hills that he was the only man in the US who could satisfy his wildcat wife in the sack.' Joan was furious, said Langford, when she discovered that Ron had even sold naughty still photographs from her movies to porn magazines: 'It was the beginning of the end. She regarded it as an awful betrayal of trust.' When Langford's allegations appeared in print after Ron and Joan had separated in 1983, Ron replied angrily that Langford knew nothing because he had been just Joan's lowly gofer, but in the American edition of *Past Imperfect* she called Langford 'my friend' and thanked him for helping her with the manuscript.

In the end Joan could not bring herself really to regret making *The Stud*. She was paid only £14,500 to make the film [£58,000] and the reviews were appalling but she was also entitled to fifteen per cent of the profits and in just ten days it took more than £500,000 [more than £2 million] in cinema ticket sales – a record for Britain then – and sales of a record of the film's music totalled £1.5 million [more than £6 million]. The movie went on to make millions more, to become the highest-selling British video ever. 'It relaunched my career,' she told Jack Tinker of the *Daily Mail* a couple of years later. 'I'd be a fool to regret that.' She added: 'I could say that ... exploiting myself in *The Stud* was a mistake. It might well have been for my own self-esteem as Joan Kass, wife and mother. But as Joan Collins, movie actress, it most definitely was not.' By 1999 she was telling Melvyn Bragg defiantly that she still thought *The Stud* was 'a really good film'. Joan's father and the critic Alan Brien came closer to the truth. Joe had never objected to Joan appearing nude on the screen but in the case of *The Stud* he wrote in his autobiography: 'Frankly I found the film distasteful. It was not my idea of entertainment.' Brien was brutal. 'Watching it,' he said, 'is rather like being buried alive in a coffin stuffed with back copies of *Men Only*.'

CHAPTER ELEVEN

TITS, ARSE AND TRAGEDY

{ 1978–1981 }

In December 1977, almost a year after Joan started to write her auto-biography, she finished it at Ron's London house in South Street, Mayfair, in such a hurry that she skimmed over the last eight years in just twelve pages and the book was littered with inaccuracies. It said, for instance, that President Kennedy was assassinated on 20 November 1963 rather than the 22nd, although any decent editor or proof-reader should have spotted that mistake.

The Kasses flew to Los Angeles, where Jackie and Oscar had bought a house and decided to spend more time for Joan to work on a film comedy, *Zero to Sixty*, in which she played a *femme fatale* who becomes involved with a car repossession man. In Hollywood one day she was lunching with Evie Bricusse at Ma Maison when David Niven Jr intro-duced them to a short, nondescript Frenchwoman, Madame Claude, who joined them for coffee and complimented them on their beauty. She wondered whether they wanted to earn some spare cash. She had many clients, she said, who preferred older women to young ones, and Joan suddenly realised that this was *the* Madame Claude, the most famous brothel madame in France, who provided rich and famous men with stunningly beautiful, intelligent call girls. 'You two girls could do very well indeed,' said Madame Claude, and 'your husbands don't have to know.' They accepted her card, promised to call her, and giggled all the way home.

In mid-February the Kasses flew back to London to shoot some final location sequences for *The Stud*, then to the Bahamas for a family holiday, and back to London for the première of *The Stud* on 11 April. The autobiography was scheduled to be published at the end of May and Joan told Rosalie Shann of the *News of the World* that writing it had changed her life. It 'was like shedding my old skin and becoming someone else', she said. 'Someone very mature and confident. I'm no longer naïve and gullible as I used to be. Thank God, I think I've finally grown up.' She was in fact more naïve and gullible than ever because when the paper serialised the book – paying her £190,000 in modern terms to do so – she was naïvely surprised and appalled to see that it had chosen to print the more lurid, sensational extracts about her sex life, promiscuity, lovers and marriages, and when she realised just how startlingly indiscreet she had been she rushed around Los Angeles trying to buy every copy of the paper that she could find to prevent her friends and acquaintances reading it.

Her astonishingly intimate revelations caused an uproar and blasted the book into the British bestseller list after she had toured eleven English cities to promote it. Most of her lovers lay low and did not react to what they probably felt was tacky, mercenary, kiss-and-tell treachery to add to the sleaze of *The Stud*, but Tony Newley, who was still earning a huge amount writing songs, appearing on American television and the US cabaret circuit and had just been voted Male Musical Star of the Year, was incensed that she had written so openly about him, their marriage and his taste for underage girls. He felt betrayed, his bitterness was to fester for years, and it infected Tara and Sacha, too. Tara was fourteen, by now wearing a rebellious ring through her nose, Sacha was twelve and suffering jeers and taunts about his flighty mother from boys at school, and both were deeply disturbed by *The Stud* and the book. With astonishing *naïvety* Joan even gave them each a copy. 'It's disconcerting to see your mother naked,' Tara said years later; 'a bit like trying to imagine your parents bonking.' She and Sacha told Joan that they no longer wanted to live with her but would rather be with Newley and his girlfriend Dareth, who was according to Leslie Bricusse 'a true delight and a natural sunny antidote to the soft cloud of gloom that always seemed to be drifting across the Newley horizon'. Tony and Dareth had established a stable family home at Lloyd Crest in Beverly Hills, where both children felt loved and secure. Joan dismissed Dareth contemptuously as 'that stewardess' but Tara and Sacha had become fond of her and saw her as an ideal, homely, loving mother, unlike their own. 'It caused a serious rift between me and the children,' Joan told Clive Hirschhorn a year later. 'It was very upsetting for all of us.' But surely she must have expected a negative reaction? 'Not really,' she said. 'Swifty, my agent, simply told me to sit down at a typewriter and let it all spill out. Afterwards, he said, I could edit out what I thought might be too personal. But once it was written I didn't have time to polish it or re-think certain sections.'

Realising that the book might damage her reputation seriously in America, she stopped Warner Books publishing it there and reluctantly returned their $100,000 advance [£156,000]. 'I wrote the book to set the record straight about the past,' she told the *Los Angeles Times*, 'but it hasn't worked out that way. It just dragged it all up again.' A year later she told David Lewin of the *Sunday Mirror* that 'writing the book was a major mistake. I shouldn't have done it. I have a fatal flaw. I am terribly naïve.' The American edition was not to be published for six years – and then only after it had been carefully sanitised – but inevitably thousands of Americans simply ordered the British edition to be sent to them. Joan's father refused to read the book, even though – again amazingly naïvely – she sent him a copy with an affectionate dedication despite the critical things she had written about him in it. He did not want to read about her affairs or what she had said about him, he explained sadly, because he was convinced that she had written the book only because she was desperate for money, '*her* kind of money.'

Joan was devastated by the children's decision to leave her but told Rosalie Shann: 'I'm not the type to slave over a stove concocting home-made soup. I want to be out in the arena of life. So now I have domestic help at home. I can't stand cleaning and cooking,' and she admitted to the *Daily Mail* that Tara had said: 'You've been out three nights in a row and we feel you don't care.' The children were much happier living with Tony and Dareth at Lloyd Crest. 'That was a really magical house,' Tara told Jane Slade of the *Mail on Sunday* in 2003. 'It had a little fountain in the front yard and a projector room where Dad used to play us Disney films he had got on the black market. We had a swimming pool surrounded by gardenia bushes, a rose garden and another where my brother and I used to catch butterflies.' They were to live there for two years. As for Katy, who was now six, she was living most of the time in Surrey with a nanny at a four-bedroom country cottage that Joan and Kass could now afford to buy in the village of Holmbury St Mary, near Dorking, though she was soon to go to Connaught House day school near Marble Arch, where she too was teased and bullied because of her mother's sexy image. 'Katy was a lovely girl,' I was told by her schoolmate Belinda Selby. 'We were great friends.' Thanks to *The Stud* and *Past Imperfect* Ron was also able to borrow £75,000 [£304,000] from the bankers Hill Samuel to buy a Georgian house in London off Maida Vale, overlooking a quiet canal in Little Venice, which allowed Janet Street-Porter to chortle in the *Evening News* that Joan had become 'Maida Vale's answer to Emmanuelle'. Once again Joan decorated the house with a surfeit of silver – it was all too theatrical, said her father – and the Kasses had by now made so much money from the film and book that they were able to sell the Los Angeles house on Carolyn Way and buy a four-bedroom mock-Tudor mansion in Beverly Hills at 2220 Bowmont Drive.

In May an ungallant debate about Joan's real age erupted in the British Press. She told several interviewers that she was about to turn forty-two, which led one reader to write to a trade newspaper that if this was so 'when I saw her some thirty-odd years ago she was the best developed eleven-year-old I've ever seen'. The *Daily Express* reported correctly that she was in fact forty-five and could not resist adding mischievously that one of Joe Collins's friends believed she was forty-seven. Joan fled to Australia and New Zealand to promote *The Stud* and returned undeterred to set up another sleazy film, *The Bitch*, which was based on a second of Jackie's steamy novels and again produced by Ron and Oscar. For that 'we want two or three Englishmen and at least one Italian stallion', she announced, but first she made another horny film, *Homework*, in which she played a mother who seduces her teenage daughter's boyfriend. She also made a television advertisement for British Airways, for which they gave her free flights for the next three years; the first of a series of witty TV ads for Cinzano with the comic actor Leonard Rossiter; two films, *Sunburn* and *A Game For Vultures*; and she appeared on television with John Gielgud in a black comedy, 'Neck', an episode of the Roald Dahl series *Tales of the Unexpected*.

In 'Neck', which was filmed in Norfolk and Suffolk in September, she played an English aristocrat's rich, promiscuous wife who seduces a series of young men who visit their country mansion at weekends. Gielgud played the disapproving butler, Jelks, who helps the cuckolded husband to take his revenge when his wife is cavorting in the garden with one of her lovers, her head becomes stuck in a hole in a statue, and he decides to free her by reaching for an axe. Joan had worshipped

Gielgud ever since she had seen him on the West End stage during her RADA days and was thrilled yet unusually shy to be acting with him. She found him elegant, charming and witty and loved hearing his theatrical anecdotes. Gielgud was less enthusiastic about the job. 'Here I am holed up in an appallingly gimcrack hotel,' he wrote from Great Yarmouth to his American lover Ed Cone. 'Sing-songs in the evening, plastic walls and unspeakable food and furniture making a ridiculous half-hour television special (!) of a Roald Dahl short story in which I do my Orient Express deadpan butler performance with Joan Collins as a randy chatelaine and one or two others. We move to Lowestoft to finish it next week and film at a dreadful 1926 stately home with Edwardian furnishings and rather pretty run-down gardens with a maze, flocked to by tourists twice a week at 70p a head while we lark amid a welter of cables and cameras in the bedrooms upstairs. All pretty boring, especially as the weather's endlessly squally and uncertain which drives everyone in and out and wastes the time of the crew. I sit about a lot and do my crossword and work desultorily on another little book of reminiscences which I've almost finished.'

Gieldgud was flattering about Joan's acting. 'People seemed to expect some kind of cataclysmic happening when Joan and I were working together,' he told *The Times*, 'but Joan is a very professional actress and we got along extremely well together. In fact, she was quite perfect in the part.' When the episode was broadcast in April 1979 they were interviewed together by David Lewin of the *Sunday Mirror*, who asked Gielgud if he had ever seen Joan acting before. 'Oh, yes,' he said. 'I went rather furtively to see her in *The Stud* when it opened. Terrible notices, but I don't see what all the fuss was about.' He revealed that he had himself just made a pornographic film about the Roman emperor Caligula. 'There was one orgy scene with twenty or thirty beautiful young girls and boys completely naked – with their hair shaved off to make them look younger, according to the director. I looked at all that naked flesh and thought: "buttocks wouldn't melt in my mouth".'

Cinzano paid Joan £20,000 [£81,000] for the first advertisement with Leonard Rossiter, the star of the TV series *The Fall and Rise of Reginald Perrin* and *Rising Damp*. In the ad he played an accident-prone buffoon who was always spilling the drink over her. At first Cinzano planned a series of ads in which Rossiter was teamed with several actresses in turn, but his on-screen chemistry with Joan was so strong that they paid her a further £13,300 a year to make several more ads over the next six years. This did not stop her sending Cinzano a cheeky bill for £20 because she had used her own make-up. A director who made some of the commercials, Terry Lovelock, found her to be utterly professional. 'She does a bit of strutting,' he admitted, 'and is constantly demanding to know what's going on. But she's not as bad as they make out.' For one of the ads they bought her a beautiful £1,000 dress [£4,000] but she was appalled that this would be ruined by Rossiter spilling Cinzano Rosé over it, so she cut a hole in a sheet, poked her head through the hole, tied a belt around her waist, and wore that instead. 'She looked wonderful,' said the art director, Ron Collins. Rossiter said later that Joan was very professional and 'a good deal firmer-breasted than I had thought'.

'How did you find that out?' she asked.

'An accidental collision, my dear,' grinned Rossiter. He added: 'Men always ask me about Joan. "Bit of a goer, is she?" they say. "Mind your own business," I reply.'

In October she flew to Acapulco to make *Sunburn* with Farrah Fawcett-Majors and Charles Grodin. 'It was not a good film but I was hungry and I had to pay the mortgage,' she told the American comedienne Joan Rivers on TV in 1986. In fact it was a much better film than most of hers, a genial comedy thriller about insurance fraud in which she appeared briefly in two short scenes as an alcoholic nymphomaniac. Then she went to South Africa – where the censors were about to ban *Past Imperfect* – to take on another tiny part in a film with Richard Harris, *A Game For Vultures*, in which she played Harris's girlfriend while he was a sanctions-busting Rhodesian businessman selling helicopters illegally to Ian Smith's white supremacist regime. Joan had suddenly become such a box-office draw that she was given top billing even though she appeared only briefly in four short, unimportant scenes and her part was utterly irrelevant to the plot. She got on well with Harris, a notorious boozer who had been sober for nearly a year, and loved going on safari at the stylishly beautiful Mala Mala game reserve in the Kruger National Park. Her acting, however, was stagey, affected, and marred by even more archness, simpering and pouting than usual, though it has to be said that a couple of the other actors were not much better. Harris, Ray Milland (as a crooked businessman) and Denholm Elliott (as a private detective) were as competent as usual but Richard Roundtree, who was meant to be a black Zimbabwean guerilla fighting in the bush, was ludicrous with his American accent and smart three-piece suit and tie, and Alibe Parsons as a sophisticated black woman was so over-the-top with her pouting, flirting and cut-glass accent that she could well have been taking the mickey out of Joan herself. As for the third film she made that year, *Homework*, it was so poor that it was not released until she became famous in *Dynasty* four years later.

The Kasses spent Christmas in Los Angeles but returned to London early in January 1979 to film *The Bitch*. Although Joan was now forty-five a poll of young British men aged twenty-five to thirty-five voted her the world's most attractive sex symbol, ahead even of Brigitte Bardot, Diana Rigg and Raquel Welch. 'A lady in her forties has more to offer than just pretty physical packaging,' she told Ivan Waterman of the *News of the World*. 'Trying to be sexy doesn't come from wearing a short skirt or letting your boobs hang out. It comes from inside. And I seem to have this tremendous energy which doesn't seem to have abated at all. I haven't done anything special to keep my looks. I keep myself busy, that's the secret.'

The Bitch, which was financed again by Brent–Walker, depicted Fontaine Khaled's sexual adventures after *The Stud* in New York and London. Her main man this time was played by a thirty-six-year-old Italian, Antonio Cantafora, who looked like a young Omar Sharif, had appeared with Joan in *L'Amore breve* in 1969, and was now calling himself Michael Coby. Joan was unhappy with the film right from the start. The script was unfinished, she said, her wardrobe incomplete, Cantafora an unknown with a voice so feeble that his entire dialogue had to be dubbed, and she had little faith in the director, Gerry O'Hara. She claimed later that once again Ron and George Walker forced her to shoot naked scenes that she did not want to do and that Walker had bellowed: 'Fuck creativity! That doesn't sell tickets. Tits and arse do!' She begged him not to call it *The Bitch* but he was adamant, and even before shooting had finished the British Press was regularly referring to her personally as 'The Bitch'. Joan insisted that she was not a bitch but the nickname stuck and it was to be four years before she persuaded the newspapers to drop it.

This time Fontaine Khaled seduces her accountant, a pop star, a waiter and her chauffeur. 'I'm not like her at all but I do like her,' Joan told Jean Ritchie of the *Sun*, 'and I think for a lot of women she acts out fantasies. There she is, seducing her chauffeur, wearing his cap and the naughtiest of undies.' She confessed that she enjoyed making sexy movies 'but I want to do other things. After all, it would be ludicrous to be prancing around in the nude at fifty.' A month later she told David Lewin that she was a frustrated comedienne: 'I want to get back to acting in the theatre with all my clothes on.' Yet two months later she was planning to film Patsy Booth's novel *The Lady and the Champ*, for which she was seeking a handsome, hunky young stud to play her eighteen-year-old lover and fully intended to shed her clothes yet again.

In May she went to the South of France to promote *The Bitch* at the Cannes Film Festival and was horrified to see a light aircraft flying across the bay trailing a banner that read JOAN COLLINS IS THE BITCH. She begged George Walker to change the slogan to JOAN COLLINS AS THE BITCH but he refused. At the end of the month she was upset again when she gave a live interview on BBC Radio Birmingham to promote the paperback edition of *Past Imperfect* and the interviewer, Alastair Yates, remarked that the book was just a diary of her sex life and that she had made Tony Newley sound like a freak. There was an embarrassed silence, Yates played a record of Newley singing 'What Kind of Fool Am I?' and Joan burst into tears and fled the studio. A week later another broadcaster, Bob Langley, offended her when she appeared on the TV programme *Saturday Night at the Mill* and she poured a bottle of wine over him.

That summer Tara and Sacha came to stay with Joan and Ron in England and Joan at last allowed Tara to go out on dates now that she was fifteen. She began work on the *Joan Collins Beauty Book* and made another half-hour *Tales of the Unexpected* TV drama, 'Georgy Porgy', this time with John Alderton, who played a Mummy's-boy English country vicar. Joan had two parts: first as his mother, a frighteningly brash, fruity, curly-red-wigged woman who terrifies him when he is small by forcing him to watch rabbits being born 'just like you and me' and then eaten by their mother; and then as a black-wigged temptress in his congregation who drives him to fantasise that every woman in his church is naked and eventually he goes mad.

The Bitch opened in Britain in September, promoted by huge posters that showed Joan in a cheeky corset, suspenders and black stockings and blazoned the slogan NOW YOU CAN SEE ALL OF ME. Katy, who was seven, was given such a rough time by her schoolmates because the posters were plastered all over London billboards and buses that she became seriously upset, and Joan screened a short film at the school that showed extracts from her more respectable roles to show the girls that she did not always play indecent parts. She also tried to give *The Bitch* some moral value by saying that in it Fontaine 'appears to have the world by the balls, but underneath she's trying to solve the problem of loneliness, which I think is the universal problem of all rich people'. But 'there comes a time when you move on', she told the *Yorkshire Post*. 'I've had enough of this type of blatant exploitation. There is no way, for my own peace of mind, that I could do any more semi-nude shots.' Inevitably the film was trounced by the critics. Typical was Judy Wade in the *Sun*. Despite the paper's salacious obsession with anything sexual, even Ms Wade was appalled by *The Bitch*. The film was tacky, tasteless and ridiculous, she said. Joan played 'the same over-ripe maneater that won her the title of Britain's top sex symbol [*but*] looks more seedy than sexy and she flops in more ways than one', she wrote. 'The film displays so much sagging female flesh, so many droopy bosoms, that only a plastic surgeon would get excited.' As for Antonio Cantafora, 'this Italian Stallion has all the pulling power of a nag ready for the knacker's yard'. Later Joan admitted that she too had thought the film was dreadful and had allowed herself and her body to be exploited, but she justified her performance by claiming that she had been very hard up and needed the money desperately. Her recurrent excuse that she made soft-porn films only because she was desperate for money seems uncomfortably similar to any prostitute's justification for her way of life.

In fact *The Bitch* was not nearly as bad as everyone said. There were indeed particularly tacky sequences that showed an underwater orgy, two lesbians fingering each other in a sauna cubicle, and another in which Joan – 'the best known cradle snatcher this side of the Atlantic'– is serviced in a shower. There is also yet another leisurely nuzzling of a nipple, but most of the sex scenes were much less explicit than those in *The Stud* and were filmed glossily and more discreetly in shadow or soft focus. There was even a sort of story involving a smuggled diamond, the Mafia, horse racing and gambling, and the bitch gets her final come-uppance at the end. Joan's acting was as self-conscious as ever but Judy Wade's claim that she looked seedy and saggy was quite unfair: in fact she looked gorgeous and most of the flesh on display was firm and succulent, though her wigs were ridiculously huge. She was even given the occasional amusing line to deliver. 'Stop sending me flowers,' she tells her Italian stallion, 'they're giving me hayfever.'

Still, Joan was now determined to clean up her image. 'I owe it to myself to get back to theatre,' she told the *Evening Standard*. 'I'm not going to suddenly turn up as Lady Macbeth – I've never been that keen on Shakespeare – but to do a good comedy on stage now is ideal,' and she told the *News of the World*: 'I'm sick of being plastered all over hoardings in black knickers and a saucy smile. I've a very good mind and a very good sense of humour and I want the public to see something of them.' She confessed to Clive Hirschhorn that she realised that almost every film she had ever made was rubbish. 'I've done fifty films in twenty-four years,' she said, 'and most of *them* I've had to live down. I came into the lounge the other day and my son Sacha was playing a video tape of a movie-of-the-week I made several years ago and I couldn't believe it. Everything about it was *dreadful*, including me. Watching it for even five minutes was a desperate act of masochism.'

One unpleasant consequence of *The Bitch* was that Tony Newley began to send her reviews of the film with the title heavily underlined. He was furious when she claimed that he was in arrears with his maintenance payments, and when he sent two first-class tickets for Tara and Sacha to fly to Los Angeles he accused her of exchanging them for two economy tickets and pocketing the difference. His bitterness was as deep as ever, even though he seemed to have found a new happiness with Dareth, whom he married in Los Angeles in October 1979 and who was to have their second child, Christopher, in April.

Joan and Ron were increasingly convinced that Brent–Walker was not paying them as much of the profits from *The Stud* and *The Bitch* as they were due. So far they had been paid only £25,000 each [£89,500] yet were convinced that the films had made millions and that an LP disc of *The Bitch* soundtrack had sold 100,000 copies in six months. Eventually they issued a writ against Brent–Walker, launching a court case that was to drag on for seven years. Another irritation was that when Joan turned down an offer from Harlech Television in January to appear in a TV programme about the Ancient Egyptian pharaoh Tutankhamun, *The Curse of King Tut*, which was to be filmed in Egypt, the channel announced that she had backed off on the advice of her astrologer because she was afraid of becoming the latest victim of the famous curse, which was said to have caused the deaths of numerous people ever since the pharaoh's tomb had been opened by Howard Carter in 1922. 'I find that a very tacky thing for them to do,' she complained, but confirmed that she had indeed declined the part because she was superstitious. She did, however, agree to play another legendary Egyptian ruler, Cleopatra, in an episode of the American TV series *Fantasy Island*, a holiday resort where any visitor's dream could be made to come true. 'It was a dreadful piece of crap,' she told Peter Conrad of the *Observer Magazine* in 1990. 'They took me to the costume warehouse and one of the dressers said, "Ooh, I think we've still got some of Elizabeth Taylor's things from *Cleopatra* here": he fished out this green rag net, a bit of tat you wouldn't even give your maid! Some of the other stuff had been worn by Cher at Caesar's Palace in Las Vegas. But I did get Claudette Colbert's jewelled helmet from the old de Mille *Cleopatra* in 1934.' It was, however, the luckiest decision of her life because it was her performance in *Fantasy Island* that was to win her the biggest role of her career, in *Dynasty*.

Joan's ambition to appear on the stage again looked as if it might be realised early in 1980 when the Forum Theatre in Billingham, Cleveland, signed her up for a play, *The Four-Poster*, in which every scene takes place in bed, but the project fell through when seven actors inexplicably declined to slip between the sheets with her. But then the Chichester Festival Theatre asked her to join Simon Williams and Elspeth March for two months in Frederick Lonsdale's 1920s comedy *The Last of Mrs Cheyney*, in which Joan was to play the title role as a beautiful but demure society jewel thief. They could pay her only a pittance, £170 a week [£515], but for once she did not care about money. She grabbed the opportunity. It was her first stage part in twenty-six years, her first since *Claudia and David* at the Q Theatre in 1954, and she was understandably nervous, especially since the rest of the cast were established West End actors who might sneer at a mere film star, but 'it's time to prove to myself that I have the talent I have always believed I had', she said bravely. When the play opened in May it was almost a sell-out for its entire run, she loved being in front of the footlights again, and although the reviews were bad she said defiantly that 'bums on seats are a bit more important than the critics'. She also insisted yet again that she was only forty-three when she was actually about to turn forty-seven, but she was indeed so good at putting bums on seats that the producers decided to take the play on a five-week tour in September and then bring it into the West End at the end of October with even more lavish costumes designed by the Russian designer Erté, Romain de Tirtoff.

That summer of 1980 was at first a golden one for Joan. Not only was she comparatively rich again and back on the stage, she also had her two elder children back at home with her. Tara and Sacha had become disillusioned living with their father and Dareth in Los Angeles and returned to England. Joan Crawford had died recently and Newley, who was by now earning the modern equivalent of £412,000 a month, had bought her crumbling old mansion in Brentwood, at 426 Bristol Avenue, which had an Olympic-sized swimming pool and its own cinema, and he had spent nearly £2.75 million in modern terms restoring the place, having the hall painted pink, the living room pink and purple, the dining room yellow and black. Newley loved the place but Dareth and the children hated it and were convinced that it was haunted. There seemed to be icy patches in some rooms, Sacha felt extremely nervous in his bedroom and became withdrawn, and even Newley could not bring himself to go down to the cellar. There were unexplained noises in the house and objects seemed to move inexplicably. Dareth and Tara, who was now seriously punk, began to argue all the time and eventually stopped speaking to each other, and the atmosphere between Newley and Dareth also became strained. The birth of their son Christopher in April erected yet another barrier between Dareth, Tony and the children, and Tara and Sacha decided to go back to Mum in England. Dareth eventually persuaded Newley to sell the house a year later, and when the new owners held an exorcism several psychics claimed that they could see ghosts, that there were as many as twenty-three restless spirits in the house, and that the cellar was the worst place of all, 'one of the portals of the underworld'. Maybe one of the venemous phantoms was that of scary old Joan Crawford herself.

When the Chichester run ended early in July, Joan made yet another TV episode of *Tales of the Unexpected*, 'A Girl Can't Always Have Everything', this time with her namesake Pauline Collins. They played a pair of hard-up repertory actresses, glamorous Suzy and homely Pat, who share a flat but can hardly pay the rent until Suzy (Joan) gets her selfish claws into a rich, middle-aged widower who gives her a mink coat and a sports car. She carries on with other men behind his back and when he asks her to marry him she turns to Pat for help, but it does not turn out at all in the way she hopes. 'Joan has a way of adding something to any scene,' said Anglia TV's head of drama, John Rosenberg. 'Her timing and professionalism are a joy to work with. She is one of our great favourites.'

On 2 August Joan, Ron and Tara, who had never been to Paris, crossed the Channel to meet Erté to discuss costumes for the tour of *The Last of Mrs Cheyney*, leaving eight-year-old Katy behind with her best friend, Georgina Duits, and her parents at their home in Crowthorne, Berkshire. That afternoon the girls were playing in a country lane when they stepped suddenly into the road and were knocked down by a car. Its eighteen-year-old driver was unable to avoid them, even though he was driving carefully at only 27 mph. Georgina broke her leg and pelvis but Katy's head smashed against a concrete kerb, her skull was fractured, and she was knocked unconscious. Both girls were rushed to Ascot hospital by ambulance but Katy's injuries were so bad that she was taken to the better equipped Central Middlesex Hospital in Acton, where the doctors and nurses reckoned she was unlikely to survive. Joan and Ron had not told anyone where they would be staying in Paris and it was 2 a.m. before her brother Bill tracked them down at their suite in the Hotel Lancaster by telephoning every major hotel in Paris. He told them that Katy was in a critical condition. Joan screamed: 'No, no, no! Not Katy! Not my baby!' She sobbed and ranted. Ron tried to book an early flight back to London but there was none until 9 o'clock. Katy might be dead by then. Joan vomited. Tara tried to console her but it was no use. Joan wept and howled. She became hysterical. She emptied a couple of miniature bottles of brandy. She began to chain-smoke. She was an agnostic but now she began to pray fervently. She telephoned several English friends who had their own aircraft but none was at home. It was Sunday morning. But at last she struck lucky when she called her father and asked him to beg one of his clients, the singer Roger Whittaker, who lived in Essex, to fly over from Stansted in his nine-seater jet and pick them up. Whittaker agreed. They met him at Le Bourget airport at 6 a.m. and he flew them to London. At the hospital they found Katy in intensive care in a deep coma, deathly white, frail and tiny, connected to a jungle of tubes, a ventilator, and with all her beautiful blonde hair shaved off. Joan asked the doctor what were her chances of survival. 'Sixty to forty against,' he said. She wept. Ironically the distraught young driver's name was also Collins – and at school Katy had recently written a story about a boy who runs into the road and is nearly hit by a car, 'and that means you must always be very careful crossing the road'.

Joan decided that the one way she might keep Katy alive was to talk to her constantly, even though she was deeply unconscious. For several days and nights she kept it up, not stopping even to put on make-up, supported by Ron, who remained wonderfully strong throughout the ordeal. Katy was his only daughter and he adored her, and to be with her and support Joan he gave up all work for a year, a rock in these darkest days of their marriage. To spend as much time as possible with Katy they lived for six weeks in a caravan in the hospital car park, and Joan talked to Katy constantly, singing to her, playing music, hanging colourful mobiles above her bed, wafting strong-smelling odours under her nose, stroking parts of her body with feathers or silk, shining a torch into her eyes. Slowly, ever so slowly, Katy began to come round, but even then Joan and Ron faced a new misery: the doctors warned them that she might be permanently brain-damaged, or blind, deaf, mute, or all three, and might have to go into a home.

On the eighth day she opened her eyes but was still semi-conscious and seemed to see nothing. Ron and Joan redoubled their efforts to stimulate her and one of Katy's favourite actors, Jon Pertwee, dressed up in his bizarre Worzel Gummidge scarecrow outfit and gave her an hour-and-a-half bedside performance to try to nudge her out of her coma. Joe came as well every day to visit his granddaughter, and slowly, day by day, she improved until after six weeks her parents were able to take her home to South Street on 13 September. She still had to learn to speak, smile, cry, walk and write again but at least she was home and improving.

Joan and Ron were exhausted physically and emotionally and hired two private nurses to look after her, one for days and one for nights, and began to try to live their own lives again. Joan had vowed to give up eating chocolate until Katy was fully recovered but to survive the nightmare she was now smoking and drinking heavily and Ron had turned increasingly to drugs and junk food to get him through the days and sleepless nights, and in five months put on forty pounds in weight. Soon after Katy emerged from her coma Joan began to keep a diary and was to use it a year later to write a deeply moving, loving, heart-rending, but inspiring blow-by-blow account of those terrible weeks, *Katy: A Fight for Life*, which was to be published in 1982. Cynics sneered that she was exploiting her daughter's tragedy to make money and to publicise herself but it was easily the finest thing she ever wrote. When she wrote from her anguished heart she could be a very good writer indeed, and she was without any doubt an incredibly gutsy, determined, indomitable woman. It was Joan just as much as the brilliant doctors – especially the neurosurgeon Robin Illingworth – who saved Katy's life. The tragedy made Joan consult in desperation several priests and rabbis as well as psychics, and Katy's recovery made her believe that maybe there is a God after all.

When the worst was over Sacha, now fifteen, was sent off to Oakham boarding school in Leicestershire. 'It was quite an experience,' he recalled years later. 'My schoolmates drummed into me what they thought of me very clearly. But I survived. I have had to parachute into new situations, so I learned how to get on with people quickly. The trick is to befriend the bullies wherever you go.' Tara, now seventeen, could not wait to leave home and went back to Paris to study languages. There she kept the names of her parents secret, but thanks to her strong Newley genes was able to earn extra pocket money playing her guitar in seedy nightclubs and busking in the Metro. 'Paris was my adventure,' she told Corinna Honan in 1994. 'It was freeing. If you don't have that stability you need as a child, you just want to get on with your own life.'

The best cure for Joan's long torment was to get back to work. Ian le Frenais and Dick Clement, the writers of the TV series *The Likely Lads* and *Porridge*, had written two scripts for a full-length film based on Joan and Leonard Rossiter's characters in the Cinzano ads, but Rossiter would not accept that the downmarket, bumbling-fool character he played would ever really meet a sexy, jet-set woman like Joan's character, and the film was never made. 'Leonard is becoming a pain in the backside,' said Joan with disappointment. 'He thinks he's Clark Gable.' But in October she did have another book to promote, the *Joan Collins Beauty Book* – ironically at just the time that she looked worse than she had ever done, old, tired and haggard – and it was serialised in the *Daily Mail*. Among her beauty tips were exhortations to eat a good breakfast; drink bottled rather than tap water and wine rather than spirits; shun tea, coffee and processed foods; and have plenty of good sex.

The new production of *The Last of Mrs Cheyney*, which had been due to go on tour in mid-August and open in the West End early in October, had to be postponed, but when Katy seemed at last to be recovering well Joan embarked on a short out-of-town tour at the end of September before opening at the end of October at the huge, 1,300-seat Cambridge Theatre in the West End. The play ran there for two-and-a-half months but the theatre, one of the biggest in London, was embarrassingly empty and made such heavy losses that she had to continue performing night after night for the final month without being paid because she and Ron had put their own money into the show.

The Kasses spent Christmas at their country cottage near Dorking. It was the happiest they ever had. Their greetings card showed Katy in a green velvet dress smiling and sitting with her favourite fluffy toy, a lamb, along with the message: 'Our dreams came true this Christmas. We hope yours will too.' The play closed on 14 January and Joan, by now utterly exhausted, went to Stobo Castle health farm in Scotland to rest for four days before she and Ron took Katy off to the Bahamas in February for a sunny, recuperative holiday. Sadly the weather was dreadful – cold, windy and cloudy at first – though Katy did learn to swim again and to run on the beach. Before returning to England they spent two weeks in Los Angeles with Ron's parents and Katy's condition improved by the week, although it was to be many months before she had completely recovered and Joan felt she could eat chocolate again.

Neither Ron nor Joan had earned much money during the past few months, and since they planned now to live mainly in England they sold the house in Beverly Hills, and to try to fill the family's empty coffers Joan made the first of several forays into the business world by launching with Philip Green a range of jeans with her signature on the back pocket. Since the jeans were made in Japan a Labour Euro MP, Derek Enright, accused her during a debate at the European Parliament in Strasbourg of being unpatriotic and threatening British textile workers' jobs and she replied by promising that the jeans would soon be made in Britain, but the company, Joan Collins Jean Co, was soon to go bust.

By now she was preparing to appear in another stage play, a thriller at the Yvonne Arnaud Theatre in Guildford, *Murder in Mind* by Terence Feely, in which for £1,000 a week [£2,700] she played a woman terrorised in her home by a gang of intruders. Her co-star was Richard Todd, who had already appeared with her in two films, *The Virgin Queen* and *Subterfuge*, but during a dress rehearsal she fell down some steps, fractured an elbow, and had to have it set in plaster. Typically she made a joke of it, claiming that moments earlier a friend had wished her good luck in the old theatrical tradition by telling her to break a leg. The play – 'a dreadful old potboiler,' she called it later – still opened the next day because it was a small-budget production and Joan had no understudy and insisted bravely that the show must go on. Although she was in agony she stuffed herself with painkillers and for two weeks performed with her arm in plaster. Her courage was rewarded by full houses and reviews that were good enough for the producers to sign her up, along with Todd and the rest of the cast, for a provincial tour in September and then a run in the West End. Joan was 'as always, very professional and wonderful to work with', wrote Todd in his autobiography. 'I admire Joan immensely both as a true, dedicated professional and as a resilient and courageous woman … She has taken some severe knocks in her time, but has come up smiling and enjoying life – *and* quite rich! She's a classic survivor, and has worked darned hard for her success.' They lunched together often and met after work for drinks and 'I learned that there were sides to her character and elements of her life which had escaped the attentions of the popular press', said Todd. 'She was always a cheerful and amusing companion, very witty and forthright, but equally kindly and compassionate, and willing to discuss her problems with refreshing candour.'

She was certainly kind and friendly towards a twenty-year-old Englishman, Paul Keylock, who wrote to her sharply that summer to complain that although he had been sending her fan letters ever since he was fourteen she had never replied. She replied with an apology and an invitation to come to Little Venice for tea with her father and Katy, and when he did she explained that his letters had not been answered because her assistant, Barry Langford, was too busy to answer every letter. Keylock offered to lend a hand, was soon running her fan club, and was eventually to become her personal assistant.

In July the Kasses flew off to Spain for a family holiday at their villa in Marbella. It ended suddenly with a call from Hollywood. Aaron Spelling, the executive producer of *Fantasy Island*, *Charlie's Angels*, *Hart to Hart* and *Friends*, wanted Joan to fly back urgently to Los Angeles and join the cast of a new weekly TV soap opera. It was called *Dynasty* and she had never heard of it.

CHAPTER TWELVE

DYNASTY

{ 1981–1982 }

Aaron Spelling had already offered the part of *Dynasty*'s champion bitch, Alexis Carrington, to Sophia Loren. She had turned it down. He had then tried Raquel Welch, but she had rejected it too, so only then did he approach Joan. Jackie believed that she was responsible for this fabulous boost to Joan's career and claimed that Spelling chose her because of the bitchy character, Fontaine Khaled, that she herself had created for Joan in her novels *The Stud* and *The Bitch*. Joe Collins agreed, but Michael Winner reckoned that it was Joan's performance as a villainous bitch in his film *The Big Sleep* that had clinched it. She had, in fact, been playing feisty bitches in films for years, but it was her performance as Cleopatra in *Fantasy Island* – that 'dreadful piece of crap' – that won her the part. 'That same camp was so necessary for the Alexis role,' Spelling told the Biography Channel in 1997. 'I said to ABC, "We've gotta go with Joan Collins," and they said, "Joan *Collins*?" Thank goodness we went with Joan because she made the role of Alexis and she made that show a hit. Can you imagine *Dynasty* without Joan playing Alexis? I can't.' Spelling's decision was endorsed by Esther Shapiro, who had originally created *Dynasty* with her husband Richard. 'The reaction was strong against her,' she told Crimp and Burstein. 'People felt her accent would not be understood and they thought she was over the hill [*but*] I thought she was the only person for the role. She has humour, and I felt the part could not work without humour.'

Joan had recently hired a new Los Angeles agent with a reputation for resurrecting fading actors, Tom Korman, to try to revive her career. 'Bluntly, she needed help,' Korman told Tony Gallagher of the *Daily Mail* in 1996. 'She was like a lot of actors who get that terribly cold moment in their lives when they are not wanted any more. She was no longer bringing in the dollars. I knew her through her second husband, Tony Newley, and I happened to like her. So when she called I agreed to work for her. No one else would touch her.'

It was Korman who telephoned her in Marbella in July 1981 to say that Spelling was offering her £220,000 [£596,000] to appear in twenty-two episodes of *Dynasty*, and they needed her immediately. 'It's a sort of soap opera,' said Korman, 'a bit like *Dallas*.' She was at first reluctant. Did she really want to schlepp all the way back to California, live in Los Angeles yet again and appear on television? She was now a proper actress again, a stage actress. But £220,000 in just five months! Ron was still not working and their debts were mounting. He too had become a casualty of Katy's horrible accident, strong at the time but crumbling now that she was getting better, and he had lost all sense of purpose and self-control. He was seriously into cocaine by now, ignoring bills and failing to return telephone calls.

Nervously he told her that she could not possibly accept the *Dynasty* offer: she had signed a contract to take *Murder in Mind* on a ten-week provincial tour in September and then into the West End. Rubbish, said Korman: this could be big, this could make you a major star; dump your lousy little limey play. Her father agreed and urged her to grab this chance of a big break, but the producer of *Murder in Mind*, Duncan Weldon, refused to release her from her contract, even though he was an old friend. He reckoned he would lose a fortune if she did not appear as promised and showed her a telegram from one theatre manager that read: 'We will not accept Joan Collins' non-appearance in *Murder in Mind* unless we have her death certificate in our hands.' She offered that when she had done her six months on *Dynasty* she would return to do two plays for Weldon for the same salary as before. He refused. She reminded him that she had gone onstage for him with an arm in plaster, that she had kept the show going at the Cambridge Theatre for five weeks for no pay. That made no difference. When she insisted that she could not lose this opportunity and was going to go to Hollywood whether he liked it or not, his company, Triumph Productions, asked the actors' unions in America and Britain not to let her work on *Dynasty*, and when that failed they sued her for £35,000 [£94,850] for breach of contract.

Her decision to go suddenly to the US also meant that she had to pull out of a couple of charity functions she had promised to attend. She apologised but was hurt by the antagonism this aroused. 'No one seems interested in the fact that I did twenty-five charity shows in the previous twelve months, and for four years I've supported financially a child in Biafra,' she complained. 'I can sympathise with Joan's hurried decision,' said Richard Todd, who had to rush back to London from his own holiday in Scotland to attend hasty *Murder in Mind* rehearsals with Joan's replacement, Nyree Dawn Porter.

Later Ron tried to claim that it was he who persuaded Joan to dump Weldon and do *Dynasty* but it was in fact her father who swayed her. She, Ron and Katy flew off immediately to Los Angeles, where Ron asked Tom Korman to book a suite for them at the Beverly Hills Hotel only for Korman to discover that he had still not paid the hotel's £3,000 bill for a previous visit. They rented instead an apartment at Century City for the six months that it would take Joan to shoot the twenty-two episodes and persuaded an English friend, Daphne Clinch, to join them to look after Katy, who was enrolled in a school that devised a special course of physical training to help repair her body. She blossomed in the warmth of California, learned ballet, to play tennis, the piano, to read music, and her academic reports were excellent. It was difficult to believe that she had been in a deep coma a year before.

Dynasty had already run for fifteen episodes, from January to the end of April, and when Joan saw them all on video she thought they were pretty dull. The show had been launched as a rival to a hugely successful soap about an incredibly wealthy Texan family, *Dallas*, which starred Joan's old RADA boyfriend Larry Hagman as the wily, scheming oil mogul J. R. Ewing, a man everyone loved to hate. But while *Dallas* was still riding high in the charts *Dynasty*, a family saga that portrayed the lives, loves and hatreds of a mega-rich, oil-tycoon Denver family, the Carringtons, had risen no higher than number thirty-eight in the ratings. Spelling and its producers reckoned it needed the injection of a tough, sexy, acid, scheming woman-you-love-to-hate to blast it to the top. Its main characters so far were the head of the family, Blake Carrington, played by John Forsythe; his sweet wife, Krystle (Linda Evans); his homosexual son, Stephen (Al Corley); and his and Alexis's spoilt, nymphomaniac daughter Fallon (Pamela Sue Martin). At the cliffhanging end of the final episode of the first series the viewers had glimpsed a mysterious, unidentifiable woman wearing a black-and-white suit, a large white black-ribboned hat with a black veil and sunglasses: a surprise witness who was about to give evidence against Blake in a trial in which he was accused of killing his gay son's boyfriend. In the first episode of the second series the mysterious witness would turn out to be Joan as Alexis Carrington, Blake's English ex-wife, whose sudden reappearance in the lives of the Carringtons after living for several years in Acapulco was to have an effect on the rest of the family similar to that of a large boulder dropped into a small pond. She was bold, beautiful, ballsy and bitchy and set out to make everyone miserable, especially Krystle, whose marriage she was determined to destroy. She wore gloriously glamorous clothes, different outfits for every scene, huge earrings, hefty shoulder pads, big hair, and ate men not only for breakfast but for lunch and dinner too. The television audience loved her. Within six weeks *Dynasty* was in the top five in the American ratings and a few weeks later had reached number one. By the end of the year Alexis was hugely popular in dozens of countries all over the world, and Joan was suddenly a bigger star than she had ever been.

No one needed to teach Joan how to play the part, Spelling told Melvyn Bragg in 1999. 'She read the first script and she had it.' Joan claimed later that she based her portrayal of Alexis on the character of her very rich, glamorous, funny, jet-set friend Cappy Badrutt, who had been her matron of honour when she had married Tony Newley but was to die of cancer a few months after Joan joined *Dynasty*. Alexis 'is absolutely ruthless, ambitious and as pure as the driven slush', she told the *Daily Star* in January 1982. 'What I'm trying to do is bring back the glamorous women we always used to see in films.' Alexis 'does what every woman secretly wants to do', she told Lynda Lee-Potter in 1998. 'She says "fuck you" to the world and to anybody who stands in her way.' Yet Joan was ambivalent about the character and told Alice Rawsthorne of the *Financial Times* in 1990 that 'Alexis was a venal bitch. I hated her with a passion. But I did identify with some parts of her character – her loyalty to a man who treated her foully; her love for her children; her strength; and her shrewdness in business.'

The saga was shot on the old 20th Century-Fox lot where she had worked more than twenty years earlier, from 1955 to 1961. She knew none of the cast except Linda Evans, whom she had met several times previously and who came into her caravan before her first rehearsal at the end of September to wish her luck and to say that everyone was rooting for her. 'I don't think I could ever be more nervous than I was on the first day of *Dynasty* when I was in a courtroom scene,' she told Judy McGuire of the *News of the World* nine years later. 'The entire cast was sitting there and I had twelve big pages of solid dialogue and it was ninety-five degrees! That was pretty nerve-racking.' That first scene consisted of a long interrogation by the prosecuting counsel in the murder trial in which Joan had to give a lot of evidence that was not easy to remember. She came through it superbly. When she made her first appearance, sitting in the witness box, removing her dark glasses and raising her veil slowly, the court gasped. She was stunning. This was a part she might have been born to play, one for which she had been destined and rehearsing all her life in role after role. SOPHISTICATED LADY JOAN IS SET TO BEAT J.R., said a headline in the *Daily Mirror*. Later in that first episode came the first of Alexis's many memorably lethal throwaway lines. When her estranged daughter Fallon remarked cattily, 'You're even more beautiful and more ugly than that grand English lady I vaguely remember, and whom I've tried very hard to forget existed these past sixteen years,' Alexis replied: 'I'm glad to see that your father had your teeth fixed, if not your mouth.'

Working on an episode of *Dynasty* every week was hard work: Joan would rise at 5.30 a.m. and claimed that during her first year on the programme she was working between twelve and fourteen hours a day, six days a week, enduring up to eight interviews and several photographic sessions a week as well and still going out at night to party until 2.30 a.m. The publicity she generated was enormous. Every newspaper in the world seemed to be obsessed by what she and Alexis were doing. Her face was splashed on the covers of scores of magazines, her every move recorded. Sue Mengers, the agent who had warned her five years previously that her career was probably over, was 'so happy she proved me wrong', she told Dominick Dunne in an interview for *The Sunday Times* a few years later. 'Even Aaron Spelling, when he cast Joan in the part of Alexis, could not have imagined how strongly the public would have taken to her – especially women. That *femme fatale* number she plays is in good fun. In her own life she has more women friends than any woman I know.'

Despite the rumours of feuds between the actors Joan always said that generally the entire cast got on extremely well. Her best friend on the *Dynasty* set was Pamela Bellwood, who played neurotic Claudia Carrington, but she was also to become very fond of John James, 'the resident hunk' who played Fallon's husband, Jeff Colby. John Forsythe turned out to be charming, considerate and fun, but despite previous claims that they got on well, Joan admitted in the *Daily Mail* in July 2007 that she and Linda Evans loathed each other.

Two days after her first rehearsal Joan flew back to London for the weekend to pick up some clothes and put the Holmbury St Mary cottage on the market for £125,000 [£338,750]. They had owned it for less than three years but despite the wonderful boost of her fat *Dynasty* salary she and Ron were still deeply in debt and she could no longer rely on him because he was now completely enslaved by his drug dependency. At one of their parties in LA the guests were fascinated to see in the throng, quaffing champagne, a huge, sinister black stranger who turned out to be Ron's cocaine pusher. Their marriage was now on some seriously jagged rocks. 'If ever Joan and I had a very bad row she would give me what I called "the silent treatment",' he told the *Sunday People* eighteen months later, after they had separated. 'Sometimes it would last a few hours, punctuated by some door slamming and big sighs – sometimes it would last longer. Once it lasted three days. Joan thought I had been playing about with another girl. Eventually I grabbed hold of her in the living room of our Mayfair home and demanded: "What the hell is the matter with you?" She stormed into the bedroom and came back with a handful of photographs. "These," she said. "These are what's the matter. Who is the floozy in these pictures?" The photographs showed a nude girl in an eyemask lying asleep on a bed. Joan was angry enough to threaten to go straight to a lawyer and end our marriage there and then. She had found a roll of undeveloped film and taken it in to be processed. These pictures were on the roll. I looked closely at them and spotted that the girl was wearing a gold chain round her waist. Then I remembered. The pictures had been taken seven years earlier. It was in Acapulco *– and the girl on the bed was Joan herself.* "It's you, you stupid woman," I shouted. "Don't you recognise your own body?" A lot of girls would have laughed at that point, but not Joan. She has never had a sense of humour about things like that.'

She did not have much to feel humorous about. He had neglected their financial affairs so badly that she was finding unpaid bills all over the place and was increasingly threatened by the prospect of writs and bailiffs. Even the newsagent's and milkman's little bills had not been paid. He had also become impotent. 'Joan wasn't the least sympathetic,' he told the *Sunday People*. 'She simply thought I was going off her.' When they split up in 1983 her friend and secretarial assistant Barry Langford told her side of the story in two long, scathing articles in the *Sun* in which he claimed that Kass had become a fat, lazy slob who had given up work all together, saw Joan as a meal ticket, exploited her, squandered her money, and gorged himself on junk food – chocolate bars, hamburgers, hot dogs, sugary drinks – as well as drugs. 'I once caught a couple of blokes breaking into Joan's Mayfair house,' said Langford. 'I thought they were burglars but they had come to turn the gas off because the bill hadn't been paid. God knows what was happening. I once found three carrier bags full of unopened bills lying around the house. Even the staff had to wait until Joan jetted in to get our money.' He added: 'Once I went to the bank for her and she had no money in her account. Can you believe that – a superstar with no cash? If she hadn't landed the role in *Dynasty* she would have been ruined completely.' Joan herself told David Wigg in 1992 that Ron had run up £500,000 worth of debts [£1.25 million] that took her four years of *Dynasty* earnings to pay off. Soon after joining *Dynasty* she was shocked and humiliated when she complained furiously to Tom Korman that Spelling had not honoured a promise to pay for ten first-class flights between LA and London only to be told that Ron had cashed the tickets and spent the money.

Joan began to turn up on set red-eyed after yet more tearful, sleepless, argumentative nights. For months, for Katy's sake, she and Ron pretended that the marriage was happy, said Langford, 'but in reality they haven't slept together for years. He began to physically revolt her. She could not bear to look at him – let alone sleep with him. It was laughable that he was rolling round telling everyone how great Joan was between the sheets when he hadn't even been there for years. He and Joan used to have terrible rows over his eating habits [*and*] it was nothing unusual for him to be bombed out of his mind, incapable of getting out of bed. He would lock the door and refuse to speak to anyone.' Now and again he would leave her and fly to London, where he would 'just sit there in this fantastic Mayfair apartment – unshaven and scruffy – oblivious to everything,' said Langford. 'Joan was under no illusions. I once heard her screaming at Ron: "You're a fucking disgrace. I'm sick of you. I'm sick of your drugs. I just want you to get out of my life." He thought the pressures on her were too great to cope with a divorce scandal – and he was right for a long time ... Few people, possibly, realise that Joan, deep down, is a very sensitive person. She's nothing like the hard-bitten Alexis.' When Joan mentioned divorce Ron threatened to 'drag her through the muck', said Langford. 'He told me he would make her life hell.'

In November she could stand it no longer and kicked him out but Katy was so miserable that Joan let him back after ten days. To add to her woes, Newley's astonishingly extravagant multi-millionaire lifestyle was causing him financial problems of his own, and he was now £20,000 [£50,000] in arrears with her maintenance payments. She had to sue him for the money and he was ordered to pay up. Leslie Bricusse had been worried about Newley and his career for some time. 'I saw Tony following a path that I knew was wrong for him – the money trail – instead of the path that his manifold talents were meant to travel,' he wrote in his foreword to Garth Bardsley's biography. 'And, when his Vegas bubble burst a few years later, he had nowhere to go.' Suddenly nobody in films, TV or cabaret much wanted to employ him, and the huge amount of money that he had made over the years had somehow evaporated – according to Newley because of all the alimony he had to pay, but in fact, said Bricusse, because of his incredibly careless extravagance. And then Natalie Wood drowned mysteriously at sea off Santa Catalina island in the early hours of 29 November after a boozy dinner with RJ and her current co-star, Christopher Walken. She was only forty-three. November had been a dreadful month.

In the second of Joan's episodes of *Dynasty* Blake Carrington was found guilty of involuntary manslaughter, given a suspended jail sentence, and Alexis decided not to return to Acapulco but to stay in Denver and make his and the family's lives hell. Was Blake *really* Fallon's father? Was he involved with a Las Vegas gangster? Did Alexis kill Krystle's unborn child, and did she see off Cecil Colby by making violent love to him and giving him a heart attack? And who was to blame for the first two vicious catfights between Krystle and Alexis, the first with cushions, the second in the lily pond, when Linda Evans nearly broke Joan's jaw? From week to week America hung on Alexis's every word, mesmerised by her wickedness and *Dynasty*'s fantasy world of vast wealth and impossible glamour, and Joan's fan mail became a deluge.

After her first seven episodes on *Dynasty* the cast took a three-week break for Christmas and she returned with Ron and Katy to London and then to the cottage at Holmbury St Mary, which was still unsold. There she invited for dinner on Christmas Day her brother Bill, his beautiful, twenty-six-year-old Guyanese model girlfriend Hazel Ganpatsingh, Tara and her boyfriend, and a couple of friends. Katy and Tara, who was now eighteen and studying at the American School in Paris, made a snowman in the garden, and after dinner Katy sang for them so beautifully that they were moved to tears.

Joan returned to California on her own in January 1982 to film more episodes of *Dynasty* and extend her *Dynasty* contract. There was no way now that Spelling and the other executives could let her leave the show at the end of her second season. She had already been nominated for the Golden Globe Best Actress Award and although she did not win she was now vital for the show's success and the show was equally vital for her career and bank balance. But she had no intention of easing off just because she was suddenly hugely successful. 'I'm absolutely dedicated to going back on stage in Britain next year,' she told Lee Bury of the *Sun*, 'and more than anything I want to do a Broadway play. I don't want to be yesterday's TV star. I mean, it's all jolly nice being the girl of the moment, the nasty lady of today. But it's not the pinnacle of my career. I don't want to coast along. I'm so aware of how precious and how short life is. I want to do so much, much more.'

At the end of January Ron joined her in LA and she was working so hard and suffering so much stress because of their crumbling marriage that she suffered sharp pains in her chest and was rushed to hospital with a suspected heart attack. She had in fact been felled by gastroenteritis, tension and exhaustion, but even when she returned to the apartment and told Ron that she was ill, and begged him to get up, he ignored her and went back to sleep. There was more tension to come: on 1 February the *Sun* published an interview with Joan that scuppered a £30,000 deal she had made with another British newspaper to serialise her book about Katy's accident. She sued the *Sun* and was then devastated to be accused of making money and publicity out of Katy's tragedy. 'The money I was raising from this book was to go into a trust

fund for Katy and to a charity for handicapped and disabled children,'
she told the *Sunday Mirror*. 'So the paper may have effectively deprived
my nine-year-old daughter and children who could well do with the
money.' The charity she had set up was the Collins Foundation, which
aimed to raise money to buy brain-scanning machines.

In February she flew back to London to make more Cinzano ads
with Leonard Rossiter and appear on Michael Parkinson's TV chat
show, but by now she was so upset about Ron, who had put on nearly
50lbs in a year, that another passenger in the first-class cabin reported
that she wept openly several times during the flight and told a stranger
that she might have to get divorced. Four days later she returned to Los
Angeles, told Ron she needed time away from him, and he returned
alone to London for a month. A few weeks later Tony Newley took
revenge for being ordered to pay Joan £20,000 [£47,500] in maintenance arrears by slapping her in turn with a writ to pay a $1,000
dental bill for Tara and Sacha. It was all too much, and she and Ron
began to have regular sessions with psychiatrists and marriage guidance
counsellors – in vain because it soon became clear that he was unable
or unwilling to give up his drugs.

In April Joan flew back to London yet again to film a British comedy
thriller with Carol White and Paul Nicholas, *Nutcracker*, in which she
played an ex-ballerina who runs a dance company where a defecting
Russian ballerina applies for political asylum. This allowed her yet again
to flaunt her body in an erotic scene when she was filmed climbing out
of a bath and into the arms of a lover. A few days later a row erupted
in America over yet another of her steamy love scenes when religious
leaders launched voluble protests over the *Dynasty* episode in which
Alexis and Cecil Colby have such vigorous sex that he has a massive heart attack. Described as 'the most explicit sex scene ever shown
on US television', it was attacked by the Rev Coy Privette of the
Christian Action League as 'no better than pornography' and the head
of the National Federation for Decency, the Rev Donald Wildmon,
complained that 'television is going to the gutter with scenes like this.
I don't want trash piped into my home and I'm sure millions of others
don't either.'

In May *Katy: A Fight For Life* was published in Britain and the *Daily
Mail* sent one of its toughest reporters, Ann Leslie, to interview Joan.
Until now, said Ms Leslie, she had always considered her to be boring

and pointless and her career to be 'thirty years' worth of mainstream mediocrity ... if you scratch the phony tinsel off her, you'll get the real tinsel underneath'. She even told Joan to her startled face that 'you didn't seem real, just a rather tacky publicity package', but then she read the book – 'a raw, unmawkish, moving and unvarnished docu-ment' – and changed her mind: all the setbacks of Joan's life 'have done little to dent her almost childlike optimism', she wrote. 'It's as though she believes that however many times she falls over, so long as she's a jolly brave and determined little girl, Mummy Fate will always kiss her knee, make it better, and let her go back to enjoying the party ... I felt like sending a message to the outraged Reverend Coy. "Despite all you've heard, and despite all those tacky things she does on screen, our Joan is really a rather good little girl at heart".'

The first episode of *Dynasty* reached British TV screens at last in mid-May, though Joan's own first episode would not be broadcast until months later, and in mid-June she flew back to Los Angeles to make two films for TV: *Paper Dolls*, in which she played the mother of a teenage model; and *The Wild Women of Chastity Gulch*, a comedy western about a quiet little town where all the men have left to fight in the American Civil War and their wives and girlfriends, including Joan as the madam of the local brothel, have to deal with the arrival of a group of randy enemy soldiers.

In July she embarked on another series of *Dynasty*, in which she was now such a huge hit that she was getting an average of twelve thousand letters from fans every week and was the only member of the cast to be given a pay rise, so that she was now earning £25,000 [£62,500] per episode. The soap was not yet nearly so successful in Britain and after the first series the BBC was seriously considering dropping it before Joan had even made her first appearance, but with commendable modesty she told Ian Harmer of the *Yorkshire Post*: 'Let's face it, we're not talking about Shakespeare here. *Dynasty* is offered as entertainment, and I think it's jolly excellent entertainment done with tremendous style and class and elegance. I had no idea the show would become such a huge hit [*but*] I have been around far too long to be fooled by any of this. There's something incredibly thrilling about the fame but I'm just putting my money in the bank and making sure my head doesn't swell.'

It was about now that a less than loving sisterly rivalry between Joan and Jackie began to smoulder and flame. Ever since childhood Jackie had felt overshadowed by Joan and now believed that Joan should have given her much more credit for helping to revive her career. Joan in turn resented the suspicion that she might well owe much of her success to Jackie. 'Jackie is the more sane and sensible of the two sisters, down-to-earth and grounded, a trusty Libra versus Joan's flamboyant Gemini,' wrote Leslie Bricusse in his autobiography. 'Both air signs, both ambitious high achievers and unspoken rivals, yet different as chalk and cheese ... Both sisters are also as competitive as gladiators.'

Joan's new fame brought other irritations too. It was four years since she had made *Homework*, the long-forgotten film in which she had played a small role as a mother who seduces her teenage daughter's seventeen-year-old boyfriend, and the movie's distributors decided that now was the time to cash in on her *Dynasty* fame by releasing it with her name above the title, even though she had spent just three days making the film and appeared in it for no more than ten minutes. Advertising posters showed her head on someone else's naked body, even though she had not been filmed nude, and extra sex scenes had been added using a naked double. She was furious, sued the distributors, forced them to cut forty seconds from the film, and eventually won $10,000.

Newspapers were increasingly running stories that she and Ron were about to divorce. She denied them vehemently. 'How many times do I have to say it?' she screeched at Rodney Tyler of the *People* at the end of October. 'How many people do I have to say it to? We are NOT getting divorced.' Three days later she was telling the *Sun*: 'I have no wish to speak about rubbish like that in front of my daughter. There is not a shred of truth in these reports. They are especially hurtful to me because I have a young child.' But the final crunch came when they flew into London on 3 November for three days to appear on a secretly arranged *This is Your Life* programme to honour her father on his eightieth birthday. They were driven by limousine straight from Heathrow Airport to the Thames TV studios at Teddington, where they were greeted on the pavement by Joe and the show's Irish compère, Eamonn Andrews. The TV cameras rolled. Joan kissed Joe. 'Happy birthday, Daddy,' she said. 'So this is your life.' Andrews stepped forward with the programme's famous red book. 'No, Joan,' he said. 'Joan Collins, this is *your* life!' For a moment she was stunned, and then the professional actress took over – and she gave one of her best performances but in her heart she was seething. Thames had assembled many of her family and friends secretly to appear on the show: Bill and Hazel, Tara, Sacha, Jackie's daughter Tracy, Roger and Natalie Whittaker, David McCallum, seven nurses who had looked after Katy after her accident, even Joan's ancient headmistress Ivy Joslin, who was in her nineties, and a thirteen-year-old Indian orphan from Bombay, Fathimary Pragasm, whom Joan had been sponsoring for years. They had also recorded tributes from Jackie, John Forsythe, Linda Evans, Gregory Peck, Leonard Rossiter and RJ Wagner, but Barry Langford reported later that Joan was incensed with Ron for not warning her. 'She would not have agreed to do the programme had she been told in advance,' said Langford. 'Ron should never have forced her to go through with it. He wanted to force her into putting on a happy face and a united family front.' Yet she too continued to pretend that all was well. 'The gossips are out to get me,' she told Garth Pearce of the *Daily Express* the next day. 'After ten years together it looks as if it's our turn for the vicious treatment. What we've done to deserve this, I just don't know. Ours is about as normal a marriage as you could wish for. It is secure and, whatever people might make up, we're staying together.' That night she attended the première of *Nutcracker* and was appalled to see that the film's publicity material showed her in a sexy leotard over a caption that read: 'In *The Stud* she sizzled ... in *The Bitch* she blazed ... Now in *Nutcracker* Joan Collins breaks all the rules.' This was just cheap exploitation, she fumed. 'It's disgusting and offensive and it makes me mad.' A spokesman for Rank admitted that the posters were exploitative but explained that 'we are trying to get people into the cinema. You need a bit of tickle,' and confessed that originally the caption had read 'Her men called her Nutcracker' but London Transport had refused to display the posters on their double-decker buses because 'they felt it had other implications'. The reviews the next day were not kind. Joan would have to stop making films soon, sniffed Derek Malcolm in the *Guardian*, 'or the make-up will finally congeal'. The *Daily Mail* gossip columnist asked her whether she had had her face, bust or bottom lifted. 'No, no, no,' she replied with a tight smile. 'You can usually tell a woman who has had a face-lift. She has a very tight smile. I haven't had my teeth capped, either.' To complete a miserable month, the Joan Collins Jean Company was wound up compulsorily in

Joan with her third husband, Ron Kass, whose original Russian name was Kaschenoff: the tall, green-eyed American boss of the Beatles' Apple Records. It was 1972 and she was pregnant with their daughter Katyana Kennedy Kass (Katy) . . . (Mirrorpix)

. . . and with her and Kass's growing tribe of children, including his three sons from his first marriage, and their nanny. (Mirrorpix)

With 11-year-old Katy in 1983, three years after the terrible car accident that nearly killed the little girl and devastated their lives. (Mirrorpix)

THERE WERE NEVER SUCH DEVOTED SISTERS: Joan with 32-year-old Jackie looking like a refugee from the Swinging Sixties, on the second day of the 1970s, at the London première of the film *David Copperfield*. (Harry Myers/Rex Features)

Joan and Jackie with the 30-year-old Swiss-Australian, Oliver Tobias, whom they chose to play the gigolo in their vulgar, soft-porn film *The Stud* in 1977. Tobias later complained that the script had been shallow, he had been paid 'peanuts', and 'making love to Joan Collins was pretty dull'. The sisters snapped that they had never really wanted him for the part and Joan sneered that he was not sexy and she hadn't fancied him at all.

(Rex Features)

JOAN THE SWINGER: sweetly demure in the 1955 movie *The Girl in the Red Velvet Swing* (*above*) and blatantly raunchy (*below*) with Mark Burns in *The Stud* in 1978. (The Kobal Collection; Ronald Grant Archive)

Joan in 1977 with 40-year-old Jackie, whom the *Daily Mail* columnist Lynda Lee-Potter described as looking like a 'tough drag queen' and 'a high-class hooker'.
(Ben Jones/Rex Features)

With the wicked Leonard Rossiter in one of the hilarious Cinzano advertisements that he and Joan made between 1978 and 1984.
(Mirrorpix)

Joan in 1978 at her luxurious Beverly Hills mansion, where she indulged her lifelong taste for flashy silver and gilt decoration, furniture and ornaments, marble floors, and mirrors everywhere. (Eddie Sanderson/Scope Features)

With Sir John Gielgud in 'Neck', a play in the 1979 TV series *Tales of the Unexpected* in which Joan played an aristocrat's promiscuous wife and Gielgud her disapproving butler. 'People seemed to expect some kind of cataclysmic happening when Joan and I were working together,' he said, 'but Joan is a very professional actress and we got along extremely well together. In fact, she was quite perfect in the part.'
(Scope Features)

... and Joan unrecognisable on TV as the wicked witch in *Hansel and Gretel* in 1983.
(Eddie Sanderson/Scope Features)

THE TV SERIES THAT
MADE HER AN ICON:

(*above*) Joan with Aaron
Spelling – the American
producer who chose her in
1981 to play Alexis
Carrington in *Dynasty* after
Sophia Loren and Raquel
Welch had turned him
down – and Joan's co-star
Linda Evans. 'Thank
goodness we went with
Joan,' said Spelling later,
'because she made the role
of Alexis and she made that
show a hit. Can you
imagine *Dynasty* without
Joan playing Alexis? I can't.'
(Craig Mathew/Associated Press)

(*right*) With Linda Evans
and *Dynasty*'s male lead,
John Forsythe
(Scope Features)

The Queen and 'the Queen of
Hollywood', as the *Hollywood Reporter*
called her, meet at a gala concert at
the Royal Albert Hall, compèred by
Joan, in 1982. If Joan's smile looks a
little forced that is hardly surprising:
earlier that evening she had been
served with a writ demanding £3,000
for a car that had been lent to her but
not returned – plus £130 for unpaid
parking fines. Embarrassed and
enraged, she threw the writ on the
ground and locked herself in her
dressing room. (Rex Features)

Joan was often accused of being vain
and wearing far too much make-up
but few women of 50, as she was,
are brave enough to agree to be
photographed without any at all and
then allow the picture to be published.
(Eddie Sanderson/Scope Features)

the High Court owing the devilishly beastly figure of £6,666, and back in Los Angeles a few days later Joan was not best pleased when she was guest of honour at a transvestite nightclub and the compère announced the arrival of the gorgeous, twenty-eight-year-old Lesley-Anne Down by saying 'and here we have the most beautiful English actress of all time'.

Back in LA she could not forgive Ron for fooling her into appearing on *This is Your Life*. After dinner one night with her agent in Beverly Hills 'Joan asked, all matter-of-fact, if I'd like to see an apartment with her', he told the *Sunday People* the following year. They drove to a luxury block of flats where Joan produced a key to one of them. 'It's beautiful,' said Ron. 'Yes,' said Joan, 'and I've paid the rent on it for three months for you.' Ron was stunned: 'Just like a hard-selling estate agent she pointed out the advantages – the view, the furnishings, the maid service, even the TV with every conceivable cable channel.' That night, at home, she made him sleep in his study, the next morning he moved out of their house and she had all the locks changed. It was the end of their marriage.

To make her even happier, she was given one of the ultimate actors' accolades a few days later when she appeared with a hugely distinguished cast on the *Night of 100 Stars* TV variety show at Radio City Music Hall in New York to mark the centenary of an entertainers' charity, the Actors' Fund of America. Among the other star performers – not just one hundred but 218 of them – were many of the biggest names in showbiz, among them Lauren Bacall, Tony Bennett, James Cagney, Bette Davis, Sammy Davis Jr, Douglas Fairbanks, Larry Hagman, Dustin Hoffman, Gene Kelly, Grace Kelly, Deborah Kerr, Burt Lancaster, Jack Lemmon, Gina Lollobrigida, James Mason, Liza Minelli, Roger Moore, Paul Newman, Gregory Peck, Ginger Rogers, Mickey Rooney, William Shatner, James Stewart, Elizabeth Taylor, Peter Ustinov and Orson Welles. Joan's contribution was to appear onstage in a silver lamé gown with Farley Granger, her co-star in *The Girl in the Red Velvet Swing*, along with a clip from the twenty-seven-year-old movie. She was hugely flattered to be included in this glittering company and spotted in the throng two of her sexiest old flames, Warren Beatty and Harry Belafonte. Joan looked lovely, Beatty tired but impressed by her fame and success. 'There are no actors so sophisticated that they do not feel the raw power of celebrity,' wrote

Beatty's biographer David Thomson. 'No other woman in Warren Beatty's life seems to have survived his quiet judgement so well or so merrily. An inspired producer would try them together now, in comedy.' When she was driven by limousine to Radio City Music Hall with her old friend Roger Moore that evening they were mobbed by crowds screaming, 'Alexis! We love you, Alexis!'

'Fame at last, Joanie,' chuckled Moore. 'It's more intense on TV than anywhere else.'

It was the most exciting night of her life and the peak of her career.

CHAPTER THIRTEEN

THE QUEEN OF HOLLYWOOD

{ 1982–1984 }

It should have been a red letter day for Joan on 13 December 1982. The American Women's Press Club gave her its Golden Apple Best Actress Award for her part in *Dynasty*, and in London she met the Queen and Prince Philip when she compèred a gala charity concert at the Royal Albert Hall and Katy presented the Queen with a bouquet. Instead it turned out to be an awful in-the-red day. As Joan arrived by Bentley at the Albert Hall a private detective handed her a writ from a car company, Henlys of London, demanding £3,000 [£7,500] for a new Mini that British Leyland had lent her eighteen months previously to promote sales and that they claimed she had failed to return. They even demanded £130 for unpaid parking fines while she had had it. Embarrassed and enraged, she threw the writ on the ground and locked herself into her dressing room, but the story was splashed all over the papers the next day and filled the front page of the *Sun*, along with photographs of her and Katy with the royals. The humiliation! She went ballistic. This was all Ron's fault, the bastard! He had told her months ago that the car had been returned. They had another blazing row.

Worse was to come. At the South Street house in Mayfair she discovered that the electricity and telephone had been cut off because bills were still unpaid after several warnings and that dozens of others, some of them years old, had not been settled either. Ron protested that he had been so damaged by the stress of helping Katy to recover from her accident that he had simply not been able to cope with everyday things, but Joan had had enough. She flew back to Los Angeles the next day for yet another row with him. They had arranged to keep up appearances for Katy's sake by spending Christmas together at the house in Little Venice but now Joan's lawyer called him to say that he was no longer welcome and that Joan would pay for him to stay in an hotel. 'I was so devastated and angry that I deliberately checked into one of the capital's most expensive hotels,' Ron told the *Sunday People* four months later. 'All through Christmas and New Year we acted out a terrible charade at our house, pretending to Katy we were living together and there was nothing wrong. I would duck out to the hotel when Katy had gone to bed, returning early the next day as though I was staying at the house. Joan went through the ritual of cooking the traditional Christmas dinner for all the family [*and*] on Boxing Day we went, as usual, to the home of Joan's dad, Joe.' They even gave each other expensive Christmas presents, but early in January Joan filed for a legal separation.

They were not brave enough to explain it to Katy themselves. 'We took her to a marriage guidance counsellor who has a superb way of telling youngsters such fateful news,' said Ron. 'She saw Katy by herself first and told her: "Mummy and Daddy don't get along so well any more. And as you know they argue a lot. They want you to know that they both love you very much and nothing is your fault. But they feel they should be living apart for a while. You will live with Mummy but you will go out for dinner with Mummy and Daddy every week and Daddy will take you out at the weekends." Some days later Katy looked at me tearfully and asked: "You *will* move back into the house one day, won't you, Daddy?"' She was to be confused and miserable for years. Joe was also upset about the split. Ron had got on well with all the family and was an excellent father to Katy, though Joe could see now that like all Joan's husbands he was not strong or resilient enough for her. A few years later Joan admitted that she might have been able to help Ron kick the drugs and save their marriage if only she had been stronger.

'It might have worked if I had made him go away to be cured for three months with the threat that if he did not succeed he would never see me again – but I was too weak to do that,' she told Rodney Tyler of the *Sunday Express* magazine in 1987. 'That is my biggest regret: that perhaps I might have been able to save him, but didn't. Everyone thinks I'm so strong. But I'm not.' In fact, she felt so vulnerable now that she was on her own that nervously she bought a shotgun and three revolvers to protect herself when she was in England.

Straight after Christmas Joan and Katy flew back to Los Angeles, and after all the unhappiness of the past few months the New Year was to bring several consolations. To fuel Joan's insatiable appetite for transatlantic travel – nine return flights in 1982 – British Airways agreed to let her and a companion fly First Class as often as she liked for free for three years in exchange for making a series of BA advertisements. The BBC decided to continue buying *Dynasty* after all and on 1 January the first episode in which she appeared – the courtroom scene – was at last broadcast in Britain. In America the show was glossier and glitzier than ever, costing £500,000 in modern values for each episode, with vast amounts being spent on Joan's and Linda Evans's sumptuous gowns, and it had overtaken *Dallas* and was now top of the ratings. At the end of January Joan won the Golden Globe Best Actress Award for her portrayal of Alexis. It was said that as a circulation booster Joan's picture on the cover of a magazine was second only to that of Princess Diana, and she began to be mobbed wherever she went and received so many letters, some of it threatening hate-mail, that the studio provided her with an armed, female bodyguard who was trained in karate.

Not that everyone raved about her and the show. Under the headline JOAN IS JUST TOO BAD TO BE TRUE! the *Sun*'s TV critic Margaret Forwood said that *Dynasty* was 'indigestible' and asked: 'Can you really believe in Alexis, as portrayed by our Joanie, any more than you can believe in the other bloodless, plastic monsters in this dreadful show? Does this rubbish really deserve to be on screen, never mind the ratings?' She suggested acidly that Joan should record John Lennon's song *Imagine* with these new lyrics:

> *Imagine I'm an actress.*
> *It's very hard to do.*
> *Imagine I'm still forty*
> *Not pushing fifty-two.*
> *Imagine all the people*
> *Loving me like I do . . .*

In America *Rolling Stone* magazine was equally rude. 'Joan Collins' favourite measurement has to be twelve inches,' it suggested. 'When you see her from that distance she really does look beautiful. But from any closer she looks a bit . . . rough. Her make-up is like a mask: her skin is covered with beige foundation, her eyes are exaggerated by thick shadow, and her lashes stand out like awnings.'

On 19 February she took her first free British Airways flight to London to make another Cinzano commercial with Leonard Rossiter – it was to win the *TV Times'* favourite commercial of the year award later in the year. Joan earned £22,300 in modern terms for just three seconds on the screen but even that sort of money suddenly seemed insignificant when she received a High Court writ for £228,514 [£546,148] from the London merchant bankers Hill Samuel, which they claimed consisted of the £75,000 that they had lent Ron and Joan in 1978 to buy the house in Maida Vale and the cottage at Holmbury St Mary, plus more than four years' compound interest that Ron had failed to pay and was now increasing by £87 every day [£208]. Joan insisted that she knew nothing at all about this loan and that Ron had forged her signature when he had applied for it. His excuse for the mounting debt was that he and Joan had earned very little when Katy had been so dangerously ill in 1980, had had to pay for expensive private nurses to look after her for twenty-four hours a day, and had simply been unable to keep up with the payments on the loan. 'It's like a bottomless pit,' he said. 'Nobody makes the kind of money they are demanding from us. It's particularly bad for Joan. Because although she is earning more than £21,000 for each episode of *Dynasty* [£50,190] she has become obsessed with money.' An added blow was that Cinzano decided not to use her in any more ads with Rossiter, thus depriving her of an easy source of income.

Her reaction to her financial crisis was to dump the agent who had negotiated her first *Dynasty* contract, Tom Korman, move to the much more influential William Morris agency, and demand that her *Dynasty* salary should be doubled to match the £40,000 [£95,600] that Larry Hagman was being paid for his part as the most popular character in *Dallas*, which was now less successful than *Dynasty*. The *Daily Mirror* reported that she was in fact demanding a rise to £50,000, though she assured the paper that 'I have no plans to leave the show. I've never walked out on a contract in my life' – forgetting that she had walked out of her *Murder in Mind* contract to join *Dynasty* and had broken her contract with 20th Century-Fox time and again by refusing to make the films that they wanted her to make. Aaron Spelling refused to pay her more, threatened to drop her all together when the current season ended a month later, and filmed three different endings to the final episode of the season, one of which would have meant the end of Alexis. But he could hardly afford to lose the actress who had made the soap such a hit almost single-handedly. It was said that more than a hundred and fifty million people in nearly eighty countries were now watching *Dynasty* every week. Bars, restaurants, cinemas and theatres all over the world were empty on the nights that *Dynasty* was screened. In Italy it was aired twice a week and in Germany, where it was known as *Der Denver Clan*, Joan was called '*Der Denver Biest*'. How could Spelling possibly drop her from the show? For two months he and Joan played a game of chicken until he gave way and agreed to pay her much more, reportedly £33,000 an episode [£78,870]. Spelling also agreed to let her wear privately the fabulously expensive clothes she wore on the show.

The new deal finally established her as the Queen of Hollywood, Robin Osborne wrote in the *Hollywood Reporter*, 'the biggest film star Hollywood possesses right now. No one creates quite the fuss and the inquiries worldwide that Joan Collins does. She looks like a star and she is probably the longest ambassador of larger-than-life glamour the town has had since the heyday of Joan Crawford, Marlene Dietrich and Lana Turner.' And in December she was to be given the accolade of her own star on the Hollywood Walk of Fame, at 6901 Hollywood Boulevard. Yet she remained modest and level-headed. 'It doesn't last, of course,' she told Bill Hagerty of the *Sunday Mirror* in May. 'OK, I'm the flavour of the month or maybe the flavour of the year, but next year or the year after another flavour will come along. The main thing is to enjoy it and reap as many of the career benefits as you can.'

She managed to earn a little extra by making an episode of the TV series *The Love Boat*, in which well-known actors were shown looking for romance on board a luxury liner, and she agreed to appear semi-naked in a series of sexy pictures for *Playboy* magazine for $50,000 [£31,000] – a brave move considering she was about to turn fifty, though once again she fibbed to Barbara Griggs of the *Sunday Express* magazine that she was only forty-seven. She also negotiated a lucrative contract with the perfume company Revlon to promote their latest scent, Scoundrel. But to add to her financial woes Duncan Weldon slapped her with another High Court writ demanding £100,000 [£239,000] in damages for breaking her *Murder in Mind* contract. To try to staunch this constant financial haemorrhage she and Ron sold the house in Mayfair, the country cottage at last, and the villa in Marbella. All that she had left was the house in Bowmont Drive and that was heavily mortgaged. She was earning a fortune and at the height of her fame but by her standards she was almost broke.

Yet she revelled in her new, Ronless freedom. In April she flew to London wearing on her lapel a saucy badge that read I'M NOT PLAYING HARD TO GET – I *AM* HARD TO GET, jocular even though she was there to see a specialist because she was afraid that she might have cancer. Fortunately this scare turned out to be simply a sinus infection, and as far as *Playboy* was concerned she *did* start playing hard to get, vacillating for weeks over whether she would let them publish her semi-naked photographs after all and finally agreeing only when they increased her fee to £66,000 [£157,740]. With potential boyfriends she played less hard to get and had several new lovers in 1983, two of them toyboys almost half her age: James Mason's twenty-eight-year-old, PR-executive son Morgan; and a muscly twenty-seven-year-old hunk, Jon-Erik Hexum, who starred with her in June in a TV film, *The Making of a Male Model*. She went out often too with the hugely wealthy British business tycoon Sir Gordon White, later Lord White of Hull – at fifty-nine one of her few older boyfriends – and in July it was reported that she was going to marry him and become Lady White. She was also seen out more than once with forty-eight-year-old Dudley Moore, Linda Evans's ex-boyfriend George Santo Pietro, Frank Sinatra's assistant Dennis Stein, and a rich property developer, Mark Nathenson, but the Press also linked her with several other highly unlikely men, among them her Beverly Hills hairdresser, Dino Gigante, whose surname made the gossips snigger but who was in fact homosexual and to die of AIDS three years later.

Ron, who was still unemployed and living in a small Hollywood flat, was even more desperate for money than Joan and decided to sell a kiss-and-tell account of their marriage to the *Sunday People*. The first instalment began 'Joan is superb as the superbitch in *Dynasty* – and she was just as good in the role when we were together at home. Long before we finally split at the end of last year we had rows in which I found myself telling her: "Come off it, Alexis" … I knew it got to her being compared with someone so scheming. She would get madder and madder. But *Dynasty was* changing her, and it was painful for me to watch as the screen image devoured the real woman.' The three-page article described their love life in explicit detail and claimed that she was now making it difficult for him to see Katy, even though Katy adored him. 'When I go to the house she tends to treat me like something the cat dragged in,' he complained. 'She can't get me out of the house fast enough for fear I might see too much. Once she snapped at me: "What are you still hanging around here for? If you don't leave now you are going to run into someone who is coming to pick me up – and you won't like that at all!"'

Joan was furious about the article and accused Ron of gross betrayal, even though she had herself written equally disloyally about her marriages to Maxwell Reed and Tony Newley. 'I cried on and off for two days,' she told Bill Hagerty. 'People have always said untrue and unkind things about me. That is one of the prices you pay for being successful. But you do not expect it from someone with whom you have shared a large part of your life. I feel so let down.' BITCH BITES BACK, shrieked the *Sun* in a front-page splash reporting that she was now determined to divorce Ron. She called his article 'a pack of lies', flew to London, sought a High Court injunction to prevent any more scandalous revelations, and won an out-of-court agreement that she could censor any subsequent articles. This did not stop the *Sunday People* running a second instalment the next weekend in which Ron claimed that right from the start of their marriage Joan had sometimes flown into 'a screaming rage', and had once hurled an ashtray at him that had smashed a huge, expensive mirror. During another row, he said, she had jabbed a lighted cigarette into his cheek. Sometimes 'she would reach a point of frenzy where she would end up stamping her feet and banging her fists'. He explained why she had become such an icon with homosexuals – 'because gay men love bitchy women' – and claimed that during their marriage she had often given him cause to be jealous. He also revealed that she wore wigs or hairpieces so often because her hair was very thin, which fuelled so many rumours that she was bald that her London hairdresser, Hugh Green, issued a public denial.

Joan's side of the story came out the next day. BITCH'S HUSBAND WAS A SECRET JUNKIE, shrieked the *Sun*, again on its front page, along with a long interview with Joan's secretary, Barry Langford, which he would surely never have given them without her agreement. 'Kass turned from a loving husband and father into a cocaine-crazed super-slob,' reported the paper. RON BLED THE BITCH DRY, howled the head-line over the second instalment of the interview. All this mudslinging led the *Daily Mirror* columnist Anne Robinson to write under the headline JOAN COLLINS AND THE SOAP OPERA THAT WON'T WASH a contemptuous article about this 'vulgar couple', whom no one could possibly take seriously, slinging public insults at each other. Joan was incandescent and wrote in reply a letter, which the paper published, in which she said: 'The amusing thing about you incompetent Fleet Street vermin is that you are far, far bitchier about me and others in my profession than we could ever be.'

The following weekend the *Sunday People* ran a third instalment of Ron's allegations – 'the steamiest series of the year' – in which he discussed his impotence, Joan's long sulks and silences, her suspicions that he was being unfaithful, and her lack of a sense of humour about herself, and he accused Langford of forging Joan's birth certificate to make it seem that she was years younger than she really was. He admit-ted that the strain of Katy's accident had led him to take drugs and that his habit had threatened to get out of hand but claimed that he had now given them up.

Along with Ron's story appeared a two-page interview with Joan's ex-chauffeur, valet and general dogsbody, John Bevan, whose wife Mena had been her cook and housekeeper in Hollywood. Bevan had always liked Ron, he said – 'he's a charming guy, easy to talk to' – and sym-pathised with him because he had tried desperately to save his marriage but that Joan was so ambitious that her 'heart could sometimes be as cold as the ashes of their love'. He reported that her house was more like a studio set than a home, with its glass tables and giant mirrors, and claimed that Joan would spend hours in her opulent bathroom 'admir-ing herself from all angles'. He went on: 'Covering an entire wall of a downstairs room are framed colour pictures of Joan. Magazine covers, photo stills and shots taken by Ron ... I remember the raised eyebrows of Robert Wagner when he wandered in as I was fixing drinks. He said nothing but his expression said "Yuk!"' Katy, claimed Bevan, was overawed by Joan and 'would never think of knocking at her mother's bedroom without checking with us to see if we thought it was OK'. Joan's bedroom was always a dreadful mess: 'Debris littered the bed, floor and furniture. Discarded dresses, wigs, stockings, suspender belts were mixed up with opened jars, bottles, tins and tubes. Joan's dressing table was like a chemist's shop after a raid. Dozens of Joan's belongings all had to be picked up and tidied away. Bottles and jars had to have their lids sorted out and put back and, in the bathroom, there were always eye make-up stains and lipstick to be cleaned off the carpet. I'm sure that her image as a sexy goddess would slip if some of her admirers knew what the little lady was like back home.'

Joan visited Sacha, who was now seventeen, about to leave school, hoping to go to Oxford, and must have been cringing with embarrassment at all this scandalous publicity. Then she flew to Paris to see nineteen-year-old Tara at the American School before returning to Los Angeles to shoot *The Making of a Male Model*, in which she played the randy boss of a modelling agency and dallied with her latest toyboy, Jon-Erix Hexum. Relentlessly the *Sunday People* ran a fourth and final instalment of Ron's memories the following weekend in which he was pictured with his very pretty new girlfriend, thirty-one-year-old Mikki Jamison, who looked remarkably like Natalie Wood, in a photograph in which he looked smart and well and not at all like some derelict junkie. By now Joan had become so fed up with all the headlines referring to her as the Bitch or Superbitch that her British lawyers wrote to several newspapers to beg them to desist. Surprisingly the worst offender, the *Sun*, agreed after consulting its readers and promised not to do it again.

Soon afterwards Joan made the most unlikely film of her entire career: a cable TV version of *Hansel and Gretel* in which she played the wicked witch as well as the evil stepmother. As the stepmother she wore a curly red wig and old-fashioned clothes, and for the part of the witch she had to endure four hours in the make-up department as they gave her a hooked nose, false teeth, warty chin and a long, filthy wig. She looked so ugly that even Katy did not recognise her and the part was so out of character that she was later nominated for the National Cable TV Association's Best Actress Award.

In July 1983 Joan flew to the South of France for a summer holiday and was robbed of jewellery worth nearly £20,000 while she was out for dinner. On her way back to Los Angeles she stopped off in England during a 90-degree heatwave and took Katy for a swim in a pool at Datchet, near Windsor, that belonged to her rich friends Jeffrey and Madeleine Curtis. Lounging by the pool was a tall, blond, blue-eyed

Swede, an ex-pop singer who was now running a computer company, Peter Sjöholm, who had shortened his surname to Holm. He was thirty-six, fourteen years younger than she, and she liked his looks, smile, the charming way he frolicked in the water with Katy, and how he played the guitar rather well afterwards. Joan asked him to escort her the next evening to the film première of *Superman III*, they went on to dance for hours at Tramp, and in the early hours she invited him to visit her in Los Angeles. She returned to California the next morning, where she resumed her affair with young Jon-Erik Hexum, but when Holm arrived from London a few days later they soon became lovers, and in September he moved in with her in the house in Bowmont Drive. It would lead to yet another doomed marriage.

At first Joan thought Holm was charming, open, honest, that they had a great deal in common – food, music, swimming – and he offered a strong shoulder on which she could lean after all the unhappiness and insecurity of the past few months. He was also reputedly extremely well endowed and a magician in bed. But unknown to Joan he had a murky history. As a teenager he had been a pop singer in Sweden in the late sixties with a group called the New Generation and they had had a number-one hit, 'Two Faces Have I', but other members of the group claimed that he cheated them out of their share of the money they had made. He decided to go solo and lived briefly in France, where in 1968 he had another number-one hit, 'Monia', by strange coincidence one of Joan's favourites at the time. For a few years he sang all over Europe and in Japan, and in 1972 he and a couple of friends opened a restaurant on a Swedish holiday island that burned down mysteriously, though the police could never prove their suspicion that it was arson. In 1975 Holm and thirteen others were arrested and charged with smuggling £1 million-worth of diamonds from Belgium into Sweden. One of his fellow accused was his girlfriend, Madeleine Sandersson, the same Madeleine at whose poolside he met Joan, but Holm jumped bail and fled to Britain, leaving her to serve six months in prison and himself liable to be jailed should he ever return to Sweden. Swedish police also suspected that Holm and Madeleine had been involved in running a call-girl racket and brothel.

In London, Holm tried several ventures that never lasted long – a recording studio, a ceramic-printing business – and moved in with another Swedish girlfriend, twenty-four-year-old Pauline von Gaffke, whose six-year-old daughter he thought was his. They lived together for nearly five years, until the end of 1980, but when they broke up, Pauline claimed, Holm registered in his own name the house they had shared and that she had helped to pay for, sold it, cheated her out of her share, and bought a three-bedroom semi-detached house in Windsor, which he had been sharing with a twenty-four-year-old receptionist, Shirley Coe, until he left her for Joan. Pauline alleged that he also cheated her out of a car, and when he met Joan two British companies were pursuing him for debts of more than £700 [£1,670].

One of Holm's later girlfriends, Kathy Wardlow, told the *Sun* in 1988 that he had confessed to her that he had never loved Joan but had set out deliberately to marry her for her money. Kathy claimed that he had boasted that Joan had fallen for him 'like a silly schoolgirl' because he ravished her three or four times a day and told him that he was the best lover she had ever known, but he admitted that he fleeced her right from the start, bugged her house and recorded all her telephone conversations so that he could control her and her friends. He had also told Kathy, she said, that he had hated having sex with Joan 'because she was old and wrinkled'; had had to think of other women while making love to her; and was constantly unfaithful with other women. 'Joan was like a big baby,' Holm allegedly told Kathy. 'All you had to do was flatter her and tell her she was beautiful – wonderful for her age.'

Unaware of Holm's track record, and inexplicably besotted, Joan canoodled girlishly with him in public, trusted him completely, and allowed him to take over her finances as soon as he moved in with her. He became her manager, sacked all her advisers – accountant, lawyer, agent – installed a powerful computer to keep track of her affairs, and within weeks had already drawn up a prenuptial agreement in the hope that she would marry him as soon as she had divorced Ron. She paid all their lavish living expenses and slipped him cash in restaurants. At first she was delighted by his efficiency. He tidied up her shambolic finances, taught her to look carefully at any new deal or offer, and began to guide her career, and at first his prudence was so successful that she was able to buy herself a maroon Rolls-Royce with an Alexis numberplate, ALXXXS. She was still working incredibly hard but now, thanks to Holm, she was keeping much more of her earnings. Up before seven every morning, sometimes at five o'clock, she would spend twelve to fourteen hours under hot lights at the studios to shoot just ten minutes of *Dynasty* every day. Despite this hectic schedule, she still managed an enjoyable social life, especially at the weekends, though she shunned the LA nightclubs because she found them boring by comparison with Tramp and Annabel's in London.

By now she had become so powerful on *Dynasty* – jokingly she called it *Dysentery* – that she was allowed to alter Alexis's dialogue if she felt that the script was not right. In 1999 she told Melvyn Bragg that at first Alexis had been gruesomely over-the-top and she had tried to make her funnier. One day that autumn she found herself sitting beside President Nixon's powerful ex-Secretary of State, Dr Henry Kissinger, at a charity ball in Denver and persuaded him to be filmed with her that very evening for a brief appearance in *Dynasty*. 'Alexis! How are you?' he was told to growl, to which she twittered: 'I'm fine, Henry. We haven't met since Portofino! Wasn't it fun?'

And whenever she had a spare moment she was putting the finishing touches to the American edition of her autobiography *Past Imperfect*, which was due to be published the following year.

Two of the men in Joan's life were deeply unhappy. Ron was so depressed without her that he was having psychiatric counselling at the University of Southern California to prevent him committing suicide. 'I don't think I've ever know such loneliness,' he told the *News of the World*. 'With Joan gone there doesn't seem to be anything left to live for.' Sacha too was depressed. Now eighteen, he had left school and wanted to study literature at Oxford but the university had just rejected him. Devastated, he flew to Los Angeles for a summer holiday with Joan and then enrolled at the London Film School to learn about making movies, but for several months in 1984 he was to take refuge in the south-western English fishing village of Lyme Regis, where *The French Lieutenant's Woman* had been filmed three years previously. There he bought a scruffy flat and became something of a recluse, but he also started to paint seriously and to make some sort of peace with himself, his childhood and his parents.

One of Joan's men, at least, was happier than he had been for ages. After several lean years Tony Newley was appearing in Los Angeles in another hit musical that he had written, this time about Charlie Chaplin, and was so prepared to let bygones be bygones that he invited her to the first night. She declined. 'We aren't on speaking terms,' he said sadly. 'We haven't been for over a decade. We don't like each other at all.'

In September and again in October Joan flew from LA to London, clocking up her thirteenth free flight of the year with British Airways, and at the end of October the Christmas issue of *Playboy*, with Joan's picture on the cover and semi-nude photographs splashed across the centrefold, reached the newsagents' racks at last and sold so well that the magazine gave her an extra £17,000 on top of the £66,000 they had already paid her to make a total of £198,000 in modern terms. 'I look better now than when I was twenty,' she boasted accurately. 'I've got a great body. Sometimes it looks terrific.'

Two weeks later the *Sun* splashed across its front page a sensational story about Peter Holm that should have alerted Joan to the real nature of the man. Under the headline JOAN'S NEW LOVE IS ON RUN, it revealed that the Swedish police wanted him to answer the diamond-smuggling charge and that he had told one of his lovers that his main ambition was to latch on to a rich woman. Across two centre pages the paper also reported that the other members of his youthful pop group had accused him of cheating them, that the Swedish police had suspected him of arson, and that his ex-girlfriend Pauline von Gaffke, who was now a fashion designer in Stockholm, had said that Holm had been constantly unfaithful to her and liked to have sex with two women at a time. 'Joan Collins should be warned – he is not the Mr Wonderful that he seems,' she said. 'Peter always told me he wanted to snare a very rich woman. Now that he is involved with Joan Collins it seems he's got his wish.' Three days later the *Sun* reported that two companies were pursuing Holm for money he owed them and it tracked down the girlfriend Holm had dumped for Joan, Shirley Coe, who told the paper that 'the only things he is interested in are money, sex and prestige, in that order. He is a greedy bastard – he's money mad.' Of Joan she said: 'He seems to be taking her for a ride like all the others.'

With astonishing naïvety Joan simply ignored all the warnings. When Rodney Tyler interviewed them together at Bowmont Drive for the *Sunday People* he reported that they sat 'entwined' in front of the fire, and when they flew to London a week later they sat holding hands in the first-class compartment. At Heathrow Airport, when they were asked by reporters about the allegations, Joan replied blithely:

'I'm not at all worried about these police charges. I never worry about anything. That's my philosophy in life.' Her family and friends worried for her instead. 'We could all see that Peter was not right for her but she wouldn't listen,' one of her girlfriends told Tony Gallagher of the *Daily Mail* thirteen years later. 'Even Jackie could see he was a clown. She disliked him intensely. But Joan and Peter would be practically fondling one another at the dinner table. I think he fulfilled her sexually, he made her feel wanted. She was blind to the faults that we could see – he was just after her money.' Four years later Joan admitted to the *Daily Express* under the headline I'VE BEEN SUCH A FOOL that she had succumbed to Holm 'because fools rush in. Because I was ecstatic when we married, madly in love, over the moon … I've always been very immature for my age.' When it was all over she asked Linda Evans to explain to her how she could possibly have been such a fool. 'You had to do it,' said Linda. 'It was such a hot romance. You were both so made for each other you couldn't help yourself.' Holm was so sure of her affection for him that he gave Rodney Tyler another amazingly cocky interview in which he admitted with relish that he was indeed interested only in money, sex and prestige, that he had treated 'hundreds' of women very badly and had never loved any of them – 'I'm a bastard to women' – and that he was keen to have sex with two women at the same time. 'I know some people might think this gives a bad impression of me,' he said, 'but you have to be honest. The good thing about me is I am straight and honest.'

The saddest result of Joan's obsession with Holm was how it affected Katy. Now eleven, she hated him right from the start, especially when he criticised or sneered at Ron. 'All of a sudden Katy felt pushed out of her mother's life,' said one of Joan's friends. Holm made no effort to win the child over and at dinner one night screamed at her: 'Your father is going to end up going to jail over all this, I can tell you.' Katy ran sobbing from the table and began to spend hours every day in her bedroom munching chocolate bars and junk food and putting on too much weight. 'Every time the phone rang Holm would rush to answer it,' her nanny told the *News of the World* four years later. 'If it was Kass he would refuse to put him through to his daughter.' Even Joe admitted sadly that Joan didn't realise how difficult things were for Katy and said that she came 'a poor third in Joan's priorities for some years – behind her pushy husband and her showbusiness career'. Neither Tara, who was now at Boston University as part of her arts course, nor Sacha was keen on Holm, and Joan's friends were already seriously alarmed that she might marry him. She ignored them all and in December she and Holm flew to London for Christmas and then to Switzerland to join several friends – Roger Moore, RJ Wagner – for a skiing holiday in Gstaad. Yet back in LA she was still photographed more than once out on the town with Jon-Erik Hexum, and her lifestyle was such that Ron went to court to demand custody of Katy, claiming that Joan was an unfit mother because of her workaholic career and promiscuous lovelife. He also claimed that he was broke and demanded that she should pay him 'spousal support'.

At the end of January Joan won the Golden Globe Award for the year's best actress in a television drama. Not everyone approved of her win. 'She started to get more precious after winning the Golden Globe,' one of the *Dynasty* cast told Tony Gallagher in 1996. 'I was on the receiving end of a few shouting matches. She knew she was on top and was not afraid to beat somebody up verbally. There was a bit of jealousy there as well.' But her position as the Queen of Hollywood was confirmed the same day when she was the 'Woman of the Year' guest of honour and victim of one of Dean Martin's televised 'celebrity roasts' at the MGM Grand Hotel in Las Vegas, during which she had to sit and smile bravely for nearly an hour while friends and enemies bombarded her with insults and scurrilous anecdotes, most of them about her notorious sex life. 'Joan looks so good because she doesn't eat fatty foods and only smokes after sex,' said Martin. 'She's down to forty a day. She's a real swinger, the only girl I know who has mirrors on the ceiling of her car.' Phyllis Diller claimed that when she asked Joan what time she went to bed 'she said at 6 p.m., 8 p.m., 11 p.m. ... She has a maid in twice a day to change the men in her bed.' The guests included Aaron Spelling, John Forsythe, Angie Dickinson, and Zsa Zsa Gabor, but the jokes became laboured and repetitive – 'Joan has been in more hotel rooms than the Gideon Bible' – although she was a good sport, took it all remarkably well, and replied stylishly at the end with a funny, feisty speech that gave as good as she had got, encouraged perhaps by the $75,000 fee [£72,000] that NBC paid her to take part.

As Queen of Hollywood she was again asked to present an Oscar at the Academy Awards in March – the Technical Achievement Award

– and she was sufficiently secure in herself to join Morgan Fairchild and Brooke Shields in an hour-long TV special, *Blondes versus Brunettes*, that poked fun at herself and *Dynasty* and allowed her to impersonate Linda Evans and Jackie Onassis. There seemed to be no limit to her fame and popularity: in May the shops were piled high with Alexis and Krystle dolls wearing real mink jackets, diamond jewellery and costing an absurd £3,400 each [£7,700] and three months later hand-made porcelain dolls of the two characters went on sale at £8,000 each [£18,000].

Work early that year of 1984 consisted first of another film for tele-vision, *Her Life as a Man*, a mildly amusing feminist comedy about an unemployed woman journalist who lands a job on a sports magazine only because she applied for the job wearing men's clothes and a false beard, which allow her to interview the powerful English woman owner of an American football team – Joan. Then in April *Past Imperfect* was published at last in America and she submitted to the usual circus of interviews and appearances to promote it. When Unity Hall of the *News of the World* came to Bowmont Drive and asked if any of the men in her life had truly loved her, she replied – even though Ron was suing her for money and Holm was living with her – 'oh, Ron. He's a good man and we had many years that were wonderful. He loved me.' Less convincingly she added: 'In my heart I'm very monogamous. I believe strongly in fidelity. I don't believe in playing around if you're with someone. I don't think it's nice. I might be old-fashioned that way, but I think if you have a proper relationship with a man you don't want to go and ruin it. Unfortunately in my imperfect past I have had a fickle heart. But over the years I have become infinitely less fickle.' The interview appeared appropriately on April Fool's Day. Ms Hall's description of Holm that day was revealing. 'I didn't get the feeling that her current chap, Peter Holm, does a great deal,' she wrote. 'He seems to sleep a lot [*and*] emerged from their bedroom at around lunchtime, munching on a banana.' Judging by his energetic noctural activities he probably needed the sleep and the calories.

The American autobiography, which was dedicated to Joan's three children and her mother, rose to number two in the US bestseller lists and stayed there for three months. Since American readers were con-sidered to be more genteel and easily offended than British ones it was a carefully edited version of the indiscreet British edition that had caused such a fuss six years earlier. Out went all mention of Joan's affairs with sadistic, homosexual Barry at RADA, with the young *Sea Wife* camera assistant in Jamaica, with Harry Belafonte and Taki Theodoracopulos. Out went the reference to Maxwell Reed inserting 'a strange soft object' into her mouth on the night that he had allegedly raped her. Out went Joan's description of the first time she and Newley had made love, when she was red-eyed and puffy in bed with the flu. Words such as *bullshit, crap* and *shitty* were deleted. *For Christ's sake* became *for goodness' sake, shit* became *damn*. The cockney sweeper on the set of *The Road to Hong Kong* was no longer allowed to say that if he had to kiss Bing Crosby he would 'rather go down' on Hitler. Newley was no longer allowed to say 'thank you' after making love to her. Katy was not allowed to be born only three months after Joan and Ron married. But this time Joan did name George Englund as one of her lovers in the 1950s now that he was divorced, and she added a long new chapter to bring her story up to date. She ended the book by claiming that if all her fame and wealth disappeared tomorrow she would still survive and be happy. She claimed that her children, especially Katy, were the most important things in her life. And she ended the book with one gutsy word: '*Onward!*'

CHAPTER FOURTEEN

MAD ABOUT THE BOY

{ 1984–1985 }

In May Joan divorced Ron Kass. After so many happy years together and so much heartache the stress was terrible, she said. It would have been even worse had she known that Peter Holm was already having an affair with a twenty-two-year-old blonde, Suzanne Anderson, though Joan was herself having a brief flirtation in New York with the hugely rich, thirty-nine-year-old German Mercedes-Benz heir 'Muck' Flick – not be be confused with his elder brother, 'Mick' Flick. 'I want to reassure Peter that it wasn't serious,' she told the *Daily Mail*. 'Anyway, I don't like the sound of Joan Flick.'

Holm had picked Suzanne Anderson up in an LA computer shop and was using Joan's money to pay her £1,000-a-month rent [£2,270] and giving her pocket money as well. 'It was always in great wads of notes,' Suzanne told the *News of the World* when the story came out four years later. 'Peter kept telling me he was only with Joan for the money and as soon as he had enough he'd leave her.' She claimed that Holm had told her he hated sex with Joan because she was 'an old lady' and that he had to arouse himself by watching pornographic films. 'He told me that Joan always wore wigs and he couldn't stand that when they were in bed,' she said, though Joan herself denies this. Suzanne added that when Joan was out all day filming *Dynasty* Holm 'liked nothing better than to dress me up in Joan's clothes before making love to me on a desk in her home. We had to do it in his office because there were always other people around in the rest of the house – security guards and Joan's secretary. And although there was no bed there we would make it on his desk, in a chair, on the floor, all over.' Holm was the best lover she had ever had, said Suzanne: 'I can understand why Joan fell for him. He's the ultimate stud, phenomenally well endowed.'

With so many staff around the house Holm must have been crazy to think that Joan would never find out. She did, invited Suzanne to a pool party at Bowmont Drive, and asked if she was having an affair with Holm. Suzanne admitted it. Joan told Holm that if he ever saw Suzanne again she would throw him out. 'The next day Peter phoned me at my place,' said Suzanne. 'He said that Joan was listening in, that he was going to marry her, and could never see me again. Of course, the day after, when Joan went off to work, he was around my place telling me Joan had made him make the call and that I should simply ignore it.' The affair was to continue surreptitiously on and off for two years, and when Suzanne became pregnant early in 1985 Holm thought he must be the father, but she was unsure because she had other lovers.

It was unlikely that Holm really found Joan old and unattractive because she looked stunningly sexy in the TV comedy film that she made when *Dynasty* took its usual summer break, *The Cartier Affair*. The chemistry between her and her co-star, the hunky, thirty-two-year-old David Hasselhoff – star of the TV series *Knight Rider* and later of *Baywatch* – was so strong that he refused to film a naked love scene with her, not trusting his own reactions. He had recently married and explained that his wife would not like it. 'It wouldn't have been proper,' he said. It might indeed have been a dangerous temptation because Joan fancied him like mad. 'He's the perfect man, that delicious body and angelic face,' she told Sue Carroll of the *Sun* in 1987. 'He is perfectly formed – the kind of man that makes you feel so small and feminine. David is exactly the sort of actor you don't mind doing sexy scenes with. He also has a great sense of humour. Any man who can make me laugh has a real chance of winning my heart.' She played an Alexis clone, an irresistibly beautiful, bitchy soap star, while Hasselhoff was her crooked new secretary who pretends to be gay, steals her jewels but falls for her. It was a genial jape in which once again she was poking fun at herself, Alexis and *Dynasty*.

She wasn't alone. In Britain, where the BBC was again thinking of dropping *Dynasty* because its popularity had slumped to number twenty-six in the ratings, far below *Dallas*, the *News of the World*'s TV critic Nina Myskow derided the way that Alexis 'pitched up once after a car crash complete with immaculate hairdo and nary a scratch'. She chortled too over Joan's purple eye make-up: 'When have you ever known her go through anything without 1½lb of purple glop slopped on each lid?'

In June the *Sun* reported that Joan had decided to marry Holm, even though she had sworn she would never marry again, and quoted her as saying that 'Peter is the first man I've ever known who wants to protect me – not exploit me'. Her friends were now desperate to prevent the marriage. Holm's idea of a fun evening was to watch a couple of videos and eat a take-away pizza in bed, and her women friends found him so dull that they changed their place cards at dinner parties so as not to sit next to him. 'Joan is upset that so many of her friends won't accept Peter,' said one. 'Frankly, he's not very well liked. He's very arrogant and treats staff like dirt. I think three or four secretaries working for Joan have walked out so far, and the rest of the staff are very, very unhappy. Joan knows Katy doesn't like Holm at all. That's another strain. So we are all trying to persuade her not to marry this man. People who know them both are sure it won't work out. But she's besotted by him.'

When Joan had signed her *Past Imperfect* contract with the American publisher Simon and Schuster she had agreed to give them first refusal should she ever write a novel, and when the book started to sell extremely well she decided to write a sexy fictional saga about working on a prime-time TV series like *Dynasty*. She called it *Prime Time*, started work on it during a skiing holiday, and when she had written three chapters she showed them to the legendary agent 'Swifty' Lazar, who sold the book immediately to Simon and Schuster for a $2 million advance [£1.9 million]. She began seriously now to write by hand on yellow legal pads – a mysterious preference of many American writers – at weekends, on aeroplanes, and on holiday, which gave her even less time to devote to Katy. Jackie was not pleased to learn that Joan had decided to invade her territory and asked her if she realised what she was taking on, but the book was not to be published for another four years because Joan was already so busy with other projects.

In August she won at last her legal battle with Ron over custody of Katy, though some family friends were quoted as saying that the child herself would rather have lived with her father than with Holm. Ron dropped his case when Joan agreed to pay him maintenance of about £9,000 a month [£20,430], though the figure was never published because the hearing was held in private. She could well afford it because by now she was earning more than £2 million a year in modern values for *Dynasty* and another £2 million from her various other TV and public appearances and endorsements. To recover from all the anguish of yet another court case Joan and Holm flew off from Los Angeles for a five-day holiday in the South of France. He was in trouble again with his creditors when bailiffs seized his house in Windsor because he had failed to keep up the mortgage payments, but he did not give a damn. He was living a gloriously lavish, carefree life, flying regularly First Class to Europe and the Caribbean, staying in the best hotels, going to the best parties, restaurants and nightclubs, meeting dozens of famous people, driving a Rolls-Royce, and spending the modern equivalent of £19,000 a month on clothes.

October 1984 was a desperately unhappy month for Joan. Leonard Rossiter died in London of a heart attack in his dressing room at the Lyric Theatre during a performance of Joe Orton's play *Loot*. He was fifty-seven. Joan burst into tears when she heard and again a week later when her young lover Jon-Erik Hexum killed himself by accident while fooling around with a prop revolver on the Hollywood set of his latest TV series, *Cover Up*, and shot a piece of his skull into his brain. He was only twenty-six. And then she was angry when it was reported that she had had an invisible hearing aid inserted into one ear: ageless film-star beauties definitely do *not* wear hearing aids.

October also saw an ominous development on the set of *Dynasty*. Its ratings were dropping and in a desperate attempt to boost them the producers started to invite famous actors to make guest appearances. One was fifty-eight-year-old Rock Hudson, the impossibly handsome, macho, heart-throb star of sixty-five movies who joined the cast to play the part of a rich stud farm owner. He looked so unwell and skeletal that for several episodes not even his fans recognised him. He had been for many years a secret, predatory, promiscuous homosexual and had known for four months that he had AIDS, but he told no one, even though he had open sores in his mouth and in one scene had to kiss Linda Evans passionately on the lips. After a few weeks he became so ill that he had to be written out of the show, and when eventually he admitted that he had AIDS Linda was terrified that she might have been infected too. He was to die in October 1985 aged fifty-nine.

At the end of October 1984 Joan flew to London to launch her new scent, Scoundrel, and denied that she was about to marry Holm.

'Marriage is for babies,' she told the Press. 'Peter is sexy, strong – physically and mentally – and right for me at the moment. But with three marriages behind me I really don't feel like taking the plunge again.' Peter had certainly boosted her confidence and finances, and persuaded her that she would make much more money if she produced and directed her own films rather than working for someone else for a fixed salary. They formed their own company, Gemini Star Productions, and embarked on a search for a sexy subject for their own TV series. Even after they divorced Joan was to admit that she had learned a lot from Holm. 'He saw a side of me that people don't often see,' she told Rodney Tyler, who was now interviewing her so often that he had become a friend. 'I learned the lesson from him to be stronger and more assertive in business and to keep a closer control over my business affairs.'

That miserable month of October ended for Joan with yet another ex-employee betraying her to the Press. Her ex-chauffeur/handyman, Ed Deal, whose Central American wife Martha was Joan's housekeeper and looked after Katy while she was away, told the *Daily Star* that Katy was dreadfully lonely, unhappy and depressed because of Joan's obsession with Holm. The paper paid Deal a reported £50,000 [£113,500] and under the headline KATY'S AGONY splashed the story on its front page along with a scrap of a facsimile letter that Deal alleged that Katy had written. The paper claimed that Katy, 'who is under the treatment of psychologists and therapists for her emotional problems, pines for her mother's attention. She sits outside her mother's bedroom door peering under it to see if the lights go on so she can grab a few moments of the busy star's time.'

Deal told the *Daily Star* that 'I'm speaking out like this because of the total difference between what Joan Collins paints in public as the picture of her relationship with Katy – and what it is really like.' He claimed that when he was driving Joan to the studio one day and said that it was sad that she was unable to spend more time with Katy, 'she stunned me when she suddenly said, "Katy is a big girl now, and I have my own life to lead." The child was just eleven at the time.' Finally, Deal alleged that Tara and Sacha both had as little as possible to do with Joan and were much closer to their father. When Tara did see her mother they were always having rows, he said, and whenever Sacha came to California he stayed not with Joan but with Newley's mother,

Grace, in her small house at Pacific Pallisades. Sacha and Joan also 'fight all the time', said Deal, and 'I remember at least on one occasion when he told her quite bluntly to fuck off ... they have little or no respect for their mum.'

Joan sobbed when she read Deal's allegations and said they were 'vicious lies' and the letter a forgery: 'I can't believe anyone would say such things about a child. This sort of rubbish can cause untold harm to my daughter.' She admitted that Katy had emotional problems but said: 'Everyone has problems. I have problems myself, just like anyone else. Whose child grows up without going through a difficult time?' The *Sun* reported that Deal had made his allegations in revenge because Joan had sacked him for allegedly beating up his pregnant wife, whom Joan had kept on as her housekeeper. She in turn told the *Sun* that her husband's allegations were 'too horrible for words. Joan is a very kind, understanding woman and has been great to me. I never once saw her mistreat her daughter. She loved Katy more than anything.' The *Sun* also quoted one of Katy's ex-nannies, Fiona Aitken, as saying that Deal's accusations were ridiculous: 'Joan loves Katy and Katy loves Joan – there is absolutely no doubt about that at all.' Joan swore to sue the *Daily Star* but obviously never did because they repeated Deal's allegations two years later when she and Peter eventually split up. Katy later admitted that her childhood had not always been idyllic. 'It was hard at times,' she told Colin Wills of the *Sunday Mirror* in 1994, when she was twenty-two, 'but I always felt loved and I feel I've come out the other end stronger.' She added: 'I grew up in my mother's wardrobe. I spent most of my childhood there, dressing up in her gowns and tottering around the house in her high-heeled shoes. So many shoes! My mother seemed to have a pair for every single second of the day. The wardrobe was like a city full of clothes. You just walked in and you were surrounded by glamorous things: silk, satin, beads, tinsel.'

Undeterred by all the denials, Ed Deal returned to the fray and told the *Daily Star* that despite her huge earnings Joan was unbelievably mean and that his and Martha's weekly wages were invariably paid late. 'She's a tightwad,' he said. 'Martha and I were each supposed to get $25 extra for catering at Joan's parties. But one day Martha wasn't paid her money. Peter told her that he and Joan hadn't liked the way the table was set. When Martha and I spent money out of our own pockets to get household things like lightbulbs or toilet paper we had a hell of a job getting the cash back. We'd have to detail every tiny thing. On one occasion Joan called in some experts to fix the electronic gates. The bill came to about £70 after the men had worked hard all day. But as soon as she saw the bill she said we mustn't pay. She was always after something for nothing – like when she did a Revlon TV commercial. Joan persuaded the Revlon executives to give her – or sell very cheaply – two rolls of ordinary carpet they used on the set. They used one at home and took the other roll to the UK with them. I drove them to the airport in a little estate car with this huge roll of carpet tied on top, hanging over each end of the car.' After Deal's accusations Joan made all her staff sign contracts with a confidentiality clause by which they promised not to talk or write about their time with her.

Three days later the *Daily Star* was at it again, this time reporting that Joan had been planning to spend most of the Christmas holidays alone with Holm in the West Indies while Katy was farmed out to friends, but that Deal's allegations had made her change her mind and include Katy after all. Joan retaliated by giving another long interview to Rodney Tyler in which she said: 'God knows I'm not the best mother in the world but Katy knows I love her tremendously. Of course there have been times when she has been unhappy or lonely or jealous or grumpy – but she has always, always known that I love her.' She admitted that after her separation from Ron she had smuggled 'two or three' overnight lovers out of the house so that Katy would not see them but denied that she was lonely and claimed that the letter she had allegedly written was either a forgery or a fantasy and that Deal had never shown it to her.

In December, despite all Joan's denials that she would ever marry Holm, despite all the advice of her friends and family, she accepted when he proposed and gave her a £100,000 [£227,000] five-carat solitaire-diamond engagement ring. When she came to sue him for divorce in 1987, and was asked why she had accepted such an expensive ring, there was laughter in court when she replied with her usual wide-eyed naïvety: 'How can you turn down a five-carat diamond?' They flew with Katy to London and on Christmas Day Joan treated the closest members of her family – Joe, Irene, Bill, Hazel, Tara, Sacha and Natasha – to lunch at Claridge's Hotel. Joe, who was now eighty-two and had had two strokes in recent months, was appalled that the bill came to £500 [£1,135]. Afterwards they returned to his house in

Regent's Park Road, where he was not impressed that Peter fell asleep in an armchair for four hours.

Tara, now twenty-one, had dropped out of Boston University, was sharing a simple flat in north London, and was about to embark on a series of lowly paid jobs – anything to avoid publicity, telling no one who her parents were. Although she loved singing and writing she was wary of doing anything that might make her famous. 'I had seen how it affects your life and how intense it is,' she said, and became a waitress, an assistant in a boutique and a record shop, a £1-an-hour gofer for a pop video company, a tape operator in a recording studio, a cashier at the London Marquee Club disco. Later she formed her own small band, first calling it Newley/Mars, then Memphis, then The Radiators, and played and sang for two years at gigs around London. 'I started wearing crap clothes, white trailer-trash stuff,' she told Colin Wills in 2000. 'I looked so shitty that one day when I left the dressing room for a quick fag they wouldn't let me back in. I said: "OK, but if you don't you won't have a concert." We played every dive going. It was all sex, drugs and rock 'n' roll. Yes, there were male groupies, God bless 'em.' She had just begun a serious, seven-year love affair, and as for drugs she confessed to Corinna Honan in 1994 that 'I've tried pretty much everything except heroin' and that her mother knew. Joan hated drugs and must have been horrified.

A few days later Joe spoke at length to Fiona Webster of the *Sun* and agreed that playing Alexis had changed Joan dramatically. 'They call her La Collins, Superstar,' he said. 'To be honest I prefer home-grown shows like *Crossroads*' because 'it's homely and true to life as I know it, which *Dynasty* is not'. He reckoned that Joan would never marry Holm, despite the engagement ring. 'She's very indulgent with her young men and husbands,' he chuckled. 'She buys and sells them.' After just four days in England Joan and Peter flew for six days to Antigua, where they welcomed the New Year as guests at the tycoon Peter de Savary's new St James's Club Hotel. Part of the deal was that they should pose for photographers but Peter refused to do so unless he was paid. Joan was furious with him and according to the *Daily Mail*'s gossip column threw her engagement ring at him but took it back the following day when he agreed to be photographed for free.

In the middle of January 1985 the *Daily Express* reported that Holm was the father of Pauline Gaffke's fourteen-year-old daughter Sabine and Joe rubbished him again. 'He's a bore,' he said. 'Joan's an idiot, too, getting tied up with him. Even without this child I didn't fancy her getting mixed up with him. He's a bum.' Yet Joan seemed to be deaf in both ears to the warnings of even her nearest and dearest. 'This is the best time I've ever had in my life,' she gushed to Rodney Tyler. 'It's the most exciting, the most fruitful and productive for work and the happiest with a man – getting to know Peter and to love each other more and more and sharing things more and more. It's the best relationship I've ever had with a man. I have someone who is very loving as well as being my best friend.' She refused to worry about his dodgy background. 'His past is totally immaterial to me,' she said. 'He could have gone with fifty girls a week for all I care. My past was imperfect too.' She admitted, however, that she was still nervous of getting married for the fourth time: 'There can be no more divorces. I absolutely cannot and will not go through that again.' There was, however, a side of Peter's character that did disturb her. Normally, she said later, he was 'helpful, kind, sweet and caring' but when she kept refusing to marry him he became 'sullen, sulky, angry and abusive. I would come home from the *Dynasty* set absolutely exhausted. He was sitting at home all day thinking about marrying me and a pre-marital agreement. It would end up with us having furious rows. Peter would go into tremendous sulks. He would not talk to me for long periods.'

By now she had let him take over her finances and business life completely and even she was denied access to his secret computer files, which were firmly locked away behind a fortress of codes and passwords. He installed a two-way mirror in his office so that he could see everyone come and go, opened all her mail, listened to many of her telephone conversations, wrote all her cheques and settled all her bills. He was even limbering up to negotiate with Spelling a huge salary increase, claiming that she was worth twice as much as John Forsythe and Linda Evans. Joan insisted that he had only her interests at heart. 'He's got rid of all the manipulating leeches in my life,' she told Rodney Tyler. 'He's forced me to be more assertive. He felt I was allowing my-self to be pushed around too much and wasn't afraid to stand and argue the ground with me. Of course we row. We have humdingers [*but*] I could never stand to be with a guy who was subservient to me.' Best of all, he had found the subject for their first independent TV mini-series, a bestselling novel by Judith Gould called *Sins*, in which the beautiful, powerful woman owner of a magazine empire is determined to avenge the horror of her experiences in the Second World War, when she was raped by a German soldier and her mother beaten up and killed. 'It's the best deal of my life,' Joan told Tyler, 'yet all along I said to him it could never be done.' Holm negotiated with CBS a basic £600,000 for Joan [£1.3 million], £100,000 [£216,000] for himself as co-producer, and a share of the profits for both of them. They began shooting the five-and-a-half-hour mini-series in the South of France at the end of February, and soon afterwards Holm set up a second series by buying the TV rights to Arianna Stassinopoulos's biography of the opera singer Maria Callas.

Joan had no idea that Peter was still being blatantly unfaithful, this time with a married, twenty-year-old Italian woman, Romina Danielson, whose Swedish businessman husband was eighty. Their first tryst was on 14 February 1985, St Valentine's Day, and after that they met regularly for sex in motels when Joan was on the *Dynasty* set. Holm called Romina his Passion Flower and persuaded her to divorce her husband, promised that he would marry Joan and then divorce her, talking half of her millions under Californian law, and would then like Romina to have his baby. He asked her to join him in Paris when he and Joan flew there in April, and although she declined she believed his promises and divorced her husband only to find that Peter had no intention of leaving Joan. He persuaded Suzanne Anderson to fly to Paris instead and dallied with her in Joan's £1,700-a-day [£3,600] six-room suite at the Ritz when she was safely out of the way filming.

At the end of March Joan and Peter returned to England to meet twenty-three-year-old Princess Diana for the first time at a lavish charity dinner and fashion parade for nine hundred guests at the Grosvenor House Hotel to mark the couturier Bruce Oldfield's tenth anniversary in the fashion business. Both women wore Oldield creations and inevitably the tabloids went wild the next day with photographs comparing their gowns and elegance. 'We love you, Joan, we love you!' screamed a crowd of women outside, and, when she met the princess, Diana said: 'You are very beautiful. I watch you on television all the time.' Joan was not convinced. 'I don't think the princess watches *Dynasty*,' she said, 'she probably watches *Coronation Street*.' She introduced the princess to Holm, who told her gallantly: 'Tonight I'm with the two most beautiful women in the world.' They sat at the same table but Diana was later said in the Press to consider Joan pushy, patronising, and keen to upstage her.

After yet another quick trip back to LA, Joan flew to Paris to film *Sins* in May and June before flying down to the South of France. She had always loved the area and bought a small house near St Tropez, at Port Grimaud – 61 rue de Fer à Cheval – where she was in future to spend one or two months every summer, and for £60,000 [£128,400] she bought a 38ft Riva speedboat to go with it and called it *Sins*. Then they went on to Venice, where Peter made a brief, egotistical appearance in the series as a TV reporter, to complete more than four months of shooting. During one lull they flew to Frankfurt in June for Joan to publicise a new BMW car, a £39,000 635CSi, for which she was to be given one, and were nearly killed when a bomb exploded in the airport's departure lounge, killing three people. Before returning to Los Angeles, Joan told Ivan Waterman of the *News of the World* how much she had enjoyed co-producing her own series. 'Now I have a real opportunity to do my own thing,' she said. 'I don't think I've ever been this excited. *Sins* has given me the chance to have some control over the finished product. There may come a time soon when I'll be truly able to direct my life almost completely. I've done enough of just being an actress. Now I'd like to be an employer again instead of only an employee.' As for Peter, she said it was wonderful to find a man who was so straight and honest: 'When you become really successful everyone wants a piece of you but he can spot a phoney at fifty paces.'

Peter was still urging Joan to marry him and suggested that they should do it romantically aboard a yacht in the Mediterranean with the ceremony performed by the captain, and at last, worn down by his constant nagging, she agreed. She asked Rodney Tyler to make all the arrangements, but when she had second thoughts and backed out at the last minute Holm refused to reimburse Tyler for all the expenses he had incurred and he had to ask Joan for the money. Back in Hollywood she embarked belatedly on yet another season of *Dynasty*, but only after a major row with Spelling. She had heard that Spelling had just signed up Charlton Heston to appear in a new *Dynasty* spin-off series, *The Colbys*, at £75,000 a week, upon which Holm demanded a rise for Joan to £80,000 an episode [£171,000]. Spelling refused. Holm telephoned him to say that in that case Joan would not be turning up for work. Spelling hung up on him. 'I'll never speak to that man again,' he said. Joan went on strike for two days. 'I will not be blackmailed,' said Spelling. 'I can't stand the way that no one honours contracts in this town.' He threatened to write her out of the series altogether and cast two sexy, younger English actresses as possible replacements for Joan: thirty-seven-year-old redhead Stephanie Beacham to play another scheming bitch, and forty-six-year-old Kate O'Mara as another possible rival to Joan. Alarmed now, Joan knew when she was beaten and turned up for work three days late, but ten days later she was back in London to be photographed at Madame Tussaud's with their new wax model of her reclining on a couch. She was beginning to feel that *Dynasty* was losing its sparkle, even though it had again just been voted the *People's Choice* best prime-time drama.

Stephanie Beacham and Kate O'Mara both came to admire Joan, though Stephanie did not always like her. 'Joan is very funny,' she wrote in *Hello!* four years later. 'She likes to have a good time and she's intelligent [*and*] always very professional, and I respect her greatly.' She admitted, however, that there was another side to Joan: she 'is like the old children's nursery rhyme: "When she is good she is very, very good. And when she is bad she is horrid" ... She is a whirlwind that can come in and delight everybody, or she can come in and ruin everybody's day. She can choose. Someone at the studio once said to me: "The essential difference between you and Joan Collins is that you go home and cry, whereas Joan makes other people go home crying." She can be so enchanting, funny, sweet and lovely ... or she can be just plain frightful. You feel like throwing her over your knee, slapping her bum and saying: "Joan, you have no right to make everybody's life so horrid."'

Kate O'Mara, who played Alexis's sister, was grateful to Joan for making British actresses and older women more acceptable in films and television. In her autobiography she said that Joan was always very kind and helpful to her, an excellent actress and completely professional. Only once did Kate suddenly see her as less than strong and dependable: unusually Joan was late to arrive on the set one day and this was so unlike her that everyone thought she must be unwell. But eventually she arrived in tears, crying: 'Nobody knows what it's like living in this goldfish bowl. My life isn't my own!' She was obviously very upset, said Kate. 'I don't know what had happened but I suspect the strain of being the world's most popular television actress and all the high-profile exposure and attention that position entailed, had finally got to her and her usual composure had cracked. To her eternal credit she pulled herself together and after apologising to me – played the scene superbly.' Joan was certainly under great pressure at times. 'Alexis has changed my life completely,' she told an American magazine. 'I get murder threats, mysterious telephone calls at night and ugly letters from thousands of women. It's made my private life horrible and I worry that this part could destroy me [*but*] I would rather be hated by millions than adored by a few thousands.' Her obsession with fame and publicity was as powerful as ever.

In July Joan and Jackie were horrified to hear that Joe had written and sold his autobiography for £30,000 [£64,200]. 'I can't see what the girls are uptight about,' he said. 'I had to write the book because people are always asking me what it is like to be Joan and Jackie's dad. Now I am going to tell them, I'll be telling everything I know, and I'll be telling the truth.' This so alarmed Joan that she demanded to see a copy of the manuscript and Jackie wrote to Joe's English literary agent, Don Short, to protest. 'She sent me a note,' Short told me, 'that said something like "Dear Don, Joan and I think Dad shouldn't be writing a book at this time. We really object to it and think somebody should have consulted us first." They were obviously frightened about what their dad was going to say about them, and as a writer herself Jackie probably didn't want to be overshadowed by her father. We sent him a copy of her letter but he ignored it, and I didn't hear from them again.'

Joan and Jackie were equally appalled to hear that Joe's youngest daughter, their seventeen-year-old stepsister Natasha, wanted to go into the British army and had applied to join the elite Royal Military Academy at Sandhurst to be trained as an officer. 'They've been saying I'm a total idiot,' said Natasha. She was in fact very far from being an idiot and had done a great deal better than either of her sisters at their old school, Francis Holland, where she had passed eight O levels, was about to pass three A levels, and was captain of the hockey team. She was later to go to Birmingham University and achieve an excellent 2:1 degree in economic history and politics before going on to Sandhurst. She was also firm and forthright and told *Weekend* magazine dismissively that 'Joan acts in trash and Jackie writes it', an opinion that did not endear her to her older sisters.

Early in August Joan and Peter had a holiday at her villa in the South of France and when they returned to Los Angeles the American scandal magazine the *National Enquirer* told them that it would pay them 'a lot of money' for photographs of their wedding if they ever went ahead with it. Joan was still dithering about marrying Holm, even though he kept pestering her, but eventually she agreed again and booked a private chapel in Las Vegas for the ceremony only to call it off once more at the last minute. She was beginning to tire of Los Angeles and feel homesick for England. Hollywood, she said, was now decidedly boring by comparison with the wild days of the swinging fifties when each party had been packed with glamorous stars and people dressed up properly. Now, she said, the 'stars' wore grunge and hardly bothered to go anywhere.

Still, at least she felt secure financially for the first time in her life. The CBS network was trying to lure her away from *Dynasty* to star in a TV series about the bitchy woman boss of a diamond firm and promised to let Peter be the producer. She was now getting nineteen thousand fan letters a week, Spelling realised that *Dynasty's* ratings might crash without her – the critics and public were becoming increasingly disillusioned with the show's ridiculous, over-the-top story-lines – and to keep her with the show he offered her a rise in salary to £50,000 per week for thirty episodes a year – a total of £3.25 million a year in modern values and £600,000 more than Linda Evans was getting. He also promised Joan an astonishing number of perks: three days off every fortnight; a huge expense allowance for clothes, travel and entertaining; all the exotic clothes that she wore on the show; her own masseuse in a refurbished luxury dressing room; a chauffeured limousine. It was an astonishingly generous deal but Joan said loftily that she would think about it. She had just pocketed £2 million in modern values as the star and co-producer of *Sins*, and earned more on top of that for occasional TV and public appearances and for advertising and sponsorships. She admitted that on clothes alone she was spending about a million pounds a year in modern values, but she was becoming bored with *Dynasty* and eventually stayed on only because Holm forced Spelling to pay her even more than he had offered: £116,000 a week in modern values, £3.5 million a year. She was now so famous that Andy Warhol persuaded her to let him paint her portrait.

Which was why she was deeply offended when President and Nancy

Reagan hosted a dinner for Prince Charles and Princess Diana at the White House in November and she was not invited, even though she had tried for weeks to wangle an invitation. To make the snub even more humiliating, Linda Evans had been invited along with several other Hollywood stars – Elizabeth Taylor, Clint Eastwood, Robert Redford, all of whom the royals had especially asked to meet – and one American magazine reported that the princess had refused to ask Joan because of her pushy, patronising behaviour at Bruce Oldfield's fashion dinner in London and had snapped: 'Just who does this woman think she is?'

By now Joan was earning altogether about £4.5 million a year [more than £9.5 million] and Holm was nagging her incessantly to marry him. She weakened at last on 6 November 1985, although she did keep her wits about her sufficiently to insist that first he should sign a pre-nuptial agreement that limited him to no more than twenty per cent of her earnings during the marriage should they ever divorce. Without telling any of her family, not even Katy, they flew by private jet to Nevada with four close friends – Joan's secretary Judy Bryer as her bridesmaid, Judy's husband Max to give her away, Peter's Swedish best man Hassa Olafson, and Joan's favourite photographer Eddie Sanderson – and they were married by the Rev Bill Sharp at 11.10 p.m. in the tacky Little White Wedding Chapel on Las Vegas's sleazy Strip. The ceremony cost $35, the music was a canned recording of the Wedding March, the candles were fake and the lights neon, but Joan wore an expensive cream silk dress, a white satin bow with streamers in her wig, and all the traditional trimmings: something old (her mother's pearl and ruby bracelet); something new (her wedding dress); something borrowed (Judy's lace handkerchief); something blue (a garter). Peter wore a white tuxedo and pink tie and slipped onto her finger a fat, half-inch-thick gold and diamond ring that was said to have cost £325,000 [£695,000]. Joan carried a small bouquet of cream roses and lilies and fibbed on the marriage licence that she had been born in 1938, not 1933, so that she was only forty-seven instead of fifty-two. Her voice trembled as she said the words 'love you, cherish you and serve you', she stuttered when she said 'to have and to hold', and at the end she giggled helplessly. The occasion was marred by one unhappy moment: when the owner of the chapel, Charlotte Richards, took a snap with her Polaroid camera Joan demanded angrily to have it because she and Peter had brought Sanderson along to take official photographs which they had already arranged to sell to the *National Enquirer* for £100,000 and to other newspapers for another £75,000 – a total of £374,500 in modern values. Peter's best man had also managed to take some surreptitious photographs that he was to sell to the *News of the World*. Afterwards Joan drank champagne, Peter quaffed some apple juice, and they sampled a strawberry mousse cake before flying back to LA, where Peter's wedding present to Joan was a £31,500 BMW [£67,400]. They did not tell Katy until the next day, Joe and Irene heard only when they were telephoned by reporters, some friends reckoned that the whole thing had been pretty tacky, and newspapers sneered that Joan had gone through with it at that particular time so as to upstage the imminent arrival in America of Prince Charles and Princess Diana. They pointed out that she had arranged to throw a big wedding party for a hundred and fifty people and to appear on every major TV channel just a couple of hours before the royals flew in. And then the *National Enquirer* refused to pay the agreed £100,000 for Sanderson's exclusive photographs because of the best man's snatched pictures in the *News of the World*.

The marriage was to last only thirteen months. 'Call it insanity,' said Joan twenty years later. 'I was obviously going through the menopause or something. It was truly stupid.'

CHAPTER FIFTEEN

FROM AN OLD HOLM TO
A NEW BUNGALOW

{ 1985–1987 }

Joan was determined to meet Prince Charles and Princess Diana during their American tour, and a week after their wedding the Holms flew to Florida to join nearly four hundred guests at a charity ball in Palm Beach where they paid £7,000 [£15,000] for their two tickets. Joan 'shamelessly upstaged Princess Diana', reported Harry Arnold in the *Sun*, 'wearing a dress that was cut so low she was almost falling out of the top of it'. The *Daily Mail*'s royal correspondent, Grania Forbes, was caustic, accusing Joan – 'dripping with diamonds' – of trying to steal the limelight with 'a spectacular gate-crashing performance': 'The manoeuvre had all the split-second timing of a military operation – and the subtlety of a sledgehammer,' she wrote. 'Her first assault came as she arrived at the hotel's main entrance in a revealing, figure-hugging black ball gown on the dot of eight o'clock, the very moment the Princess was to have gone through the same door ... When the princess arrived twenty minutes later it was clear that the fifty-two-year-old actress, in her own distinctive style, was challenging Diana in the fashion stakes. The soap queen's dress, with frills and flounces and cut low to reveal much of her bronzed bosom, was to say the least eye-catching.' Only thirty-two couples were due to meet the royals – they had each paid £35,000, five times as much as the Holms, for their special tickets – but Ms Forbes reported that Joan simply gate-crashed the event, hogged the photographers' cameras, and that eventually Princess Diana found Joan's antics 'a huge joke and giggled into her napkin'. Finally, Ms Forbes reported, 'Miss Collins pulled her greatest stroke when it came to the dancing. As a fellow guest, twenty-six-year-old Kiki Courtelis, notes, it was no accident that she bumped into the prince on the dance floor. "She just managed to position herself next to him and immediately started talking. She asked him to dance not the other way round.'" Harry Arnold reported that Holm fell asleep during Prince Charles's speech and had to be nudged awake while 'the whole table laughed with embarrassment', and added: 'The presence of Joan Collins put the princess on edge from the start. There is little love lost between the two superstars. I can reveal that when Diana was told of Joan's marriage she asked who her new husband was. And when she was told remarked: "I suppose that's the best she can do at her age."' After the ball, said Grania Forbes, the royals slipped unnoticed out of a back door while 'the soap queen left in a blaze of flash bulbs by the front entrance'. In fact, the reporters were not being fair: Prince Charles greatly enjoyed his dance with Joan and told his biographer Jonathan Dimbleby not only that *he* had asked *her* to dance but that 'she was very amusing and with an unbelievable cleavage, all raised up and presented as if on a tray. Eye-wander was a problem.'

Three days later the Holms flew to London, where their arrival was marred by a front-page splash in the *Sun* and a two-page interview inside with Peter's ex-lover, Pauline Gaffke, who claimed that he had cost her £100,000 [£214,000] during their eleven years together. 'Peter's not a real man,' she said. 'He always has to have a rich woman to look after and protect him. He may look big and strong but really he's a weak, pathetic apology of a man who cannot stand on his own two feet. He's hardly done a proper day's work in his life. He's dull company and excruciatingly boring. The only thing he is good at is making love.' She forecast that the marriage would not last and said: 'I suspect Joan will begin to suss how shallow he is within a matter of months. That's exactly how long it took me.'

At the end of November Joan switched on the twenty-three thousand Christmas lights in Regent Street and was told to her delight that she had attracted an even bigger crowd than Princess Di had done. The following night Madeleine and Jeffrey Curtis, around whose swimming pool Joan and Peter had met, threw a lavish party for a hundred and thirty people at Stocks nightclub in the King's Road to celebrate their wedding with a remarkably varied crowd of guests that included Michael Caine, Faye Dunaway, Lady Falkender, David Frost, Soraya Khashoggi, Bruce Oldfield, Lord and Lady Rothermere, Sir Clive Sinclair, Lord Weidenfeld and Susannah York. The next night Joan hit an even higher social jackpot when she and Lauren Bacall acted as compères at a Royal Variety Show at the Theatre Royal in Drury Lane and met the Queen. When Joan claimed afterwards that she had been so nervous that her knees had been knocking throughout the show, Joan Rivers remarked: 'I didn't think she could get them that close together.' Two days later she earned £20,000 from Littlewoods Pools for spending just twenty minutes at Harrods to present a cheque to one of their winners, and a couple of days later the *News of the World* reported that she had made almost £86,000 [£178,000] in one day when she flew to Munich to appear on a TV chat show for £4,900; visit a furrier's shop, for which she was given a white mink cape worth £13,250; a jeweller's shop, for which she was presented with a £7,700 gold and emerald necklace; a BMW showroom in exchange for two cars worth £55,280; and the Hilton Hotel, where she earned £4,800 by drawing a winning lottery ticket.

Joan told Paul Callan of the *Daily Mirror* on Christmas Eve that Peter had changed her life and she had never been so happy, and Zsa Zsa Gabor was appalled when she invited them to a dinner party for the exiled King of Tunisia and 'throughout the whole evening Joan was draped all over Peter and insisted on sitting next to him during dinner – which is completely contrary to the European custom of seating husband and wife separately', she wrote in her autobiography. 'She spent the entire evening holding Peter's hand so tightly that he could hardly eat.' But Holm's behaviour changed rapidly after the wedding, as though he no longer needed to pretend to love her. He became bossy and dogmatic, criticised Joan in public, sneered at her looks, and made snide remarks about her age. He lost his temper much more than before, was often cold, arrogant or sulky, became increasingly secretive about the contents of his computer files, and took to carrying a two-foot-long padlocked bag wherever he went. When she asked him what was in it he replied mysteriously: 'Explosives and gold bars.' Her bank account seemed to have sprung a major leak – she told a friend once that he was helping himself to £6,000 [£12,420] a day – and because of their agreement that she would give him twenty per cent of her gross earnings she paid him more than a million dollars in just six months from February to October 1986, even though she was also paying all their living expenses. Their rows became worse than ever and eventually, she claimed, he became violent, hurling her precious contacts book across the room so that hundreds of pages were scattered, and attacking Katy's teenage nanny, Madelaine Kipps, 'grabbing her forcibly, throwing her about and shoving her outside the door, where she fell as he screamed profanities at her'. The girl was so terrified that she quit her job. Holm also lashed out at Robert Kass, Katy's stepbrother, shrieking as he accused him of taking his parking space, ordering him out of the house, and telling him never to return.

Equally unhappy were the viewing figures for *Dynasty*, which had crashed to number seventeen in the ratings thanks to some utterly ridiculous plotlines, most notably an end-of-season wedding scene in which the entire cast was mown down by terrorists wielding machine guns so that the viewers had to tune in the next season to see who had survived. 'I've been saying for four months that the storylines are wrong but nobody took any notice of me because I was just one of the actors,' Joan told a Los Angeles Press conference to launch *Sins*, which finally reached the TV screens early in February. Increasingly she was also saying publicly that she did not want to stay in *Dynasty* for much longer.

To publicise *Sins* she appeared on Joan Rivers' TV chat show, where she said she regretted making *The Stud* and *The Bitch* and admitted that she was not a very good mother. She startled Rivers by confessing that as a teenager she had been a slut. 'You're supposed to be one of the great women in bed,' said Rivers. Joan blushed. 'Well, yes,' she said. 'Am I good in bed? I'd rather be that than a good cook.' She was never in any danger of being a good cook. Rivers asked her which husband had been the best lover. Joan demurred. 'Come on, Joanie,' said Rivers.

'Yours, darling,' she said.

Rivers was stunned, and during the advertising break said nervously: 'Is it *true*? Did you *really* sleep with Edgar?'

'Of *course* not,' said Joan. 'Are you *mad*? He's *much* too old for me!'

She was still determined to have her fair share of *The Stud*'s profits and early in February she and Ron buried the hatchet, joined Jackie and Oscar in suing Brent–Walker in the High Court in London, and settled for £147,233 [£304,772] before the case came to court when Brent–Walker agreed to pay more if an independent audit found it to be justified. Tragically Ron's pleasure at winning the case after so long was destroyed when he was diagnosed with cancer of the colon and had to have an operation in Los Angeles in March. Joan visited him in hospital and all the bitterness between them evaporated, but he had only seven months to live. Her feud with Tony Newley, however, was not so easily healed, even though he too had recently had an operation in Los Angeles to remove a cancerous kidney. When he appeared on Terry Wogan's chat show Wogan asked him whether he ever watched Joan these days. 'No,' said Newley, 'I watched her for eight years and that's enough.'

Another feud erupted in March when *Dynasty* won the American People's Choice Award for the favourite TV drama. The cast agreed that at the televised ceremony John Forsythe should receive the award and thank the viewers for their votes, but Joan moved in and grabbed the limelight by doing both. When she then handed the microphone to Forsythe he snapped: 'What is there left to say? You've said it all, haven't you?' and for months he and Linda Evans refused to talk to Joan except on camera.

A couple of days after admitting that she was not a very good mother Joan told Paul Callan that 'Katy is the most important person in my life and we spend a great deal of time in one another's company. I cannot tell you how wonderful it is for me to care for and love someone like her. She is slightly shy and rather reserved. But she loves coming down to the set of *Dynasty* and watching me work.' Unfortunately she undermined her credibility by fibbing that 'my marriage to Peter Holm is great, and he and Katy have formed a really special relationship'. It was special, all right: she hated him with a specially deep loathing and was extremely unhappy.

Sins was savaged by the American critics. 'We may finally have reached saturation point where Joan Collins is concerned,' wrote Tom Shales in the *Washington Post*. 'The Joan Collins fad is passing.' In the *Los Angeles Herald Tribune* Elvis Mitchell was so repelled by Joan's heavy make-up that he suggested the series should carry a credit for 'make-up by Earl Scheib', the owner of a chain of car paint-spray shops that boasted that they could turn 'old clunkers' into shiny new beauties. *Sins*' cast included Steven Berkoff, Timothy Dalton, Gene Kelly and Lauren Hutton but despite its soft-focus photography and glitzy settings – Paris, Venice, a French château, New York – it was shallow, amateurish, stilted and clichéd. The story was dreary, the dialogue crass. Like *The Stud* and *The Bitch* the soundtrack was deafened by raucous music and the reviewers were particularly critical of one scene in which a pregnant woman was tortured. Once again Joan blamed others, as she had done when criticised for her tacky scenes in *The Stud* and *The Bitch*. 'I, who loathe and detest violence, did not want that scene in,' she told the *TV Times*. 'I tried to get it out, but they wanted it for the American audience because, sadly, violence sells.' She never seemed prepared to accept responsibility even for a series where she was the producer, and she was sufficiently hypocritical as to tell *Globe* magazine in February that she was 'one of the few people in the world who really believe in censorship [*since*] I think there is so much unhappiness among the young today because they are allowed to see so much sex and violence.' Four months later she was blithely telling *Woman's Own* magazine that 'sexual freedom was abused by women ten, fifteen or even twenty years ago, feeling they had to be good sports and jump into bed with anybody. Hopefully women are more discriminating now.' Well, it was exactly fifteen years ago that Joan had herself been cuckolding Tony Newley with Ron Kass, nineteen since she had been betraying him with a cameraman, and twenty since she had been having her adulterous fling with Ryan O'Neal. Whether she liked it or not she was now so firmly identified in the public mind with sexual promiscuity that one British dial-a-joke telephone line was carrying the following joke until Members of Parliament complained and had it removed:

Question: What does Joan Collins put behind her ears to make her attractive?

Answer: Her legs.

After *Sins* the Holms had planned to co-produce their TV mini-series about Maria Callas, but Joan's voice was clearly not up to the task and they dropped the project. 'Stick to the kind of opera you know, dear: soap,' remarked one of her friends. They embarked instead on a second mini-series with a Second World War theme, this time only three hours long, *Monte Carlo*, which began in Monaco in 1940 with Joan playing a gorgeous half-Russian cabaret singer who was also a British spy. The cast included George Hamilton, Malcolm McDowell, Lauren Hutton, Peter Vaughan, Philip Madoc and Leslie Phillips, but once again it was slow, shallow and pedestrian despite its glamorous scenery, costumes and glossy photography. Joan admitted that her singing in the series was not good enough but again denied that it was her fault. 'It was a bone of contention between Peter and me,' she told the *TV Times*. 'I wanted to take some training for the role and he kept on insisting that I didn't need it. He won, and I was right.' When the series was broadcast towards the end of the year the *New York Times* critic John O'Connor said that it teetered 'on a thin line between being outlandish and being obscene. It manages, in the end, to be merely silly.' As for Joan's performance, he said, she 'seems to have finally reached the stage in her career where she looks totally unreal. She is a walking air-brushed photograph.'

Yet by now she was making so much money – an estimated £3.5 million in 1986 [£7.25 million] – that in April she bought for £1.5 million [more than £3 million] an enormous Beverly Hills mansion in Cabrillo Drive, high above LA, with huge white entrance pillars, a marble hall, vast windows, five bedrooms, five bathrooms, a pool, two-storey guest house, 13ft wall all around, spacious gardens and a spectacular view over the city. The main reception room could take three hundred and fifty guests for a party or a hundred and sixty people for dinner. The house had once belonged to her old chum Laurence Harvey, who had died thirteen years earlier, in 1973, of stomach cancer, aged only forty-five. 'It's a typically tasteless movie star's house – the sort the public imagine stars to live in, but fortunately they usually have better taste,' sneered a local estate agent. Joan admitted that by the time she had finished doing it up her way it was typically glitzy over-the-top Hollywood. 'This was my *Dynasty* house,' she told a Fellow of All Souls College, Oxford, Peter Conrad, when he interviewed her in 1990 for the *Observer Magazine*. 'One spent all one's life in that very unattractive studio, surrounded by lights and cables, with only a trailer to get dressed in; there was no glamour to the work at all. I wanted to have a house like this, just once.' After ten or twelve hours a day on the *Dynasty* set she wanted to relax in a glamorous, lavish, spacious home. Although she was usually deeply superstitious, bravely she ignored the local belief that the house was jinxed because after Harvey's death two more of its owners had died young, both at the age of only forty-nine: the comedienne Totie Fields and David Janssen, star of the TV series *The Fugitive*. It was said that Janssen had dreamed one night that he saw a coffin being carried out of the mansion, asked who had died, and was told 'some actor called Janssen', and two days later, they said, he had died of a heart attack. Over the next three years Joan was to transform the place, spending another £750,000 [£1.5 million] to add a breathtakingly sumptuous bathroom, jacuzzi, vast wardrobes for her mountain of clothes, a home cinema, games room, computer room, a bar with an aquarium with dozens of rare tropical fish, acres of glass and mirrors as always, upholstered walls, peach or white carpets everywhere.

Early in June the Holms were in England for the Epsom Derby, where they joined the Roger Moores and Michael Caines, and the *Sun* reporter Harry Arnold recorded that 'fabulous filly' Joan 'paraded around the paddock [*and*] even the royal party took a good look at the soap star. The Queen checked out her condition through a pair of binoculars and Princess Di joined her mother-in-law in grinning widely at Joan's publicity canter.' Her clothes benefited nowadays from the expert touch of an experienced film dresser, Jaleh Falk, a thirty-five-year-old Persian who persuaded her to buy some outfits from a new South Molton Street couturier, Anthony Price. 'At home in her apartment, without a wig, she was a nice, normal woman and I liked her,' Mrs Falk told me, 'but as soon as she put on her wig and dark glasses she became Alexis and a pain in the arse. She's the most insecure person on this planet and she didn't like it at all when a Lord whom I knew socially came into the shop and started chatting with me. She hated it that I knew him, dropped some clothes deliberately on the floor, crooked her finger at me, and said, "Pick that up, Jaleh," so I said, "Do you want one of your corsets, Miss Collins?" I was never allowed to call her Joan but I wasn't going to have her treat me like that, and two gays in the shop ran over in a tizz to pick up the clothes. I can't say I liked her, and she was so avaricious that I couldn't believe it. We did a shoot for a Littlewoods mail-order catalogue and I had to arrange a bedroom to look like a 1930s boudoir so that she could pose in it in negligées and pyjamas with a glass of champagne. After the shoot she said, "Jaleh, you're such a clever girl: that champagne glass is exactly the same as a set I have at home," and she got her chauffeur to take the glass as well as all the negligées, underwear, pyjamas, even the cheap sheets on the bed and my own iron, pointing at all the stuff like Alexis as he did so. She even wanted to take the bed but I had to tell her it was rented. On another occasion, when we were doing a shoot for an airline, she made me buy a pile of expensive luggage from

Harrods and just took it all afterwards.'

In April, back in LA, Holm had rekindled his affair with Suzanne Anderson, who had recently had a baby boy by another man, and their fling was to continue for three more months. 'It was all very exciting,' she said. 'Peter was a born stud.' When he and Joan flew to the South of France in June to start filming *Monte Carlo* Katy went to school in London and to live there with Joan's London secretary, Cindy Francke, and Holm telephoned Suzanne in Los Angeles and begged her to join him in France. 'He said Joan was being so temperamental on the set that he couldn't go on without me,' she claimed in the *News of the World* a year later. 'Peter paid for me to stay in the fabulous Hotel Negresco in Nice and came to make love to me every day. Sometimes it was in the morning, sometimes the afternoon, and occasionally at night, whenever he could get away, or when Joan was working. The trip was fun, but when I returned alone to Los Angeles I somehow felt so sad that I decided to end things with Peter.' Despite or because of his own infidelity he began to suspect Joan's close friendship with her co-star, George Hamilton, and flew into a jealous rage on the set one day, screaming at Hamilton 'you're a fucking Casanova!' when he saw them kissing rather too enthusiastically during a love scene. He stormed off the set and spent the rest of the day sailing his boat and water-skiing, as he did almost every day while Joan was working up to fifteen hours a day. To publicise *Monte Carlo* Joan gave interviews to David Lewin of the *Daily Mail* and Geraldine Hosier of the *News of the World* and claimed that she had always been a puritan and 'completely faithful' to her husbands. Politely both journalists managed to keep straight faces.

In public she pretended that the marriage was perfect. 'Peter makes me so happy,' she fibbed to Tico Medina of the *News of the World*. 'I admire and love him. Our relationship is a normal and very happy one.' But when they returned to Los Angeles in mid-July they had a huge row, she accused him of being an idle layabout and sleeping for much of the day while she was working her guts out, and he walked out to stay with a friend. She broke down, sobbing, on the *Dynasty* set, and he returned after five days, but already the marriage was on the skids. It did not help that while Joan loved parties, champagne, wine and cigarettes, Holm was a non-smoking teetotaller who drank only Evian water or fruit juice and preferred to stay at home. They fought about everything, especially the renovation work on the new house, arguing even over the height that the aquarium should be. He claimed later that on one occasion she slapped his face and screamed: 'I hate you! Get out of this house!' and she said he had yelled at her and twisted her arm painfully. She became increasingly frightened of him and warned him that if he continued to be so horrible she would divorce him. 'If you divorce me you'll see what'll happen to you,' he said with menace. 'I'm prepared. I've taken the steps and I'm ready to deal with you.' She fled, moving in with Jackie for three days and seeing her doctor because she was suffering palpitations due to her constant stress and anxiety.

There was more unhappiness when her hairdresser and walker Dino Gigante died of AIDS in August, and again when Ron visited his first wife, Anita, in Switzerland, suffered a stroke, and had to be rushed into intensive care at Lausanne University Hospital. Joan paid for two of his sons to fly to Switzerland to see him and for Ron to fly back to Los Angeles, and for the last two months of his life, as he lay dying of liver cancer, she paid all his medical bills, furnished a flat for him near the hospital, and tried to ensure that he was as comfortable as possible. Holm went berserk when he found out. 'Don't waste our money on Ron Kass!' he screamed.

'I'll spend *my* money the way I want to,' she shrieked.

Katy, now fourteen, was devastated to be told that her father had only weeks to live, and Joan's unhappiness was compounded when Ron's parents, Joe and Gertie Kass, criticised her bitterly in a long interview with Neil Wallis of the *Daily Star* at their home in Los Angeles. 'I'm afraid that Katy is the typical Hollywood kid,' said her eighty-four-year-old grandfather, who was still working. 'Practically every kid with parents in showbiz is a mess – and Katy is no exception. Such kids tend to be neglected. They don't get the love they need. They suffer – and Katy is suffering, too.' Katy's seventy-five-year-old grandmother told Wallis that 'She has her career and she is making a lot of money. So she takes care of that.' Joe added sadly that Katy was 'a very shy kid who doesn't say much. And she's lonely, I suppose. She doesn't have too many friends around because they live way up in the hills.' The old man said that there were times when Joan was just like Alexis Carrington 'but she's always been like that, even before she started playing the part ... she's not my favourite person but then she's a lot of people's "not-favourite-person" too. Is she hard? You said it!' He revealed that Joan was never very friendly with him and Gertie: 'She was very hard to get to know all the years she was married to my son.' He said that Jackie was much nicer than Joan: 'Jackie is such a straightforward person. She still wears the dresses she bought a year ago. She doesn't dress up all the time, and she doesn't go out every night to eat the way Joan does. Joan just has to, for some reason. She did it even when she was living with my son and it's no different today.'

Wallis also tracked down and interviewed Lee Bergere, who had played the Carringtons' butler in *Dynasty* for two years and disliked Joan as much as her in-laws did. He claimed that she was always having tantrums on the set. 'Joan is always lashing out at the world,' he said. 'She is filled with anger at the way she believes the world treated her before *Dynasty*. She had to do trashy films like *The Stud* and *The Bitch* to survive. She can't forget that. It haunts her.' On the third day Wallis interviewed Joel Fabiani, an actor who had appeared in two series of *Dynasty*, who reported that Joan was so arrogant, demanding and selfish that many of the cast and crew disliked her intensely and nicknamed her The Cow.

At the beginning of September – just as Joe Collins's breezy autobiography was published in Britain – Katy flew at her own request to London to begin the new term at an English boarding school. She could no longer bear to live with Peter Holm and the tension at home, but her long suffering at his hands was about to come to an end. His cruel cold-heartedness towards Ron was finally to persuade Joan that she could put up with him no longer. She had just about had enough of *Dynasty*, too, and was fed up with the long hours and planned to give it up soon to produce her own films.

Ron Kass died in Los Angeles on 17 October 1986. He was only fifty-one. Joan sobbed when she heard and wept again at his Jewish funeral at Forest Lawn cemetery, where she shared a pew with Katy, who was dressed in black and helpless with tears, and with Ron's ex-wife Anita and his last girlfriend, Anne Wallace. Afterwards Joan sprinkled soil onto his coffin, whispered 'goodbye', and paid for the ceremony. 'Ron was a sweet, lovely, gentle man until he started snorting the nose candy,' she told the *Daily Express* six months later. 'Those days when Katy was born and Sasha and Tara were at school in London were the happiest. The most terrible night of my life was when my stepson,

Robert Kass, told me his father was dying.' By now she had forgiven Ron for all the cruel things he had said about her after their separation. 'He did it for money,' she sighed. 'People will stoop to all sorts of things for money.' She knew only too well that she had stooped pretty low herself at times.

After her dreadful experiences with Peter Holm she was so nostalgic about Ron and all their happy years together that she could barely bring herself to go into the stylish Georgian terrace house they had shared in Mayfair, on which they had lavished £100,000 over the years they had spent together but which had now not been used for three years and had fallen badly into damp disrepair with holes in the walls and wallpaper hanging off them. She became convinced that it was haunted by his ghost and ordered it to be sold as quickly as possible. 'I felt Ron's presence every time I went into the building,' she said. 'It was as if he still lived there.' One of the estate agents reported that Joan's alterations to the house had been 'in incredibly bad taste. To be absolutely frank, Joan ruined what was a perfectly lovely Georgian house by turning it into something more like a gin palace.' The drawing room had been smothered in expensive black velvet, the main bedroom ceiling in naff white satin. There were mirrored walls everywhere, and a film-star sauna. 'It was a weird experience,' recalled the agent, 'as most of their belongings had just stayed totally untouched for years. There were even satin sheets still on the huge double bed Joan and Ron shared – they were crumpled and dirty since no one had been living there for so long. And all these little personal touches gave the house a really creepy feeling.' Considering how short of money Ron had been for so long, it was a mystery why the place had not been sold before. It was bought now for a paltry £30,000 by the Duke of Westminster's Grosvenor Estates and sold eighteen months later for £425,000 to a developer who renovated it tastefully and sold it for £1¼ million in 1989.

There was at least one happy consequence of Ron's death: Joan and Tony Newley realised that life was too short to bear grudges for ever, met for lunch, became friends again, and she was soon reminded that one of the reasons she had loved him was his perky, cockney sense of humour. When she picked him up in a *Dynasty* studio limo he grinned. 'Yeah,' he said, 'I remember when the limo used to be for me.'

In November *Monte Carlo* reached American TV screens but the viewers switched off or over in their millions and for some reason Joan blamed Holm for the flop rather than herself or the director. *Dynasty* was in trouble again, too, plunging to twenty-ninth in the US ratings, and so was Peter Holm. Joan telephoned him on 8 December and asked him to meet her for lunch at the Studio Grill on Santa Monica Boulevard, but when he arrived there was no sign of her. Instead he was approached by an official acting on behalf of the notoriously fearsome Hollywood divorce lawyer Marvin Mitchelson, who served him with an inch-thick pile of divorce papers. Dazed, he returned to the mansion in Cabrillo Drive to find that Joan had moved in at last and to be greeted by a team of security men who refused to let him in even to pick up his toothbrush or passport and who were throwing all his expensive clothes and shoes carelessly into the back of a pick-up truck. Another security expert was changing all the locks and the code for the electric gates. Stunned, and accompanied by his twenty-seven-year-old personal assistant, Jim Garay, who reckoned generously that Peter needed him now more than Joan did, Holm returned to the house in Bowmont Drive, where he told the Press that he loved Joan deeply and hoped for a reconciliation.

Garay, who had worked for the Holms for nine months, was convinced that Peter really did love Joan. 'I grew to like both of them enormously,' he told the *News of the World* magazine. 'In her divorce papers the reasons Joan gave for seeking an annulment were alleged fraud and mismanagement. And she also claimed she feared for her life. How she could make such claims I do not know. One of the things that I would like stated is that Joan was unappreciative of what Peter had done for her financially. I could be completely misled, but I think he was just doing his best to protect her so she did not get ripped off. I don't think she really knew how much work and effort he put in on her behalf. The original accusation from Joan was that there was a missing million dollars [about £660,000]. As the matter goes on, I think she will come to realise that all the money has been properly spent. Peter did collect a fee of nearly twenty per cent of Joan's income, which gave him nearly a million dollars last year. But this was the figure agreed formally between him and Joan and a very normal percentage for a business manager who also acted as executive producer for her.' So what went wrong, if Holm was not entirely to blame? 'My own view is that the marriage got lost in the responsibilities of one being a major world television star and the other being her business manager,' said

Garay. 'I don't think Peter could turn off from the business and I don't believe she could ever turn off from being a star. And that, as a man who knows them both, is very, very sad.'

Under Californian law divorcing couples were normally forced to split their wealth 50:50 unless they had signed a prenuptial agreement, as the Holms had, but Joan's first plan was to avoid honouring even that by having the marriage annulled on the grounds of irreconcilable differences and fraud, which would mean in effect that it had never taken place and would therefore render invalid the prenuptial agreement. The prospect of having to pay Holm twenty per cent, let alone half of everything she had, was horrifying because by now, on top of all her acting and writing, she was making TV commercials for Revlon, Sanyo kitchen appliances, Canada Dry soft drinks, and Tequila. She had also launched her own ranges of cheap jewellery, hats, spectacles and home videos and was about to branch out into fashion, nightwear and lingerie, and she made dozens of personal appearances at £5,000 a time, though it is fair to say that Holm had negotiated fiercely almost every one of those lucrative deals for her and undoubtedly deserved a slice of the action. In December the *Daily Mail* calculated that she had probably made about £7 million in the past year, but even Holm estimated that it was more like £3½ million [£7¼ million].

The day after he was served with the divorce documents Joan broke down and wept on the *Dynasty* set, told her colleagues she was getting divorced, and filming was stopped for the day. Mitchelson sent workmen to Cabrillo Drive to break down the door into Peter's computer room and remove boxes full of his papers and secret printouts, Joan hired a burly armed bodyguard to protect her, and in London her father said happily: 'I'm delighted the marriage is over. He's a bum. He was no good for Joan.' Katy, too, was ecstatic that she was rid of her nightmare at last. On 12 December a Los Angeles judge granted Joan a restraining order forbidding Holm to approach her even by telephone, or her children, staff, or the mansion in Cabrillo Drive, but he was comforted by the arrival from London of Madeleine Curtis, who had flown to Los Angeles to look after him and cheer him up. He also tried to revive his affair with Suzanne Anderson, telling her that he had finally left Joan and wanted her back, but she too had had enough of him, was to marry another man the following year and to have a second child.

To celebrate her freedom Joan threw a huge party and David Niven

Jr presented her with a T-shirt emblazoned with the slogan HOLMLESS, and on 30 January there was a hostile truce during which representatives of both parties collected legally agreed items and records while Joan flew to Paris to join Leslie Bricusse's fifty-sixth birthday party. Back in London and at a loose end, she telephoned her property developer friend Charles Delevingne and said she would like to meet some attractive, lighthearted young guys with whom to have a bit of fun while she was in town. He invited her to lunch at his office in the Fulham Road on 3 February along with two possible candidates, John Lorimer and Bill Wiggins, telling the men that he wanted them to meet a beautiful, unmarried, twenty-three-year-old millionairess. Forty-year-old Wiggins – handsome, manly and blue-eyed – arrived forty minutes late, panting after a hard game of squash but still charming, mischievous and smiley. Joan, who was perched sideways on a bannister, took one look at him and went weak at the knees. He took one look at her, recognised her instantly, and thought she was stunning. 'I'm sorry,' he said wickedly. 'I didn't quite catch your name.' She giggled and they kept laughing for two hours, all the way through lunch. By the end of the meal she was hooked. To make their meeting even more perfect, she discovered that his friends called him 'Bungalow' Bill because it was said that he had nothing much up top but a hell of a lot down below. After all the misery and traumas of her failed fourth marriage naughty, jolly, virile young Bungalow Bill was just the tonic she needed.

CHAPTER SIXTEEN

WIGGY AND WIFFY-WOO

{ 1987 }

Bill Wiggins was just the age that Joan liked her men: a juicy thirteen years younger, like Peter Holm. He had been born in Kent the youngest of a builder's four children, given the names Herbert William, and his family and some of his friends still called him Herbert or Herbie though most of them, including Joan, called him Wiggy. He had been educated at Sutton Valence boarding school, a less than top-notch boys' establishment near Maidstone, where he was considered to be not very bright but distinguished as a crack shot in the cadet force. He had left school at seventeen with only four O levels and without attempting A levels, and now ran a small property company, Ironjade, from a cluttered little office in Chelsea, which was sufficiently successful for him to live in a small mews house in Pooles Lane, near Chelsea Harbour, drive a Porsche, and whisk girls off for sexy holidays in the South of France, the Caribbean and Swiss ski resorts.

He was a roguish, love-'em-and-leave-'em, heavy-drinking, man-about-town bachelor whose friends nicknamed him Bonking Billy as well as Bungalow Bill because he had enjoyed dozens of affairs, was always game for another, and was said to have bedded a girl just fifteen minutes after meeting her. One of his girlfriends, Caroline Gould, a thirty-year-old model, told the *News of the World* that when they had first gone to bed together she had been 'shocked at what a big man he was but I must say he's a very good lover. Even when he was drunk out of his skull on wine or champagne he could always make love. He always wanted to do it twice a day.' She called his favourite organ 'Wiffy-Woo' and its impressive size inspired his friend Nigel Dempster, the *Daily Mail* gossip columnist, to invent his Bungalow Bill nickname after they had been playing a game of squash. 'It was a very hot summer's day,' Wiggy told me, 'and we got out of the shower and I was standing there, head covered by a towel, and a girl walked past the door, which happened to be open to let a bit of draught in. "Hello, Wiggy," she said. Dempster was amazed. "How the hell did she recognise you with your head covered?" he said. He thought it was very funny and the next time he wrote about me he came up with Bungalow Bill.' I asked Wiggy if he really did have an enormous penis. 'Well, it's not small!' he said, and roared with laughter. After lunch, for the purpose of research, I followed him to the gents' lavatory but at the *moment critique* could not bring myself to look.

Wiggy thought Joan was the funniest woman he had ever met as well as quick, brazen and gloriously good-looking, and he loved her starry aura and zest for life. She in turn fancied him like mad and arranged for a mutual friend to invite them both to a dinner party where they barely spoke to anyone else and hardly stopped laughing. Bill cheered her up immensely, distracted her from brooding over the divorce, and at the end of the evening she asked him to take her out alone the following night. He agreed, but was then invited by a friend, Bertie Brookes, to dinner that night. Wiggy said he had a dinner date already. 'Bring her too,' said Brookes, expecting him to turn up with some blonde bimbo, but when he arrived with Joan, Brookes was stunned and one male guest jumped up and cried excitedly: 'Fuck me, it's Joan Rivers!' Joan was such fun that Wiggy's friends took to her immediately and she enjoyed the sort of ordinary, unglitzy evening she had not known for years. She found Bill's unpretentious, celebrity-free milieu hugely refreshing, though there was one uncomfortable moment when one of the women, who had clearly had a drink or two, started making snide remarks about old hags who tried to cling on to their looks and did not know how to grow old gracefully. 'It's all right, dear,' said Joan crisply, 'I can remember the first time I had a drink myself.' After dinner they went to Tramp, danced until the early hours, and when Wiggy took her back to her suite at the Ritz they became lovers.

A few days later she flew to Los Angeles and asked him to come and stay there with her soon. A wonderfully lively, carefree new romance had begun, but despite Wiggy's fling with Joan he was still dallying with his TV producer girlfriend Sue Birbeck, a former live-in lover who had wanted in vain to marry him, and Lindy Field, a dusky, thirty-two-year-old former Miss Barbados whose main claim to fame was that she had recently had a fling with the English cricketer Ian Botham.

When Wiggy's eighty-five-year-old father heard that his son was having an affair with Joan Collins he was shocked. 'What the devil do you think you're doing going out with this tramp from Hollywood?' he exploded. The shock was too much for him. 'I think that finished him off and he decided he'd had enough of this world,' Wiggy told me. 'He died soon afterwards and Joan sent a great big wreath to his funeral.' Bill's elder brother Peter was just as unimpressed as their father. Wiggy's relationship with Joan 'will soon fizzle out because he's so girl-mad', Peter told the *Sun*. 'Joan would be very foolish to hang her hat on him because he's always been the same and will never change his ways. He will never settle down. I don't know of anyone who he has even thought of marrying. All he has ever done is chase girls. It's been his life-long hobby and he's never really been interested in anything else. When he was a kid the big joke used to be that he was the first heterosexual at his boarding school! Basically he's never grown up.'

Back in LA the war with Peter Holm resumed. Early on the morning of 6 February Joan's agent Ben Casey turned up at Bowmont Drive with three armed security men to seize more goods and documents from Holm, who started video-taping the intruders, and when Jim Garay turned off the electricity to prevent them driving out of the electric gates they simply smashed their vehicles through them. Six days later Joan and Peter were facing each other in a Los Angeles court, where he demanded to be given £35,000 a month living expenses [£60,500], the Bowmont Drive house, the villa in the South of France, his BMW car, the documents Casey had seized, and that Joan should be sent to jail for ten days for contempt of court because she was refusing to return the documents. She in turn wanted the £1 million [£1.73 million] that she claimed he had stolen, the furniture at Bowmont Drive, the Christmas decorations, even the groceries in the fridge at Bowmont Drive. Eventually proceedings descended into an undignified squabble over minor possessions – desk lamps, wastepaper baskets, video tapes, CDs, indoor plants – and Holm even demanded custody of a drawerful of screws. 'That's the last screw he'll be getting from me!' snapped Joan. In the end the court decided that Joan could keep the French villa but that Peter should have the car, so he promptly increased his demand for maintenance to £50,000 a month [£86,500].

A few days later she flew back to London and spent much of the time with Wiggy, and when she returned to LA he followed her two weeks later, paying for his own ticket, to stay with her for a fortnight. When he arrived he was greeted at the airport by a barrage of photographers, moved into the mansion at Cabrillo Drive, and suddenly found himself in a world of startling opulence and glamour. The house was fantastic enough but Joan also threw a party that first night at which she introduced him to Linda Evans, Ryan O'Neal, Farrah Fawcett and Angie Dickinson. Joan wined and dined him in the smartest restaurants every night – Spago's, Morton's, Le Dome – and introduced him to numerous other friends, including the cast of *Dynasty*. She even encouraged him to become an actor, introduced him to her agent, told him he had a wonderful voice, arranged for him to have a screen test for a TV commercial, and there was talk of him appearing in an episode of *Dynasty*. She took him to Swifty Lazar's post-Oscars party, where he sat next to James Stewart and chatted with Lauren Bacall and Shirley MacLaine. He would have been less than human had he not revelled in all this unaccustomed luxury, the first-class travel, the best hotels and restaurants, the famous friends, being treated like royalty wherever he went, but he was always to deny that he was ever Joan's kept man because sometimes he paid for himself and much of the travel and other perks came free because he was with her. Towards the end of March she returned to London to present an award at a BAFTA ceremony, attend a royal film première, and see Wiggy again. They went together to Paris for Yves St Laurent's fortieth anniversary party, she decided that she would like to take a break from work for a few months and spend more time with him in London, and she rented for £1,700 a week [£2,941] a six-bedroom Mayfair apartment in Mount Street for herself, Katy, a nanny and a maid.

When she flew back to Los Angeles on 24 March for the next divorce hearing she became enraged at Heathrow Airport when two British Airways check-in girls told her that she was too late and that her and her secretary's first-class seats had been given to another couple on the standby list, the film director David Puttnam and his wife. First reports said that Joan had been five minutes late but BA later claimed that she had been thirteen minutes late and had arrived at the check-in desk just thirty minutes before take-off. Joan shrieked that she had been flying with BA an average of twice a month for six years, and a senior ground hostess, Patsy Butcher, was summoned to tell her that the rules stipulated that if a first-class passenger had still not checked in forty-five minutes before take-off her seat could be sold to someone else. Joan and her secretary would have to travel in Club Class instead. 'You fucking old cow!' shrieked Joan. Miss Butcher – who was fifty-three, the same age as Joan – walked away. 'I don't take that sort of language from anyone,' she said, 'especially not from you, *young* lady.' Joan burst into angry tears, swore loudly that she would never fly by BA again, and when an official tried to calm her and called her 'Joan' she snapped: 'My name is Miss Collins!' Eventually she accepted four club-class seats so that she and her secretary could spread themselves out, but she was still angry, loud and aggressive. 'How the hell can I stretch out here?' she complained. Other passengers reported that in fact she was able to stretch out across the two seats and sleep very well but she was still complaining loudly when she reached LA. 'It was a disgrace, a damned disgrace,' she fumed. 'I've never been so humiliated in my life.' She demanded that the two check-in girls at Heathrow should be disciplined and instructed her agent to approach the American airlines Pan-Am and TWA to see what they would pay her to advertise their flights instead.

To be fair, her arrogant Alexis-like behaviour was probably fuelled as much by stress as by self-importance, for she had to appear on the set of *Dynasty* at 6 a.m. the next morning and again in the Los Angeles Supreme Court three days later to suffer the indignity of having to produce a list of all the dates over the past three and a half years that she and Peter Holm had *not* slept together – an impossible and humiliating task. He was now demanding £53,000 a month – £640,000 a year [£1.1 million] – because, he said, she had accustomed him to living the high life, spending more than £13,000 a month [£22,500] on clothes, and living in six-room suites at five-star hotels. Joan was also involved in three other worrying court cases: two involving the illicit sale of pictures of their wedding, and a third in which a cheeky photographer was suing her for $1 million for restricting his right to take pictures of the wedding and so depriving him of the chance of making a fortune out of them.

The chairman of British Airways, Lord King, tried to mollify her by sending her a huge bouquet and a handwritten letter of apology, and Bill Wiggins flew again by British Airways to Los Angeles on 30

March to join her for a week. But she returned to Britain by TWA and then, when she was meant to fly back to LA by Pan-Am, she failed high-handedly to check in for her flight at all or to cancel the two first-class seats she had booked. 'We are a little put out that she didn't let us know she wouldn't want the seats,' said a Pan-Am spokesman but they still refunded her money. Joan eventually issued a statement regretting her tirade and admitting that she would have to continue flying by BA because 'Concorde to New York is the only game in town'.

On 1 April she dispatched Marvin Mitchelson to Paris to bid on her behalf in a sale of the late Duchess of Windsor's fabulous jewels, where he bought for her a diamond and sapphire pendant for £210,000 [£363,000]. Ten days later she and Wiggins returned to London by TWA and she moved for three months into the flat in appropriately named Mount Street and relished the chance to relax a little at last and enjoy going to the West End theatre, the National Gallery, Christie's and Sotheby's, weekends in the South of France.

One night soon afterwards the traffic around Joan's new flat was so heavy that Wiggy took her back to his little mews house in Pooles Lane, which was part of an eighteen-dwelling development. 'As we drove in through the automatic gates,' he told me, 'Joan said "you *are* modest, Wiggy: it's *huge*." She thought that I owned all eighteen houses! The next morning a friend of mine, a very big man, was in the kitchen when she went down to make some tea, looking tiny in her dressing gown. He recognised her. "What the hell are you doing here?" he said, and she said: "well, he wouldn't come back to my place."

'We had a *fantastic* time together,' Wiggy went on. 'We had a riot. We were a great team and she certainly did a lot for me. I became a very well-known person and it was great. I loved it and it opened doors for me, and I had a great time with people like Roger Moore and Michael Caine. They were really nice. Everything was fine all the time that things were going Joan's way but she can turn if they're not going her way and sometimes she had a spiteful tongue. If something upsets her she can be extremely cruel.'

As their affair developed he discovered a much softer, vulnerable side to her character. He saw her often first thing in the morning and was charmed to see how girlish she looked underneath all the superstar clag she had worn in public for so long. Under the strain and worry of the divorce and the fun of being with a carefree man like him, she started to drink much more than before and became quite chubby and her face bloated. She was also always self-conscious about her thin hair and deeply hurt when one newspaper claimed that Wiggy was so turned off by it that he made her wear a wig in bed. He denied it, but in Monaco in June she read an item in the *People* in which two women claimed that while she was dancing energetically at Tramp one night her hairpiece had slipped and exposed a 'large, bald area', and she was so upset by this story that she cried for ages. She could be over-sensitive and highly emotional, Wiggins told David Jones of the *Daily Mail* nine years later, but also so self-important that she refused to believe she was ever wrong and needed desperately to be noticed. As they left a film première one night Joan suddenly panicked when she saw the crowds outside. 'Oh my God,' she cried, 'there's no one here to protect us.' Wiggy told her not to be silly, to take his arm and all would be well, but she shouted and demanded a police escort across the road. 'The moment she started panicking it was like a jungle,' said Wiggy, 'and the whole crowd stampeded towards her. I couldn't help thinking that she had to have this crowd reaction.' Yet in New York once she avoided attention by wearing no make-up and dressing as an old woman. 'That's the contradictory aspect of her personality,' he said. 'She doesn't want attention but she craves it.'

Another contradiction was that although she could be extremely generous she could also be cruel. One evening she gave a party where one of the guests brought along a friend, an Italian lawyer, Carlo Colombotti, a quiet man who was invited to stay for a couple of nights. Colombotti was the sort of man who preferred to listen rather than to be the heart of the party, and three days later Joan suddenly exploded: 'Listen, who the fuck are you? You've been at my house for three nights and you've hardly said anything.' Colombotti was deeply hurt, said Wiggy, and left immediately. He also claimed that Joan could be dreadfully arrogant on the *Dynasty* set and used to sneer at Linda Evans. 'Joan is such a mixture of fragile ego and insecurity,' said Wiggy. 'She wanted me to become more famous, but then didn't like it if some of the limelight descended on me.' In a restaurant in the South of France he was once mobbed by a group of young girls asking for his autograph. No longer the centre of attention, Joan announced that they were going, *now*, and when he continued signing she snapped:

'I don't *believe* it. That shit Wiggins is signing autographs and keeping me *waiting*.' He told Jones: 'Joan didn't like being upstaged by anyone and I suspect that I was the only person she had met for a long time who had told her what I thought was wrong with her. I'd say: "You can't talk to waiters like that." I think in a certain way she liked that. She liked to be dominated – but only for ninety-five per cent of the time and when it suited her. Because of me she went through a period of being treated by a group of people as a normal human. After Los Angeles, that was refreshing. And whatever her attitude now I can tell you that she had one of the best times of her life when she was with me. Drunken and debauched, but fun. We were rarely in bed before 3.30 a.m. and Joan loved it. She told me she loved me many times, and I told her I loved being with her. I'm not sure I knew what love was, to be honest. I was fond of her. She made me laugh, and that was enough.'

Her vulnerability did not stop him having affairs with other women even when she was in London. One was a beautiful, thirty-two-year-old blonde model, Jilly Johnson. Joan tried to be philosophical about her when the *News of the World* outed him. 'Boys will be boys,' she said. 'He was at a friend's stag night and bumped into his old flame. He was very drunk' – but she struggled to come to terms with Wiggy's insistence that he should be free to sleep with anyone he liked. She in turn embarked on a gentle, platonic relationship with a twenty-eight-year-old art dealer, Robin Hurlstone, a very tall, elegant, handsome, blond whom she had met at a London dinner party just a day after meeting Bill Wiggins in February. Discreetly they lunched and dined together regularly and after months of friendship were eventually to become lovers.

Meanwhile Wiggy revelled in some aspects of his new fame. It helped his business and he persuaded Joan to join him in investing £100,000 in a Knightsbridge bed-and-breakfast joint that he proposed to turn into a luxury hotel. He was invited to all sorts of exclusive social occasions, to play in celebrity tournaments, and to become a Radio 2 disc jockey for a day, but he was often irritated when his every move was reported, photographers stalked him, and strangers kept asking for his autograph. 'Nine-tenths of the time it's very tiresome,' he said. 'I can't get any peace and quiet. I can't even speak to a female friend without her being listed as my next date.'

In May they flew to New York – by British Airways Concorde – to deliver to Simon and Schuster the typescript of the novel she had been writing on and off for four years, *Prime Time*. Her editor, Michael Korda, swore that every word of the book was hers: 'There is no ghostwriter, no helper, no hidden person. Her concentration is remarkable, given all the things going on in her life.' It would in fact have been much better had she had some serious editorial help because it was a dreadfully amateurish schlock novel, but because of her fame an English publisher, Rosie Cheetham of Century Hutchinson, bought the British rights for a huge advance of £360,000 [£623,000] without even reading the book. 'You've got to remember that at this time Joan was probably the most famous woman after the Queen, mobbed wherever she went,' Mrs Cheetham, now Rosie de Courcy, told me, 'and I thought: "My word, this is going to be huge." When her agent, Swifty Lazar, came to London I went to see him at his hotel. He was a terrifying legend, this absolutely tiny, *minute* little person in a silk dressing gown, like the Mekon in the *Dan Dare* comic strip. He had huge, black-rimmed spectacles like the bottom of jam jars and a completely bald head. He had never heard of Century Hutchinson but he growled, "OK, $750,000 and it's yours." I said, "What, just like that?" and he said, "Yes."'

When Jackie protested that Joan was invading her territory as a novelist Joan replied: 'Come off it. You started your career acting when I was already doing it, so why shouldn't I have a bash at a bestseller?' Michael Korda told Rosie that Joan was 'a warmer person than Jackie and a better writer', but she told me: 'When I met Jackie I thought she was terribly nice, instantly warm, instantly fun.'

Towards the end of May Joan and Wiggy took ten of her family and friends – Tara and her boyfriend, Elizabeth Taylor and *her* boyfriend George Hamilton, Vivienne Ventura, Regine – to a five-star hotel in Marrakesh for a long weekend to celebrate her fifty-fourth birthday. Wiggy wore a black T-shirt with the slogan MEN OF KENT DO IT BETTER and they canoodled like honeymooners, kissing on the dance floor, holding hands everywhere, nuzzling, gazing into each other's eyes, though Joan did stamp back to their room one day when he spent ten minutes chatting with a young blonde by the swimming pool.

Meanwhile, back in Los Angeles, Marvin Mitchelson appeared in court yet again to claim that Joan could not possibly pay Holm what he wanted because, he said, she owed the taxman £700,000 [£1,211,000]. In return Holm claimed that he was still waiting for Joan to return his BMW. When she put the Bowmont Drive house up for sale, where he had been living since they had separated, he took a lot of her furniture, paintings and books with him, threatened to open the house to tourists, flew to London and told the Press: 'I'm here to haunt the bitch.' With the agreement of an American judge Joan hired two private eyes to follow him everywhere to try to track down her possessions, and in July there was yet another court hearing, this time when Mitchelson applied successfully for an order for Holm to be evicted from the house because it had been sold to a film producer for £450,000. When police and bailiffs arrived to throw him out he barricaded himself in, threatened to shoot them, and yelled: 'Nobody's coming in here! There'll be a bloodbath!' But soon he surrendered and shouted as he left the house, 'This Bungalow Bill Wiggins character can't hold a candle to me!' A local TV station put him up in an hotel for the night but he told the *Sunday Mirror*: 'I don't know what I'm going to do. I have nowhere to live. Joan is behaving in real life far worse than Alexis on television. I think the role has affected her.' At a later hearing he demonstrated outside the court by waving a placard that read pathetically: JOAN, YOU HAVE OUR $2.5 MILLION, 13,000-SQ. FT HOME WHICH WE BOUGHT FOR CASH DURING OUR MARRIAGE. I AM NOW HOMELESS. HELP! And so the undignified squabbling went on and on.

After Marrakesh, Joan and Wiggy flew to the South of France to spend the weekend at her villa in Port Grimaud and returned in time to sparkle on 3 June at the Epsom Derby with Roger Moore and Sir Gordon White. A fortnight later they were at Ascot races, where Joan was barred from the Royal Enclosure because her application form had not arrived, though she managed to nobble Princess Diana for a few minutes in the Turf Club bar. Then it was off with Wiggy and Katy to the South of France again to celebrate Katy's fifteenth birthday; back to London for a royal film première with Princess Diana; and off again with Wiggy and his friend Malcolm Fraser to the South of France, where she hired armed guards in case Peter should turn up in search of revenge.

In mid-July Joan flew back to Los Angeles to face yet another court appearance, during which she claimed that all four of her husbands had bled her dry and that none had ever been able to support her

– forgetting that she had depended entirely on Tony Newley for years when the children were small – and she broke down and sobbed so loudly that the judge called for a recess. Peter claimed truthfully that when he had met her she had had few assets, was living in a heavily mortgaged house and owed twelve years of back taxes, but that after three years of his handling her affairs and managing her career she was rich, owned three unmortgaged houses, and was earning much more than ever before – all thanks to his skilful negotiations. He did however admit the next day that she had always paid for everything and that he had spent £812,000 [£1½ million] in just thirteen months.

In court the next day it was just like Joan's first episode of *Dynasty* when a surprise witness was suddenly called to the stand: Peter's mistress Romina Danielson gave evidence that they had been having an affair for more than two years until just two weeks previously, and said she thought she was pregnant. She broke down, sobbed, collapsed, and had to be carried out on a stretcher. Nor did it help that back in London Wiggy was misbehaving again with Jilly Johnson. Joan retaliated by canoodling with a thirty-eight-year-old Spanish lawyer, Spencer Seguero, but her love life had by now become such a public joke that the *News of the World* reported that the Duke of Westminster had named his new spaniel puppy 'Joan Collins' because 'she's always on her back'. Even her old friend Paul Newman was chuckling publicly about her promiscuity: when he launched his Newman's Own Old-Fashioned Roadside Virgin Lemonade that summer he claimed that 'Joan Collins was restored to virginity after drinking four quarts of it'.

In August she returned to *Dynasty* for what she said would be her final series. The US ratings had plummeted so far that it was now wallowing at number thirty-two. Not surprisingly: one recent ridiculous storyline had Fallon Carrington Colby abducted by a UFO and impregnated by an alien.

On 25 August Joan was granted her divorce at last. 'I don't want any more husbands,' she said with relief. 'What I need is a wife.' But the nightmare was not yet over: Holm was still demanding alimony of £53,000 [£91,700] a month, yet another court hearing was fixed for 7 October, and now he was threatening to write an explicitly sexy book about their life together. Eventually, on 2 November, his claim was dismissed and Joan finally had to give him £100,000 [£173,000] and the car. 'I will say this for Peter Holm,' she told Valerie Grove of *The*

Times three years later. 'Even though I ended up paying him $180,000 that was minuscule compared with what he'd done for me in the way of good deals in real estate and mini-series.' He had, in fact, made her £1.5 million out of *Sins* alone, so she could perhaps have been more generous towards him and forgiving than she was. She did not always treat her ex-husbands or boyfriends kindly.

In the first week of September *Sins* appeared on British television and Joan flew to London to promote the series. Reporters asked her about the qualities she sought in men. 'Humour,' she said, 'kindness, caring about other people, a sense of dignity about their own profession whatever it is, a lack of vanity.' Then she giggled. 'Sounds just like Bill Wiggins!' Less amusing was the reaction of the public to the first episode of the series and its gruesome scenes of children being tortured, a young girl being raped by Nazi thugs and a pregnant woman murdered, especially since it was broadcast before the adult watershed at 9 p.m. and only three weeks after the Hungerford massacre, when a gunman had strolled through a small town in Berkshire slaughtering sixteen people.

Back in California the earth moved for Joan on the morning of 1 October when Los Angeles was hit by an earthquake that threw her out of bed, lasted for two minutes, killed seven people and injured a hundred and eighty-seven. She was terrified and fled with her staff into the garden, but Wiggy was undeterred and joined her there again for two weeks. At the end of the month she and Katy were back in London for her father's eighty-fifth birthday. No matter how much she had always blamed Joe for being an unaffectionate male chauvinist pig, she loved him dearly until the end of his life. A few days later she was jetting off to Mexico for the Acapulco Film Festival, where she flounced out of a grand dinner because she said she was utterly bored by the people at her table, among them the President of Mexico and the opera singer Placido Domingo, who was said to have remarked afterwards: 'She's a bitch, darling. What more can you expect?' She returned to Los Angeles and then to London to join Wiggy and the Duchess of York at a charity ball. At fifty-four her constant travelling and stamina were as astonishing as her smooth looks, which kept the gossips searching for any face-lift scars. Journalists continued to ask her to admit that she had had plastic surgery but she always denied it and threatened to sue the *Sun* and the *News of the World* when they claimed in November that she had recently paid a Californian surgeon £9,000 to have her breasts enhanced with silicon implants. 'I'm more against plastic surgery than anything else I can think of,' she told the *Daily Mail*. 'It's abhorrent to me,' and both papers retracted their stories, apologised, and paid several thousand pounds in damages.

Her affair with Wiggy was dwindling and she began to accept that it could not last for ever. 'Eventually I would basically like *The Mate*,' she told Rodney Tyler, 'the person who is there for ever, the friend, • the lover, the one you live with and share everything with. For the time being I have accepted that The Mate is not to be, but that does not mean to say I would like to be without a mate at sixty-five. I know from my track record that my problem is that I expect far too much from a man and that I have compromised in all the long-term relationships I have had and then I have ended up hating myself for compromising. In time I hope the sort of relationship I shall need later on will create itself. In the meantime I am giving myself eleven years for it to happen!'

She spent Christmas in England with Joe, Irene and her children, and then flew with Wiggy to Acapulco to stay briefly with her hugely wealthy oilman friend Ricky di Portanova and his wife Sandra at their magnificent cliffside mansion that overlooked the bay and was serviced by eighty-four live-in staff. Many people believed that Joan wanted to marry Wiggy, but he told me that they had never discussed marriage. 'I'd decided that I was going off with my friends to South Africa and she wanted me to stay with her in Acapulco,' he said. 'Things were getting a bit strained and there were lots of other people in my life that were younger, and I said to her: "Look, I think you're absolutely amazing, I'm very fond of you and I always want to remain fond of you, but I think it's time we cooled our relationship. I'm going to spend two or three weeks in South Africa and whatever happens I'd like to remain your friend." There were a lot of tears and she said she wanted to continue a much more serious relationship, but marriage was never discussed. When I left the next morning she was in tears, and I said, "I'll be back in three weeks and we'll see one another again and see how things go on," and she said, "I can't believe what you're doing. Without me you're nothing." I'll never forget those words. I told her that I had been nothing all my life, so nothing would change. That's what she was like when she wasn't getting her own way, and she'd got used to getting her own way.'

Nine years later Wiggy told David Jones of the *Daily Mail* that he had explained to Joan that there was no long-term future for them 'because if I ever settled down it was probably going to be with someone who could give me children. I told Joan that I wasn't prepared to play a Mr Collins role for ever, that I wanted to retain my own identity, and I thought it was time to change our relationship, though I would always want to be her friend. When the time came for me to leave she was holding on to my shirt as we walked up the steps outside the villa where my courtesy car was waiting. "I can't understand you," she wept. "Why would you do this? With me you can have anything you want in your life. Without me you're nothing." Then I walked down the steps and our relationship was effectively over.'

Joan's version of the end of the affair was different. 'He was terribly good for me as the antithesis of Peter – outgoing, loved people and parties,' she admitted to Jean Rook of the *Daily Express*, 'but if I'm with a bloke I'm with a bloke. And he'd better be with me. If he goes chasing every bit of skirt around he gets the elbow.' Gallantly Wiggy allowed her to claim that she had dumped him. 'I couldn't give a damn about the fact that she says she broke up with me,' he told me, 'but it's completely untrue. *I* broke up with *her*.' Joan's revenge was to claim dismissively that she had had a fling with Wiggy only because she had been deeply unhappy after the end of her marriage, had started to drink too much, and her judgement had been affected.

Wiggy flew to Cape Town and Joan went off to Barbados to welcome the New Year with her still-platonic young admirer Robin Hurlstone, who was staying with Carole and Anthony Bamford at their superb house on the stylish west coast of the island and had asked them to invite her too. At twenty-eight he was very much younger than even Holm and Wiggy – twenty-five years younger than Joan and young enough to be her son – but they had been seeing a lot of each other throughout her affair with Wiggy and Joan without a man was like a bike without a pump. On New Year's Eve, at the future American ambassador Pamela Harriman's party, Joan was asked to do the traditional countdown to midnight, glanced at Robin, and suddenly wondered whether maybe he was The Mate she had been seeking all her life. They were to live together for the next thirteen years.

CHAPTER SEVENTEEN

ROBIN AND *PRIME TIME*

{ 1988–1989 }

Robin Hurlstone was the most unlikely of all Joan's many lovers. Not only was he twenty-five years younger, he had also twelve years previously lived for eighteen months in London, Suffolk and Paris with the notoriously dissolute, homosexual, seventh Marquess of Bristol, who was to boast of having enjoyed two thousand rent boys, whom he called 'twinkies'. Bristol was an alcoholic drug addict who had pumped himself so full of booze, cocaine and heroin that he was to squander his entire inheritance of £30 million before dying in 1999 of multiple organ failure at the age of forty-four. 'I was in the same house as his brother Nicholas at Eton,' Hurlstone told Anthony Haden-Guest for an article in the *Observer* in 2006. 'He looked at me and told Nicholas: "He's the one I want." I was eighteen, he was twenty-one.' One of their friends told the *Sunday Express* in 1996: 'I have little doubt that Robin was Bristol's great love. I don't know if it was returned, but when Robin went his own way, Bristol was devastated.'

At Eton Robin had been a pretty boy, 'very well-dressed and fastidious about his appearance' one of his friends told the *Daily Mail*. 'But he was never a physical person. He rarely played sports.' In his teens he had inherited a fortune and an estate in Wales, and he had become a dealer in pictures – not antiques, as the gossip columnist Nigel Dempster reported in a cheeky joke about Joan's age. Robin and Joan shared a strong and similar sense of humour but otherwise he seemed to be the complete opposite of boozy, sporty, extrovert Wiggins, who claimed that he and Joan had used to laugh at Robin. 'I certainly did not regard him as a ladies' man,' he said. The gossips whispered that Joan's relationship with Robin was friendly rather than sexual. 'He was a very kind, gentle character but I'd say that he was Joan's walker, not her boyfriend,' I was told by Joan's Persian couturier, Maryam Rokny-Owji, who had recently been introduced to her and was to design more than two hundred outfits for her over the next twelve years.

It would be easy to understand if Joan chose after Holm and Wiggy to settle exhaustedly for an affectionate chum rather than a lover, but Jackie believed that theirs was a genuine romance, and one of Robin's friends told me that he had not had an affair with another man for many years and had indeed had several affairs with women. Yet the tittle-tattle about his sexual orientation was so widespread that when he and Joan started living together she made a point of insisting publicly that he was her lover 'in every way', although thirteen years later, when their affair was over, she told Lynda Lee-Potter that they had never actually lived together and that although they had shared a bed 'there's sharing a bed and sharing a bed'. This was 'a complete lie', one of Robin's friends told me. 'He kept his flat in South Kensington but spent almost every night with Joan. She denied it only to fend off any claim that Robin might make as her common-law husband and to ease what Sacha described as "her suffocating guilt" about the way she ended their affair. In fact Joan asked Robin to marry her as early as March 1988, just a few weeks after their affair began, and she kept on nagging him about it for years. She was amazed when he wouldn't marry her. It was the only thing they ever really argued about but he could never see the point of marriage since obviously they couldn't have children.'

In London she continued to see Wiggy occasionally, in Los Angeles she dated George Hamilton, who had split up with Elizabeth Taylor, and it was reported that she enjoyed brief romances with three other men before settling for Robin. One was an American oil tycoon, James Letsos, of whom she said to a friend: 'I think this is it. I think the world of James – and you can't say he wants my money.' Then came a forty-two-year-old Greek, an electronics multi-millionaire appropriately named Alexis, Alexis Mardas, who had been a friend of John Lennon and Ron Kass. Then a friend of Wiggy's who had holidayed with them in the South of France, the thrice-married property developer Malcolm Fraser, although later Joan denied that they had been lovers and all three may have simply been camouflage to protect Robin.

In January she flew to Milan to do a TV interview and was accused by an Italian immigration official of having altered her passport to show her date of birth as 1938, rather than 1933, so as to suggest that she was only forty-nine rather than fifty-four. 'Your discourtesy is devastating,' she said, and produced a driving licence with the same spurious date. It was on this trip that she and Robin became lovers at last and he introduced her to his old friend Gianni Versace, the most generous of couturiers, whom she came to adore and who was to give her armfuls of fantastic clothes over the years. But she was cross again to read in the Press that both Holm and Wiggy were planning to write about their romances with her. Wiggy was said to be asking £100,000 and Holm to be hawking around American publishers the synopsis for a book for which he wanted £416,000 [£790,000]. Wiggy's project was 'in very bad taste', Joan told the *Daily Mail*. 'I had been hoping that we could stay friends.' As for Holm, she told the *Sunday Mirror* that 'it's sad and pathetic for anyone to reveal secrets about the most intimate relationship anyone can have – their marriage – apparently forgetting yet again that she had herself written two sensationally revealing autobiographies that had trashed her first two husbands, and was soon to embark on a third.

Her first novel had already earned her £2 million [£3.8 million] even before publication and she was about to sign another hugely lucrative deal with Simon and Schuster to write two more. This did not please Jackie, whose own eleven novels had sold an estimated sixty-five million copies in thirty languages and were also published by Simon and Schuster and edited by Michael Korda. 'Jackie can't help but feel Joan is crowding her territory,' said Korda. Jackie's agent, Morton Janklow, admitted that the sisters had had 'flare-ups' about Joan's trespass and Swifty Lazar agreed that 'certainly there is sibling rivalry at times'. When Dominick Dunne wrote a piece about them for *The Sunday Times Magazine* in April he was instructed by Joan's close friend and publicist Jeffrey Lane that the sisters must be given exactly the same amount of space and that if he used Joan's name first in one sentence he must use Jackie's first in the next. Both women denied that there was any sense of rivalry. 'We're not in each other's pockets, but we're good friends,' Jackie told Dunne. 'We're not the kind of sisters who call each other every day, but she knows I'm there for her.' Joan agreed and said that their lives and tastes were completely different: 'I like Los Angeles but I'm more European than she is in my outlook. I like staying up late. I like sleeping late. I like two-hour lunches, with wine. I do not like tennis, golf, lying by the pool. What I like doing here is to work very hard and then leave.' Joan's idea of a perfect afternoon and evening in LA would probably have been hell for Jackie: she liked to go to the Universal Studio cinema complex and see three films, one after another. She admitted to Melvyn Bragg eleven years later that they had drifted wide apart. 'You can choose your friends but you can't choose your family,' she said. 'I love my sister but I'm not as close to her as I used to be. I don't think she was thrilled when I started writing.' One witness who had once been close to both women told me that 'Joan and Jackie actually loathe each other and always have done, and Joan is jealous of Jackie because Jackie is so much richer than she is'.

The long battle between Joan and Peter Holm – who was now living with Kathy Wardlow, the twenty-six-year-old daughter of a rich, retired music industry executive – rumbled on and seven months after Joan had been ordered to pay him £100,000 she had still not done so and his lawyer had to seize cash from her bank account and threaten to have her *Dynasty* wages sequestrated. Holm's penury was not, however, to last much longer: he was soon to inherit millions when his wealthy father died, and henceforth Joan was always to refer to him contemptuously as 'The Swede', forgetting how much she had apparently loved him once and how much he had done for her.

Joan's father was unwell too and in March had to have an operation for kidney stones. She flew to England to see him and was shocked to find that he had lost the will to live, all interest in his old enthusiasms, and was reluctant even to eat or drink. She found him at home in bed, staring at children's cartoons on television and although she had brought him some smoked salmon he could not bring himself to taste it. She was never to see him again. In her third volume of autobiography, *Second Act*, she claimed that while he was dying she had had to fly back to Los Angeles to work and was there when he died. In fact she flew off to the South of France for a few days' Easter holiday with Tara, Katy and Robin and was there when on 1 April he died of kidney failure and a heart attack. He left her a Dunhill cigarette lighter and everything else to Irene. Joan flew back to London to join more than a hundred mourners at the traditional Jewish funeral on 5 April at Golders Green crematorium, and despite her complicated relationship with Joe she told the Press that 'we did have a wonderful relationship and a full life together'. She wept copiously at the funeral and the card with her huge, heart-shaped wreath read: 'Goodbye Daddy – I will remember you with love – Always Joan x.' Jackie stayed in Los Angeles but sent a wreath of hyacinths with the message. 'We love you'. In fact 'Jackie *hated* Joe', I was told by one of her friends, and from what she said about him in later years it seems that she had still not forgiven him for something that he had done or not done, despite all that he had done to educate her, launch her career and support her well into her twenties. Seven years later she was to deny that she had been deeply hurt by his open contempt for her books. 'My father never read a book in his life,' she told Lester Middlehurst in 1995, 'so I can hardly be insulted by that. And, besides, he just didn't understand what I was about.'

A couple of weeks after the funeral she did fly to London to promote her latest novel, *Rock Star*, and told Sara Barrett of the *Daily Mail* that 'the only reason I didn't go to my father's funeral was because I knew it would be a terrible media circus. I spoke to him the day before he died and we had a wonderful conversation.' She claimed that she, Oscar and their three daughters 'had a little memorial for him at home, besides. My three girls were his grandaughters, they were *very* upset by the news. The last thing I was going to do was fly off and leave them. And anyway, Daddy wasn't alive to know if I was there or not.' Her three girls – Tracy, Tiffany and Rory – were twenty-six, twenty-one and eighteen at that time and could surely have been left in LA or even flown with her to the funeral. A year later Jackie said in an interview that when she was a teenager Joe had made her life a misery and she repeated her false allegation that he had thrown her out of the house when she was sixteen. 'I wanted to be a journalist,' she said, 'and my parents just laughed in my face – especially my father who was a domineering and difficult man.'

In 1999 Jackie told Melvyn Bragg that although both she and Joan had suffered difficult relationships with Joe she had been able to come to terms with it, but Joan had not. 'I think she was constantly searching for the man of her dreams who would be not a *father* figure but who would *replace* the father figure ... Maybe that's why she's been married a few times!' Wickedly she told a *Daily Mail* reporter that 'Joan's men come and go, mine come and stay'. Five months later Joan discussed

Joe with Roald Dahl's daughter Tessa, who was writing a profile for *You* magazine and also claimed to have been psychologically damaged by her father. Joe had been 'detached, cold, hard, critical, difficult, acerbic, and everybody had to please him', said Joan, but she had never managed to please him, so 'there comes a time when you think, "Hang on, it's time to stop proving." Even though he never gave me credit, even if he didn't say it, I'd think: "I wonder if he's going to see this, I wonder if he'll realise how successful I am, whether he knows I am the most famous television star in America, if not the world, whether I have achieved this or achieved that." All I got was, "How can you be out with that Swedish creep?" Always the ready criticism but never the praise. I think that both Jackie and I were brought up by a man who didn't know how to tell us that we were lovely, clever, pretty wonderful girls.' Two months later Joan admitted to the *News of the World* magazine that Joe's death had changed everything, 'although I miss him tremendously. For the first time in my life I am completely free. I don't have to be anything I'm not. Also I don't have to ever ask anybody for anything. I can go where I like and do what I like. It's great.' She admitted, however, that she still needed a father figure, so she appointed eighty-one-year-old Swifty Lazar to the post.

Three days after the funeral she slipped out of London for a weekend in Paris with Robin, but when she returned she was seen canoodling with Wiggy again in a nightclub until the early hours. This may have been something of a smokescreen because he was once again romancing one of his old girlfriends, Debbie Klonaris, the dusky daughter of a black American father and white English mother, with whom he was soon to live and have two children. 'Debbie's great fun,' Wiggy told me. 'I call her Mrs Woggins and we sign our Christmas cards Wigs and Wogs. That's how all this business of racism ought to be treated.' Ten days later Joan was dining, dancing and holding hands at Annabel's with Malcolm Fraser again while Wiggy was once again out on the toot with Jilly Johnson. 'I have an interesting life, with men friends but no specific man in my life,' Joan told the *News of the World* magazine. 'I have a man for all seasons – a man for all diversions! I don't need a man, I just like to have one. So having six or seven works out very well.' She added: 'Sex for me is one of the most natural things in the world. I never have to stay at home for lack of company.'

In April she decided to put down stronger roots in England, rented out the mansion in Cabrillo Drive for three months for £27,000 a month [£51,300] to Paul Hogan, the Australian star of *Crocodile Dundee*, and on Wiggy's advice bought a first-floor flat in a highly fashionable and expensive area of London at 15 Eaton Place for £700,000 [£1,330,000]. At the end of May she was off to Marrakesh again and was paid by La Mamounia $50,000 to take a crowd of friends to join three hundred 'celebrities' on a lavish five-day freebie to mark the opening of its new casino. Robin shied away from going on such a vulgar jaunt but she took three other boyfriends – Wiggy, Malcolm Fraser and George Hamilton – as well as Ned Ryan, Charles and Pandora Delevingne, and Viviane Ventura. After Marrakesh she, Robin, Sacha and Katy went off for another holiday, this time to Hydra to stay with Alexis Mardas. On another jaunt, to Cannes, Joan and Wiggy were invited to a party where 'Joan wanted to rekindle her romance and she asked me to come to bed', Wiggy told David Jones eight years later. 'I said no and she stormed off. Her stepson, Robert Kass, kept his eye on me and reported to her next morning that I had slid off with another young lady whose name I won't mention. Joan was furious and called me all kinds of names.' The young lady involved was Joan's old boy-friend Lord ('Gordy') White's twenty-seven-year-old daughter Sita, who was later to have a child by the Pakistani cricketer and politician Imran Khan. Yet in July Joan and Wiggy were still going out regularly together, smooching in public and visiting each other's flats. She also seems unwisely to have encouraged the lust of a twenty-four-year-old Italian actor, Antonio Zequila, who claimed that he was her latest toyboy and had enjoyed several wonderfully raunchy encounters with her in London, Venice and Cannes. Joan denied it furiously, and when Zequila kept pestering her at a party she threw a glass of red wine over him. 'She'd obviously been flirting with him at some time,' Wiggy told me. 'He was all over her, asked her to go to bed with him, she pushed him away and asked me to protect her, and he carried on, totally ignoring me, and she threw the wine over him. She got very upset about this and he went absolutely *berserk*: "Mamma mia! Bitch! How could you possibly do this to me, the beautiful me?" She grabbed me and said, "I'd very much like you to come to my bedroom tonight," and I said, "not tonight, Joanie," because I was having too much fun.'

At the end of August Joan flew back to Hollywood to make what she had decided definitely would be her final *final* season of *Dynasty*.

By now she was thoroughly fed up with the show, which was sinking fast in the ratings and all but dead. When Stephanie Beacham rejoined it in September after two years' break it seemed completely bizarre. 'I felt as if I'd fallen asleep on the sofa watching it and dreamed that I was working on it,' she told *Hello!* 'Nothing seemed real. It was as if time had suddenly stopped.' After seven years in the show Joan was bored and felt that it was the complete rubbish that others had always said it was. 'We started to make bricks without straw, struggling valiantly with dreadful dialogue,' she told Valerie Grove a year later. 'And there was always that thing of not being in control of your own life. "Yes, Mr Spelling, I'll be there." They could work you till ten o'clock in the evening. That's all very well when you're twenty-five but at a certain point you want to say you're in charge of your life.' She decided that she had had quite enough of Hollywood, too. 'You go to a dinner party there and you never hear anything other than what the box office on this film is, what the grosses on that film are, what this or that star is up to in private, who's hot and who's not,' she told the *Sunday Mirror* magazine a year later. 'That's all you hear – business, business.' She hated even the weather in LA and decided that she would rather live in England, return to the theatre, and write more novels. She had already written several chapters of her second, *Love and Desire and Hate*, but when *Dynasty*'s desperate executives offered her a rise of £25,000 a week to stay on for one more season, which would bring her salary up to £75,000 [£142,500] per episode and make her the most highly paid woman in television, she weakened and agreed. 'I had to stay a year and a half longer than I wanted to,' she told Mrs Grove. Well, she didn't *have* to but the money was just too tempting.

Towards the end of 1988, when *Prime Time* was due to be published, Joan hired Jackie's London PR lady, Yvonne de Valera, to work with her temporarily for three months at her flat in Eaton Square and to handle some publicity and secretarial work for her. 'I thought she was tremendous, a darling,' Ms de Valera told me. 'She was *really* fun – that's the key thing about her – and just gorgeous.' Joan's couturier Maryam Rokny-Owji agreed. 'Joan was down-to-earth, jolly and fun to work for,' she told me. 'And she was positive. She became my main client and we became friends. She's a bit *too* careful about the financial side of everything. Although I was competing with Valentino and Nolan Miller from a small London attic Joan used to pay me peanuts, usually a quarter of the proper price: £250 for an outfit instead of £1000, £2000 instead of £8000. I wouldn't say she's mean but she cares for money, probably because she's half-Jewish. Some people *blow* money but she doesn't.' As for Joan's beauty, 'she looks fake and artificial with so much make-up, but the moment she's at home she removes her wig and make-up and takes her shoes off. As I was giving her a very private, personal service I got to know her body very well. She didn't have enough hair – she was never bald but it was very weak and thin – but she looked pretty and natural without make-up because she has gorgeous bone structure and of course fake but natural-looking teeth.'

When *Prime Time* was finally published early in October 1988 Joan was interviewed by the novelist and playwright John Mortimer for the *Daily Telegraph* magazine and told him that she had not been so excited by anything since the birth of her first baby. In America her new daddy, Swifty Lazar, launched the novel with a lavish party at Spago's; in Britain she was mobbed by fans during a signing session at Harrods, and the book shot within a few days to number three in the bestseller lists.

It was hardly a novel at all, more like non-fiction, because it was so relentlessly autobiographical. It told of a beautiful, stylish, forty-year-old English actress, Chloe Carriere, who lands the coveted role of a super-bitch who is just like Alexis in a new prime-time American TV soap, *Saga*, that is just like *Dynasty*. It becomes America's most popular soap of all time and Chloe becomes a household name and begins to earn a fortune. Her husband, Josh, is half Newley, half Kass: a charismatic but difficult cockney singer who is compulsively unfaithful with underage girls and is destroying himself with booze and drugs. Chloe files for divorce and takes up with a sexually insatiable but moody Peter Holm clone who becomes her manager, bores all her friends, but keeps nagging her to marry him.

There is not much of a plot. Chloe has a secret illegitimate daughter and is stalked by a mad young man who has raped and murdered a Central American actress who was so promiscuous that she was nicknamed The Mexican Open. 'The Mexican Open! What an insult!' It is all pretty dreary, unconvincing stuff that shows only too well how dreadfully dull and unglamorous Hollywood was in the 1980s. Even the biggest stars are depicted as being boundlessly selfish, shallow, self-obsessed, bitchy, jealous, greedy, devious, discontented and bladdered with drink and drugs, the characters are all so deeply unpleasant that it is impossible to care about any of them, and it is equally difficult to become even mildly excited by the regular cold injections of sexual scenes. 'He played her like a Stradivarius,' we are told, and there are regular explicit dollops of 'cocksmanship' and cunnilingus, with one 'blonde young Adonis ... playing a concerto on her clit' for more than an hour. A father shows his ten-year-old son 'what a real man is like' by masturbating in front of him, howling like a wolf and slumping against the wall. A female 'star' lies on 'an exquisite white ermine cloak' under the ceiling mirror in her bathroom and masturbates in 'a delicious frenzy' towards five orgasms. A Spanish maid spies on her lesbian mistress and her latest lover. A male homosexual 'star' dies of AIDS after cursing his boyfriend – 'who've you been fucking, you lousy little faggot?' – for giving him the disease: 'Don't fucking give me the fucking tears routine you mother-fucking queer.' Hello, Rock Hudson.

Joan's father would have hated the book, yet still she dedicated it to him both mawkishly and pretentiously:

For every actress
who has ever suffered the slings and arrows
of outrageous fortune
that are such a part of our lives ...
and for Daddy, who was
such a part of mine

The book was so tacky that it made Joan seem as sadly sleazy and unstylish as Jackie's books.

There are, thank goodness, occasional glimpses of Joan's naughty sense of humour. One actress's up-and-coming young lover is not nearly up and coming enough to satisfy her. Another woman finds fellatio so repugnant that the only way she can bear to perform it is to pretend that she is enjoying an ice-cream cone. But in the end the book is utterly thin and bogus. Most ridiculous of all is how at the end of it both Josh and Chloe's blowsy, down-and-out, has-been actress rival Emerald suddenly recover miraculously from serious alcoholism, health problems and terminal failure to bounce back out of the gutter and become inexplicably huge TV stars all over again. And the sudden, schmaltzy happy ending is truly ludicrous.

Joan's British editor, Rosie Cheetham, commented, 'I didn't have time to edit it myself but had to take it the way it came from America,' she told me. 'I was shocked that Michael Korda hadn't given her more help. He's a very good editor and writer and I thought he would have sorted it out, but I overlooked that Joan would be absolutely determined to do it herself and that although she presented this very sophisticated image she is not in fact a particularly cynical person, and because she's always been the centre of attention she has never watched people or listened to how they talk, so a lot of her writing seems very naïve and clichéd. She's a person of the moment who's always looking forward, not back, and that's a wonderful strength but also a weakness in a novelist, whereas Jackie is a *huge* gossip, *fantastically* interested in other people, always watching and listening.'

The critics were savage. Paul Golding wrote in *The Sunday Times* that it was 'unrewarding nonsense ... dreary ... stilted ... ill-written sentimentality'. The anti-pornography campaigner Mary Whitehouse called it a 'combination of violence and obscenity ... phoney ... trash'. The romantic novelist Barbara Cartland said it was 'filth ... lewd and disgusting ... determined to go worse than her sister Jackie, [*she*] has scraped the bottom of the gutters with both hands for this book and wallowed in the cesspools'. Miss Cartland added: 'It seems to me in-credible that, when she already has millions, she is prepared by this dirty, evil book to risk destroying the innocent purity of young girls who idolise her.' Bryan Appleyard, who interviewed her for *The Times* in her suite at Claridge's, described the book as 'nasty', and did not take to her at all. 'She wears black high heels, black tights, a short black skirt and a white blouse,' he wrote. 'Her hair tumbles in the approved fashion. The lipstick is applied to create a sharp downward V-shape on her upper lip and her no-coloured eyes are savagely outlined by thick pencilled curves which form two dagger-like points at the out-side edges. She is swathed in thick gold chains and her forearms are armoured with a huge collection of bangles. She looks like an ageing sado-masochist's dream. Except, that is, for the curiously large head, which seems imperfectly balanced on the startlingly fragile body and the thin, actressy voice which emerges from the whole terrifying con-coction.' When he suggested that the novel was perhaps just a bit too autobiographical she said that she no longer gave a damn what anyone thought except the public: 'The eyes, the only visible organic surface on her entire face, stare back, waiting to be challenged. She is wary and defensive, ready to stamp on the slightest sign of a cheap crack or a trick question.' When she said that no one could possibly admire the British tabloid Press he said that he did and she was horrified. 'The irony of her position appears to escape her,' he wrote. 'She is a tabloid queen made by the tabloids and happy to feed their fantasies, yet she wants to sneer at them too.'

Jackie was under the impression that *Prime Time* sold very few copies and was reported by *TV Guide* as having said at a party that 'the poor dear's book just seems to have sunk', but in fact it sold a very respectable fifty thousand copies in hardback and later three hundred thousand in paperback, Mrs Cheetham told me: 'We got all our $750,000 advance back, mainly because of a huge serial deal and because Joan's first novel was a news event. Whenever there was a signing session they were literally queuing around the block. But then we made the mistake of signing her up for two more novels for even more money. Even then we felt slightly uneasy but it was a crazy time and publishers were paying enormous sums of money. Like now, the lust for celebrity had gone through the roof. It was a time of madness for poor Joan: she was really sometimes quite frightened by the pressure of the crowds.'

Now that her father was dead Joan spent Christmas 1988 in Beverly Hills for a change with Tara (who was still singing with her group), Sacha (now painting portraits but living a reclusive life in his flat in Lyme Regis), Katy (now sixteen), Jackie, Oscar and their daughters – and Robin Hurlstone, who finally emerged from his shy shadows to be acknowledged as Joan's regular beau. When he flew to Los Angeles to join her just before Christmas the *National Enquirer* quoted her as gushing, 'I've never been in love like this before – it's wonderful,' and him echoing, 'I adore her.' Wiggy was consigned to history, possibly because Joan was furious that she had just lost the £100,000 that he had persuaded her to invest in the London bed-and-breakfast joint, and although he too lost money and protested that he had advised her in good faith she hated losing money and ordered her advisers to demand that Wiggy should reimburse her. He refused to accept responsibility for the loss and told me that 'she didn't mention the fact that I found her the flat in Eaton Place that she's probably made £2 million out of'.

Joan was never to forgive him, even though he resisted for years the temptation to sell her letters or to accept a £650,000 offer he received to write a book about their affair. When she published eight years later her third volume of autobiography, *Second Act*, she did not mention him at all and when she was asked about him by Michael Parkinson on television she said: 'Bill *who?*'

Her coldness upset him. 'We had some great times together and we laughed a lot, so I don't see what the problem is,' he told Lina Das of the *Daily Mail's Weekend* magazine fifteen years later. 'It's a real shame because I always wanted to remain her friend after we split up. But then Joan has always been the sort of person who could place bits of her life into compartments.' He added: 'I learned more about human nature in those fourteen months than you would in fourteen lifetimes. I made a lot of friends very quickly and lost them all again overnight. The whole experience gave me an insight into how celebrities are – they're no better or worse than us normal people but they're probably a damn sight more insecure.' Three months after the end of their friendship he became briefly a disc jockey with a Cambridgeshire radio station, where he began his first programme by saying: 'Hi, all of you out there. I'm Bungalow Bill. If you read the newspapers you'll know I'm the latest candidate in the Joan Collins Youth Training Scheme.' He settled down at last with his dusky girlfriend Debbie Klonaris, 'Mrs Woggins', who had already three sons by two previous relationships. By 2007 they were living happily in Kent and sending their own two sons to an expensive private school. 'Debbie's great fun,' he told me, 'and she has a wicked sense of humour.' She had indeed: she used to call Joan 'Gerry', short for Geriatric.

Determined to leave Los Angeles, Joan put the Cabrillo Drive mansion up for sale at an asking price of £3.25 million [£5.75 million] and when Robin was staying with a friend in the South of France two months later he found a beautiful, half-built dream house that he urged her to buy, a place that would not keep reminding her of Holm and where they could spend a couple of months every summer. It was a peach-coloured, six-bedroom villa with a swimming pool set in twelve acres in a serene, peaceful forest of oaks and pine trees high in the hills above St Tropez, between the villages of Gassin and Ramatuelle, with a wonderful view of the Mediterranean. Joan flew to Nice, loved the house, bought it for £900,000 [£1,584,000], and they named it Destino. She put the house at Port Grimaud on the market for £500,000 [£880,000], they moved into Destino on Bastille Day, 14 July, and Robin set about decorating and filling it with pictures and furniture. For many summers there they were to revel idyllically in the lazy peace and sunshine to the tinkling of ice and the laughter of their friends. 'I really think I should have been born French,' said Joan a year later. 'I have come to love living in France. It's a much more gentle life than in Hollywood. More cultured. I like a certain amount of gracious living – eating properly in nice restaurants, going to parks and art galleries and wonderful shops, people dressing properly for going out to dinner. Conversation is important to people in Europe. Yesterday we went to the country to see friends and we talked about flowers and food and wine and it was all ... well, harmonious.' She did however suffer one moment of panic when she left the first half of the manuscript of her next novel, *Love and Desire and Hate*, hanging in a plastic bag on the back of a luggage trolley at Nice airport and did not realise it was missing until she reached London. Luckily British Airways and the airport managed to track it down and return it.

She made her final episode of *Dynasty* in March, a ludicrously bathetic finale in which Blake Carrington was shot dead by a madman, Alexis plunged to her death from a balcony, Fallon fell down a mine shaft, Sable became pregnant by Alexis's husband, and Krystle went bonkers and into a coma in a Swiss hospital. Even so, Joan and some of the cast and crew were in tears on the last day. She treated them all to champagne and a cake decorated with the message '*Dynasty* 1981–1989. It's been the best. I love you all. Joan.' But there was one member of the cast whom she was never to forgive for a remark that he made just before the show ended: Michael Nader, who played her final *Dynasty* husband, Dex Dexter, and was heard to sneer that Joan preferred to quaff champagne and guzzle caviar in her dressing room while the 'real' actors did all the work. She was to bear a grudge against him for years.

Foolishly she signed an agreement whereby she accepted a one-off payment of £225,000 [£396,000] in exchange for waiving her right to any future *Dynasty* repeat fees, residuals, foreign rights or profits. That decision, she said years later, was to cost her millions because somehow there was life after death for *Dynasty*: it was screened again and again all over the world on cable TV, video and DVD. The astute

Peter Holm would never have let her sign that deal. 'I will always be grateful for what Alexis did for me,' Joan told the *Sunday Mirror* magazine a year later, 'but playing that hard character for eight years, with everyone thinking that's how I was – except those who knew me well – obviously had an effect on me.' Even some of those who knew her well – Ron Kass, Peter Holm, some of her staff, some of the *Dynasty* team, maybe Tony Newley – would have argued that she had become just as hard and cold a ball-breaker as Alexis, but women acclaimed her. Lynda Lee-Potter wrote in the *Daily Mail* that Joan deserved the respect and gratitude of all women: 'She's given a lot of fun over the years, and sometimes we've laughed at her. But she's proved that if women are bold enough they can have everything. They can enjoy all the door-opening courtesies without playing "poor little me".' Mary Riddell wrote in the *Daily Mirror*: 'Self-important she may be, tasteless possibly, but as she begins the run-up to sixty her achievements outweigh her flaws,' and she quoted a social psychologist, Dr Maryon Tysoe, as saying that 'a woman in her fifties who presents herself as seriously up-and-running, independent and having a good time has to be a good model, especially for older women. It's not so long since women thought that, at fifty-five, they should retreat into a baggy cardigan and a pair of old carpet slippers.' Joan herself admired strong, assertive women like Margaret Thatcher, Mother Teresa of Calcutta, Princess Anne and the Queen, 'women who are compassionate, dedicated to a cause and not afraid to be themselves even if it sometimes makes them unpopular'. People either liked her very much or not at all, she told Jackie Modlinger of the *Daily Express* magazine. 'I am the first to admit that I do have faults, but they are often exaggerated by the Press. I am honest, unsubtle, completely transparent, and I am both intolerant and impatient. All of these things have contributed to my reputation as being bitchy and vindictive. I know that I have these qualities and that they are perhaps fifty per cent, but the other fifty per cent is not like that.'

At the end of April she flew back to Britain with twenty-six pieces of luggage – a mountain of suitcases, hatboxes, parcels and five huge trunks. 'It might *seem* like a lot,' she said hilariously, 'but I'm here for nearly three months'. She was once again to attend the Derby and Ascot races, where she persuaded Malcolm Fraser to let her wear his estranged wife Joanna's pass into the Royal Enclosure but was stopped by a steward who recognised her immediately and knew very well that she was not Mrs Fraser. 'She threw a tantrum like a two-year-old,' one witness told the *Daily Express* and one of the stewards told the *Sun* that 'she was in a furious temper. You'd think Joan would have realised she didn't have the slightest chance of getting in on someone else's ticket. After all, she has one of the most famous faces in the world.' To make the story even jollier, Mrs Fraser was in fact nowhere to be seen: the badge in her name was being used for most of the day by one of her husband's other girlfriends, who had no right to wear it either.

In June Joan recorded her second *Desert Island Discs* radio interview and chose this time Luciano Pavarotti singing 'Come Back to Sorrento'; Dame Vera Lynn's poignant wartime song 'We'll Meet Again'; 'The Wonder of You' by Elvis Presley; Frank Sinatra singing 'Come Fly With Me' (down to Acapulco Bay, of course); Puccini's 'Intermezzo' from *Manon Lescaut*; Steve Barton and Sarah Brightman singing 'All I Ask of You' from *The Phantom of the Opera*; another Puccini piece, 'O mio babbino caro' from *Gianni Schicchi*; and Lionel Richie's 'Love Will Conquer All', which in Joan's case was pretty optimistic. As a book to read on her desert island she chose *The Picture of Dorian Gray* by Oscar Wilde, and her luxury was a large bottle of moisturiser to protect her skin against the tropical sun. 'Life isn't easy,' she told the interviewer, Sue Lawley, 'but you bloody well make the best of what cards you've got to play and play them as well as you can. I have a sort of enthusiasm for life and I don't ever want to lose it. I like my life. I like who I am and what I do and I'm quite at peace with myself.'

In July she was given what she thought would be another accolade when London Weekend Television invited her to appear on an hour-long programme, hosted by Michael Aspel, called *The Trouble With Joan Collins*. Instead of being the fanfare for her career that she expected, it quickly degenerated into a scurrilous Aunt Sally show even crueller than Dean Martin's *Celebrity Roast* five years earlier. To her horror they showed a dreadfully embarrassing screen test – 'Hilarious,' said the *News of the World* – that she had made thirty years earlier when she had been considered for the lead in *Cleopatra*. Her *bête noire* from *Dynasty*, Michael Nader, turned up and claimed that her greatest talent was shopping, and *Dynasty*'s creator, Esther Shapiro, revealed that ABC had feared that geriatric old Joan would turn it into a crumblies' saga. Her old jazz chum from RADA days, George Melly, accused her of settling for glamour in rubbishy films and programmes rather than quality in her work, and she was for some reason upset when she was described as a 'camp icon', even though by now she was indeed to such an extent that the camp TV performer Julian Clary was calling himself the Joan Collins Fan Club. Nor was she best pleased to see that Wiggy was also there in the audience guffawing at the rude jokes about her. She was grilled about all the fibs she had told about her age and cynically questioned as to whether she was telling the truth about never having had plastic surgery. She gritted her teeth, smiled tightly throughout, and replied when Aspel asked her at the end what was the *real* trouble with Joan Collins: 'The trouble with Joan Collins is that she's very thirsty and she thinks it's about time for a glass of champagne.' But beneath her unruffled exterior she was furious and demanded afterwards that the programme should be scrapped. LWT refused and it was broadcast two months later.

At the end of the month Tara, who was now twenty-four and living in north London with her designer/musician boyfriend Chris Ellis, gave her first major concert with her band Newley-Mars – for which she and the group's guitarist, Matthew Marrs, had written all the songs – at the trendy Rock Gardens in Covent Garden, where The Police, U2 and Dire Straits had started out. She sang with a voice that was 'a cross between Kate Bush and Siouxie and the Banshees', said the promoter, Sean McDonnell. When later she played at another gig, in Islington, Joan turned up incognito, disguised as a hippy, to support her.

At the end of July 1989 Joan and Robin flew to the South of France, moved out of the house in Port Grimaud and into the new villa, and enjoyed a Mediterranean cruise on the Italian couturier Valentino's yacht. Joan raved about a beautiful wedding dress that they saw when they went ashore in Sardinia for dinner and the newspapers reported that they were planning to marry. 'I'm so very very close to Robin, and very much in love,' she told Baz Bamigboye of the *Daily Mail*. 'He is very special and makes me very happy. But that doesn't mean I want to get married again,' she fibbed, and added: 'He's a very private man and doesn't like to be in the spotlight.' She told another interviewer: 'I quickly realised that Robin was the man I had been waiting for all my life. He was somebody who didn't want anything from me except the me he loves. He loves me for myself, as a woman, and not – as some people might imagine – because I am an actress or star. It is the real me he sees – someone who is basically quite simple, a down-to-earth regular sort of person.'

It was not the first time that Joan had met Bamigboye. 'I was in First Class on a flight from Los Angeles to London in about 1989 and she was sitting across from me,' he told me. 'She was wearing a posh track suit, dark glasses and a silk scarf, and a British Airways flunkey carried a suit bag and make-up case on board for her. An hour before we landed in London Joan popped into the loo with her gear and twenty minutes later she returned to her seat in a Chanel suit, hair looking fabulous, full make-up, looking a million dollars. I told her how fab she looked and she smiled and said: "Darling, you've got to understand that you're never not on show. I knew there wouldn't be photographers at LA but I know for sure they'll be at Heathrow. This is my uniform, my protection." It was that word *protection* that always intrigued me. I guess that when she's in public and dressed up to the nines the Chanel suit and all that hair and make-up is her armour. When she was in the middle of that nasty divorce from Peter Holm I had to chase her around LA and it was the most hellish time for her, but whenever she appeared in public she was always well turned out and gracious. She must have been going through hell but that movie-star look was her protection.'

And her professional badge of honour. 'My sense of Joan has always been her professionalism both on and off the screen,' said Bamigboye.

CHAPTER EIGHTEEN

AFTER *DYNASTY*

{ 1989–1993 }

In September 1989 Joan flew to America to launch her new collection of jewellery and a perfume called Spectacular. In New York she was ushered around by Donald Trump but in Little Rock, Arkansas, a local reporter, Adriaane Pielou, said she looked 'like a *Thunderbird* puppet, with a big shiny head, all dark hair and glistening lip gloss, and a little matte body'. She flew on to Sydney to launch the Australian edition of *Prime Time* and on her way back stopped off in Hong Kong, went on board a junk in the harbour for dinner with friends, and was terrified when a storm suddenly blew up, the vessel started rolling crazily and caught fire, and the engines exploded in clouds of thick black smoke before the junk was towed to safety.

Her equally stormy relationship with Tony Newley had calmed to such an extent that he invited her to the first night of his West End revival of *Stop the World – I Want To Get Off* at the Lyric Theatre in October. Years of his instability, depression, suicidal fantasies, barmy psychic consultations, and an affair with a nineteen-year-old girl had destroyed his third marriage and he and Dareth were soon to be divorced. Now fifty-eight, Tony and his mother, Gracie, had returned to live together in London and his children were there for the first night, too, though Sacha made a snide remark to a *New Standard* reporter when he said of Joan: 'We tend to have a metaphysical relationship with each other. It's very rare when we appear together and it does tend to coincide with rather a lot of cameras.' Sadly the revival of the show was a disaster – even Leslie Bricusse thought it was abysmal – and it closed after just five weeks, losing more than £600,000 [more than £1 million]. Joan and Tony had become so reconciled that they spent Christmas together and then he and Gracie returned to Los Angeles, where Dareth divorced him and went to live in Florida with their fifteen-year-old daughter, Shelby. Tony and his mother, by now comparatively poor, returned yet again to live in England.

In mid-January Joan was back in LA herself to host a TV chat show and was furious when her old friend Zsa Zsa Gabor told a TV audience that La Collins was bald. She swore never to speak to Zsa Zsa again. Then it was back to England before returning to Los Angeles in March for the Oscars. Even after *Dynasty* her life was as hectic as ever, though she did make one concession to the approach of old age by starting to take Hormone Replacement Therapy.

Ever since she was at RADA Joan had dreamed of one day playing the lead in Noël Coward's *Private Lives*: the spoiled, feisty, thirty-year-old divorcee Amanda Prynne, who meets her ex-husband when they are both on their second honeymoons and staying at the same hotel. She achieved her ambition at last when the impresario Michael Codron agreed to stage a production that would open at the Theatre Royal in Bath in September and then after two weeks move into the Aldwych Theatre in London. Her salary would be tiny by comparison with *Dynasty* – just £3,000 [£5,280] a week for six performances – but she was thrilled at the prospect of returning to the West End stage after nine years. At first she wanted her leading man to be in his thirties or forties – Nigel Havers, perhaps, or Charles Dance – but Codron felt that it would be absurd to cast someone so much younger as her ex-husband and she had to settle for Keith Baxter, who was at fifty-seven a month older than she.

To make up for her sudden drop in income Joan signed up for two hugely lucrative television projects – a TV mini-series based on *Prime Time* and a series about astrology – but they fell through in April and May when the producers of both accused her of being ridiculously greedy. The producer of the astrology series, Rissos Kyriakides, claimed that at first she agreed to accept a princely £500,000 [£880,000] for just two weeks' work on it but then demanded a further £100,000 [£176,000] plus six per cent of the earnings. 'I was quite angry when she put her price up,' he said, and his fellow producer Chris Raphael claimed that 'nothing was good enough for her. We had a deal to stay at the Crillon in Paris, she demanded the Ritz. We had a deal with Valentino to do the wardrobe, she wanted someone else. She ran up a £45,000 expenses bill and spent £5,000 on wigs.' They told Joan to go jump and gave the job to Stefanie Powers instead, and a few months later a company called Wig Specialities sued Joan for £2,786 [£4,903], which they claimed she owed them for wigs she had ordered for the show in January. The producer of the *Prime Time* series, Roy Medawar of ION Pictures, claimed that Joan had charged £25,000-worth of dresses [£44,000] to the film's budget without telling him. 'We tried to tell her it wasn't *Dynasty* but she wouldn't listen,' he said. 'She's plain greedy and outrageous.' He also accused her of rewriting huge chunks of the script and refusing to let him cast younger actresses like Jacqueline Bisset and Ann-Margret as well because 'she wanted to be the biggest name in this movie'. Joan retaliated by claiming that ION owed her £177,000 [£311,520] in salary and sued the company in LA for £3 million [£5.25 million] for 'defamation of character, slander and lies'.

To forfeit nearly £700,000 in two months barely dented Joan's fortune, which was estimated that summer to be worth about £20 million [£35 million], but just as she lost a fortune with one hand she made an even bigger one with the other. Swifty Lazar persuaded her to leave Simon and Schuster once they had published her second novel, *Love and Desire and Hate*, and move to Random House, which had offered to pay her £2.5 million [nearly £4.5 million] for her third and fourth novels, with a first advance of £800,00 [£1.4 million] up front. She agreed and was assigned by Random House to a notoriously tough, ambitious editor, Joni Evans, who told Lazar that 'I want her so bad I can taste it, and I don't care how much it costs'.

In June Joan went to Ladies' Day at Ascot races again. Robin always avoided any occasion where there were likely to be photographers, so although she told the *Sunday Mirror* magazine that 'I cannot imagine not having him in my life – he's a most wonderful man' she was squired again by Malcolm Fraser as a guest of the football pools millionaire and racehorse owner Robert Sangster and his wife Sue, but when she tried to reach the Sangsters' private box by strolling through the Royal Enclosure she was stopped again by a steward because she did not have the right badge. 'It's the same every year,' sighed a racecourse official, Laura Thompson-Royds. 'She never stops trying. She's a silly woman. I don't know why she doesn't get herself organised. All she has to do is apply in the usual fashion for the Royal Enclosure in January.'

In July she and Robin enjoyed a Provençal holiday at Destino but she was devastated when Malcolm Fraser died suddenly after a severe asthma attack. He was only forty-eight. 'Something like that makes you think about your own mortality,' she told Judy McGuire of the *News of the World* magazine, 'but I'm terribly glad I'm not young any more. I really am. I think life is tougher for young people now and I don't envy them at all.' Tara's and Sacha's lives were 'much more difficult in many ways than mine was because of all the divorces and having a famous mother. That has got to be hell! It must be awful having a celebrity mother.' But Tara was still enjoying composing and singing; Sacha, now twenty-five, had just joined the London International Film School in the hope of becoming a director; and Katy, now eighteen, had a steady boyfriend, Jeff Stewart, a thirty-three-year-old actor who was three years older than Robin Hurlstone and playing PC Reg Hollis in the TV series *The Bill*, and she had just enrolled at a college in Paris to study French and journalism.

Private Lives opened in Bath at the Theatre Royal in September. By now, said the gossips, Joan and Keith Baxter disliked each other so much that they could barely look at each other, but Robin was there to support her, every one of the thousand seats was sold, and the audience loved her and exploded with applause. 'When they were queueing up to buy tickets they weren't asking to see *Private Lives*,' said one of the theatre staff. 'They were asking to see Joan Collins or Alexis. I wish we had someone like Joan to pull the crowds every night.' One of the audience, Mrs Sue Moore, told Rebecca Hardy of the *Daily Mail*: 'I couldn't take my eyes off her. She has such charisma. Everyone has always said she has presence and now I've seen it for myself.' When the play moved to the West End two weeks later the first-night audience included Tony Newley; Coward's old lover and heir Graham Payn; Princess Margaret's ex-husband Lord Snowdon as well as her lover Roddy Llewellyn; the actors Michael Caine, Jenny Seagrove, Vivienne Ventura, Barbara Windsor and Susannah York; the directors Ned Sherrin and Michael Winner; the politician and scribbler Jeffrey Archer; the broadcaster Gloria Hunniford; the singer and composer Lynsey de Paul, and even the legendary landlord of the Coach and Horses pub in Soho, Norman Balon, whose famously drunken establishment was that very evening the setting of the award-winning comedy *Jeffrey Bernard is Unwell*, starring Peter O'Toole, which was still running after a year at the Apollo Theatre and which Joan hated even though most people thought it was hilarious. On her own first night she was given a five-minute standing ovation, five curtain calls, and afterwards there was a glitzy party at the Ivy where Graham Payn gave her a tortoiseshell pillbox inlaid with gold that Coward had owned and said that Noëlie would have loved her performance. 'I found her funny and touching and Noël would have approved,' Payn told Valerie Grove.

Three national newspaper reviewers were equally enthusiastic. The *Daily Telegraph* said: 'She gives a supremely confident performance, sparkling in repartee, and quite superb in the splendidly choreographed fight at the end of Act II. She sings the cheap but potent "Someday I'll Find You" with the same endearingly off-key quality as Gertrude Lawrence [*and*] looks superb and wears her clothes elegantly.' In the *Evening Standard* Milton Shulman enthused that Joan had been 'irrepressibly naughty, adorably sulky, wittily volatile and outrageously provocative.' The *Sun* said that she had given 'a bitchy, witty, wonderful perormance ... brilliant ... Joan knows exactly how to please her adoring public. *RATING: Magic!*' And in the *Daily Mail* Baz Bamigboye, who had seen Elizabeth Taylor's performance as Amanda when she and Richard Burton had starred in a disastrous production of the play on Broadway, reported that Joan was much better. Few of the other critics, though, were impressed and most reckoned that Joan had been acted off the stage by Sara Crowe, a twenty-four-year-old unknown who was playing her squeaky flapper rival, Sybil. In *The Times* Benedict Nightingale reported that Joan had been 'sadly superficial' and 'bland'. The *Daily Express* said that while the production was 'stylish and witty' Joan was 'more suited to Carry On comedy than Noël Coward subtlety [*and her*] comic timing is distinctly erratic'. And Jack Tinker wrote in the *Daily Mail* that by comparison with Sara Crowe 'Miss Collins can only speak the lines in her cool, professional fashion and watch scene after scene run away from her. It is not that she is not good in the role, it is simply that she is not quite good enough. She knows the words but cannot find the music.' Valerie Grove offered a perceptive explanation for the widely differing reviews. 'The truth is, both critics are right,' she wrote. 'The witty repartee of the honeymooning couples never stales and Tim Luscombe is a clever director. But first nights are tricky and a television mega-star on stage is very tricky. In the tension caused by an audience agog at the glittering Collins, the icy little voice of the comedienne Crowe as silly Sibyl is such a tension-reliever the audience roars its applause.'

Joan had her own theory about her popularity with ordinary theatre goers rather than critics. 'I loathe the stupid word but I've been a *star* since I was eighteen and I know that if you start taking yourself seriously you're as dead as a doornail,' she told Andrew Duncan of the *Sunday Express* magazine. 'One thing that appeals to the public about me is that they know, in spite of all the brouhaha, that I'm a down-to-earth woman and probably a better actress than I'm given credit for.' She added: 'I'm very normal, totally unneurotic and extremely sensible – three qualities few actors have. I won't knock my profession, but so many of them are hopelessly messed up by drugs, drink, screwing around and terribly exaggerated ideas of their own importance.' However snooty some of the reviewers had been, *Private Lives* was to run for four-and-a-half months at the Aldwych.

In October Joan's second novel, *Love and Desire and Hate*, was published in Britain. Unbelievably it was even worse than her first: utterly absurd and appallingly written. It told of six horribly selfish, shallow, obsessive characters who come together in Acapulco in 1955 during the filming there of a Hollywood epic. They are a male English film star, a reformed French prostitute, a young Greek film director, a sixteen-year-old French actress, her ugly ballet teacher and a sinister, sadistic Italian producer. The ex-whore, director and ballet teacher all have good reason to hate the Italian producer, who has been during the Second World War the brutal military governor of the Greek island of Hydra, yet has somehow since then become hugely rich and escaped prosecution as a war criminal even though he has not bothered to change his name. The fact that these four should all turn up unsuspectingly on the same film set ten years after the end of the war is only one of several ridiculous coincidences in the book. As one character remarks to herself: 'This was too much, much too much. It simply couldn't be true, it just wasn't possible.' Quite so.

The characters were all ludicrous caricatures. The English film star is 'The Most Handsome Man in the World' and blessed with a penis that is contantly twitching, bulging, popping up and straining at the leash so that he can fornicate five times a day. The reformed prostitute is the original Golden-hearted Whore: stunningly beautiful, fresh and loving despite having been used and abused for years by much of the German army in Paris during the war as well as the occasional Italian officer and a sizeable portion of the English aristocracy. The sixteen-year-old French actress is just an ordinary, demure schoolgirl in St Tropez but suddenly and absurdly becomes an insatiably randy Hollywood star. Her teacher is not only an ugly virgin but also a mad, murderous virago who becomes obsessed by the English film star and masturbates frantically eight times a day with the assistance of his sweaty shirt. And the toad-like Italian ex-general – a Mussolini lookalike, of course – somehow becomes an instantly brilliant film producer despite his lack of experience and tiny 'Lilliputian penis', a shortcoming that inspires him to beat women up while attempting to ravish them. In one highly unpleasant scene the Italian monster assaults the French whore with a giant dildo and almost kills her – a crude, vicious scene that Joan described in extremely nasty detail with unseemly, gloating relish.

The book is punctuated with numerous explicit but utterly unerotic descriptions of sexual congress, fellatio, cunnilingus, masturbation, sadism, masochism, rape, an attempted gang-bang and even a castration, and in one memorable passage Joan wrote: 'At last his moans were becoming faster and Inès knew it must be ending. His hot breath scalded her shoulders and his saliva dripped on to her face. "Yes, yes, you *whore*! You filthy French *cunt* – you disgusting bitch. This is for *you*!" he cried with a scream of satisfaction. He gave her a final vicious thrust, at the same time punching her in the face until she lost consciousness.'

Still, Joan did come up with a few extremely handy sexual tips, as you might expect from such an experienced woman. A limp penis, she reported, may be aroused by immersion in a mouthful of ice followed by a mouthful of hot water. Ice cream can apparently do the trick too, and sometimes a smack on the 'bottie'. Most useful of all for any girl who cares about her complexion is this piece of homely advice that came originally from Mae West: after making love she should 'deftly' massage her lover's semen into the skin of her face and neck.

Apart from Mae West, several other real people pop up in the book. Picasso ogles the prostitute in a Paris café. Laurence Olivier, Vivien Leigh and Noël Coward burst into the English film star's dressing room to tell him in the most ludicrous dialogue how *divine* he was in *Hamlet*. Ava Gardner, Lana Turner and Liz Taylor all fancy the star rotten and another actress remarks that no man since Gary Cooper has made her come so often and '*so* deliciously'. He was, she said, much better than Frank Sinatra or Errol Flynn. And Hermione Gingold, who had appeared with Joan in two films in the 1950s, *Cosh Boy* and *Our Girl Friday*, is portrayed savagely as a greedy, boozy, 'smug bitch' and 'vicious backbiting cow' whose husband molests young boys and is 'as queer as a seven-pound note' and 'camper than a row of tents'. No one was going to sue Joan for libel: Gingold had been dead for three years and her husband for twenty-one.

Clichés infect page after page of the novel. Girls pout prettily, tables groan with food, a sow's ear becomes a silk purse, a shoe is on the other foot, people are always wending their way, laughter is the order of the day, and the English film star has a body and face that even a Greek god would envy. Joan's galumphing style was hilarious. Try this: 'If Ramona could have managed a maidenly blush, she would have summoned one up, but her thespian gifts were not that munificent.' And she kept lapsing affectedly into French or Italian for no obvious reason. There are huge holes in the plot – one major movie appears to have been filmed in just one week – and it would be tedious to list all the ludicrous incidents, unbelievable developments and careless mistakes. *Love and Desire and Hate* is a book that must surely have embarrassed Robin, whose refined artistic sensibilities must have been badly bruised when Joan dedicated it 'To Robin, For all his patience, love and support'. It is not a book that anyone with any style, sensitivity or subtlety would want to have dedicated to him.

Joan invited lonely Tony Newley yet again to spend Christmas with them in Cumbria and persuaded him to join her in two of a TV season of eight one-act, half-hour Noël Coward plays in which she was to appear on television and produce, *Tonight at 8.30*. In one of them, 'Red Peppers', they played a bickering couple of faded, third-rate music hall stars in red, white and blue sailor suits and curly red wigs. In 'Fumed Oak' they were a nagging suburban housewife and her husband, and a few months later Tony was to confess that he wished they had never divorced. 'We could have stayed together,' he said. 'Joan is marvellous. She's lost none of her *joie de vivre*.' Sacha confirmed that 'when I see them together, which is quite often, they adore each other as friends and they have great repartee'. In the six other Coward TV plays she was among other roles a repressed spinster, a barmaid and a hard-up social climber, and she appeared with actors as distinguished as John

Alderton, Jane Asher, Miriam Margolyes, Siân Phillips, Dennis Quilley, Joan Sims, John Standing and Simon Williams.

Joan's sense of taste and style, however, came under fire again in February when she criticised British designers like Vivienne Westwood and stores like Harrods and Selfridges for selling 'revolting' clothes. 'When it comes to cheap, Joan Collins is an authority,' snapped Harrods' spokeman Michael Cole. 'Her remarks should be seen in the light of our decision to discontinue the sale of her jewellery, which did not sell and was regarded by our customers as vulgar.' He pointed out that Harrods had also rejected her perfume and failed to sell many copies of her books, and added: 'Miss Collins's taste and sense of style is obvious for all to see and to be criticised by her is quite a compliment.' Vivienne Westwood was equally feisty. 'I was not aware that anyone, not even she herself, considered Joan Collins to be a pundit of good taste,' she sniffed.

By now *Private Lives* had reached the end of its run at the Adelphi and after more than four months on stage, as well as making eight TV plays in eight weeks, Joan was exhausted. She took a holiday in Acapulco and then presented Joni Evans at Random House with an outline for her third novel. Ms Evans did not like it much so she, Joan and Rosie Cheetham met in Beverly Hills to thrash out alternative ideas for the next book, which was eventually to be called *A Ruling Passion*. They settled on a novel about two sisters, one similar to Princess Diana, the other similar to Princess Grace, that was set in a principality like Monaco. 'We spent a week sitting every day beside Joan's pool and working out the plot,' Mrs Cheetham told me. 'Joni said she could fix everything, cooked up this fantastical plot, and at the end of each session would type the synopsis out, but I didn't see how this was going to work. It was getting far too elaborate. It was absolutely crazy. I didn't think even Tolstoy could do this. We were mad to ask Joan to do something that was so far out of her experience. We were asking her to do something impossible.'

Joan went into hibernation in the South of France to write the new novel but had to fly to Los Angeles at the end of June to make yet another *Dynasty* programme. When the show had come to an end two years earlier many of its fans complained that too many loose ends had been left untied, so the producers miraculously resurrected all the dead, dying maimed characters for a final, *final* three-hour sequel, *Dynasty:*

The Reunion. Alexis bounced back after falling to her death from the balcony, Krystle emerged as good as new from her coma, Blake recovered from his fatal gunshot wounds, and the whole rubbishy nonsense went on as absurdly as before, with Alexis as unattractive, predatory and ballbreaking as ever, made up like a clown and with eyebrows as aggressive as fat caterpillars.

Back in France at the end of July to work again on the novel, Joan was appalled to be photographed – sunbathing topless in her garden and undressing in her bedroom – by a long-distance snapper whose snatched pictures were published soon afterwards in the American supermarket tabloid *Globe*. She sued the magazine for gross invasion of privacy and demanded £13 million [£21 million] in compensation but settled out of court two years later for a reported payment of £300,000 [£438,000]. Although she was later to claim that the trauma of that intrusion had seriously delayed the completion of the new novel, she finished it in fact amazingly quickly and delivered a vast, 694-page manuscript to Joni Evans at Random House at the end of September.

That summer Tara seemed to be on the brink of making a major breakthrough as a singer when she formed a group called E-zee Possee and was taken up by Boy George, whose record label More Protein published her debut disc, 'Breathin' is E-zee', and who reckoned that she could become 'a huge star'. Soon afterwards she was to cut her first solo record, 'Save Me From Myself', but sadly she was never to become the rock star she dreamed of being. To promote the record she gave an interview to Linda Duff of the *Daily Star* in which she said how lonely she had been as a child and how much she had hated having famous parents. It was like 'having a Gorbachev-sized birthmark on my forehead', she said. 'It's been like a millstone hanging around my neck.' She lost a great deal of weight and felt so damaged by her childhood that her father persuaded her and Sacha to go into psychoanalysis for two years. 'Learning about yourself is indeed one of the most terrifying things you can do,' she said. 'There is nothing fun about it. But it helped me work out my fears.' Even so, when she left her boyfriend, Chris Ellis, that month after living with him for seven years she chose after ten years of independence to flee back to Mummy and live with Joan again. 'Mum is only too happy to buy me a place to stay and give me money,' she told Gill Pringle of the *News of the World* magazine. 'She has helped me out of corners. I owe her so much.'

At the end of September 1991 Joan's half-sister Natasha – who was twenty-three, had passed out of Sandhurst, was now a 2nd Lieutenant in the Women's Royal Army Corps and serving with the Royal Engineers in Germany – married a fellow officer, twenty-seven-year-old Lieutenant Patrick Coxen, in a smart white wedding at the village of Newnham, near Faversham, in Kent. Joan and Jackie were both invited but stayed away. Joan said that she needed a dental check-up, sent a pretty vase as a present, and went instead to join Britt Ekland and LaToya Jackson at a party that Madeleine Curtis was giving at her home in Datchet.

In October she took Robin and *Private Lives* on a gruelling, six-month tour of eleven American cities with Simon Jones as her male lead, starting in Denver and going on to Dallas, Houston, Sacramento and San Francisco, sometimes receiving standing ovations, sometimes desultory applause. In December they opened in Beverly Hills to another standing ovation and the *Los Angeles Times* reported that 'even seven and a half years of *Dynasty* has not diminished her ability'. The *Hollywood Reporter*, too, was full of praise and said that Joan's performance was 'a triumph on many levels. She delivers the ultra-glamour most audiences will anticipate, but also comes through with an Amanda who's much more confident, full-blown and stage-wise than most will expect.' Sadly the good reviews were not enough to keep the show going over Christmas and it closed early in Beverly Hills because of poor ticket sales. To publicise it she gave an interview to one of the gossip tabloids that she purported to hate, the *National Enquirer*, and gave them a list of the seven things that a woman should do to guarantee true love: never marry the man you love ('marriage tends to bring on complacency'); never trust him completely; don't give in to him too easily; never discuss your ex-lovers; choose much younger men because their ideas are more liberal; always look good; and act younger than your age. She also advised women to keep going to discos. No wonder all her marriages had failed.

In the new year the play travelled on to Miami, where she gave an interview to Mary Kemp of the *People*, hooting with laughter as she told her a recent joke she had heard: 'This guy with the biggest schlong in the world is standing with another guy on a bridge, both peeing into a river. "God, this water's cold," he says, and the other says: "Yeah, and deep too."' The play went on to Washington, Seattle,

Pittsburgh and finally in February to New York, where the reviews were lukewarm and the fearsome 'Butcher of Broadway', Frank Rich of the *New York Times*, said that the performance was 'not remotely satisfying' and that 'Joan Collins turned Noël Coward's intoxicating comedy *Private Lives* into a sobering experience'. His malign influence was such that ticket sales were poor and the play closed two weeks early in March 1992 after just thirty-seven performances, but only after it had prevented Joan attending Jackie's husband Oscar's funeral in Los Angeles on 6 March. He had died at home in Beverly Hills at the age of sixty-five after nearly twenty-six years of happy and faithful marriage and after fighting prostate cancer for five years. Jackie was devastated. 'He was the love of my life,' she said.

Joan and Robin did manage to fly to Los Angeles a few days later for Swifty Lazar's lavish annual Oscars party for three hundred of the most powerful and famous people in Hollywood at the ultra-fashionable Spago restaurant on Sunset Boulevard. At dinner Robin sat next to thirty-three-year-old Madonna Ciccone, the singer, who had recently been having an affair with Warren Beatty. She sniffed and licked each dish before tasting it, spent much of the meal blowing pink bubblegum, and suddenly asked Joan: 'Did Warren fuck Vivien Leigh?'

'Well, I was engaged to him at the time,' said Joan, 'so it's hardly likely he would have told *me*.'

'Well, he *says* he did,' said Madonna. 'Warren's always had this great knack of going with the right actress at the right time.'

For six months there had been an ominous silence from Joni Evans at Random House. Then came a terrible shock: in March 1992 she rejected Joan's novel. It was not nearly good enough to be published, she said. 'It was very primitive, very much off-base,' she said. 'It was jumbled and disjointed. It was alarming. I didn't believe it. It was dull. It was clichéd.' These were odd complaints to make since both Joan's previous novels had also been primitive, jumbled, disjointed, dull and clichéd, yet Ms Evans had been so desperate for her to write another that she had said she could 'taste it'. Joan was astonished by her reaction and claimed that she had written the book that they and Rosie Cheetham had agreed, although she had known and expected right from the start that Joni would need to do a lot of editing and rewriting to make it publishable, as she did for many of her other authors. Normally Joan would have turned to Swifty Lazar for advice, but at eighty-five he was suddenly showing alarming signs of senility – 'Your tits are too big,' he told her suddenly one day, 'you should have them lopped off' – so she started to write her fourth novel, *Hell Hath No Fury*, the story of a spurned wife's revenge, so that once that was done she would at least have fulfilled her two-book contract with Random House and earned their huge advance.

At the beginning of May she and Robin flew to Johannesburg for eight days to help raise funds for a South African charity, Operation Hunger, and she broke down in tears when she appeared on a TV variety programme, *Revue Plus*, and was insulted by a former England soccer goalkeeper, Gary Bailey, and three South African actors, Clive Scott, Frank Opperman and Jeremy Crutchley. None of them was on the show but in recorded comments one called her 'a sexy old auntie' and 'a nice package which is empty inside', while another said she was just 'a silicone sex symbol'. She was however applauded by the audience, one of whom stood up to apologise on behalf of all decent South Africans, and the TV channel also apologised and cut the offensive remarks before they were broadcast. She toured Munsieville, a poor black township outside the city, helped to serve maize, meatballs and spaghetti to some of the residents, ducked into one of the little corrugated iron shacks and was appalled to learn that it was home to fifteen people. She hugged and cuddled some of the black children and said that they were 'so sweet. If I was Mia Farrow I'd have already adopted all of them.' At a charity dinner she auctioned two of Alexis's dresses for £8,000, donated £1,000, sold autographs, and eventually helped to raise more than £10,000. She and Robin visited a religious mission, joined a safari, and spent a few days in Cape Town before flying home, where she immersed herself again in her new novel.

In June she was involved in yet another noisy rumpus at the races, this time at the Epsom Derby, where she arrived late, fifteen impolite minutes after the Queen, because she had not been on time at Battersea heliport to catch the helicopter that she was due to share with George Hamilton and they had left without her. She caught another helicopter a few minutes later but when she reached the racecourse and Hamilton came smiling to greet her she shrieked unfairly: 'George, you're a *shit!*'

Joan flew off to Argentina to promote a Spanish edition of *Love and Desire and Hate* before settling down to several serious months of work on *Hell Hath No Fury*, interrupting her literary labours only once to appear in an episode of the fat, rude comedienne Roseanne Arnold's American lower-class TV sitcom *Roseanne*, in which Joan played Roseanne's cousin and hated every minute of it.

It was eleven years since Joan had last made a film for the cinema and she was tempted back by the English actor, director and writer Steven Berkoff, who had played a Nazi villain in *Sins*. He wanted her for a movie in which he planned to star and direct, *Decadence*, which was mainly a two-handed, class-ridden sexual fantasy in which they both played two parts. Joan was a rich, snooty but foul-mouthed, kinky, upper-class bitch as well as a plain, sluttish, four-letter, *nouveau-riche* cockney woman. Berkoff played the two women's yobbish lovers, one of them the cockney woman's husband. Joan had long played elegant bitches – though this time she had to appear in a basque, suspenders and stockings and wield a riding crop while riding Berkoff as if he were a horse – but as the crude *nouveau-riche* woman her acting ability was seriously tested and she acquitted herself well in a part utterly unlike any other she had ever played. It was, however, a weird, pretentious movie, so stylised and pleased with itself that all the dialogue was in rhyming couplets, and so self-indulgent that I began to wonder whether 'Berkoff' might be cockney rhyming slang. She and Berkoff flew to Luxembourg to shoot *Decadence* and Joan found that whereas he had been a darling as a mere actor in *Sins* he was extremely difficult as a writer, director and star and at one stage the crew nearly resigned en masse. Joan too marched off the set in a rage after one row too many and caught a plane back to London, but Berkoff admired her performance and told Melvyn Bragg in 1999 that she was a much better actress than people thought she was and that if you scrape off all that veneer and gloss and make-up and lipstick and silicones or whatever else she's got, plastic, underneath there is more silicone and plastic but then you scrape that off and then underneath that is a real live human being and a very vital one and a highly intelligent one. He was less amused by the phalanx of Joan's friends – Christopher Biggins, Michael Winner – for whom she wangled small parts in the film. 'She had an entourage,' said Berkoff, 'like a kind of Snow White and the Seven Dwarves.' Despite their row – and Berkoff cutting the film so that he dominated every scene – he persuaded her to join him to promote the film at the Cannes Film Festival in May, but when he asked her a few months later to appear in another film he had written, this time about John Bobbitt, the American whose wife had cut off his penis, she declined.

A few days after returning from Cannes Joan had to face the appalling fact that on 23 May she would be sixty, an Old Age Pensioner, eligible for a state handout of a few pounds a week, a free bus pass and a winter heating allowance to prevent her dying of hypothermia. Every British newspaper, from *The Times* to the *Daily Mirror*, greeted her milestone birthday with a fanfare of interviews, tributes and profiles. 'She is a Hollywood star of the old school – perhaps the last we have,' said the *Sunday Telegraph*. In the *Daily Mail* Lynda Lee-Potter wrote that 'if she truly hasn't had a face-lift I can only say she's the only sixty-year-old I've ever seen who hasn't got a single line or a wrinkle. She certainly has none of the tough drag-queen look of her younger sister.' The only journalist who was not at all impressed by Joan was the feminist writer Germaine Greer, a woman strikingly different in every respect, who wrote a savage piece about her – 'the pouting pensioner' – in *The Sunday Times*. Joan's film career, she said, 'has produced more turkeys than Bernard Matthews. Her emotional life has been equally B-rated. She can probably claim the distinction of being the worst judge of men ever to survive to the age of sixty.' Nor was Ms Greer impressed even by Joan's good looks, pointing out that as long as twenty years previously, when Joan had been only forty, carelessly staged photographs had shown her 'sagging arms and gnarled elbows. Nowadays Miss Collins knows better than to bare her upper arms for daylight shots and is seldom shot in daylight at all.' Even Robin did not escape Ms Greer's acid pen: 'We are expected to believe that after more than forty years with a tendency for going to bed with creeps she is now going to bed with an old Etonian who is much too much of a gent to take her money and spend it on younger women.' Ms Greer finished her article with brutal contempt: 'The images of Joan Collins that have proliferated for the past twenty years do not express sensuality and tenderness but hard-edged glamour, sterility and loneliness: Miss Collins bewigged, bepainted and bejewelled, sticking red roses on a designer Christmas tree in her hideous house in Beverly Hills; Miss Collins's bulging white satin bed, a dais for performing on rather than an inviting place to sleep; Miss Collins's dressing table, an ice cave blazing with wrinkle-erasing light; the mask of Miss Collins, staring wide-eyed into her key-light out of rouged eye-sockets and a froth of micro-powder. Miss Collins the trouper has never had the time or inclination to discover how to live.'

Even Alexis Carrington might well have been lost for a cutting reply to that, and it was to be six years before Joan was able to answer in kind. 'If Germaine Greer had had a child she wouldn't have ended up so bitter,' she told *OK!* magazine in 1999. 'If she'd raised a son she might have understood a bit more about men.' The truth was, of course, that flinty-eyed, wrinkled old Germaine Greer probably understood men only too well and a great deal better than dear old naïve, girly, starry-eyed Joan.

CHAPTER NINETEEN

THE OLD AGE PENSIONER

{ 1993–1996 }

When Joan turned sixty in May 1993 Steven Berkoff told the *Sunday Telegraph* that she had become an icon, the most famous actress in the world, and indeed she seemed to have everything she could possibly desire: global recognition, vast wealth, two satisfying careers as actress and novelist, a young lover who adored her, three healthy children, a doting ex-husband, and many powerful friends. Tara had just landed a job in Manchester with Granada TV hosting a late-night show for teenagers, *Juice*, on which she discussed dildoes, condoms and gay clubs, and she was living happily in a flat in Didsbury with a new boyfriend, her twenty-seven-year-old co-presenter Johnny Bramwell. Sacha had just graduated from the London International Film School after directing an acclaimed thirty-minute black-and-white comedy, *Yvette*, starring Rex Harrison's granddaughter Cathryn Harrison, had painted recently a highly praised portrait of the actor Nigel Hawthorne in his film role as King George III, and was now doing Joan's portrait and accepting commissions. And Katy, who was about to celebrate her twenty-first birthday with a party at the Pizza on the Park, was still living with Jeff Stewart, had been working for a publishing company, and was about to become Joan's couturier Maryam Rokny-Owji's assistant. 'Katy was very genuine, calm, kind and loving,' Mrs Rokny-Owji told me. 'She would help me with administration, inviting guests and making phone calls. She had no influence on making the clothes but she was always good when we had a fashion show or special project.' Even though Maryam had given Katy a job Joan insisted that she should not make any more clothes for Britt Ekland: 'Stars like Joan don't want to give their couture de-signer away because they want to shine in the crowd. Britt was very upset and bitter when Joan forced me to stop designing clothes for her.'

Yet Joan's life was not as perfect as it seemed. Robin was restless. After five years as her acknowledged lover he was finding her shallow, demanding and dependent, and he was close to ending the affair. 'He had loved her very much and it had been a very happy relationship for years,' one of their friends told me, 'but it shouldn't really have lasted much more than a year. I don't think she ever really loved him. She loved *him* loving *her*.' His discontent became obvious to their friends, and her Greek ex-lover Taki Theodoracopulos took her to dinner at Annabel's and asked her to go to bed with him again. 'I'd love to, darling,' she said, 'but I'm in a relationship' – and so she still was, for Robin could never quite bring himself to dump her.

As if Joan did not already have plenty of writing to do on her fourth novel, she also agreed to compile a book of beauty tips, *My Secrets*, and hired a young writer, Cindy Blake, to help her finish it at Cabrillo Drive. Ms Blake was terrified. 'I overheard her on the telephone talking to someone with whom she was greatly displeased,' she reported later in the *Sunday Telegraph*. 'Her tone of voice carried that kind of calm fury which makes you wonder if she throws knives at small rodents in her time off. I came to understand that the most egregious sins on her list were disloyalty and stupidity [*and*] she was not one to be crossed, not one to suffer fools, not one to be working for if you didn't know what on earth you were supposed to be doing – which I didn't.' Yet there was also a soft side to Joan that surfaced when she chatted – looking 'endearingly girlish' without any make-up – about men and love in Hollywood. 'No one is better at girl-talk,' wrote Ms Blake. 'I never knew whether the vulnerability she displayed was calculated, but it certainly had me believing she was neither Bitch nor Sweetheart but an intriguing combination of both.'

At the end of June Joan and Robin were invited to Jeffrey and Madeleine Curtis's daughter's wedding in Datchet and Joan was disconcerted to see that Peter Holm was there as well. She managed to avoid him all evening but Mrs Curtis told a *Daily Express* gossip columnist that 'of course Peter was invited. He has known my daughter most of her life. If he and Joan still have something to sort out it's up to them' – which suggested that the Curtises, at least, did not consider Peter to be anything like the monster that Joan had claimed he was.

That summer she appeared in a BBC TV comedy play, *Mama's Back*, by Ruby Wax, in which she played a TV soap star who is sacked and has to return to her husband (Michael Gambon) and a boring life as an ordinary suburban housewife. It was a gem of a comedy, said David Wigg in the *Daily Express*: 'There are some hilarious moments for Joan as she gives her own tongue-in-cheek impressions of Florence Nightingale and St Joan.' She also accepted with relish the challenge of guest-editing the Christmas issue of *Marie Claire* magazine, and finally delivered nervously to Joni Evans the completed manuscript of her fourth novel, *Hell Hath No Fury*.

The mansion in Beverly Hills had been on the market for four years and Joan was desperate to sell it, since she was now spending much more time in Europe than in LA. The original asking price had been £3.25 million but in November she accepted an offer of only £1.3 million [£1,872,000], less than she had paid for it seven years earlier, just to get rid of it. A few weeks later Los Angeles was struck by yet another major earthquake. 'I have to be the luckiest woman,' she said. 'I would never have sold it after that.' Her luck lasted barely a few weeks because the American tax authorities had noticed that she had made no tax return for 1987 and were demanding a million dollars plus interest, and she had to send them a cheque for $1.3 million – £674,000 – about half of what she had made from the sale of the house.

She and Robin spent Christmas in Barbados but she suffered a heavy blow when Swifty Lazar died on 30 December, aged eighty-six, and left her with neither a father figure nor a shield against Joni Evans and Random House, which informed her six weeks later that they considered *Hell Hath No Fury* to be just as amateurish and unpublishable as *A Ruling Passion* and demanded the return of the £800,000 advance that they had already paid her for the two books. The publishers would never have dared to treat her like that had Swifty still been alive, she said: 'He was so powerful, one phone call and they'd have backed off.' The problem for Random House was that *Dynasty* was no longer on television, Joan's fame as Alexis was likely to fade fast, the public was losing its taste for schlock novels by celebrity authors, and in the new climate they could never hope to recoup the £2.5 million that they had agreed to pay her. The only way out for them was to claim that the book was so bad that it simply could not be published, which would mean that she had broken the contract. Joan's reaction was splendidly feisty: not only did she resist the demand that she should return the £800,000, she also insisted that Random House should pay her the unpaid balance of £1.75 million since she claimed that she had now delivered two completed novels and so had fulfilled her part of the contract. With glorious cheek and stunning self-confidence she started to write her fifth novel, *Too Damn Famous*, even though her third and fourth were still unpublished. The legal battle was to last for two nerve-racking years. 'We'd go out to dinner and have a lovely time with friends and then we'd come back to my flat and there would be some ghastly fax from the lawyers detailing the latest antics of Random House,' she told David Wigg in 1996. 'It was all very stressful.'

At least she still had Rosie Cheetham to help her with the new novel. 'She would write and then I would take it away and for twenty pages a night I'd have a go at it,' Mrs Cheetham told me. 'But she was very, very particular and a lot of what I wanted to do would come back crossed out or changed. Joan really loved writing, she worked very hard at it, and because she was being paid a fortune and people were falling over themselves to flatter her, she thought the reviewers were simply against her just as they had always been about her acting. The worst thing was always the lack of time: we were always up against it with deadlines. But Robin was very helpful during those years. He had literary taste and didn't want her to be writing the novels. "I love her dearly," he said to me. "I *really* love her, but they're just childish."' And sleazy, I suggested. Well, said Mrs Cheetham, 'she may have felt she had to do that because Jackie did, and it was the sex-and-shopping era, but I don't think she was that comfortable doing it.'

During their hours of writing and editing together Rosie Cheetham discovered an unexpectedly cosy side of Joan's nature. 'I saw a lot of her and came to like her hugely,' she told me. 'You'd think she might not be nice to other women but she is. She's a man's woman but she does very good girl gossip too and many's the time that I've turned up at that lovely flat in Eaton Place and found her without a scrap of make-up and her hair in just a kind of turban but looking terrific. She was really nice and cosy during those sessions, not at all arrogant, although she could turn quite quickly into being imperious. But then I think a lot of great beauties can be like that, and people who have been very flattered all their lives, but basically she's a *terribly* down-to-earth woman and could be so simple and girly. I like her *very* much.'

At least Joan was making some money from one of her books: *My Secrets*, which was published in January 1994 and serialised at length for five days in the *Daily Express*. It was packed with tips about the right foods to eat, the right exercise to take, the right clothes and make-up to wear, and she recommended plenty of good sex and a zest for life. And she came up with some nice lines. 'Women go to bed with men so they can talk to them,' she wrote. 'Men talk to women so they can go to bed with them.' From birth to the age of eighteen a girl needs good parents, she told Peregrine Worsthorne of the *Sunday Telegraph*, then 'from eighteen to twenty-five a girl needs good looks. From twenty-five to fifty a girl needs a good personality, and from fifty onwards a girl needs cash.' She undertook a British publicity tour, during which she clashed with a BBC Radio Scotland interviewer, Jackie Bird, who asked her if she had written her beauty book because she had turned sixty.

'How old are you?' snapped Joan.

'Thirty-one,' said Jackie.

'I thought you looked older.'

'I was going to say the same thing about you.'

Joan was further upset when Ms Bird claimed that she had never been much of a success in the cinema, sneered at *The Stud* and *The Bitch*, and called her a 'soft-porn queen'. Joan marched out of the studio only to find herself up against another woman interviewer who took no prisoners, Judy Rumbold, who gave her lunch at a smart Mayfair restaurant and printed afterwards a devastating profile in the *Guardian* magazine:

'Christ!' shrieks Collins at lunch. 'That looks *horrible*.' A flustered waiter beats a swift retreat to the kitchen carrying an aesthetically disastrous tomato salad. 'I want *half* that amount, and can't you put some oil on it or something?' She sits and fidgets, pursing her lips just so, patting her souffléd hair, batting her eyelashes, before announcing with a firm slap of the table, 'I'm sorry. I can't sit here. Those people,' she says, jerking her head towards a small group of businessmen who are generating – at most – the noise level of a gnat, 'they're putting me off.' She stands up and sweeps across the restaurant to a corner table while a flurry of waiters and a noxious cloud of Spectacular by Joan Collins follow in her wake. 'I can't understand it,' she says, 'the other times I've been to this place, it's been like a *tomb*.' She settles herself and looks across at the restaurant – a mirrored bordello-like place reminiscent of the strobe-lit backdrops of her early films – to see how many people noticed this flawless performance. 'I can't help it,' she says. 'I'm a Gemini, a butter-fly. I am very easily distracted.'

The main course arrives. She's having spinach. You can tell by the look on the waiter's face as he propels the limp green stuff towards her that the dish is doomed. 'Oh no, I don't want *this*,' she says, as if addressing a plateful of sheep's gonads. She points to my plate. 'I want *that*.' Broccoli; she must have it. Now. Urgently. Right away. We negotiate a swap and the waiter, by turns quaking and awestruck, sweats and apologises. He calls in reinforcements and they embark on some needlessly complex rearranging of table furniture. What, you wonder, as spinach and broccoli are shuffled round the table like chips in a game of roulette, would Susan Hampshire make of all this?

Collins gets out a cigarette and a waiter hovers by her with a box of matches. 'What are you doing?' she barks, as if he were preparing to administer colonic irrigation with a garden hose. 'I was going to give you a light,' he says limply. 'Oh, go on then.' Then she gets up, saying she's going to the Ladies 'to have a cough'. The truth is – and the kitchen staff responsible for eliminating the scarlet smears from every glass that comes within puckering distance of Collins's mouth will back me on this one – it's her second lipstick mission in less than an hour. And who can blame her? At her age, lipstick matters.

In February Joan flew off to Barbados for two weeks to make on the beach a sixty-minute exercise and fitness video based on her beauty book. She and Robin stayed again with the Bamfords, who invited the opera singer Luciano Pavarotti to dinner. He sat next to Joan, shared her chocolate pudding, and afterwards sang 'Nessun dorma'. They also lunched with one of Joan's favourite old actresses, ninety-year-old Claudette Colbert, at her house near Speightstown. Then Joan flew on to Canada, Los Angeles and Australia to promote the beauty book, but when the video reached the shops in May it sold badly.

Sacha did better when he held his first professional exhibition of about thirty drawings and watercolours at the Halcyon Hotel in Holland Park: both his parents and Tara turned up to support him and the show sold out, making him some decent money for the first time.

'I'm so proud of my little boy,' said Joan. 'He's wonderfully talented.' He was soon to go and live in Los Angeles and to paint portraits of the film directors Oliver Stone and Billy Wilder and the writer Dominick Dunne. Joan was also proud of both her daughters. Tara was writing songs and a TV sitcom, had found a new boyfriend – a photographer, Jonathan Millais – and had become so successful as a television presenter that a month later the *Daily Mail* devoted a page and a half to an interview with her by Corinna Honan in which she confessed that she had once resented the fact that Katy was her mother's favourite child but that 'going into analysis has made me come to terms with these things. I feel very level-headed about it all now. There were times in my life when I was bitter and angry. I'd like to think I've grown up a bit now and put that behind me.' Like her mother she kept trying to reassure herself that she was not as naïve as once she had been, and like Joan she was unconvincing.

In July 1994 Joan bumped into a spectre from the past, Bill Wiggins, at a charity function where one of the lots to be auctioned was a twosome dinner date with her, so she was flattered as well as flustered to hear wicked Wiggy bid £5,000 for her. Luckily he was outbid by a businessman who paid £1,000 more, or who knows what might have happened. She believed that another phantom, this time malignant, was haunting her when she and Robin joined Carole Bamford and some other friends for a few days in a rented *palazzo* in Venice, which they were convinced was home to an evil poltergeist. Although it was a hot September Joan was chilled by an inexplicably icy draught, and in one spot in the dining room the hair on the back of her wig suddenly stood on end. Scores of sugared almonds seemed to have arranged themselves on the floor in the shape of a body, Robin was convinced that somebody had been lying across him during the night and claimed that a huge, bronze jardinière had moved across the drawing room and that a carving knife had flown through the air. They left in a hurry.

At the end of December they flew to Barbados again to welcome the New Year with Michael Winner, John Cleese, Sir David and Lady Frost, and Robert and Sue Sangster, and then it was back to the States for another author tour to promote the beauty book. The year ahead was to be particularly busy, too. Joan made a cinema film, two movies for TV, published her fifth novel, and began to write another autobiography, *Second Act*, with Robin's help. The cinema film, *In the Bleak Midwinter*, which was retitled *A Midwinter's Tale* in America, was a triumph even though her part was small. Written and directed by Kenneth Branagh, it was a delightfully witty, lighthearted and very English movie about a cast of neurotic, unemployed English actors who decide to stage a charity production of *Hamlet* just before Christmas, which resurrects all manner of memories and emotions. The characters were excellent – Joan played an elegant, cynical agent opposite Jennifer Saunders as a tough Hollywood agent – while Richard Briers, Celia Imrie, Michael Maloney, Julia Sawalha and John Sessions played the 'resting' luvvies who were harassed throughout the film by a taunting rendition of Noël Coward's sardonic song '*Why* Must the Show Go On?' All in all it was a wonderfully cheery, affectionate, insiders' mickey-take of actors and went on to win an award at the Venice International Film Festival in September.

Joan's new novel, *Too Damn Famous*, was published in June. It was easily her best, partly because it described in down-to-earth fashion what she knew best, her own life and problems rather than some silly, melodramatic plot, and partly because she had had Rosie Cheetham's help. Joan's heroine, Katherine Bennett, is a clone of herself: the most famous TV star in the world, 'the woman they loved to hate', who plays the part of a venemous, unscrupulous bitch in a prime-time TV soap, lives in a huge, soulless Hollywood mansion, and divorces her drunken, drug-addict husband after many years only to marry a sexually insatiable but sinister, moody control freak who takes over her life. Despite her fame and wealth, Katherine is lonely, has few real friends in the shallow goldfish bowl of Hollywood, and is desperate to find a man who might really love her – but not an actor, most of whom are egomaniacs desperate to be loved but unable to give love in return. Actresses, too, are generally pathetically desperate for applause: 'It's a stupid profession, really. Marlon's right.' Katherine is, in fact, just too damn famous for her own good. The media hound and lie about her, she is mobbed wherever she goes and sometimes overwhelmed by the pressures of her fame and demands of her fans. She feels responsible for her Ron Kass-like ex-husband, whom she is still supporting and who is living in a filthy, chaotic apartment, drinking two bottles of vodka a day and about to be struck down by cancer. She feels guilty too about her troubled, morose, teenage son, who has been badly affected by her divorce, believes that she cares more about her career, clothes and publicity than about him, and is at one stage in a coma. The vulnerable Katherine falls for a golden-haired, fabulously well-hung Frenchman, like Holm an ex-pop star who pleasures her five times a day but sacks her staff and advisers, takes over her business and finances, tries to control her whole life, eventually becomes a nightmare, and turns out to be a con-man.

Thankfully this time Joan resisted the temptation to splatter the book with dozens of explicit sex scenes, though one of them, about an actress who is so promiscuous that she is nicknamed The British Open, deserves a place in any schlock anthology: 'Carefully, as though taking precious eggs from their nest, he removed first one breast, and then the other. His hand cupped one, while his skilful lips caressed the other. Throwing back her head, but careful not to dislodge the massive blonde wig, she began to let out little moans ... He found her panty-less and moist ... His fingers worked swiftly. He'd done this many times, and knew exactly how to bring her to fulfilment. This time, it was something of a record – even for her. It was less than a minute, before her back arched, and she gave the high-pitched little scream which meant that she had reached a climax. Dirk carefully put her manufactured breasts back in place, and handed her a wad of Kleenex. "Feeling better?" he asked, noting how her face fell, as she searched in vain for a swelling in his trousers.'

The book was dedicated again 'FOR ROBIN With all my love' and the British reviewers were kinder than usual. The book was 'perfect holiday reading', said the *Daily Mirror* and 'like a huge bar of chocolate ... irresistible,' said the *Sunday Telegraph*. 'I loved every minute.'

Two weeks later Joan was finally allowed into the Royal Enclosure at Ascot thanks to some serious lobbying by her racehorse-owner friend Robert Sangster, who managed to persuade the authorities to give her a badge of her own. She took pleasure in not using it except for spending only ten minutes in the enclosure and then reporting in *Second Act* that it had been no big deal.

In July Tara started work as a presenter on the first day of London's new women-only radio station, *Viva!*, and interviewed 'my darling Mummy' on her morning chat show. Joan revealed that she would like Tara to start having babies now that she was nearly thirty-two. 'What, we wonder, will she do for an encore?' asked Vanessa Feltz in the *Evening Standard*. 'Tomorrow? "My darling Daddy, Anthony Newley, warbles 'What Kind of Fool Am I?'" And the next day? "My darling Auntie Jackie Collins gives us three hundred different words for whanger".'

The first TV movie that Joan made that year was a story of blackmail and murder, *Hart to Hart: Two Harts in Three-Quarters Time*, with her old friend RJ Wagner and Stefanie Powers, and in July and August she worked on the second, *Annie: A Royal Adventure!*, a Little Orphan Annie sequel in which she was given top billing despite again having only a small part. Allegedly a children's comedy, it told of an apparently 'cute' but actually eminently smackable, red-haired American child and her two equally nauseating friends who sail for England on the *Queen Mary* along with an evil, conniving, over-the-top society widow, Lady Edwina Hogbottom (Joan), who plans to blow up Buckingham Palace and become Queen. Joan camped it up outrageously and in one scene even shrilled like Lady Bracknell 'a *sand*-wich?' It was not one of her finer roles.

In September Joan and Robin sought refuge at Destino, where they resumed work on the autobiography. She had also ventured into journalism, writing an article for *Chic* magazine in which she warned that Britain was a sick, yobbish society heading towards anarchy and deplored the increase in crime, the vulgarity of modern life, the prevalence of grungy clothes, and the disappearance of good manners and correct speech. This was unexpected from a woman whose own behaviour 'is not always in the best possible taste', suggested Colin McDowell in *The Sunday Times* under the headline LOOK WHO'S TALKING. 'How could we forget all those prima-donna performances at airports, restaurants and social occasions from the races to garden parties, which have so enlivened our lives and so endeared Miss Collins to us over the years?' He went on: 'This is the actress, remember, who starred in such notable movies as *The Stud* (yes, she really did bare all at the age of forty-two) and *The Bitch*.' He concluded: 'The nice thing about Collins is that she has always managed to dress precisely as the woman next door would had she won the pools and gone out to spend, spend, spend. I've always felt Joan – Essex woman exalted to the world stage – could have avoided the unhappiness of her failed marriages if she could have found a builder called Len and lived – all mod cons, en suite and heated pool, mind you – in Chelmsford ... She invariably manages to look like that successful Chelmsford builder's wife, no matter what she wears or what the occasion.'

A year after Oscar's death Jackie had found happiness again with one of his friends, a fifty-three-year-old LA businessman, Frank Calcagnini, who soon moved in with her, and since he was five years younger she insisted that she too was fifty-three, not fifty-eight. 'But why, then, did a newspaper recently publish her birth date as 4 October 1937?' Lester Middlehurst asked her: '"I've no idea," she growls, "but they were wrong. So please get it right. I'm fifty-three."' No she wasn't: she was two months short of fifty-nine and nearly six years older than her new lover. Jackie had finally followed Joan's example and found herself a toyboy.

Joan's right-wing Conservative opinions resurfaced when she was interviewed for the *Daily Telegraph* by Boris Johnson, who was later to become the editor of the *Spectator*, a Conservative Member of Parliament, and was mesmerised by her beauty and smouldering sexuality, the wide, sparkling eyes, the breathy little English voice, the tiny waist, the 'heaving poitrine … the … crikey … Yes, the mind has been more or less turned to putty,' he wrote, but he did manage to hear what she said about politics. 'It's the really wet way that we treat criminals,' she said, 'and victims are treated worse than criminals. Yesterday a thirteen-year-old girl was raped by an illegal immigrant, and he's now walking free and this poor little girl is cowering in her house, and there's nothing they can do, and he's an *illegal immigrant*! That's the sort of thing that drives me crazy so often that I think we need more of a police state. I'm *huge* on law and order. I think I'm part of the silent majority.'

After spending Christmas in London Joan and Robin flew to New York to face a Supreme Court jury on 67th Street and the legal battle with Random House, which was to be televised live by a local cable channel, Court TV. She was hugely apprehensive and told her friend Sarah Standing that if she lost the case she would have to sell the flat in London or the house in the South of France. The first shots were fired on an icy winter morning on 6 February when the publishers' lawyer, Robert Callagy, told the jury that Joan should be made to return the £800,000 advance she had been paid for two novels because she had not fulfilled her contract since the manuscripts were so bad that they were unpublishable and consequently unfinished. 'If you sign a contract, you live up to it,' he contended. 'If you don't perform, you have to pay the money back.' Joni Evans had left Random House, was now working for the William Morris literary agency, seemed at the age of fifty-three to be as tough and ruthless as Alexis Carrington, and gave evidence that Joan's first manuscript, *A Ruling Passion*, had been 'extremely dated, melodramatic and a little bit Gothic. It was not very modern. I was concerned it did not have the edge of her previous books. This was a manuscript in no shape at all. It was all over the map with many themes not quite gelling. It was totally not credible, jumbled and alarming.'

Joan's lawyer, Ken Burrows, who was married to the author Erica Jong, began her defence by denying that Joan owed Random House anything and claiming that in fact *they* owed *her* almost £1.75 million: the unpaid balance of the agreed £2.5 million advance, because she had delivered two manuscripts and thus fulfilled her side of the contract. Nowhere did the contract stipulate that the money would be paid only if Random House approved the manuscripts. If Random House wanted the novels to be better then they should have given her the expert editorial help that all publishers give to 'celebrity' authors if necessary. Joni Evans had admitted, for instance, that she had spent six weeks helping Jeffrey Archer to rewrite his novel *Kane and Abel* and had devoted a great deal of time to polishing books by Michael Caine and Walter Matthau, so why had she not done the same for Joan?

On the morning of the third day Joan told reporters that she could not repay the £800,000 anyway because she had spent it all. 'It sounds a lot but it actually isn't,' she said. As for Joni Evans, 'she wanted me as an author desperately. The woman seduced me like a man trying to get a woman into bed. She told me how wonderful I was. How terrific. She kept telling me I was the greatest thing since sliced bread.' In court Callagy ambushed her by suddenly calling her unexpectedly to the witness box and producing a statement she had made four years previously when she had sued *Globe* magazine over the topless photographs they had published and had claimed then that the pictures had upset her so much that she had been unable to complete the book for Random House. So had she really finished the book, as she was claiming now, or had she not, as she had claimed in a sworn deposition in the *Globe* case? One of the statements had to be a lie. Which?

'You were under oath,' said Callagy. 'You swore to tell the truth?'

'Yes.'

'You know what telling the truth means?'

'Yes.'

She tried to explain how one sworn statement could completely contradict the other.

'Just answer the questions,' snapped the judge, Ira Gammerman. 'Just say yes or no.'

'No.'

'Read what you said at the time,' insisted Callagy.

'I'm looking for it,' snapped Joan.

Several times she said 'I can't remember' and finally Callagy moved in for the kill: 'So you tell the *Globe* one thing when you are suing them, and you say another thing when you are suing Random House.'

'No, no!' said Joan.

'Have you no shame?' he said quietly.

The judge admonished him for this. Joan wiped her eyes, dabbed her nose and retired to a room nearby where she was said to be deeply distressed. Some cynics believed that she was giving the greatest acting performance of her life but Rosie Cheetham, who was about to be called as a witness, told me that Joan's tears were 'utterly genuine. She was mortified. That evening we convened in her suite with her two lawyers: sweet, mild-mannered Ken Burrows and Don Zakarin, an absolute Rottweiler. Joan was looking dazzling, wearing the prettiest black dress and looking lovely, but Sarah Standing said, "I think we could lose this case." Joan, looking a very pretty picture of woe with tears sparkling in her eyes, said: "I'm just a forward-looking person. They tie me up in knots trying to make me remember things from six years ago. I *can't*. I'm a *Gemini*, I don't bother to worry about the past. Give me twenty-five lines of dialogue, I can learn it, but then it's gone and I'm on to the next thing." So her Rottweiler of a lawyer, Don, said, "Joan, shuddup and listen to me. You think this is *your* case. It is *not*. It is *my* case. I do not permit people to lose my cases for me. You want dialogue, you're gonna *get* dialogue, starting tonight." And she looked at him with big eyes and said "Gotcha!" and from that moment on she was Alexis Carrington in court. He coached her what to say and she slayed them in the witness box. But she had certainly told two versions of the truth.'

Mrs Cheetham, who had now left Random House in London to

help her husband Anthony launch a new publishing giant, Orion, gave invaluable evidence on the fourth day that may have finally won the case for Joan when she said that Joan had had every right to expect Joni Evans to give her close, line-by-line, page-by-page editing. Whatever Joni Evans might say, said Rosie, *A Ruling Passion* was a 'fast, page-turning read'. It needed a lot of work on it, she admitted, but 'it could have been turned into a successful work of commercial fiction'. Ten years later Rosie confessed to me that she had exaggerated 'a bit' in court, that she had been 'extremely optimistic' in claiming that a decent editor could have made *A Ruling Passion* publishable, and that editing it would have been 'a long, difficult job and I wouldn't have wanted to do it. But if Joan's books were really bad then it was our fault: her publishers. Blame us. It was unfair to ask her to do something that was not based on her own life. People wanted to read about Joan's life, not about made-up princesses in some made-up principality.'

Many authors, publishers and literary agents were convinced that Random House had targetted Joan because they realised that they had agreed to pay her far too much and knew that they could never recoup the advance because readers had become much less interested in 'celebrity' novels. On the fifth and final day of the trial the jury took nearly two hours to reach their verdict while Joan sat sipping coffee nervously in a nearby café with Rosie, Judy Bryer and Sarah Standing. 'For all her starry sophistication, here was one very vulnerable woman,' wrote Ms Standing in the *Daily Express*. When the jury returned, Joan dived instinctively into the Ladies to put on her armour, more lipstick. Back in court the jury announced that it had decided unanimously that she had indeed delivered one complete manuscript, *A Ruling Passion*. As the TV camera zoomed in to record her reaction she adopted a series of wonderfully actressy expressions that were worthy of *Dynasty*: apprehension, bewilderment, hyperventilation, sudden understanding, joy. Her victory was not total, however, for the jury agreed with Random House that she had not delivered a second novel because *Hell Hath No Fury* had been just a rehash of *A Ruling Passion*, and they left the judge to decide how much Random House still owed her. Judy Bryer hugged her, lifting her off her feet, and Joan thanked the jurors, who gave her a standing ovation, shook hands with them all, signed their copies of her manuscripts, and outside the courthouse she punched the air triumphantly for the photographers.

Joan and her Swedish fourth husband, Peter Holm, whose real name was Sjöholm and who was fourteen years younger than she, in love on the French Riviera in the summer of 1985, five months before their wedding ... (Sipa Press/Rex Features)

... and Holm two years later, after their divorce, demonstrating outside a courtroom in Los Angeles and pathetically begging for a share of Joan's fortune. (Topham Picturepoint)

In 1983, when she was 50 and still
married to Ron Kass, Joan had at
least three toyboy lovers: 36-year-
old Peter Holm, 26-year-old Jon-
Erik Hexum (*left*) and James
Mason's 28-year-old son Morgan
(*below*). Hexum starred with her in
a TV film, *The Making of a Male
Model*, but died after a tragic accident the following year when he
was fooling around with a prop
revolver and shot a piece of his
skull into his brain. (Private collection;
Time and Life/Getty Images)

In 1987, when Joan was 53 and still
married to Peter Holm, she had a
rip-roaring affair with 40-year-old
'Bungalow Bill' Wiggins: a jolly,
rugged, handsome man-about-
London who had earned his nickname because it was said that he
had 'not much up top but a hell of
a lot down below.' For more than a
year they had a huge amount of
fun on both sides of the Atlantic
before he decided to cool the affair
and live with another woman.
(Bill Wiggins)

After Bill Wiggins, Joan fell for yet another handsome man who was much younger than she: tall, elegant, 28-year-old art dealer Robin Hurlstone. They lived together in London and the South of France for more than ten years until she suddenly dumped him in 2001 for her fifth husband, Percy Gibson. (South West News Service)

Despite all Joan's lovers and husbands, and despite all the difficulties of their relationship, this was perhaps the man whom she loved most of all: her 85-year-old father, Joe, just before he died in 1988. And judging by the framed photographs of her beside him, he adored her too. (Chris Davies/Arena PAL/Topfoto)

Life looking extremely rosy and sparkling in 1988: the Collins sisters with the world (and American star photographer Annie Leibovitz) at their feet. Gorgeous, elegant, successful and famous, they were both also self-made multi-millionaires. Who said that life should be fair? (Annie Leibovitz)

Joan with her 22-year-old
artist son, Sacha, on holiday in
Greece in 1988 ...
(P Anastasselis/Rex Features)

... and her rebellious teenage
daughter, Tara. (Mirrorpix)

Joan reconciled at last with her once-bitter ex-husband Anthony Newley, together with Tara, Katy and Sacha at the launch party for Joan's third volume of autobiography, *Second Act*, in 1996. (Richard Young/Rex Features)

Joan in 1998 with Nigel Hawthorne in *The Clandestine Marriage*, a rumbustious 18th-century comedy in which she played a vulgar, snobbish, *nouveau-riche* widow and he a dotty, lecherous, impoverished old aristocrat. 'She can be a very good actress indeed,' he said, and 'the real lady underneath it all is very, very warm.'
(BBC/British Screen/The Kobal Collection/Alex Bailey)

Joan and her Peruvian fifth husband, 36-year-old Percy Jorge Gibson Miguel Monaghan Mueller Parra del Riego, in Los Angeles in March 2002, a month after their wedding . . .
(Rose Prouser/Reuters)

. . . and with her third grand-child, Ava, Sacha's daughter, in 2004. You would never believe that Joan was 71.
(Eddie Sanderson/Scope Features)

Joan as she will always be remembered:
as Alexis Carrington in *Dynasty* in
1982. She was 49. (MPTV)

'Justice was done,' Rosie Cheetham told me, 'because it was totally and utterly our collective fault as publishers. I felt that Joan had been very hard done by, that it was madness, unfair and wrong, and that Random House and Joni Evans behaved very badly. At first she had been totally behind the plot of *A Ruling Passion*. Random House fired her before the court case but we knew what the deal was when we did business with Swifty Lazar. He said it right upfront: "I will not get my stars to come to the table if they think it's going to be dependent on a publisher's judgement of what they finally produce. They are *not* writers. It is up to you to find ghost writers, editors, and it's your job to turn them into publishable books. Therefore, I insist that the delivery advance is paid whether you like it or you don't.' Every Swifty contract from time immemorial had that in. It was nasty but it was there. Random House would *never* have taken Joan on if Swifty hadn't died. They would never have dared. So it was *entirely* our fault. We were silly enough to pay an enormous price for the books because we were caught up in the hype.'

Because the second novel was just a rewrite of the first, the judge ruled that Random House should pay Joan only £616,000 plus interest instead of the £1.75 million that she had demanded, and because they now owned *A Ruling Passion* the book would never be published, which was probably just as well judging by some of the pretty awful extracts that emerged in court. A couple of weeks later the American edition of *Too Damn Famous* was published by Dutton Press under the title *Infamous* – the word *damn* would apparently upset sensitive American readers – but it was to be six years before she published another novel.

Joan and Robin went off to Barbados to recuperate after two years of legal anguish, but her euphoria at winning the case evaporated when the *Sunday Mirror* published five days later an unhappy claim about Katy's relationship with her forty-year-old boyfriend, Jeff Stewart, with whom she had recently broken up after five years. Joan was apoplectic, but there was nothing she could do about it.

Joan was upset again in May when *Vogue* ran a four-page photo feature along with an affectionate interview by Vicki Woods, who wrote that although Joan was the most photogenic person she had ever met, in ordinary daylight 'she looks like an older, frailer shadow of her former self and the camera-ready make-up – black-rimmed eyes and jammy red lips – looks forced'. Ridiculously and inaccurately, Joan's London PR lady, Stella Wilson, complained to the editor, Alexandra Shulman, that the piece had been 'gratuitously nasty'. Worse was to come. In August Bill Wiggins spilled the beans about their affair at last when he gave a long, in-depth interview to David Jones of the *Daily Mail* and claimed that it had been he, not she, who had ended it. 'So what is the real Joan Collins like?' asked Jones. 'The answer is as complex as she is. Iron-willed on the outside, weak and racked by terrible insecurity and self-doubt inside. Competitive, bossy – on villa holidays she has been known to leave notes on the fridge designating tasks to other guests – she has a compulsive need to always be on top. Her attention span is notoriously short, especially if people are not talking about her.' Wiggy was still baffled by Joan's determination to deny his existence and not to mention him even in her new autobiography, *Second Act*, perhaps because Robin had done so much to help her write it. 'That hurt me,' Wiggy told me. 'I still like her and think she's a Good Thing but I'm hurt that she's taken this attitude towards me. I've been as loyal as I possibly could be and more loyal to her than most.' Hell hath no fury, he told Jones, 'but I don't believe I scorned her. Unlike others, I never ripped her off, but now I hear she is going around saying that I lived off her for five years afterwards. It's just not true, and it grieves me greatly.' Four days later the *Daily Mail* ran a profile of Joan by Tony Gallagher, who claimed that Wiggy had said that he did not think she was happy because she had never been taken seriously as an actress nor as a writer. Gallagher claimed that Joan was lonely because Tara and Sacha were away and Jackie was now estranged because of their rivalry as writers.

Second Act covered much of the same ground as *Past Imperfect* but brought Joan's life story up to date, expanded parts of it, and added extra anecdotes. It was published in September and serialised over five days in the *Daily Express*, which chose surprisingly to repeat many of the old stories that she had already told in *Past Imperfect*. Amusingly she confessed that she had had 'at least a dozen lovers'. She had previously admitted to twenty-three and I reckon there had been at least seventeen more. In fact the book was much more circumspect than *Past Imperfect*, offered fewer intimate revelations, and said nothing about Maxwell Reed allegedly raping her nor Tony Newley's taste for jailbait. She dedicated the book to the memory of her mother and chose as its epigraph a quote by the American journalist William Allen White: 'I am not afraid of tomorrow, / For I have seen yesterday / And I love today.' Like the American edition of *Past Imperfect*, which had ended ebulliently with one word, *Onward!*, the new book ended with *En avant!*

Three days after it was published she returned to Francis Holland to open her old school's new indoor swimming pool and was greeted like royalty, as befitted the most famous and successful Polished Corner of them all. With her on the stage was the school's patron, the Bishop of London, the Right Reverend Richard Chartres, which allowed the chairman of the school council, Miss Madeline McLaughlan, to joke about the bishop and the actress. Then she went off to Harrods to sign copies of *Second Act* and with Robin to the South of France for their usual summer holiday, where their peace was disturbed when the *Daily Express* claimed that she had just spent £90,000 having her breasts enlarged and she had to instruct her lawyers to deny the allegation and force the paper to retract it. In St Tropez, to publicise the book, she gave an interview to Rebecca Tyrell of the *Sunday Telegraph Magazine* in which she claimed that she had never been unfaithful to any of her husbands. Oh, really? When she was married to Maxwell Reed she had committed adultery at least with Sydney Chaplin and Arthur Loew. She had cuckolded Tony Newley with at least a film cameraman as well as Ryan O'Neal and Ron Kass; Kass with at least Jon-Erik Hexum, Morgan Mason and Peter Holm; Holm with at least Bill Wiggins – and there may well have been others. She also claimed that she had had an affair with a married man only once. This was quite untrue. There were at least six – Harry Belafonte, George Englund, Rafael Trujillo, Tony Newley, Ryan O'Neal and Ron Kass – and if she had indeed had an affair with Bing Crosby in 1961, as had been claimed, he too had been married at the time. Joan's bold attempt to rewrite history was glorious to behold and there is something wonderfully endearing about her optimistic belief that she could get away with the most blatant fib even when it could easily be disproved. Optimism was indeed one of her most attractive traits. 'I never get depressed,' she told Rebecca Tyrel. 'Isn't that awful? How can *you* be depressed when children are dying of malnutrition? When people are walking around starving? When people are being sent to concentration camps? How *can* you be depressed? For most people life can be pretty bad. So, if you are living a pretty good life, enjoy it. A lot of people can criticise me for skating over my problems, being too superficial, not being deep enough to really suffer. I have certainly suffered, but suffering is different from depression.'

In October she flew alone to America to make a guest appearance in the long-running TV sitcom *The Nanny*, in which she played a rich New York family's bossy stepmother. She also landed a starring role in a new Aaron Spelling prime-time TV series, *Pacific Palisades*, decided that once again she needed a base in Beverly Hills, and rented herself yet another apartment high above the city so that now, once again, she occupied properties in London, the South of France and LA.

Joan returned to London to find that Tara, who was now thirty-three, was earning a reputation almost as raunchy as her own. She had left Viva! radio, become a TV presenter on the adult porn Fantasy Channel, and told the *Sunday Mirror*: 'Mum has been great. My new job is probably not exactly what she would want me to do for a living, but she is a hundred per cent behind me. She has been giving me advice on the sort of things I can do on the show.' These included interviews with pimps, prostitutes, strippers and transsexuals. 'My mother's been a liberating force for many women,' said Tara, 'and I feel as if I'm carrying on her work. She made the idea of the woman taking control acceptable and in my interviews I will be trying to show sex from the woman's point of view. Men often have a strange idea about what women want. I hope to set the record straight.' Soon afterwards she was photographed naked from the back for the January issue of *Tatler* to publicise the protests of an anti-fur charity, People For the Ethical Treatment of Animals, which had adopted the slogan I'D RATHER GO NAKED THAN WEAR FUR. Joan protested too, not about Tara's nudity − 'that's fine' − but about her objection to wearing furs, pointing out that she wore fur herself. Tara explained her naked protest by announcing grandly that 'the point of being a celebrity is being able to do something for the good of society', which inspired the *Evening Standard* to point out that she was not a celebrity and to suggest sarcastically that what she really meant was that 'if I show society my bottom I live in hope of becoming a celebrity'. Still, it added, 'we should not be too hard on Tara. After all, she is genuinely committed to preserving an endangered species: Offspring of Formerly Famous Performers In Search of Stardom, otherwise known as OFFPISS.' Tara had also just taken on a second job as an adviser on an adult magazine, *For Women*, where she planned to publish pin-ups of men with erections. 'Men can ogle to their hearts' content at pictures of naked women,' she told the *People*. 'It really pisses me off. The best we get is a picture of a dishy bloke grinning inanely at the camera. It's not very exciting to look at and it's obvious the man is not turned on.' She announced that she loved sex and that her perfect day would be to be 'locked in the bedroom with an Italian lover and a supply of food', but complained that she no longer had a boyfriend and had 'gone without nookie' for more than a year. Unlike Tara – and Joan for decades before her – Sacha and Katy sensibly resisted the temptation to discuss their sex lives with the tabloids. Katy had recovered from her broken, unsavoury love affair with Jeff Stewart, was now romancing a twenty-six-year-old businessman, Paul Robinson, and was soon to live with him in London. At twenty-four she was still searching for a proper career, had abandoned her job as Maryam Rokny-Owji's assistant, and was taking a course in photography at an adult education centre.

Joan received at last the public recognition for which she had sought so desperately all her life when she was awarded the OBE in the 1997 New Year Honours list 'for services to drama' and became an Ordinary Officer of the Most Excellent Order of the British Empire. This did not give her a title – she was not suddenly a Dame, as Elizabeth Taylor was to become two years later – but the medal reassured her that although she might sometimes suspect that her career had been shallow and undistinguished it had perhaps been of some value after all, and maybe Daddy would at last have been proud of her.

CHAPTER TWENTY

GRANNY DODO AND THE
YOUNGEST TOYBOY OF THEM ALL

{ 1997–2001 }

In February 1997 Joan flew to Australia and New Zealand to promote the new book and was the guest of honour at a huge charity dinner in Christchurch on St Valentine's Day. Her visit was marred by reports that she behaved arrogantly. One New Zealander told me that she had been impossibly high-handed, had demanded first-class return air tickets for five people, and had insisted that all the hotel rooms on the floor beneath hers should be empty. None of the allegations was true: they were merely examples of the gossipy lies that she had had to put up with for years. Her host that evening, Sir Allan Wright, who was chairman of the fund-raising committee of the Cancer Society of New Zealand, did tell me that she was 'a real prima donna and thought she was royalty, though she made a nice speech', but the society's chief executive, Pamela Williams, told me that Joan was 'charming, very warm and not hoity-toity at all'. Both agreed, however, that it had been unwise to sit her beside an outback sheep farmer, Jim Morris, who had never heard of her. 'She ignored him all evening and left early,' said Sir Allan.

In March she went with Sacha to Buckingham Palace to receive her OBE from the Queen. 'I've lived in America for a long time,' she told the Press, 'and my friends ask me why I haven't become an American citizen. It's because I love everything that goes with being British and this is one of the things that makes me so proud.' Back in Hollywood she started to earn £25,000 [£32,250] per episode in Aaron Spelling's new soap about the greedy, randy 'beautiful people' living in the fashionable Los Angeles suburb of *Pacific Palisades*, in which she played yet another Alexis Carrington clone, a rich, jet-setting man-eater, but the show was axed after just eight episodes because of low viewing figures.

Fortunately Joan had a happy celebration to take her mind off the flop: Tara had decided to marry her own toyboy, a twenty-eight-year-old French composer and music producer, Michael Nadam, who was five years her junior and dropped the N of his surname to call himself Adam. She learned Hebrew, adopted Judaism, and they were wed on 15 June in a glitzy, four-hundred-guests wedding at a synagogue in Sceaux, near Paris, that was pictured and reported at glossy length in *Hello!* – always a risky business since it was widely believed that any marriage covered 'exclusively' by the syrupy magazine was inevitably doomed to suffer 'The Curse of *Hello!*' and end in tears. Tara's parents were both there – although Newley, who was still living with his mother in Esher, looked frail after another six weeks' chemotherapy treatment for cancer of the kidney. Sacha, now thirty-two, was having his first major American exhibition of portraits at the Chateau Marmont in Los Angeles; and Katy, now twenty-five, was living happily with Paul Robinson in London, although she was still unsure what to do with her life and was soon to give up photography, work in a bookshop and then as an assistant at Harrods.

At the end of the month Joan gave an interview to Richard Barber of the *Daily Telegraph* to publicise *Second Act* and talk about politics. She still hero-worshipped Margaret Thatcher – 'I loved that woman' – but was less impressed by the current leader of the Conservative Party, William Hague, of whom she said cruelly, wrinkling her nose: 'Oh, darling, he looks like a foetus.' As for the newly elected New Labour Prime Minister, Tony Blair, she despaired of him: '"Call me Tony, indeed!" *Much* too blokeish. He's the Prime Minister, for heaven's sake! As for Gordon Brown wearing a lounge suit at a black-tie dinner, that's just downright disrespectful. Whatever next? The Queen opening Parliament in a headscarf and trainers?' Her disapproval, however, was nothing by comparison with her anger when the Princess of Wales was killed in a car crash in Paris three days later. In a powerful article in the *Daily Express* she blamed 'jackal' paparazzi photographers for hunting Princess Diana to death and urged that they should be banned by law.

Joan had long hinted that she would love to make a guest appearance on *Coronation Street* and was granted her wish at last in September when she played a cameo role in a Christmas video edition of the programme. It was a parody of her Cinzano advertisements: the drink was spilled on one of the *Coronation Street* characters and Joan reassured her by saying: 'Don't worry, darling, it washes out.'

For Joan 1998 was to be a memorable year: she was invited by Petronella Wyatt, the deputy editor of the *Spectator*, to write an eleven-hundred-word diary column; she was to appear in a film with two fine actors, her new friend Nigel Hawthorne and Timothy Spall, *The Clandestine Marriage*; and she was to become a grandmother. She was also to compile a book called *My Friends' Secrets*, a collection of interviews about beauty with twenty famous woman over forty – among them Shirley Bassey, Shakira Caine, Diahann Carroll, Jerry Hall, Joanna Lumley, Ali MacGraw, Ivana Trump and Twiggy, whom she called the 'zest generation'. The *Spectator's* editor, Frank Johnson, was so impressed by her article that he, like others, wondered whether someone had written it for her. Johnson was to ask her to write more diary pieces for the magazine during the years ahead. Her first article caused a stir because she accused dress designers and glossy magazine editors of treating women with contempt because they designed and promoted fashions only for 'anorexic, androgynous teenagers' that no 'real women with real bodies' would dream of wearing. She also criticised British Airways' decision to replace the patriotic Union Jack tailfin design on its aircraft with ugly 'ethnic' designs. A month later her second column admonished those readers who suspected that her first must have been ghosted; complained about illogical political correctness that treated smokers like pariahs yet tolerated predatory, cruising homosexuals; and reported that New Yorkers were now so obsessed with Viagra that they said you had to swallow it quickly to avoid a stiff neck. The *Daily Telegraph* was so taken by her light, witty style that she was asked to review two London restaurants in an article in which she described a bottle of Chilean wine as 'bright and fruity, perfect for lunch, rather like Christopher Biggins' – though Joan was perfectly capable of holding her own in any serious discussion. At one *Spectator* lunch Michael Heseltine, the Conservative ex-Cabinet minister, criticised Tony Blair for not taking Britain into the European single currency and 'Joan argued correctly that it would be disastrous if Britain was tied to the euro', Frank Johnson told me. 'She gave the classical case against the single currency and I thought: "Good old Joan".'

To mark her sixty-fifth birthday the *Daily Mail* published an affectionate tribute by Lynda Lee-Potter, who had by now become a friend but still referred to Joan's 'colossal ego' as well as her 'vulnerable streak underneath. She's never been very good at being on her own, which is perhaps why she's such a bad picker when it comes to chaps … time and again she's selected men who have exploited and abused her. It's why women like her so much. There's nothing more alienating than a female who appears to have a perfect life. If an incredibly beautiful, smart woman can do stupid things, the rest of us feel better about our own mistakes.'

At the end of August Joan excelled herself in her fourth *Spectator* diary column when she defended President Clinton for his 'penchant for bonking trailer park trash' – 'Slick Willie's just doing what has always come naturally to most men of power, position and wealth' – and suggested that his lover Monica Lewinsky's lewd antics involving a large Havana cigar should have her nicknamed the Count of Monte Cristo 'give or take a vowel', another joke of Robin's.

In September Joan began filming *The Clandestine Marriage*, a rumbustious eighteenth-century comedy by George Coleman and David Garrick in which a vulgar, snobbish, *nouveau-riche* widow (played by Joan) and her common-as-muck brother (Timothy Spall) hope to marry off their elder niece to the son of an impoverished old aristocrat (Nigel Hawthorne) but find their plans thrown into disarray when the young man prefers the younger niece, his besotted old father decides he fancies her too, and she is already secretly married. The critics were savage when the film was released, inexplicably so because it was a charming romp with splendid atmosphere, scenery, costumes and photography, and the three main characters were memorably portrayed. Hawthorne, leering, staggering about and wearing thick make-up, a huge, curly red wig and red velveteen suit, was splendidly lascivious, unsavoury and decrepit. Spall was wonderfully plump, prosperous and pompous yet unsure of himself socially, and Joan was excellent as the pale, wrinkled, social-climbing old battleaxe with a ridiculously affected accent and dirty teeth. Even her voice had lost its usual shrill, squeaky tone, and good sport that she was she allowed an excellent joke against herself, appearing in one scene flying to and fro on a swing decorated with flowers just like the one she had ridden naked in *The Stud*. It was one of her best performances, a delightful piece of nonsense brimming with jollity and *joie de vivre*.

The movie was shot at Stanway House, a beautiful Jacobean stately home in Gloucestershire, but it was plagued for four nerve-racking weeks by financial problems when promised money never arrived, unpaid bills piled up, cheques bounced, the cast and crew were not paid, and the whole project teetered on the brink of collapse. Joan and Hawthorne, however, had enough faith in the film that they saved it from disaster by borrowing nervously £450,000 [£580,000] between them to pay the crew and keep the film going until the expected funds finally arrived. It was a brave gamble but eventually their investments were repaid.

Joan's behaviour was not always quite so angelic. 'At a peak in her career, she felt entitled to bouts of pique,' wrote Stanway House's tenant, Peter Hillmore, in the *Mail on Sunday* a few months later. 'She demanded a local girl be employed as her "gofer", fetching and carry-ing for her. She knew when to throw the judicious tantrum that goes with stardom. She had to have her tea in a special blue patterned mug. Her gofer brought tea out to her half a mile away in a cup, and it was sent all the way back. The cup went missing once when Lord Neidpath [*the owner of Stanway House*] accidentally and unforgivably used it for his breakfast. A complete house search was ordered by Miss Collins. And, because she was always professional in front of the cameras, everyone on the set was mightily satisfied that a star was behaving like stars are supposed to.'

Hawthorne was impressed by her acting and told Melvyn Bragg on *The South Bank Show* the following year that with plenty of direction she could be an excellent actress but that she seemed afraid to explore the depths of her real self and expand her repertoire because she felt safest clinging on to her usual role as a 'society bitch'. 'I rather am inclined to dread the warpaint going on because it's almost as though she paints on Joan Collins. The real lady underneath it all is very, very warm.' Their admiration was mutual and when Hawthorne was given a knighthood at the end of 1998 she wrote in the *Spectator* that he was the most brilliant actor of his time.

In London on 5 October 1998 Tara gave birth to her first baby and named her Miel Celeste, French for 'Heavenly Honey'. Joan and Tony Newley arrived at the hospital within fifteen minutes of each other to see their first grandchild and Joan photographed him with the baby. 'I'm so glad I saw him that day,' she told Lynda Lee-Potter the following year, 'because my last memory of him is with pure joy on his face looking at his eldest daughter holding his first grandchild.' The cancer was to kill him six months later. Tara risked the Curse of *Hello!* again by inviting the oleaginous magazine to take exclusive photographs and devote seven glossy pages to pictures of the baby, mother and beaming grandmother, who announced that she would refuse to answer to the names Granny or Nan but would rather be called Dodo, the name that her brother Bill had given her as a child.

Joan's smile faltered, however, a few nights later when she and Robin went with the food critic Adrian Gill and his girlfriend to eat at Gordon Ramsay's restaurant and were thrown out because Ramsay said that Gill had been running a maliciously personal campaign against him and his restaurants for three years. They left the place in a loud, embarrassed silence. 'The cult of chef as demigod has been allowed to escalate into sheer madness,' fumed Joan in her *Spectator* diary a few days later, calling Ramsay an egomaniac and his menu pretentious. Still, she rarely bore grudges for long: little more than a year after she had sneered at Tony Blair he invited her and Robin to dinner at Chequers and they were won over. 'I was very taken with him,' Joan told Lynda Lee-Potter. 'He was mesmerising, and Robin thought he was fabulous. He was charming beyond belief. He wore an open-necked blue shirt and he was so attractive.' Ramsay too would eventually be forgiven.

Early in 1999 Joan and Robin spent ten days in Acapulco and then went off for another holiday in Egypt, where they sailed up the Nile with a group of friends on a big chartered boat with a crew of fifty. Joan loved the country and the dignity of the people, the elegance of their turbans and djellabas, the river with its dhows and palm trees, the biblical countryside with its mud huts, shepherds and flocks of sheep. They returned to Los Angeles for her to work on a Steven Spielberg movie, an animated humanoid cartoon about a Stone Age family, *The Flintstones in Viva Rock Vegas*, in which she played Fred Flintstone's prospective mother-in-law from hell, Pearl Slaghoople. It was a silly, unfunny film but Joan was suitably dragonly in a series of garish leather costumes that made her look remarkably attractive for a granny of sixty-six. Physically she was still in astonishingly good shape but mentally beginning to show just a few early signs of grumpy old age, complaining in the *Spectator* about mobile phones, modern technology, the impossibility of learning how to use a computer, and deploring the decline of individuality and glamour among modern young actresses in Hollywood. Why, she asked, did no one nowadays have even a fraction of the allure of Grace Kelly, Ava Gardner, Lana Turner or Elizabeth Taylor? Why did none of the men come anywhere close to the smouldering masculinity of Clark Gable, Spencer Tracy, James Stewart or Gene Kelly? Perhaps old Granny Dodo was in danger of becoming extinct.

Back in England she joined the cast of a lively new video production of the Tim Rice/Andrew Lloyd Webber children's musical *Joseph and the Amazing Technicolor Dreamcoat* to play two very small parts: as the stern, prim music teacher playing the piano at a school production of the musical; and as Mrs Potipher, the wicked, randy wife of a rich Egyptian. Despite appearing only briefly she was given third billing after Donny Osmond and Richard Attenborough, but she performed well enough and it was a splendidly colourful fantasy, though not all the catchy music should have been credited solely to Lloyd Webber, as it was. The prettiest song, 'Any Dream Will Do', had in fact been composed more than ninety years earlier by an American, Kerry Mills, for a 1907 hit song, 'Little Redwing', which was later adapted by First World War soldiers as 'The Moon Shines Down on Charlie Chaplin', each verse of which ends 'Before they send him / To the Dardanelles'. Lloyd Webber was perfectly entitled to hijack the melody when he wrote the musical in 1967 because Mills had died in 1948, the song was out of copyright and had been in the public domain for four years, but it would have been generous had the original composer been acknowledged.

Tony Newley died of cancer on 14 April 1999 in Florida – where he had gone to seek treatment and live with an old girlfriend, Gina Fratini – and Joan said she cried for two days and would miss him terribly. He was sixty-seven. His ninety-seven-year-old mother Grace, Tara and Sacha flew to Miami to join Gina and Dareth for a small funeral three days later, but Joan did not go because she had agreed to be in Hollywood that day to make a TV commercial for Olympus cameras for £100,000 [£129,000] and felt she could not let the crew down. 'Dad loved Mum,' Tara told Colin Wills of the *Sunday Mirror* eighteen months later. 'I talked about it with him as the end drew near. He deeply regretted ruining their marriage because of the other women. If he'd had his time over again I know it would never have happened. Even after the divorce, Dad and Mum were never off the phone to each other. I don't think Mum could have borne going to the funeral. Seeing Dad being put into that memorial wall the way they do in America.'

Newley left a net estate of £641,408, which would be worth about £790,000 in 2007 – not much considering how many millions he had earned at the height of his career. He left the house in Esher and its contents to Grace to use until she died; the apartment in Florida and a share of his company Tellisford Music to Gina; his papers to Boston University; £1,000 to Leslie Bricusse's son Adam; and whatever was left to go into a trust fund to be shared by Gina and his four children.

When *My Friends' Secrets* was published in May, Joan was interviewed yet again by Lynda Lee-Potter for the *Daily Mail* and swore that she had never had a face-lift, no matter how much people might disbelieve her: 'I'd be frightened and face-lifts don't last. I've seen people who've had them three years ago and they look the same as they did before.' But for the first time she admitted that she might just have plastic surgery one day and probably would 'if I was doing a series and they said, "We're finding it difficult to photograph you."'

Sacha was all over the British newspapers too that week because two more exhibitions of his paintings had just opened in Brighton and London. By now he had painted portraits of Gore Vidal, Steven Berkoff and two of Joan, one of them showing her tense and haggard, 'absolutely hideous', she told Lee-Potter, 'a picture of Dorian Gray, the one that's in the attic'. She much preferred the gentler, glamourised second one, which showed her reclining on a sofa, but Sacha disagreed, saying he preferred the 'brutal' one because 'I was painting her psyche, her energy'. By now he was charging £9,000 for each portrait and had begun an affair with a woman who was eight years older, the film star Michael Douglas's very wealthy forty-one-year-old wife Diandra. Sadly Tara's marriage had already succumbed to The Curse of *Hello!* and ended after less than two years. The London divorce court granted her a decree nisi on 24 May but she had to wait another year for the decree absolute while she and her husband fought over custody of the baby. 'I loved being a Jewish wife, the cooking and the cleaning,' she told Mary Riddell of the *Daily Mail* later. 'I was happy to be a mother and a housewife. Shall we just say that things changed drastically after we got married.'

That summer Joan fell out irreparably with her couturier Maryam

Rokny-Owji. 'Being a demanding lady she wanted me to put her first and all my other clients second,' Mrs Rokny-Owji told me. 'Evie Bricusse asked me to make a dress for her for Valentino's party in St Tropez and we picked an Yves St Laurent fabric for it, but when Joan saw the roll of fabric she said: "Oh, fantastic, I would love to have something in the same material." I said, "This is Evie's," so Joan chose a different colour, and because she was in London for only a week she said: "Maryam, please drop Evie's now and make mine first because I'm going to the South of France. You can make hers later." So I stopped Evie's, finished Joan's, gave it to her, finished Evie's, and gave it to her a couple of days before the party. A couple of days afterwards Joan left a message on my answerphone saying: "How *dare* you make the same outfit for Evie?" It was Evie who ordered that dress first and being a proud Persian I thought, "I'm not going to put up with this," and told her agent Peter Charlesworth that I would not make any more clothes for Joan unless she apologised. Of course she didn't and that was the end of it.' But Joan still claims that Maryam broke their exclusivity agreement.

In November Britain's cultural guru Melvyn Bragg devoted an hour-long programme to Joan on his highly regarded TV arts programme *The South Bank Show*. The contributors included Aaron Spelling, Steven Berkoff, Nigel Hawthorne, Sacha and Jackie, though Joan was disconcerted when Bragg revealed indiscreetly that she had not wanted Jackie to appear at all. 'That's hitting below the belt, isn't it?' she said, but admitted that she and Jackie did not get on very well. Jackie in turn remarked that Joan could sometimes be difficult: 'We all know what actresses are like: when they're *on* they're a pain in the ass! But when she's just being herself she's a lot of fun.' For once Joan looked far from her best, with deep bags and creases under her eyes despite being caked with make-up, black panda eyes, very thick lipstick and heavily painted eyebrows. She told Bragg that she had always known that life would often be hard and occasionally unjust but that you have to make the most of it and 'when they give you lemons you try and make lemonade.'

Sacha explained that his two portraits of her were so different because apart from the superstar he saw her as also 'extremely vulnerable, still starry-eyed, still I think a trifle amazed that she is who she is, still very much the twelve-year-old girl who used to fill scrapbooks with cuttings of Clark Gable that, I think, is the ballast that keeps her from tipping over into the stardom side.'

Bragg asked her if she thought that she had fulfilled her potential. 'I wish I'd done a really good film,' she confessed. 'I wish I could say I did *Sons and Lovers*, which I should have done.' But she pointed out that in *Dynasty* she had become the best-known actress in the world and that she had never wanted to play a serious role like Hedda Gabler anyway.

In a post-mortem in the *Mail on Sunday* two days later Elizabeth Sanderson reported that the antagonism between Joan and Jackie went right back to their childhoods and quoted one of their friends as saying that 'Joan was older and a hundred and twenty times prettier. Jackie was always fun, clever, one of the boys, but people said: "Joan always looks absolutely fabulous, whereas Jackie can look a bit like a man in drag."' Nor did it help that because Joan had always been so extravagant, and Jackie so thrifty, Jackie was now a great deal wealthier than Joan. Ms Sanderson quoted another friend as telling her that another big difference was that 'Jackie's a superb mother. Her children absolutely adore her. She purposely had no help around the house when she was bringing up the kids. I think you'd have to draw a map to get Joan into the kitchen. She wouldn't know how to boil an egg. Joan likes staying in bed late in the morning, having lunch with wine, then going out and going to bed late. She's a star. Jackie likes her home.'

Joan had long dreamed of meeting the notoriously randy President Clinton and her wish was granted in November when she went to the White House and was amused when an intern announced that the President used the Oval Office mainly for business 'but also for private matters'. There was no sign of any Havana cigars, but as soon as Clinton strolled into the room Joan was smitten by his gift for immediate intimacy, his beautiful, expressive hands, and his enormous feet – always apparently a promising sign in a man. He also had 'wonderful breath', she informed readers of her *Spectator* diary a couple of weeks later, though she was less enchanted by Buddy, the First Dog, which immediately attempted to ravish her right leg. Pets, of course, soon come to resemble their owners.

In November Tara and Miel returned from Paris to live in a flat in north London but on the first day of the new millennium some domestic crisis made her grab the baby and flee barefoot to the safety of her Uncle Bill's house in Belgravia. It was not a happy start to the twenty-first century but Joan was staunch in her support. 'She offered to stay with me at night,' Tara told Mary Riddell. 'She was on the phone every day. She helped me in every way. She found me a solicitor and said: "Darling, just call this person." She and my gran sent food and chicken soup.' Joan also sent her money. 'If it weren't for my mother and my grandmother, Miel and I would have been in deep financial trouble this year.' Miel's birth, Newley's death and Tara's broken marriage combined to bring mother and daughter closer than they had been for many years. 'My mother has been really brilliant,' Tara told Michael Prestage of the *Mail on Sunday*. 'I think she loves being a gran.' Joan drew the line at changing nappies but 'she carries around pictures of the baby and will show them to anybody who will look'. Tara added that despite her attempts to become a singer or TV presenter: 'I have never said I wanted to be a star or a celebrity. I don't think it brings happiness. The road to success seems littered with heartache and I don't want to go down it.' But before long she was back on television as the presenter of Granada Breeze's programme *Style Guide*.

In March Joan flew to Los Angeles to make a cameo appearance in the TV sitcom *Will and Grace* and then in April began a seven-week tour of California and the southern states in A. R. Gurney's stage play *Love Letters*, first opposite George Hamilton and then with Stacey Keach. The play was a two-hander, the actors playing lifelong friends – Andy, a pompous United States senator, and Melissa, an unhappy, rich, bored alcoholic – who sit onstage at a table and read out alternately the notes, postcards and letters they have written to each other over fifty years, and react to them and each other. When the play reached Austin, Texas, in May, Ada Calhoun wrote in the local *Chronicle*: 'Is it my imagination or was the house a little less full after intermission?'

On 30 April Jackie was devastated when her lover, Frank Calcagnini, died of cancer at fifty-eight. Robin's beloved seventy-five-year-old mother, Lydia, was dying of cancer too and needed him to be with her in England, so he was unable to join Joan on the tour of *Love Letters*. But watching her onstage every night was the company's tall, dark, thirty-four-year-old manager, Percy Gibson, who had been born in Peru, the son of a once-rich Peruvian businessman and a forty-three-year-old Scottish teacher. Percy had been splendidly named

Percy Jorge Gibson Miguel Monaghan Mueller Parra del Riego, had wanted to become a priest or an actor, and at seventeen had won a scholarship to study theology and the theatre at Bard College in New York. Realising that he was not a great actor, he had become instead a freelance theatre manager, had married an out-of-work American actress and become a US citizen, and although they were childless and had separated after eleven years they were still sharing a New York apartment from time to time, meeting for lunch or dinner, celebrating birthdays together and their wedding anniversary, and had recently gone on holiday together.

Joan was twice Percy's age but he thought she was gorgeous, funny, full of life and always laughing. After the first Sunday matinée in San Francisco, when she and George Hamilton came off the stage for the interval, Hamilton said despairingly, 'Joanie, they're not laughing,' and she replied: 'That's because this play's not fucking funny!' Watching Hamilton clowning around and Joan squealing deliciously with laughter, Percy thought: 'You're adorable, just adorable.' Nearly two years later he would become her fifth husband, but when the tour ended in Houston in May they went their separate ways, he to return to other theatre companies, she to London for Royal Ascot and to decline an invitation to play Mrs Robinson in a West End stage version of *The Graduate*, for which she would have had to appear completely naked in one scene, as Kathleen Turner was doing then and Jerry Hall about to do. 'It's unseemly to undress on stage,' sniffed Joan, even though she would have had to be nude for just twenty seconds on a darkened stage. 'I don't remember her wearing very much in *The Stud* or *The Bitch*,' said Jerry Hall, but Joan went even further when she told the *Daily Mirror* that it made her 'sick to see naked people' on television. This sudden attack of puritanism so irritated *The Sunday Times* that it named her an 'Enemy of the People', pointing out that never before had she shown much reluctance to drop her knickers.

To promote the paperback edition of *My Friends' Secrets* Joan gave an interview to Hazel Courtney of the *Daily Mail*, who asked her what she would take to keep herself young should she be shipwrecked on a desert island. 'Robin,' she said sweetly. 'I would take Robin.' Did she mean it? Maybe. She also presented a series of TV programmes based on the book and signed a deal with a British publisher, House of Stratus, which agreed to pay her an advance of £150,000 [£178,500] for her next novel, *Star Quality*, and yet another volume of autobiography. Her old friend and editor Rosie Cheetham was no longer prepared to publish her novels. 'I told her agent that the figures didn't add up and I didn't want to offer her an insulting advance,' Rosie told me.

Joan's next movie was meant to be a light-hearted jest in which she, Shirley MacLaine, Debbie Reynolds and Elizabeth Taylor – combined ages 269 and with sixteen ex-husbands between them – poked fun at themselves and each other in *These Old Broads*, a TV film in which they played four old harridans very like themselves: a Hollywood agent and three old actresses who hate each other but are forced to make another movie together because they need the money. Joan played a man-eating bitch who has a red velvet swing and undergoes plastic surgery every few years. 'You tramp!' says Debbie Reynolds. 'No wonder they call you the British Open!' Shirley MacLaine mocked her own wacky New Age beliefs and superstitions, Debbie Reynolds her own goody-goody image, accusing Elizabeth Taylor of running off with her husband, which indeed she had in real life when she had bolted with Eddie Fisher forty-two years earlier. And Liz Taylor, who amazed Joan by insisting haughtily that everyone should call her Dame Elizabeth, played the agent, a woman with a pet asp called Cleopatra. All of this should have been amusing fun but the film turned out to be slow, dull and completely humourless.

Throughout the summer and autumn of 2000 Joan and Percy Gibson kept bumping into each other in Los Angeles, New York or London, and when she flew to Los Angeles in January 2001 to appear again in *Will and Grace* she asked him to help her edit the final twenty thousand words of her new novel. He agreed, and was with her when she had a row with the producers of *Will and Grace* and burst into tears. He put his arms around her. The effect was electric. 'It was a *coup de foudre*, like being struck by a thunderbolt,' she told *Hello!* later. He agreed: 'The physical contact triggered something in both of us. I think it caught both of us by surprise.' They became lovers, and Joan faced several weeks of agonising soul-searching. Was this madness? Did she really love Percy more than Robin? What about the huge, thirty-three-year age gap between them? She was almost old enough to be his grandmother.

She had to fly to New Zealand again for a fortnight in March to film with Rachel Hunter a children's comedy about a boy who befriends a koala bear, *Ozzie*, and finds himself up against a couple of bumbling villains. She asked Percy to go with her. Everyone thought he was her assistant but they lived as man and wife and 'it was idyllic', she told *Hello!* later. 'It felt like being in Never-Never Land.' They went swimming and on picnics, played Scrabble, and 'spent a huge amount of time talking about what was happening to us. I think we were both a little scared. We had to consider my children, Percy's family, my friends, his friends. I warned him that we would be attacked remorselessly by the media.' She had to take sleeping pills to relax, and when they returned from New Zealand she spent five days at a health farm 'and stared at the ceiling for most of the time', wondering what the hell she ought to do. When she emerged she knew what she wanted. She wanted Percy.

CHAPTER TWENTY-ONE

THE LATIN FROM MANHATTAN

{ 2001–2002 }

Telling Robin that she was going to dump him after so long was traumatic. 'I love Robin and will always love Robin,' she told *Hello!* 'We had a relationship that lasted for thirteen years and was wonderful in so many respects. But, in the end – there's no easy way to say this – my feelings for Percy were stronger.' He was stunned. 'Robin and I were both very upset,' she told Lynda Lee-Potter later, 'but I wanted to be with Percy. In the final analysis one has to live for oneself.'

Robin's friends believed that the end was neither that simple nor that touching. 'She treated him appallingly,' I was told by one who insisted on remaining anonymous. 'It was all to do with his mother dying. He adored his mother. The last year of her life was ghastly, so he couldn't go off with Joan on the tour of *Love Letters*, and that's when she met Percy. Joan always needed and wanted Robin's attention and he just couldn't give it to her. His mother died in December 2000 and he was very, very upset, but just one day after the funeral Joan snapped at him: "For God's sake, Robin, people's parents die. Get over it." So it was a double whammy when she said soon afterwards that she was dumping him. She doesn't care about anyone else and is utterly ruthless. Sacha was absolutely right when he said: "My mother travels through life with emotional hand luggage only." The end with Robin was really unpleasant, absolutely vile, and so sudden – "it's over and that's that". I think she just got bored and wanted a change.' It was not in fact a complete surprise because during the filming of *These Old Broads* Elizabeth Taylor and Shirley MacLaine had both told him that they thought Joan was having an affair.

'Robin had loved Joan deeply for many years and was absolutely devastated when she dumped him,' I was told by another friend.

'He loved her so much that he would have been happy to look after her for the rest of her life. She stashed away sums of money in bank accounts that she asked him to run for her and he increased her wealth dramatically.'

Rosie Cheetham (now de Courcy) told me that 'Robin's a very nice man and Joan did very much want to marry him but he didn't feel comfortable about that. We went to stay with them at Destino and I think he was genuinely very much in love with her, there was no doubt about that, and she with him, but I think he struggled with the nature of her fame and the vulgarity of that world.'

Katy, now twenty-eight and working for a charity, was still living happily with her boyfriend, but Joan's elder children's lives were in turmoil too. Tara, now thirty-seven and living in Maida Vale, had found a new boyfriend, television actor Darren Day, but had lost her job as a roving interviewer of famous people for the daytime TV programme *Celebrity*, which had just been axed, and was frustrated that she did not yet have her own TV show and was not yet famous. To add to her woes she was mugged at a bus stop and robbed of a £7,000 gold Cartier watch that her mother had given her. London was now the crime capital of the world, Joan complained in the *Spectator*, and no one was doing anything to solve the problem. Sacha's life, too, was going through an upheaval. He and Diandra Douglas had recently broken up after she won a £44 million divorce settlement from Michael Douglas and her wealth proved to be too much for Sacha. 'It was like a beautiful suit, but I just didn't feel comfortable in it,' he told David Wigg of the *Daily Mail*'s *Weekend* magazine. He admitted that her rich, materialistic, jet-set life was very glamorous and seductive, but maybe it was too much like Joan's: perhaps by breaking up with Diandra he was also rejecting his mother's hectic, hedonistic way of life. 'To have been Diandra's partner I would have to have taken over the role of master of the house,' he said. 'And that's a lot to take over. There are three houses and an enormous bonds portfolio. That just didn't interest me.' He had also come to realise that he was painting very little and partying and travelling too much. Tara admired him for turning his back on such riches. 'Sacha could have had a really easy ride there,' she told Mary Riddell. 'It would have been a very cushy situation,' but to make the break-up easier he had just met the girl he would eventually marry: a beautiful, thirty-one-year-old jewellery designer of Italian descent, Angela Tassoni, who had once been a model and had appeared in three small films. When he moved to New York she followed him and soon they were living there together.

In March Joan went to the Oscars ceremony as usual and reported in the *Spectator* that although most of the women were decently dressed and coiffed for a change she was appalled to see the singer Björk wearing 'a creation that wouldn't have looked out of place perched on a Skegness landlady's spare loo roll' and the silicone-breasted Pamela Anderson in tiny 'trailer-trash' hot pants and a skimpy shirt, 'revealing all the taste and refinement of a hooker on holiday'. She said, however, that she was delighted that Russell Crowe had won the Best Actor Oscar for *Gladiator* and Benicio Del Toro the Best Supporting Actor Award for *Traffic* because they were the only macho actors left in Hollywood.

She flew back to New York to spend Easter with Percy, appearing with him for the first time in public at an American Gay Lesbian Alliance ceremony where Joan – by now an adored gay icon – presented an award. Percy moved in to live with Joan and she put the word around that he was 'like a tiger' in bed and that her sex life was the best it had been for years. She had never been shy about discussing such intimate matters openly but cynics remembered that when she had started living with Robin she had insisted that he was her lover 'in every way' but had later appeared to deny it. When reporters tracked down Percy's wife, Cynthia, she admitted that he was not particularly good in bed, they had hardly ever made love, it had never been 'combustible'. He was also a kind, gentle, liberated New Man who was happy to help with the housework, so perhaps Joan had found at last the wife that she had said she needed.

When Percy telephoned Cynthia to confess that he was having an affair with Joan Collins she was 'completely shocked and bewildered', she told Sharon Churcher of the *Mail on Sunday* ten months later. 'It was as if my world had fallen apart. It just didn't seem possible I was hearing this from the man I'd spent ten years of my life with. I was embarrassed, ashamed and humiliated that he was associating with a woman like Joan who, to me, represents the worst of commercial American culture. I believed he still loved me and I thought of him as my only real family.' But 'Joan isn't the first elderly woman Percy has taken on as a responsibility', she said. 'His mother, Bridget, is just eight years older than Joan and has Alzheimer's. Percy is very close to her but I can't imagine Joan will find it easy having her around. She'll be a constant reminder of how cruel the ageing process can be.' Cynthia added ominously: 'His mother is the most important person in his life – more important than me, more important than Joan.'

The Press went into a frenzy to record the story of Joan's latest toyboy, and Marcelle d'Argy Smith wrote an admiring profile in the *Independent on Sunday* in which she argued that it did not matter that Joan could neither act nor write well: what mattered was that she was a star who 'glitters, gleams and decorates every room she goes into', and that was enough. She also commented: 'You would be hard-pushed to meet a man who has ever seriously fancied Joan despite how terrific she looks. Whether it's lack of depth, lack of soul, her asexual Englishness, a lack of sensuality or absence of mystery, heaven knows. Men say things like, "I don't find her physically attractive", "she has a tinny voice, no allure", "her life is all about her", [*and*] some people consider her "masculine, for all her endless female trappings".' But as Melanie McDonagh wrote in the *Sunday Telegraph* a few weeks later, 'Collins is someone who cheers you up simply by being bad. And the thing about her badness is that it lives right down to our expectations about how film stars ought to behave.'

Although Percy and Cynthia were not to be divorced for four more months, he proposed to Joan on 23 May, her sixty-eighth birthday, and gave her an antique, heart-shaped, diamond engagement ring. She celebrated by telling *Hello!* how deliriously happy she was. The magazine usually paid large fees to celebrities who co-operated in producing its long, grovelling photo-feature interviews and once again she allowed it to parade her private life across six glossy pages. Percy was 'more in tune with me than anybody I've ever met', she gushed, echoing what she had said at first about every one of her husbands. 'I feel more myself with Percy Gibson than I ever have with anyone. I really feel looked after.' She claimed that her family all liked him but avoided mentioning that Sacha was appalled and embarrassed that his elderly mother was behaving yet again like a naïve teenager and had just dumped Robin, of whom he had become extremely fond, for a toyboy the same age as he was. 'Robin's a fabulous guy,' he told *The Sunday Times*. 'I thought they were going to go on for ever. He was one of the four corners of my world. I thought they were so suited.' But there was not much point in disapproving openly of Percy. 'If I wanted to go into a sulk about all of this, I could have done,' he said, 'but I thought, "What's the point? It wouldn't help anyone."' Joan was as starry-eyed as ever at the start of yet another new romance. 'I just want to live in the now, while Percy and I are having a wonderful time, while we adore each other,' she said. 'Somebody summed up my attitude in a favourite saying of mine: "Yesterday is history, tomorrow's a mystery, but today is a gift. That's why it's called the present."' She was to wheel out the quote in future in almost every interview she did.

At the end of all Joan's marriages and long relationships she had treated her rejected men with an unattractive lack of kindness or generosity – Reed, Newley, Kass, Holm, Wiggins – and Robin Hurlstone was no exception. As Melanie McDonagh wrote in the *Sunday Telegraph* she was 'in that rare class of actresses who seem to consume their mates like black widow spiders'. In July she considered putting the French villa on the market and according to the *Mail on Sunday* contacted a local estate agent, but the question arose whether she would give Robin a share of the proceeds – or even an acknowledgement of all he had done for her – because he had found, furnished and decorated it and had poured years of love into it. 'Robin was devastated by the split from Joan,' one friend told Wayne Bodkin of the *Mail on Sunday*. 'He was very tearful. But he is shocked by the news that the house is for sale. He put his heart and soul into it. He would expect a share.' I was told by another friend that at first Joan agreed to pay Robin half of the profit when she sold Destino, but that then she claimed that he was demanding the entire proceeds. 'That was nonsense,' another friend told me. 'It was an appalling debacle. She took such advantage of Robin, knowing that he wasn't the sort of person who would sue her even though he was encouraged to do so by a very eminent QC, knowing he would never sell his story for thirty pieces of silver – or more like half a million. He never spoke to her again and even today, five years later, he absolutely despises her. He calls her "that ghastly woman" and loathes her betrayal and all her broken promises.' In the end she decided not to sell the house anyway. More than a year later he was to find new happiness with a beautiful society model who was fifty years younger than Joan, twenty-year-old Marina Hanbury, in a love affair that was to last for nearly three years. 'Marina was absolutely gorgeous,' one of his friends told me, 'but like Joan she wanted to marry him. He's had more proposals of marriage than any man I know! Women are constantly asking him to marry them.' Marina went on to have a romance with Prince and Princess Michael of Kent's twenty-six-year-old son, Freddie Windsor, and by the end of 2005 Robin was enjoying an affair with a Russian journalist.

In August Joan and Percy had a holiday on a friend's yacht in the Mediterranean and then flew to London to rehearse another stage play, *Moon Over Buffalo*, but once again it seemed that her literary career was jinxed when the House of Stratus, which was due to publish her new novel, *Star Quality*, early in September, admitted that it could not afford to pay her the final £50,000 of her agreed £150,000 advance and publication had to be postponed for several months while they sorted out their financial problems. But her disappointment paled into insignificance when in America on 11 September nineteen Arab terrorists hijacked four giant passenger jets and crashed two of them into the twin towers of the World Trade Center, killing nearly three thousand people. Until now Joan was still not sure whether she should marry Percy but the horror of that day persuaded her to go ahead. Death could come at any time and you had to make the most of every minute. They began to plan for an extravagant wedding five months later.

Moon Over Buffalo was a farce by Ken Ludwig, set in the New York town of Buffalo in 1953, in which a couple of old, married, has-been actors, George and Charlotte, hear that a big-shot Hollywood director is coming to see them onstage with the idea of possibly casting them in his next movie. Chaos erupts, exacerbated by the discovery that George has made one of the cast pregnant and has hit the bottle, Charlotte has decided to run off with their best friend, and the company has no idea whether it is meant to be putting on *Private Lives* or *Cyrano de Bergerac*. Directed by Ray Cooney, co-starring a Broadway actor, Frank Langella, and with Percy as the company manager, the play gave Joan yet another chance to appear onstage scantily dressed in a lacy basque and peach-coloured suspenders. It opened in Guildford on 18 September, went on to Bath, and reached the Old Vic in London on 15 October. To publicise the play she gave an interview for the *Sunday Telegraph* to Gyles Brandreth, the TV personality and an ex-MP, whose newly elected Conservative Party leader was Iain Duncan Smith. Brandreth found that 'her eyes were awash with mascara, her lips are ablaze with scarlet gloss but, at close range, she looks less the drag queen and more the star-about-town than you might expect'. He also found her 'surprisingly normal, not the least intimidating. Could it be that she overrates the awesome nature of the Collins persona because she spends a fair bit of her time in the company of acolytes (and "screaming queens", in theatre parlance) who play up to it?' Brandreth said he admired her and reckoned she was 'enormous fun and gloriously uncomplicated. She is not deep, literary or political. "I don't go in for introspection, I'm not religious, I don't think about death, I can't remember the last book I read and I know nothing about the new leader of the Conservative Party except that someone called Smith can't be all bad. I want to enjoy myself and entertain people, that's all."' He asked her what was the secret of her success. Energy, she said, and exercise, optimism, hard work, and an ability to live for today. 'Remember,' she said, 'yesterday's history, tomorrow's a mystery, today is a gift. That's why it's called the present.'

She also gave an interview for *The Times* magazine to Ginny Dougary, who went to the first night in Guildford and reported that one woman in the audience had said to her: 'Looks good, doesn't she? Although I suspect that she's been under the knife a few times.' No matter how often Joan denied it, women refused to believe her. Ms Dougary reported that Joan's performance had been 'rather marvellous in a slightly camp way, all wide eyes, pouts and flounces'. During their interview, she said, 'there is something very girlie and flirtatious about her. Even the way she sits, slipping one denim leg beneath the other, leaving a smooth, bare foot dangling, makes one think of a Lolita-ish teenager. This should be slightly creepy in a woman who is practically a septuagenarian but for some reason it's not; perhaps because there is always a suspicion of knowingness or irony in her projection ... No wonder she's a hit with gay men, with that arch, exaggerated femininity so beloved by drag queens.' Joan complained about welfare state spongers, immigrants, and people who were jealous of her money, claiming that she had never made a fortune and that TV actors were paid much more nowadays. 'You know what people get on *Friends*?' she asked indignantly. 'They get like $150,000 to $250,000 an episode. Kelsey Grammer gets half a million. I got $15,000 a week on *Dynasty* for the first year.' Joan pleading poverty was something of a novelty but her openness was disarming: 'I do love drinking,' she said enthusiastically. 'I even love getting smashed.' Asked if she had become 'a baby person' now that she was a grandmother she said: 'No, not really. I mean, I much prefer them to animals but ...' and then threw back her head and laughed. And finally, of course, 'Yesterday's history, tomorrow's a mystery, today is a gift. That's why it's called the present.' Ms Dougary ended her article by writing: 'You know, I'm no drag queen but I think I may just have joined the Joan Collins Fan Club.' The West End critics, however, had not. When the play, re-titled *Over the Moon*, reached the Old Vic they savaged it. One called it 'excruciatingly laboured and wearisomely frenetic' and some criticised Joan for allowing it to be publicised by posters showing her 'parading around in her underwear'.

Sacha was also in London to open his latest exhibition at the Catto Gallery a week after Joan opened at the Old Vic. He had grown to look uncannily like his father but had also inherited his father's melancholy and pessimism and told *The Sunday Times* that he believed most people have miserable lives and can expect only a few moments of happiness. His mother, of course, with her eternally youthful optimism, refused to worry much about anything, least of all her effect on other people. 'What she does is enjoy life,' said Sacha, 'and she doesn't give too much painful reappraisal of the past or of motives. I think all that baggage, all that psychological stuff, is what ages people. She just lets it all go. There's a downside to that, of course, which is that sometimes you need cumulative lessons and learning from your past.' At thirty-six he still called Joan Mummy and admitted to David Wigg that at times he felt intimidated by her.

Because of the dreadful reviews *Over the Moon* closed six weeks early, on 1 December, but as usual Joan refused to fester with regret, put the flop firmly behind her, looked ever-optimistically to the future, and two weeks later threw an engagement party where she announced that she and Percy had decided to marry in February. 'I wouldn't be doing this if it wasn't for keeps,' she told her friends. 'I'm very happy and very much in love.' When one of the British newspapers telephoned Bill Wiggins to ask if he could offer Percy any advice about living with Joan, he said wickedly that 'since Percy has already been married he will have noticed that with his wife every twenty-eight days or so he'd have been getting four or five days off, but not with our Joanie he won't!' To me Wiggy said: 'With the greatest respect to

Joan, what full-blooded guy of thirty-five is going to marry a woman of sixty-eight?'

Despite Joan's fear of computers and modern technology she agreed that it was time she had her own website and had one designed at www.joancollins.net, where for years her home page showed her reclining on a couch in a black, lacy dress with the invitation ENTER just below her waist, though the site was redesigned in 2007.

In January she and Percy enjoyed a sunny holiday in Acapulco before returning to London to plan their lavish wedding. Percy's ex-wife was convinced that the marriage was doomed. 'This relationship is not going to be good for Joan or Percy,' she warned Sharon Churcher two weeks before the wedding. 'We spoke last week and I said: "Percy, what are you doing? This has train wreck written all over it." And what happens to Percy if Joan loses interest in him? Or if she dies? He'll look up in fifteen years when he's fifty-one and say, "My God! I've had no life except taking care of an elderly mother and an elderly wife. And I'm known around the globe as a gold-digging toyboy."' Joan's family became alarmed when she was said to believe there was no need for a pre-nuptial agreement with Percy, despite her expensive experiences with Peter Holm, and one of her closest friends said helplessly to another: 'What the hell is she doing marrying the fucking *help*?' Joan's publicist, Stella Wilson, was quoted in the *News of the World* saying that it was Percy's idea to have a pre-nuptial agreement because 'he's been hurt by the accusations that he's a gold-digger.'

The cost of the wedding, at Claridge's, was eased by *Hello!*'s glossy rival *OK!*, which paid Joan £375,000 [£431,000] for exclusive coverage and photographs that would sprawl across fourteen pages of the magazine. It was estimated that the happy couple would make as much as another £1.5 million from worldwide syndication of the pictures. They invited a hundred and eighty people but upset Joan's old friend Nicky Haslam, a writer for *Hello!*, when they then disinvited him because *OK!* did not want a *Hello!* columnist at 'their' wedding. AM I MIFFED ABOUT BEING UNINVITED TO JOAN'S NUPTIALS? he asked in a huge *Evening Standard* headline three days before the wedding. DARLING, I'M FAR TOO YOUNG. Haslam was, in fact, over sixty but enraged by Joan's behaviour. She had not even explained the situation to him herself but had ordered Stella Wilson to leave a message on his answerphone telling him he was no longer welcome at the wedding.

'It's not as though I haven't looked after the old bat over the years,' he complained. 'I've escorted her to film premières and society events, not to mention introduced her to just about everybody I know.' He ended his tirade with a splendidly bitchy pay-off: 'By the way, darling, I do think your idea of having the royal piper playing his bagpipes as you walk down the aisle is rather brilliant. It'll be so nice for the guests to hear the wedding march without the help of their hearing aids.' Joan retaliated in the *Spectator* by sneering that Haslam was an 'F-list celebrity [*and*] rather pathetic. Get a life, dear.'

The wedding, at 5 p.m. on 17 February in Claridge's ballroom, was said to have cost about £100,000, and the guests included Princess Sally Aga Khan, Shirley Bassey, Christopher Biggins, Cilla Black, Rupert Everett, Freddie Forsyth, Gina Fratini, Jerry Hall, Gloria Hunniford, Roger Moore, Sir Tim Rice, Sir Cliff Richard and Ruby Wax. Another was the actress Arlene Dahl, who was also an astrologer and convinced Joan that she and Percy had known each other in a previous life 'and had unfinished business together. It seemed to make sense,' said Joan. 'We had such a powerful affinity for each other – we felt as if we'd known each other before.' She arrived a few minutes late, wearing a lilac silk gown designed by *Dynasty*'s couturier Nolan Miller. Percy wore a Buchanan tartan kilt in honour of his Scottish mother, and his best man, Chris Pennington, a Flower of Scotland kilt. Joan was given away again by Judy Bryer's husband, Max, and Judy herself was again her matron of honour. The ceremony lasted only fifteen minutes and when it was over, reported *OK!*, 'Joan and Percy kissed each other passionately to loud cheers and wolf whistles'. *Wolf* whistles? Nicky Haslam would certainly not have approved. After a long, gourmet dinner, and Percy's speech, the bride rose to make a speech as well and said she was so happy because she had finally found her soulmate, and they danced until 2 a.m.

Had Joan been an American woman who had married five times, and had her husbands all kept their original surnames, she would now be Joan Collins Reed Newley Kaschenhoff Sjöholm Mueller Parra del Riego. Sadly she was just plain Joan Gibson when they went off on honeymoon to Malaysia for two weeks at a luxurious resort on a wonderfully romantic little island in the Straits of Malacca, Pangkor Laut, where the best rooms were elegant wooden huts perched on stilts above the sea, where iguana trotted along the beach, peacocks strutted through the main dining room, and sandpipers flitted between the tables. I had stayed there myself five years previously and decided it was a five-star Garden of Eden, as had Luciano Pavarotti, who had fallen in love here with his young secretary Nicoletta Mantovani and had said when he opened the resort in 1994: 'I almost cried when I saw how beautiful God had made this paradise.'

Back in London, looking tanned and relaxed, Joan gave a radio interview to promote her new novel and joked about the difference between her and Percy's ages: 'Look,' she shrugged, 'if he dies, he dies.' *Star Quality* was published at last in March, not by House of Stratus but by Robson Books. It was a romantic saga, set between 1917 and 2002, about four generations of women in one family who all become famous in some branch of showbiz because they all have that feisty, indefinable something special, star quality. One of the women is a vicious, foul-mouthed, drug-addicted, lesbian monster who is gang-raped after going to a seedy bar and has a daughter by a black, bisexual, drug-addict gigolo: 'He fucked her on the bearskin rug in front of the fire, then he fucked her on her bed. When she begged for more he took her on the cold marble bathroom tiles, then he poured bubble bath into her jacuzzi tub and took her again under the foaming hot water. Lulu lost count of the number of times she came.' Why did Joan feel that she had to write such tacky scenes? The book is all pretty dreary and the ending so hurried, with the final fourteen years swiftly put out of their misery in just fifteen pages, that it seems even she had become thoroughly bored by her own tale. Absurdities abound. Two uneducated young working-class women remark of one man that 'he's indefatigable' ... 'he's a perfectionist and he's got inexhaustible energy'. In 1953, two years before Princess Margaret had to abandon her hope of marrying Peter Townsend because he was divorced, one of Joan's characters miraculously marries a gay duke in St Margaret's Church at Westminster, even though she has been divorced twice. Most ridiculous of all, after her disgrace in the lesbian club the monstrous drug addict lands a part in her mother's TV soap and no one recognises her for ages, even though just a year earlier she was the world's most famous supermodel whose face had appeared on every magazine cover. But the saddest aspect of the book is that all the male characters fall into one of the following categories: robotic sex machines who can fuck all day and night; ugly, sweaty losers; or vicious, perverted bastards who hate women and torture them with callous brutality. Joan may not always have taken up with the nicest of men but she must surely have met at least some decent ones.

To promote the book she gave another interview, to Cassandra Jardine of the *Daily Telegraph*, who informed her that Russell Crowe had just refused a Variety Club Award because she had been the previous winner. 'He must have been drunk,' snapped Joan. 'He was the only time I met him,' when Crowe had apparently been some 'drunken lout who came up to our table in a dirty T-shirt'. So much for his being one of Hollywood's few macho actors. Another man who found Joan less than wonderful was the British scriptwriter Barry Cryer, who complained that she had commissioned him to write for £3,000 an amusing monologue about her career for a possible one-woman show but had paid him only £1,500 because although the speech had gone down well with an after-dinner audience she had been too nervous to remember all his jokes and therefore felt she did not need to pay him for those she had not used.

It was not long before the *Daily Mail* reported her first public row with Percy, in New York just two weeks after the honeymoon, when she objected to finding him deep in conversation with a woman at Liza Minnelli's fourth wedding. However, they denied this story was true. She claimed that someone 'who used to be in my life' had been spreading 'all kinds of derogatory and defamatory things about Percy and I ever since we announced our engagement' and was sending emails to newspapers alleging that theirs was a sexless marriage and that they slept in separate beds. Joan's American PR man, Jeffrey Lane, denied the rumour. 'I've been staying in the guest room of Joan's apartment in Los Angeles since February,' he reported, 'and I can one hundred per cent confirm that they share a bedroom and live as a couple. This is a fact. It's a total nonsense to suggest otherwise.' Asked how he could possibly know what went on when the bedroom door was closed, he replied: 'Obviously I'm in my bed and they're in their bed. They have a perfectly normal relationship. I see them go to bed together every night, and in the morning, when we're all having breakfast, they're like a normal romantic couple, holding hands and all that sort of thing.'

Joan was increasingly disturbed about Britain's growing yob culture and in April wrote an article for the *Sunday Telegraph* deploring the modern 'ladette' culture, which encouraged girls to sleep with scores of men, dress like whores, swear like navvies and get so drunk that they were sick. 'The British Open' had come a long way since she had herself been castigated for immorality in the 1950s and early 1960s.

Because Percy – 'my Latin from Manhattan' – was about to manage a play in New York and she was herself about to join the New York cast of a daytime soap, she left her apartment in Los Angeles and bought another for £2 million on the eighth floor of a block on the Upper East Side of Manhattan, which she intended now to be her main base. Even so, she kept her London flat and still spent two or three months every year in the South of France, where she loved eating at the fashionable Club 55 on Pampelonne beach and frolicking with the likes of Liam Neeson and Natasha Richardson, Rod Stewart and Penny Lancaster, Ivana Trump and Regine. She decided not to sell Destino, which was now worth about £4 million, because she loved it so much, and she went there again in August to start writing a screenplay, *Best of Enemies*, about two feuding actresses. 'I love my house,' she told David Wigg. 'I love the surroundings – the hills and the trees. And there is a light here that doesn't seem to exist anywhere else in the world. There's an incredible, soft, wonderful light in Provence, even when the sun shines.'

A month later she and Percy flew off to New York for Sacha's wedding to Angela Tassoni, of whom Joan approved, in the Cathedral of St John the Divine on 17 September, and a week later she made her first appearance in *Guiding Light*, a long-running, afternoon family saga aimed at pensioners and housewives, in which she played yet another rich, glamorous, manipulative bitch called Alex. Back in London at the end of September she gave yet another interview to Lynda Lee-Potter to coincide with the publication of yet another of her beauty and lifestyle books. This time she admitted that she had had about two dozen lovers – double her previous estimate but still not nearly the true total – 'but don't forget that I was with most of the men in my life for a very long time,' she said. 'I'm a serial monogamist.' She claimed yet again that 'in all my relationships and marriages I've been the one who's left. No one has ever left me.' In truth Warren Beatty, Tony Newley and Bill Wiggins, at least, had effectively left her first. 'Cross my heart and hope to die, I have not had a face-lift,' she insisted, but 'I find it almost impossible to believe she hasn't had a few tucks,' wrote Mrs Lee-Potter, 'because why do her arms look older than her face?'

Joan knew from previous interviews that Mrs Lee-Potter did not like Jackie much and asked her why. 'I say that Jackie looks stunning in a high-class hooker sort of way but I think her books are diabolical,' wrote Mrs Lee-Potter. 'I can't understand why they sell and Joan is a far better writer. At this point Joan, who never wants to upset her younger sister, leans towards my tape recorder and says: "Joan Collins makes no comment about that remark."'

Her new book, *Joan's Way: Looking Good, Feeling Great*, was full of feisty advice for women, whom she urged to assert themselves vigorously and speak their minds, even if they were called bitches for doing so; to stop worrying about hurting other people; to refuse to be manipulated; and to love themselves.

Back in London she earned herself a neat £100,000 by making a forty-second TV advertisement for Marks and Spencer's Christmas campaign, for which she posed apparently naked but dripping with jewellery, wearing a fake fur, and remarking that what she liked best about Christmas was 'a nicely roasted bird'. Then it was back to New York to launch her new American publisher Hyperion's edition of *Star Quality*. When an American interviewer expressed amazement at her energy and productivity – two books, the daily soap, the filmscript, the TV ads, the travelling – Joan said: 'My dear, this is what life is about, taking everything you can from it, making the best of what you have, making what you have *better*. I'm a totally forward-thinking person. I feel inordinately blessed with everything I have, personally and professionally, and always optimistic about what is around the corner.' *What a woman*, wrote the reporter. In fact the soap had become too much for her and she left it after just three months. *Dynasty*, where fifty minutes of film had had to be shot every six days, had been exhausting enough, but *Guiding Light* was a daily show and much more stressful for the actors, who had to learn every day as many as forty-five pages of dialogue, many of which might be changed at the last minute, shoot fifty-five minutes of film, and there was no time for proper rehearsals. She told *Vanity Fair* that it was the most difficult acting she had ever done. The stress became apparent when, in November, she fell out for good – after many years of friendship – with Jeffrey Lane, following a row when she asked him one night if her car was waiting outside and he snapped 'that's not my job' before launching into a tirade of screaming at her. They never spoke again. A few days later the *Mail on Sunday* claimed that the pressure she was under was also affecting her marriage, that at a recent party she had had another row with Percy, and that when he had tried to calm her by touching her arm 'she yanked it away and hissed: "Don't touch me," and stormed off.' Thirty years earlier she had told Clive Hirschhorn of the *Sunday Express* that 'the thing about marriage, at least my experience of it, is that it tends to make you more selfish. I mean, the more you marry, the more selfish you become.' Now that she was almost seventy and in her fifth marriage it was perhaps time to slow down, take on less, and stop rushing about quite so much. There must surely be a limit to how much even Joan Collins could do as she moved into her eighth decade.

CHAPTER TWENTY-TWO

A NATIONAL TREASURE

{ 2003–2006 }

Joan did begin to slow down in 2003. She appeared on a couple of TV chat shows in Britain and in America on an *Intimate Portrait* TV tribute to mark her seventieth birthday in May, but there were no new films, plays or books. She marked the start of her eighth decade – two months after the American and British invasion of Iraq – with a party in New York and a ten-day holiday with Percy in Mauritius while her half-sister Natasha, now Captain Coxen of the British army, was serving in Kuwait as a United Nations operations officer. The British newspapers, which Joan had long believed had it in for her, published affectionate tributes. 'It's official,' wrote Paul Callan in the *Express*. 'Joan Collins is a national treasure – as English, in her own way, as Derby Day and HP Sauce, rainy Sundays and green countryside, *Woman's Hour* and village cricket, pubs and the Cup Final, Page Three Girls and donkey rides on the beach.' Callan asked Michael Winner what it was that had made Joan so popular. 'She has the spirit of a child and a great love of life,' he said. Joan made no mention herself of her dreaded milestone birthday in the diary column that appeared in the *Spectator* the next day – God forbid – but she did tell a nice story against herself. She and Tara had been browsing around an East End antiques market in Bermondsey, she wearing her disguise of raincoat, baseball cap and no make-up, when Tara heard one of the stallholders say to his sluttish wife: ''ere, Trace, did you see that was that Joan Collins? Gor blimey, even you look better than what she does!'

Tara was now writing columns for the *Financial Times* and *Good Health* magazine and had recently found her own toyboy, Richard Skeates, a homely country-lad finance administrator who was several years her junior and lived in Somerset in the quiet seaside resort of

Weston-super-Mare. She had met him at the funeral of her old nanny, Sue Le Long, who had often taken her and Sacha to Weston as children to stay with her sister, Richard's mother. Richard had a five-year-old daughter, Anicia, and was about to change Tara's life dramatically. She abandoned her dream of becoming a showbiz or TV star, went to live with Richard in a modest, three-bedroom house on a modern housing estate in Wick St Lawrence, near Weston-super-Mare, and gave birth in Bristol to his son on 8 September. They named the baby Weston, after the town, a decision of which Joan did not entirely approve.

Inevitably her second grandchild made her more family minded and Tara, Richard, Anicia, Miel and Weston joined her and Percy in July at Destino, where she romped with the children on the beach, and on Miel's fifth birthday took her to Disneyland near Paris. By August Joan had become so proper and respectable that she admitted to Ruby Wax on television that she wished she had not been so unfaithful to her previous husbands, and two weeks later she exhibited more of her new puritanical streak in her *Spectator* diary when she attacked the TV presenter Ulrika Jonsson for accusing in her recent autobiography a previous lover, John Leslie, of having raped her brutally six years earlier. 'Why wait years to report it?' asked Joan. 'To get more book sales?' Yet she had herself waited twenty-six years before writing her own autobiography and accusing Maxwell Reed of raping her. 'I don't believe John Leslie is a rapist,' she wrote, forgetting that some did not believe that Reed had been a rapist either. She redeemed herself, however, by ending her column with another splendid blast at modern, yobbish Britain: as a child her mother had been taken to the circus by her grandmother to see the fat lady and the tattooed man, she wrote, and now they were everywhere. She lamented, too, the demise of her favourite aircraft, Concorde, and when she and Percy joined the last commercial flight from New York to London she asked: 'So what if Aunt Maisie's windows get blown in just because she lives under the flight path?'

She attacked vulgar ladette excesses again in an interview with yet another *Daily Mail* writer, Mary Riddell, at the end of November, and complained that 'this sexual stuff they do now, like "roasting" sessions with young girls and footballers, is demeaning, degrading and horrible. I have old-fashioned values. I had a wild period, but I never did anything like that, and nor, thank God, did my children. Now girls walk around with FUCK ME written on a T-shirt or flash their bottoms. What real, decent man is going to want to marry a girl like that? I don't understand the fascination of getting as drunk as possible and having as many partners as possible. Is this what the suffragettes worked for? For women to become slags?' Ms Riddell was convinced that Joan must have had plastic surgery, noticing that 'her softening arms and the alabaster face appear not quite to match. '"Do you think I need it?" she asks, perhaps evasively. I wonder whether her quest for youthfulness may actually be rooted in a fear of mortality.' Of course it was, one of Joan's friends told me: 'She has such a terror of old age and death. There's no faith there at all and there's not a big spiritual aspect to her.' In fact Joan's face was looking increasingly like a tight mask and in her interview with Ruby Wax she bore an uncanny resemblence to Mae West in old age, with her rigid visage and little glittery eyes.

Joan and Percy enjoyed a double Christmas that year: first in England with Tara, Richard, their three children, and Percy, bless him, cooking the turkey and all the trimmings; then in New York with Sacha and Angela before going on to Aspen for some snow and Acapulco for nine days in the sun. There Joan allowed her old friend Eddie Sanderson to invade their privacy yet again by taking dozens of photographs to sell to *OK!*, which published them across six pages.

Flying so often had become increasingly irritating because of the strict new anti-terrorist security procedures at American airports, where Joan complained that she seemed always to be picked out for especially intimate searches 'due to my obvious resemblance to Mr bin Laden, no doubt'. She had to endure another frisking when in February they returned to England to rehearse her next play, *Full Circle*, a comedy by Alan Melville, with which she and Percy (as the company manager) were to embark in March on a fifteen-week tour of British theatres. Set in Paris in the early 1950s, *Full Circle* told of a rich lady novelist (Joan) who confesses to her three children that the man they always thought was their father was not, and that they are in fact all illegitimate and all by different fathers. She decides to make them respectable by inviting their three fathers to her elegant apartment so as to choose which should become the children's perfect official father. In Joan's own life Percy had become the perfect partner. 'He's the man I've been looking for all my life,' she told David Wigg. 'He's a perfect husband in every way.' Because of him, she claimed, she had even given up her once limitless appetite for going to parties night after night. 'To me, you go to parties to meet somebody else,' she said. 'There's not really much point in that because I've met the person I want to be with. He looks after my every need without being in any way a doormat. He likes taking care of me.'

Her performance in *Full Circle* earned her a rave review from Charles Spencer of the *Daily Telegraph*. 'What an astonishing woman Joan Collins is,' he wrote. 'Age cannot wither her, nor custom stale her infinite lack of variety.' Was it really possible that she was almost seventy-one? 'As she sweeps on to the stage of the New Wimbledon Theatre, wearing a deliciously silly picture hat and clutching a bunch of freshly cut flowers, she is a vision of eternal youth. Her dark eyes sparkle with mischief. Her smile is irresistibly roguish. Her cheekbones are to die for, while her cleavage, as T. S. Eliot (one of her most devoted admirers) put it, holds out the promise of pneumatic bliss. Keats (could he, too, have been one of her early lovers?) got Joan Collins in a nutshell when he declared: "A thing of beauty is a joy for ever: its loveliness increases." I don't think anyone could maliciously accuse Joan Collins of being a great actress [*but*] she can do glamorous villainy. She can do charm. She can do light comedy. I don't think her range goes much deeper or wider than that, but why on earth should it? One of Joan Collins's many admirable qualities is that she has always known her limits.' He concluded: 'The night belongs to Collins. She treats the piece with exactly the lightness of touch and hint of mockery that it deserves and wears a succession of over-the-top costumes with superb aplomb. The final spectacular frock-coat-and-bustier combination in lilac and black (designer Hugh Durrant) draws audible gasps of amazement from the audience. And anyone who doubts La Collins's ability to act should feast their eyes on the matchless display of false modesty with which she takes her final curtain call. Irresistible.' She had always insisted that she was best at light comedy and here at last was a critic who agreed.

Less welcome was *The Sunday Times*'s annual Rich List in April, which showed that while Jackie was the sixteenth richest British film and TV millionaire and estimated to be worth £66 million, Joan was nowhere to be seen.

Early in May she ventured into politics again when she wrote a long article for *The Sunday Times* under the headline THEY'RE TRYING TO

KILL MY ENGLAND in which she said how proud she was to carry a British passport and urged readers to resist every attempt to subjugate England to the European Union and the Brussels bureaucrats. This led one of the leading members of the small UK Independence Party, her old friend Robert Kilroy-Silk, to invite her to become a patron, which she did at a public meeting in Nottingham at the end of the month. Her sudden appearance on the political scene caused hilarity in political and journalistic circles, which led her five months later to announce that although she was still a patron of UKIP she did not necessarily agree with their policies or intend to vote for them. This caused more tittering, and wisely she returned to her political home when she agreed to be a prize in a Conservative Party raffle.

On 12 May Angela gave birth in New York to her and Sacha's first child, a girl they named Ava Grace. They were living now in an apartment overlooking Central Park and he had a studio in Greenwich Village where he had just completed a powerful triple portrait of the paralysed *Superman* actor Christopher Reeve, which the Smithsonian's National Portrait Gallery in Washington was about to buy for its permanent collection. Explaining his unflattering, sometimes brutal pictures, Sacha, a great admirer of Lucian Freud, told the *Sunday Express*: 'I had enough sensibility as a little boy to see that my parents were often surrounded by false people and that showbiz didn't make them or me happy. My mother loves being a star but my father helped me see through it.' Despite his distrust of shallow showbiz values, he was still prepared to give an interview to *Hello!* and let it splash pictures of the baby, Joan, Angela and himself on its cover and across eleven inside pages. Perhaps they paid him a lot of money, but the family's apparently insatiable taste for intimate, exhibitionist, glossy magazine publicity belied its apparent distaste for intrusive 'reptile' tabloid reporters and photographers. Joan was at it again a few days later, spread-eagled this time across six pages of colour photographs in the *Sunday Telegraph Magazine* and an interview with Nigel Farndale, in which she said 'with a glint in her eye' that Jackie was a fantastic mother and grandmother: 'She's got hundreds of grandchildren. I shouldn't have said that. She won't like that.' Impertinently Farndale suggested that perhaps Joan was a touch superficial. She agreed immediately. 'I like superficial things,' she said, 'fashion, theatre, reading thrillers, television, walking, children, food, drink, friends – if that's superficial then I guess I'm superficial.'

Her tour of provincial theatres inspired her to write again in the *Spectator* about her despair at the mounting evidence that British society was being destroyed from within by yobbish behaviour, bad manners and violence. As she went around the country, she said, she had seen drunken yobs on the loose, vandalising cars, swearing foully, assaulting passers-by and attacking the police. She blamed this distressing collapse of British pride, civilisation and society on the 1960s, when young people had begun to rebel against all rules and every form of authority.

In October 2004 she published yet another novel, *Misfortune's Daughters* – her fifth to be published – and dedicated it 'For my darling husband Percy. *Never ever change.*' It told of two rival sisters, Atlanta and Venetia Stephanopolis, the daughters of a cold, ruthless, billionaire Greek tycoon, a kinky sado-masochist who has murdered their beautiful mother because she admitted having an affair with a younger man. The elder daughter, Atlanta, is fat and cruelly ugly with a big nose, thick lips and eyebrows, the beginnings of a moustache and beard, and black hair all over her body. She is so ugly that her father rejects her, whereas he adores her sister Venetia, who is beautiful, blonde and very feminine. Atlanta decides to have plastic surgery and after just one three-hour operation becomes miraculously beautiful and a famous actress who is pursued by almost every man she meets. We are not told how this miracle has been achieved nor how all Atlanta's body hair has suddenly disappeared and never grows again. But despite Atlanta's unlikely transformation she soon realises that an actress's life is empty and amoral, so without any training or experience at all she becomes instead – instantly – a brilliant journalist and editor and marries a rich Australian publisher. Venetia, by contrast, becomes a spoilt socialite bitch addicted to ecstasy, cocaine and crack, marries a bisexual pervert, and is so promiscuous that she is nicknamed 'The Greek Open'. Was that ancient joke beginning by now to wear a bit thin?

This time the sleaziest sex scene describes Venetia's pervy husband in the middle of a disgusting orgy, heavily made-up, bombed out of his skull on drugs, lying on a table, smiling happily, and being sexually molested:

> He was naked except for garlands of black leather and chains around his neck and wrists. Crawling over and around him, almost humming like insects as they did so, were half a dozen of the most degenerate

looking men and women ... Drag queens in full make-up and wigs, bull-dykes with forearms bigger than a stevedore's, transvestites, and half naked gay hustlers, they were all intent on doing something to the inert body. Some were kissing him or fondling him, one was even masturbating over him ... the pack crawled over him like maggots on rotting fruit.

It is a remarkably silly, dreary, uninspired book whose unbelievable characters have neither depth nor humanity. None has any credible hinterland, and the allegedly Greek characters might just as well be Hottentots for all the Hellenic attributes they exhibit. While the French and Italian characters keep lapsing absurdly into unnecessary French or Italian, the Greeks appear to be utterly ignorant of their own language. There is not even one *kalimera* or *kalinikta* among them, let alone a *parakalo* or *efharisto*. And the book's unlikely slushy happy ending is pure Mills and Boon.

The absurdities in *Misfortune's Daughters* are almost endless. A young Mexican man is called Kristobel. An Italian says *buon giorno* 'in a charm-ing Italian accent'. Atlanta begins her unbelievable journalistic career by selling her socialite friends' secrets to a gossip column yet no one suspects that she might be the nark, even though she is always at the same parties as the spy and writes for the same magazine under her own name. Later, to research an article, this rich, gorgeous young woman lives on the streets among the tramps, bag-ladies and down-and-outs and is completely accepted by them without even one asking who the hell she might be.

The book is stuffed with clichés: 'the paparazzi went into feeding frenzy'; 'there were plenty more fish in the sea'; 'It was a piece of cake for Maximus to stroll over'; the 'cosmetic surgery that had turned that sow's ear into a ravishing silk purse'. It is also so carelessly written that one character drives from Cannes to Cap d'Antibes via the inland A8 motorway, a journey twice as long as the direct route along the coast, and Atlanta drives from Nice airport to Cannes (which is to the west) via Cap Ferrat, which is to the east. And so it goes on: careless, slipshod, uninspired garbage. Worst of all, the style of writing is as crude as ever: one renowned Hollywood Casanova, for example, is 'this living legend, this phallus on legs' and says: 'You love sex, Atlanta, don't you? I knew that night on your island that once you got rid of your virginity, you'd be horny as a little toad.' Another woman is so keen on Venetia's husband that 'he's got her practically creaming her panties'.

It is all so tacky. Why would a woman as stylish, elegant and witty as Joan write and publish such sleazy rubbish? Could she not see that her books were just as gross, vulgar, moronic and uncivilised as the violent yobs and vomiting ladettes of whom she so disapproved? Some of the tit-flashing FUCK ME girls might even be her own readers.

On 20 October the *Daily Mail's* star columnist Lynda Lee-Potter died. She had interviewed Joan so often and so fairly that they had become friends and Joan wrote a warm tribute that appeared in the *Mail* the next day. She was also to attend Mrs Lee-Potter's memorial service in St Bride's church in Fleet Street seven months later and in the *Spectator* to applaud her down-to-earth common sense and honesty. Yet such moments of kindness and generosity were offset by a very different side of Joan's character a few days later when security staff at Heathrow airport insisted that she should remove her hat, jacket and shoes as she went to board her flight to Los Angeles. The *Sun* reported that she was furious and snarled at a security woman. Later, she explained that airport security staff targeted her to humiliate her, 'but it was funny seeing this big star standing there furious in her bare feet,' one witness told the *Sun*. She was so angry that she wrote an article about her humiliation in the *Mail on Sunday* under the headline WELL, DO I *LOOK* LIKE AN AL QAEDA BOMBER?

She was still giving numerous interviews to publicise the new novel. Deborah Ross, who grilled her for the *Spectator*, asked what she thought of Tony Blair. 'Not a lot,' said Joan, who no longer considered him as gorgeous as she had when he had invited her and Robin to dinner at Chequers. 'Somebody told me last night he dyes his hair. Is that true? God, we need a leader, don't we? Desperate, desperate, desperate for a leader.' She told the *Independent* that if a film were ever made of her life she would want to be played by Catherine Zeta Jones, and in yet another *OK!* photo-feature she said that she found it difficult to write the sex scenes in her novels 'because it's very easy for them to become clichéd'. When the paperback was published ten months later she told the *Mail on Sunday* magazine that she had taken three years to write the book 'and it was a labour of love because I adored it'.

After another family Christmas with all her children and grand-children at her flat in New York, Joan and Percy flew again to Acapulco to stay with Evie and Leslie Bricusse for their usual January holiday. Her life slowed down a lot in 2005, though she and Percy still travelled a great deal: Las Vegas for two days in February to check out the cabaret acts; London to make a speech at a gala celebrating RADA's hundredth anniversary; St Tropez in May, June and July; London in August; LA, San Diego and New York in September; London again in October. She appeared on a dozen TV chat shows, in March on a celebrity episode of the quiz show *Who Wants to be a Millionaire?*, and in May on the American programme *This Morning* when another guest, Dr Alex Karidis, an eminent London plastic surgeon and Fellow of the Royal College of Surgeons, became convinced that she had had 'extensive' plastic surgery.

When he told the *Daily Mail* about this, the paper was forced to apologise and retract the story. But a few months later Joan was to admit to Barbara Ellen of the *Observer Magazine* that she had indeed had her forehead injected with Botox but still denied that she had had a face-lift.

There were no new films or plays in sight but she did appear in one episode of a BBC TV series about the staff of a five-star hotel, *Hotel Babylon*, in which she played a most unlikely part as a frumpy, elderly widow who carries her small dog around and fancies the hotel doorman. In July she was asked if she would make a guest appearance in two episodes of the trashy TV series about the wives of a team of soccer players, *Footballers' Wives*, in yet another Alexis Carrington role as a rich, sarcastic, manipulative bitch. She read the script, decided that the show was 'quite like *Dynasty* in its way [*because*] it has fabulous locations, great clothes and is glamorous', and agreed to play the part. Her decision was a huge mistake because it was an unbelievably awful series, woodenly written, appallingly acted, stilted and disjointed, about a deeply unattractive group of vulgar, shallow, Essex-girl women whose breasts were all hoisted to shoulder level and whose husbands were all tattooed yobs. Joan's horrible, predatory, ball-breaking character, Eva de Wolffe, was allowed to have a toyboy but he must surely have been half blind because she looked as grotesque as a pantomime dame, com-pletely unsexy, and suddenly every bit as old as her seventy-two years. She should never have agreed to appear in such a base show when she was already immensely rich and could hardly have needed the money. Even she admitted when it was screened that she had been 'ghastly' in it. 'I was terrible, awful, horrible,' she confessed to Cosmo Landesman of *The Sunday Times*. 'I've never been so embarrassed.'

Still, her status as a National Treasure was never even dented by the dreadful parts she so often accepted and it was confirmed in October when she and Percy were invited to Margaret (now Baroness) Thatcher's eightieth birthday party at the Mandarin Oriental Hotel in London along with six hundred and seventy 'celebrity' guests, among them the Queen, Prince Philip, Tony and Cherie Blair, and Sir John and Lady Major. A few days later they were off to Venice to celebrate another birthday, Michael Winner's seventieth, at the Hotel Cipriani. A couple of days after that they were in New York chatting with Prince Charles and his wife Camilla at a British consulate drinks party, and then it was Palm Beach, Florida, for Donald Trump Jr's wedding. At least some of the hassle of air travel had been removed because after months of application Joan had just been granted at last an American green card, which made her a US resident alien and allowed her to float through US customs and immigration without being fingerprinted, photographed or interrogated.

In November she and Percy were back in Britain, where she and Gordon Ramsay kissed, made up, and he apologised for having thrown her and Adrian Gill out of his restaurant seven years previously by inviting her to appear on his TV programme, *The F Word*. 'My mother has never forgiven me for telling you to leave my restaurant and told me off for being rude,' said Ramsay. In December Joan was back on TV, all girly and coquettish in a bright scarlet trouser suit on *The Paul O'Grady Show* and then chairing one edition of the quick-witted comedy programme *Have I Got News For You?*, in which she was surprisingly funny and held her own well against the two mischievous regular panellists, Ian Hislop and Paul Merton, though she was shrill and squeaky and looked uncomfortable with a terrible chestnut wig and small, pouchy eyes set in a rigid face. Hislop asked her impishly why she had been persuaded to support UKIP. 'I was in Newcastle and bored,' she said. She ventured again into the world of politics when Richard Barber asked her for the *Daily Mail*'s *Weekend* magazine what she thought of the Conservative Party's young new leader David Cameron and she replied with shrewd political acumen: 'He's got a face like a pudding, hasn't he? He's not as good-looking as Tony Blair ... As a matter of fact I wanted William Hague to return as leader.' Obviously she no longer thought that Hague resembled a foetus.

In March she and Percy flew to Los Angeles to enjoy several Oscar awards parties and she joined John Forsythe, Linda Evans and others of the old *Dynasty* cast to make a final nostalgic programme to mark its twenty-fifth anniversary, *Dynasty Reunion*, but she agreed to do it only if Michael Nader, who had been rude about her acting seventeen years earlier, was barred from joining them. Sometimes she did bear grudges.

Then it was back to Britain to embark for a month on a nationwide tour with a one-woman show that she had put together, *An Evening With Joan Collins*, directed by Percy, in which she talked about her life, told some of her favourite anecdotes, showed photographs and clips from her films, and was accompanied by a musical group called Four Poofs and a Piano. It opened in Cardiff in April and went on to twenty-four cities, including Birmingham, Edinburgh, Manchester and Oxford. *The Times* critic Clive Davis was completely seduced when he saw the show in Basingstoke. 'La Collins has built a career out of tat,' he wrote, and 'I was dreading having to sit through this show. But, surprise, surprise, the woman who once plied her trade under the soubriquet "the coffee-bar Jezebel" turns out to be a terrific storyteller. It comes as a huge relief to find she has a gift for not taking herself too seriously. She is Gloria Swanson blessed with a sense of the ridiculous, tossing out one self-deprecating anecdote after another as examples of her less than glorious screen appearances go hurtling past on the screen. Marilyn Monroe and Bob Hope, tart memories of Bette Davis and an oversexed Darryl Zanuck, and some riveting footage of Collins hamming it up during a courtroom battle with a publisher anxious to rake back an absurdly inflated advance. Not a dull moment.' Equally impressed was an old Francis Holland classmate, Diana Patten, *née* Naismith, who saw the show in Hastings and was invited backstage to meet Joan. 'Percy was an absolute sweetie,' Mrs Patten told me, 'and Joan was lovely. We weren't very good friends at school but she had been great fun then, recognised me now, and was not at all snooty. She never was.'

The *Daily Mail* discovered that Joan and Tara had very different ideas about how to raise a child and asked them to debate the issue.

Joan confessed that she was finding Tara's two-year-old son, Weston, increasingly wild. In a restaurant recently he had smashed a glass, stolen her sunglasses and spent the rest of the meal lying on the floor or running around the room while Tara ran exhaustedly after him. Joan could not understand why parents nowadays seemed to have such trouble controlling their children. 'I believe children should do what they are told,' she said. Tara disagreed, retorted that Joan's generation had never understood 'the psychological implications of parenting', accused her of often having been an absentee mother, and claimed that she herself had a much closer, more loving and understanding relationship with her children than Joan had ever had with hers.

After the tour Joan and Percy flew off for their usual summer holiday in the South of France, where she was saddened to hear on 24 June that Aaron Spelling had died the previous day in Los Angeles after a stroke. Surprisingly she saw fit to write a remarkably bitchy, gossipy item about Spelling, his wife and daughter in her *Spectator* diary a month later and suggested that he had in fact died of a broken heart. While Spelling was dying, said Joan, his wife Candy had invited an ex-jailbird, Mark Nathanson, to move into their mansion and had been seen cavorting with him all over Hollywood, New York and Las Vegas. Because of this, said Joan, the Spellings' daughter, Tori, had not spoken to her mother for more than a year, her father's friends had found it impossible to contact him, and few were invited to his funeral. Considering Joan's contempt for journalists who peddled such stories to the muck-raking tabloids, it was astonishing that she saw fit to emulate them, though she was kinder when she reported in the same column that her 'dear mother-in-law', Percy's eighty-one-year-old mother, Bridget – 'a wonderful lady' who was living in an old folks' home in Glasgow – had also just died.

Before returning to America Joan and Percy appeared on another 'celebrity' edition of the TV quiz show *Who Wants to Be a Millionaire?* to raise money for one of her favourite charities, the Shooting Star Children's Hospice, of which she was the patron. She looked fresh, attractive, and was on good form. When the quizmaster, Chris Tarrant, reminded her that they had last met when she had been looking for the right man to play opposite her in *The Stud* she trilled: 'Did you audition for it?' She was not nearly as quick when it came to the questions and surprisingly neither she nor Percy could answer when Tarrant asked them which Shakespeare play was set during the siege of Troy: *Romeo and Juliet, Hamlet, King Lear* or *Troilus and Cressida*. They asked for two of the four possibilities to be deleted but were still baffled and had to resort to the 'phone a friend' option to be told correctly that the answer was *Troilus*. It seemed incredible that neither Joan, who had been to RADA and an actress for nearly sixty years, nor her theatre manager husband could answer such a simple theatrical question. They were finally floored when Tarrant asked them which Member of Parliament was currently the 'Father of the House' of Commons: John Selwyn Gummer, Alex Salmond, Tam Dalyell or Menzies Campbell. Any member of UKIP could probably have answered correctly 'Dalyell' but, 'I've never heard of any of them,' confessed Joan and she and Percy escaped with a comparatively measly £16,000 for the hospice.

They returned to North America to embark on a marathon eight-month tour across the continent with *Legends!*, a twenty-year-old comedy by James Kirkwood about two famous old has-been actresses who hate each other but are conned into joining the cast of a play because they are told that Paul Newman has agreed to star in it. Joan came up with the inspired idea of casting her old *Dynasty* friend and rival Linda Evans to play the second actress and the match seemed perfect: as in *Dynasty*, Joan's character was a sexy old bitch who was used to playing tarts and baddies, Linda's a warm, sweet old date used to playing good girls and nuns. The play opened in Toronto in September, moved south to Philadelphia six weeks later, and then went on for one- or two-week gigs in seventeen more towns – including Washington, Los Angeles, Denver, Chicago and Cleveland – and was eventually destined for Broadway in May 2007 if all went well.

All did not go well. The critics hated it, and it did not help that Linda had never acted on stage before but only in front of the camera. A STEAMING TURD was the savage headline above a review by a Toronto actor, director and producer, Mike Mackenzie, who said that Joan's performance was 'wooden, charmless and boring' and the production 'fundamentally awful ... an atrocious piece of theatre ... the show doesn't need more work, it needs never to be seen again.' In *Variety* Richard Ouzounian agreed: 'The grave would be a more appropriate resting place for this dead-on-arrival comedy,' he wrote, adding that Joan seemed 'to be playing the audience rather than the part.' John Coulbourn reported in the *Toronto Sun* that 'the stink of a bomb clings to it like a hooker's perfume', and Paul Isaacs wrote in *Eye Weekly* that 'the script is dross, the two leading performances have all the comic timing of advanced rigor mortis, and the whole show appears to have been directed by a metronome with the power switched off'. The tour still had six months to run, and the hope of it ever reaching Broadway became feebler by the week.

Relations between Joan and Linda Evans were not good. In a devastating article in the *Daily Mail* in July 2007, Joan claimed she had never wanted Linda in the play. She accused Linda of being bitchy, jealous, a dreadful actress, unprofessional and without any stage presence, despite the fact that she had won a Golden Globe in 1982, and been nominated every year for the next four years. Having originally said good things about the play, she now admitted that the script and direction were poor, and they were hoping the *Dynasty* connection would ensure a great response.

Any other seventy-three-year-old actress would have been so devastated by such contemptuous reviews that she would surely have decided that it was time to hang up her wig and retire. Why should she slog away night after night onstage to entertain people who sneered at her? But a woman like Joan would never even consider giving it all up. 'I need to keep busy,' she had told Andrew Duncan of the *Sunday Express Magazine* in 1990. 'I shall be like Daddy. He was eighty-four, in robust health, and he stopped eating and drinking when he got tired of life. I'll do the same. One day I'll say: "That's it."' She had never been a quitter and had always had immense confidence in herself, perhaps because she simply did not have the imagination to realise that maybe her acting and writing really were abysmal. She would tell herself that her fans still adored her, that ordinary people relished her acting and her books, that it was only the snooty, over-intellectual critics who sneered at her. In the *Spectator* in December she hit back at the critics who had been so savage about *Legends!*, calling them 'legless men who teach running' and quoting RJ Wagner's remark that 'they remind me of soldiers who arrive after the battle's been fought and shoot the wounded'. And perhaps she was right to be so dismissive about the reviewers and to retain such brash self-confidence, for she still gave pleasure wherever she went. She was still idolised by thousands, mobbed by hundreds, stalked by the paparazzi, reported and interviewed in the newspapers. If she gave up acting and writing who would she be?

Defiantly she gave yet another American TV interview at the end of October in which she claimed that she looked so young because she and Percy were having so much sex, and defiantly yet again she denied having had any plastic surgery, calling it 'the plain woman's revenge'. Even when the *Daily Mail* reported that the TV talk show host David Letterman had recently joked on air that security at the Emmy Awards had been 'tighter than Joan Collins's face', she insisted that Letterman had in fact said it was tighter than Joan Rivers's face. She had long boasted that her motto had always been a quote by the optimistic American journalist William Allen White: 'I am not afraid of tomorrow, for I have seen yesterday and I love today.' Even at seventy-three the woman was indomitable.

Onward!

SHE

{ 2007 }

Carl Jung believed that buried deep in every man's subconscious lies his *anima*, the female aspect of his soul, his feminine side, without which he would not be fully human, and he said that the embodiment of the *anima*, the archetype of womanhood, was Ayesha, the heroine of Rider Haggard's 1887 African adventure novel *She*. Sigmund Freud agreed, describing Ayesha as 'the eternal feminine'. In the novel she is She Who Must Be Obeyed, the fantastically beautiful, mysterious, immortal, white queen of an East African kingdom that has long been lost in ancient catacombs. Thousands of years old, she is a sorceress both desired and feared, 'with a certain snake-like grace that was more than human', utterly selfish, amoral and uncaring about others' lives and feelings and so infinitely powerful and ruthless that she will destroy anyone who displeases or obstructs her. In a paper published in 2004 in an international journal of Jungian studies, *Harvest*, the Australian academic Dr Sue Austin suggested that Queen Ayesha embodied the eternal feminine dilemma of having to choose between love and power. Could it be that no woman can have both?

Ayesha was evil and Joan Collins, of course, is not, but perhaps it is not too fanciful to imagine that Joan, like Ayesha, embodied something of the prototypical *anima*, the essence of femininity, the eternal female. She was beautiful, seductive, alluring, elegant, bright, naughty, funny, vain, flighty, self-indulgent, changeable and emotionally vulnerable, and she wielded an immense power over men. Yet she also exhibited virtues and failings that are usually associated with masculinity: strength, courage, hard work, independence, determination, aggression, impatience, rudeness, recklessness, success, selfishness, amorality, sometimes cruelty. Jung would not have been at all surprised by such contrasts, for along with a man's *anima* he believed that in each woman there lurks in her subconscious an *animus*, the male aspect of her soul.

All of which might partly explain why Joan appealed so strongly to women as well as men and especially to homosexuals and transsexuals, who would see in her the embodiment of both *animus* and *anima* because although she had numerous masculine traits she had become almost a caricature of exaggerated femininity with her small stature, huge hair, mask-like face, thick clown-like make-up, big blackened eyes, sumptuously glossy scarlet lips, large breasts, tiny waist, slender legs, little feet. She was Eve and Ayesha, the eternal woman. She was Tony Newley's friend Herbert Kretzmer's *She* in the song that Kretzmer wrote with Charles Aznavour in 1974:

> *She may be the beauty or the beast*
> *May be the famine or the feast*
> *May turn each day into a heaven or a hell*
> *She may be the mirror of my dream*
> *A smile reflected in a stream*
> *She may not be what she may seem*
> *Inside her shell*

In the novel Ayesha finally persuades her lover to enter the Fire of Life with her and so become immortal too, not realising that the Fire can remove as well as confer immortality, and in seconds the flames restore her to her true age and after thousands of years of life she crumbles to dust. God forbid that anything similar might happen to Joan.

Whenever Joan was asked what her epitaph should be she replied with a gloriously feminine choice: She Had Her Cake And Ate It Too. She told the *Daily Mail* in 1998 that she would like to be remembered by her friends as somebody who 'brought a little joy and fun into their lives' and she told the *Sunday Express* in 2002 that she would like to be remembered 'for bringing pleasure into people's lives, whether it's my family or friends, or people who watch me on the stage or TV. I'd like to be remembered as a life-enhancer.'

She will. She will not be remembered for her acting or writing, she was not the perfect mother to Tara and Sacha, she could be incredibly selfish, arrogant, shallow and materialistic, and when she was finished with her lovers she treated them with a ruthless lack of loyalty or compassion. But she was also a warm, feisty, funny, self-deprecating, immensely human woman who made us laugh and cheered us up with her outrageous antics, absurdities and startlingly disastrous mistakes. She always said 'yes' to whatever life offered her, often when she should have said 'no', and her indomitable optimism and *joie de vivre* are a glorious example that should give hope to us all.

'Life's quite simple, really,' she told Barbara Ellen of the *Observer Magazine* in 2006. 'Be content with what you have. Try to find happiness in your life, whether it's looking after chickens or your husband or your children or grandchildren.' But she also realised how lucky she had been to be born with what she called 'the happy gene': 'Percy said that to me the other day. We were looking through old photographs and he turned to me and said, "Oh look, Joan: you're always laughing."'

So will he for many more years, with any luck – unless, of course, she meets some gorgeous, hunky, irresistible eighteen-year-old when she's ninety-three.

FILMOGRAPHY

LADY GODIVA RIDES AGAIN (British Lion/London Films, 1951) Pauline Stroud, Dennis Price, Stanley Holloway, Kay Kendall, John McCallum, Diana Dors. Screenplay by Frank Launder and Val Valentine. Produced by Sidney Gilliat. Directed by Frank Launder.

THE WOMAN'S ANGLE (Associated British, 1952) Edward Underdown, Cathy O'Donnell, Lois Maxwell. Screenplay by Leslie Arliss. Produced by Walter Mycroft. Directed by Leslie Arliss.

JUDGMENT DEFERRED (Associated British, 1952) Hugh Sinclair, Helen Shingler. Screenplay by Barbara Emary, Walter Meade and Geoffrey Arme. Produced and directed by John Baxter.

I BELIEVE IN YOU (Rank, 1952) Cecil Parker, Celia Johnson, Laurence Harvey, Harry Fowler, Ursula Howells, Godfrey Teale. Screenplay by Basil Dearden, Nicholas Phipps, Michael Relph and Jack Whittingham. Produced by Michael Relph. Directed by Basil Dearden.

COSH BOY (Rank, 1952), aka THE SLASHER, THE TOUGH GUY James Kenney, Hermione Gingold, Hermione Baddeley, Betty Ann Davies. Screenplay by Lewis Gilbert and Vernon Harris. Produced by Daniel Angel. Directed by Lewis Gilbert.

THE SQUARE RING (Ealing, 1953) Jack Warner, Robert Beatty, Maxwell Reed, Kay Kendall, Bernadette O'Farrell. Screenplay by Ralph Peterson and Robert Westerby. Produced by Basil Dearden and Michael Relph. Directed by Basil Dearden.

TURN THE KEY SOFTLY (Rank, 1953) Yvonne Mitchell, Kathleen Harrison, Terence Morgan, Glyn Houston, Geoffrey Keen, Thora Hird. Screenplay by Maurice Cowan and Jack Lee. Produced by Maurice Cowan. Directed by Jack Lee.

DECAMERON NIGHTS (Columbia, 1953) Joan Fontaine, Louis Jourdan, Godfrey Tearle. Screenplay by George Oppenheimer and Geza Herczeg. Produced by Mike Frankovitch and William Szekeley. Directed by Hugo Fregonese.

OUR GIRL FRIDAY (Renown Pictures, 1954) aka THE ADVENTURES OF SADIE George Cole, Kenneth More, Robertson Hare, Hermione Gingold, Hattie Jacques. Screenplay by Noel Langley. Produced by George Minter. Directed by Noel Langley.

THE GOOD DIE YOUNG (United Artists, 1954) Laurence Harvey, Richard Basehart, Gloria Grahame, Stanley Baker, Margaret Leighton. Screenplay by Vernon Harris and Lewis Gilbert. Produced by Jack Clayton. Directed by Lewis Gilbert.

LAND OF THE PHARAOHS (Warner Bros, 1955) Jack Hawkins, Sydney Chaplin, James Robertson Justice, Alexis Minotis, Kerima, Dewey Martin. Screenplay by William Faulkner, Harry Kurnitz and Harold Bloom. Produced and directed by Howard Hawks.

THE VIRGIN QUEEN (20th Century-Fox, 1955) Bette Davis, Richard Todd, Herbert Marshall, Jay Robinson, Dan O'Herlihy, Lisa Daniels. Screenplay by Harry Brown and Mindret Lord. Produced by Charles Brackett. Directed by Henry Koster.

THE GIRL IN THE RED VELVET SWING (20th Century-Fox, 1955) Ray Milland, Farley Granger, Glenda Farrell, Luther Adler, Gale Robbins. Screenplay by Walter Reisch and Charles Brackett. Produced by Charles Brackett. Directed by Richard Fleischer.

THE OPPOSITE SEX (MGM, 1956) June Allyson, Ann Sheridan, Ann Miller, Dolores Gray, Joan Blondell, Agnes Moorehead, Leslie Nielsen, Dick Shawn. Screenplay by Fay and Michael Kanin. Produced by Joe Pasternak. Directed by David Miller.

SEA WIFE (20th Century-Fox, 1957) aka SEA-WYF AND BISCUIT Richard Burton, Cy Grant, Basil Sydney. Screenplay by George

Burke. Produced by Andre Hakim. Directed by Bob McNaught.

ISLAND IN THE SUN (20th Century-Fox, 1957) James Mason, Joan Fontaine, Harry Belafonte, Patricia Owens, Stephen Boyd, Dorothy Dandridge, John Justin. Screenplay by Alfred Hayes. Produced by Darryl F. Zanuck. Directed by Robert Rossen.

THE WAYWARD BUS (20th Century-Fox, 1957) Jayne Mansfield, Dan Dailey, Rick Jason, Dolores Michaels, Betty Lou Keim, Larry Keating. Screenplay by Ivan Moffat. Produced by Charles Brackett. Directed by Victor Vicas.

STOPOVER TOKYO (20th Century-Fox, 1957) Robert Wagner, Edmond O'Brien, Ken Scott, Larry Keating. Screenplay by Richard Breen and Walter Reisch. Produced by Walter Reisch. Directed by Richard Breen and Walter Reisch.

THE BRAVADOS (20th Century-Fox, 1958) Gregory Peck, Stephen Boyd, Albert Salmi, Lee Van Cleef, Henry Silva, Kathleen Gallant. Screenplay by Philip Yordan. Produced by Herbert Swope. Directed by Henry King.

RALLY 'ROUND THE FLAG, BOYS! (20th Century-Fox, 1958) Paul Newman, Joanne Woodward, Jack Carson, Tuesday Weld, Gale Gordon, Dwayne Hickman. Screenplay by Claude Binyon and Leo McCarey. Produced and directed by Leo McCarey.

SEVEN THIEVES (20th Century-Fox, 1960) Rod Steiger, Eli Wallach, Edward G. Robinson, Michael Dante, Berry Kroeger. Screenplay and produced by Sidney Boehm. Directed by Henry Hathaway.

ESTHER AND THE KING (20th Century-Fox, 1960) Richard Egan, Denis O'Dea, Sergio Fantoni, Rik Battaglia, Gabriele Tinti. Screenplay by Raoul Walsh and Michael Elkins. Produced and directed by Raoul Walsh.

THE ROAD TO HONG KONG (United Artists, 1962) Bob Hope, Bing Crosby, Dorothy Lamour, Robert Morley, Frank Sinatra, Dean Martin, Peter Sellers, David Niven. Screenplay by Norman Panama and Melvin Frank. Produced by Melvin Frank. Directed by Norman Panama.

LA CONGIUNTURA (Columbia, 1965) aka ONE MILLION DOLLARS and HARD TIME FOR PRINCES Vittorio Gassman, Jacques Bergerac. Screenplay by Ruggero Maccari and Ettore Scola. Produced by Mario Cecchi Gori. Directed by Ettore Scola.

WARNING SHOT (Universal, 1967) David Janssen, Eleanor Parker, George Sanders, Stefanie Powers, Lillian Gish, Walter Pidgeon. Screenplay by Mann Rubin. Produced and directed by Buzz Kulik.

SUBTERFUGE (Commonwealth United, 1969) Gene Barry, Tom Adams, Suzanna Leigh, Richard Todd, Michael Rennie. Screenplay by David Whittaker. Produced by Peter Snell. Directed by Peter Graham Scott.

CAN HEIRONYMUS MERKIN EVER FORGET MERCY HUMPPE AND FIND TRUE HAPPINESS? (Universal, 1969) Anthony Newley, Milton Berle, Connie Kreski, Bruce Forsyth, Tara Newley, Sacha Newley. Screenplay by Anthony Newley and Herman Raucher. Produced and directed by Anthony Newley.

IF IT'S TUESDAY, THIS MUST BE BELGIUM (United Artists, 1969) Suzanne Pleshette, Ian McShane. Screenplay by David Shaw. Produced by Stan Margulies. Directed by Mel Stuart.

L'AMORE BREVE (Cinegal, 1969) aka STATE OF SIEGE and BESIEGED Mathieu Carrière, Faith Domergue, Michael Coby. Screenplay by Gianfranco Galligarich. Produced by Felice Testa Gay. Directed by Romano and Romolo Scavolini.

THE EXECUTIONER (Columbia, 1970) George Peppard, Judy Geeson, Nigel Patrick, Keith Michell, George Baker, Charles Gray. Screenplay by Gordon McDonnell and Jack Pulman. Screenplay by Jack Pulman. Produced by Charles Schneer. Directed by Sam Wanamaker.

THREE IN THE CELLAR (American International, 1970) aka UP IN THE CELLAR Larry Hagman, Wes Stern. Screenplay by Theodore Flicker. Produced by James Nicholson and Samuel Arkoff. Directed by Theodore Flicker.

QUEST FOR LOVE (Rank, 1971) Tom Bell, Laurence Naismith, Denholm Elliott, Juliet Harmer, Lyn Ashley. Screenplay by Terence

Feely. Produced by Peter Eton. Directed by Ralph Thomas.

REVENGE (Rank, 1971) aka INN OF THE FRIGHTENED PEOPLE, TERROR FROM UNDER THE STAIRS, AFTER JENNY DIED and BEHIND THE CELLAR DOOR James Booth, Sinead Cusack, Kenneth Griffith, Tom Marshall, Ray Barrett, Zuleka Robson. Screenplay by John Kruse. Produced by George Brown. Directed by Sidney Hayers.

FEAR IN THE NIGHT (Hammer Films, 1972) aka DYNASTY OF FEAR and HONEYMOON OF FEAR Judy Geeson, Ralph Bates, Peter Cushing, Gilliam Lind, James Cossins. Screenplay by Jimmy Sangster and Michael Syson. Produced and directed by Jimmy Sangster.

TALES FROM THE CRYPT (Cinerama, 1972) Ralph Richardson, Peter Cushing, Nigel Patrick, Richard Greene, Martin Boddey. Screenplay by Milton Subotsky. Produced by Max Rosenberg and Milton Subotsky. Directed by Freddie Francis.

THE MAN WHO CAME TO DINNER (TV, 1972) Orson Welles, Lee Remick, Don Knotts, Marty Feldman. Screenplay by Moss Hart, George Kaufman, Sam Denoff and Bill Persky. Directed by Buzz Kulik.

TALES THAT WITNESS MADNESS (Paramount, 1973) Michael Jayston, Kim Novak, Jack Hawkins, Donald Pleasence, Georgia Brown, Peter McEnery, Donald Houston, Suzy Kendall. Screenplay by Jay Fairbank. Produced by Norman Priggen. Directed by Freddie Francis.

DARK PLACES (Film International, 1973) Christopher Lee, Robert Hardy, Jane Birkin, Herbert Lom, Jean Marsh. Screenplay by Ed Brennan and Joseph Van Winkle. Produced by James Hannah Jr. Directed by Don Sharp.

DRIVE HARD, DRIVE FAST (TV, 1973) Brian Kelly, Henry Silva, Karen Houston, Joseph Campanella. Screenplay by Douglas Heyes and Roy Huggins. Produced by Jo Swerline Jr. Directed by Douglas Heyes.

L'ARBITRO (Documento, 1974) aka THE REFEREE, FOOTBALL CRAZY and PLAYING THE FIELD Lando Buzzanca. Screenplay by Sandro Continenza, Giulio Scarnicci and Raimondo Vianello.

Produced by Gianni Hecht Lucari. Directed by Louis Philippo D'Amico.

ALFIE DARLING (EMI, 1975) aka OH, ALFIE! Alan Price, Jill Townsend, Hannah Gordon, Rula Lenska, Annie Ross. Screenplay by Ken Hughes. Produced by Dugald Rankin. Directed by Ken Hughes.

I DON'T WANT TO BE BORN (Rank, 1975) aka THE DEVIL WITHIN HER Ralph Bates, Donald Pleasence, Eileen Atkins, Caroline Munro, John Steiner, George Claydon. Screenplay by Stanley Price. Produced by Norma Corney. Directed by Peter Sasdy.

IL RICHIAMO DEL LUPO (Pacific International, 1975) aka CALL OF THE WOLF and THE GREAT ADVENTURE Jack Palance, Fred Romer. Screenplay by Juan Logar. Produced by Joseph Allegro and Elliot Geisinger. Directed by Paul Elliotts.

THE BAWDY ADVENTURES OF TOM JONES (Universal, 1976) Nicky Henson, Geraldine McEwan, Georgia Brown, Trevor Howard, Madeline Smith, Arthur Lowe, Terry-Thomas. Screenplay by Jeremy Lloyd. Produced by Robert Sadoff. Directed by Cliff Owen.

IL POMICIONE (Collectives I, 1976) Luciano Crovato, Argia Esposito, Gabriella Lepori. Screenplay by Adriano Asti and Roberto Bianchi Montero. Directed by Roberto Bianchi Montero.

EMPIRE OF THE ANTS (American International, 1977) Robert Lansing, John David Carson, Pamela Shoop, Jacqueline Scott, Albert Salmi. Screenplay by Jack Turley and Bert Gordon. Produced and directed by Bert Gordon.

POLIZIOTTO SENZA PAURA (Promer, 1977) aka FEARLESS, FEARLESS FUZZ, FATAL CHARMS and POLICE AT THE SERVICE OF A CITIZEN Maurizio Merli, Franco Ressel, Gastone Moschin, Jasmine Maimone, Alexander Trojan. Screenplay by Franz Antel, Gino Capone and Stelvio Massi. Produced by Franz Antel. Directed by Stelvio Massi.

THE BIG SLEEP (ITC, 1978) Robert Mitchum, Sarah Miles, Edward Fox, Oliver Reed, Candy Clark, James Stewart, John Mills.

Screenplay by Michael Winner. Produced by Elliott Kastner. Directed by Michael Winner.

THE STUD (Brent Walker, 1978) Oliver Tobias, Sue Lloyd, Mark Burns, Emma Jacobs, Walter Gotell, Doug Fisher. Screenplay by Jackie Collins. Produced by Edward Simons, Ron Kass and Oscar Lerman. Directed by Quentin Masters.

ZERO TO SIXTY (First Artists, 1978) Darren McGavin, Sylvia Miles, Denise Nickerson, Dick Martin. Screenplay by Judith Bustany, Lyle Richardson and Peg Shirley. Produced by Kathie Browne. Directed by Darren McGavin.

SUNBURN (Paramount, 1979) Farrah Fawcett, Charles Grodin, Art Carney, Eleanor Parker, Alejandro Rey. Screenplay by John Daly, Stephen Oliver and James Booth. Produced by John Daly and Gerald Green. Directed by Richard Sarafian.

A GAME FOR VULTURES (Columbia, 1979) Richard Harris, Ray Milland, Richard Roundtree, Sven Bertil-Taube, Denholm Elliott. Screenplay by Philip Baird. Produced by Hazel Adair. Directed by James Fargo.

THE BITCH (Brent Walker, 1979) Michael Coby, Carolyn Seymour, Sue Lloyd, Mark Burns, Pamela Salem, Kenneth Haigh. Screenplay by Jackie Collins. Produced by Edward Simons, Ron Kass and Oscar Lerman. Dircted by Gerry O'Hara.

NUTCRACKER (Rank, 1982) Finola Hughes, Paul Nicholas, Carol White, William Franklyn, Leslie Ash, Geraldine Gardner. Screenplay by Raymon Christodoulou and Max and Yvonne Roman. Produced by Panos Nicolaou. Directed by Anwar Kawadri.

PAPER DOLLS (TV, 1982) Joan Hackett, Marc Singer, Jennifer Warren, Darryl Hannah, Alexandra Paul. Screenplay by Leah Markus and Casey Mitchell. Produced by Michele Rappaport. Directed by Edward Zwick.

HOMEWORK (Jensen Farley, 1982) Michael Morgan, Shell Kepler, Wings Hauser, Betty Thomas. Screenplay by Maurice Peterson and Don Safran. Produced and directed by James Beshears.

THE WILD WOMEN OF CHASTITY GULCH (Aaron Spelling Productions, 1982) Priscilla Barnes, Pamela Bellwood, Lee Horsley, Howard Duff, Morgan Brittany. Screenplay by Earl Wallace. Produced by Shelley Hull. Directed by Philip Leacock.

THE MAKING OF A MALE MODEL (TV, 1983) Jon-Erik Hexum, Roxie Roker, Jeff Conaway, Kevin McCarthy, Arte Johnson, Ted McGinley. Screenplay by A. J. Carothers. Produced by Lynn Loring and Elaine Rich. Directed by Irving Moore.

HANSEL AND GRETEL (TV, 1983) Bridgette Andersen, Paul Dooley, Rick Schroder. Screenplay by Patricia Resnick. Produced by Bridget Terry. Directed by James Frawley.

HER LIFE AS A MAN (TV, 1984) Robert Culp, Marc Singer, Robin Douglas. Screenplay by Joanna Crawford and Diane English. Screenplay by Joanna Crawford and Diane English. Produced by Mimi Rothman. Directed by Robert Ellis Miller.

THE CARTIER AFFAIR (Hill/Mandelker Films, 1984) David Hasselhof, Telly Savalas. Screenplay by Eugenie Ross-Leming and Brad Buckner. Produced by Joel Dean and Christopher Nelson. Directed by Rod Holcomb.

DYNASTY: THE REUNION (Worldvision, 1991) John Forsythe, Linda Evans, John James, Heather Locklear, Emma Samms. Screenplay by Richard and Esther Shapiro, Edward de Blasio and Robert and Eileen Pollock. Produced by Elaine Rich. Directed by Irving Moore.

DECADENCE (Mayfair Entertainment, 1994) Steven Berkoff. Screenplay, produced and directed by Steven Berkoff.

IN THE BLEAK MIDWINTER (Castle Rock, 1995) aka A MIDWINTER'S TALE Richard Briers, Hetta Charnley, Nicholas Farrell, Mark Hadfield, Gerard Horan, Celia Imrie, Michael Maloney, Julia Sawalha, John Sessions. Screenplay by Kenneth Branagh. Produced by David Barron. Directed by Kenneth Branagh.

HART TO HART: TWO HARTS IN THREE-QUARTERS TIME (TV, 1995) Stefanie Powers, Robert Wagner, Daniela Amavia, Sebastian Koch, Jeff Kaake, Tara Slone. Screenplay by Mart Crowley and

Donald Ross. Produced by Steve McGlothen and Stefanie Powers. Directed by Michael Tuchner.

ANNIE: A ROYAL ADVENTURE! (Columbia/Tristar, 1995) George Hearn, Ashley Johnson. Screenplay by Trish Soodik. Produced by Wendy Dytman. Directed by Ian Toynton.

SWEET DECEPTION (TV, 1998) Kate Jackson, Joanna Pacula, Jack Scalin. Screenplay by Joelle Harris. Produced by Mark Harris and James Shavick. Directed by Timothy Bond.

THE CLANDESTINE MARRIAGE (Portman Entertainment/BBC Films, 1999) Nigel Hawthorne, Timothy Spall, Tom Hollander, Paul Nicholls, Natasha Little, Emma Chambers. Screenplay by Trevor Bentham. Produced by Steve Clark-Hll. Directed by Christopher Miles.

THE FLINTSTONES IN VIVA ROCK VEGAS (Universal, 2000) Mark Addy, Stephen Baldwin, Kristen Johnston, Jane Krakowski, Thomas Gibson, Alan Cumming, Harvey Korman. Screenplay by Deborah Kaplan, Harry Elfont, Jim Cash and Jack Epps Jr. Produced by Bruce Cohen. Directed by Brian Levant.

JOSEPH AND THE AMAZING TECHNICOLOR DREAMCOAT (Universal, 1999) Donny Osmond, Richard Attenborough, Maria Friedman. Screenplay by Tim Rice. Produced by Andrew Lloyd-Webber. Directed by David Mallet.

THESE OLD BROADS (Columbia Tristar, 2001) Shirley MacLaine, Debbie Reynolds, Elizabeth Taylor. Screenplay by Carrie Fisher and Elaine Pope. Produced by Lewis Abel. Directed by Matthew Diamond.

OZZIE (Daybreak Pacific, 2001) Spencer Breslin, Ralf Moeller, Rachel Hunter. Screenplay by Michael Lach and Lori O'Brien. Produced by Grant Bradley and Dieter Stempwierwsky. Directed by William Tannen.

ELLIS IN GLAMOURLAND (2004) Linda de Mol, Chris Tates. Screenplay by Mischa Alexander. Produced by Alain De Levita and Johan Nijenhuis. Directed by Pieter Kramer.

THE MONEYCHANGERS (NBC, 1975)
Kirk Douglas, Christopher Plummer, Anne Baxter, Lorne Greene, Susan Flannery, Jean Peters. Screenplay by Dean Riesner and Stanford Whitmore. Produced by Ross Hunter, Jacques Mapes and Marvin Miller. Directed by Boris Segal.

DYNASTY (ABC, 1981–1989)
John Forsythe, Linda Evans, Gordon Thomson, John James, Jack Coleman, Michael Nader, Heather Locklear, Pamela Bellwood, Pamela Sue Martin. Created by Esther and Richard Shapiro. Produced by Aaron Spelling.

SINS (Gemini Star Productions, 1986)
Jean Pierre Aumont, Marisa Berenson, Joseph Bologna, Capucine, Timothy Dalton, Giancarlo Giannini, Gene Kelly, Neil Dickson, Lauren Hutton, Steven Berkoff. Screenplay by Laurence Heath, Produced by Steve Krantz. Directed by Douglas Hickox.

MONTE CARLO (Gemini Star Productions, 1986)
George Hamilton, Lisa Eilbacher, Lauren Hutton, Robert Carradine, Malcolm McDowell, Philip Madoc, Leslie Phillips, Peter Vaughan. Screenplay by Peter Lefcourt. Produced by Gerald Abrams. Directed by Anthony Page.

TONIGHT AT 8.30 (BBC, 1991)
Eight Noël Coward plays: *Ways and Means, Still Life, The Astonished Heart, Shadow Play, Red Peppers, Family Album, Hands Across the Sea, Burned Oak.*

PACIFIC PALISADES (1997)

Natalia Cigliutti, Kimberley Davies, Travor Edmond, Jarrod Emick, Greg Evigon, Finola Hughes, Brittney Powell, Jocelyn Seagrave, Michelle Stafford, Lucky Vanous. Produced by Aaron Spelling.

THE GUIDING LIGHT (CBS, 2002)

Chaz Brewer, Kim Zimmer, Robert Newman, Beth Ehlers, Bradley Cole. Series created by Irna Phillips.

FOOTBALLERS' WIVES (ITV, 2006)

Gillian Taylforth, Zoe Lucker, Alison Newman, Chad Shepherd. Executive Producer: Brian Park.

THE MAN FROM U.N.C.L.E., *The Galatea Affair* (CBS, 1966) Robert Vaughn, David McCallum. Screenplay by Jackson Gillis. Directed by Darrell Hallenbeck.

THE VIRGINIAN, *The Lady From Wichita* (NBC, 1967) John Cliff, John Damler, Ann Doran.

BATMAN, *The Wail of the Siren* and *Ring Around the Riddle* (ABC, 1967) Adam West, Burt Ward.

STAR TREK, *The City on the Edge of Forever* (NBC, 1967) William Shatner, Leonard Nimoy. Screenplay by Harlan Ellison. Produced by Gene Coon. Directed by Joseph Pevney.

MISSION IMPOSSIBLE, *Nicole* (CBS, 1969) Greg Morris, Bob Johnson, Peter Lupus, Peter Graves, Martin Landau. Screenplay by Paul Playdon. Produced by Stanley Kallis. Directed by Stuart Hagmann.

THE PERSUADERS!, *Five Miles to Midnight* (ITC, 1971) Tony Curtis, Roger Moore, Robert Hutton, Laurence Naismith. Screenplay by Terry Nation. Produced by Robert Baker. Directed by Val Guest.

FALLEN ANGELS (Anglia, 1974) Susannah York, Sacha Distel.

SPACE: 1999, *Mission of the Darians* (ITC, 1975) Martin Landau, Barbara Bain, Nick Tate, Paul Antrim. Screenplay by Johnny Byrne. Produced by Fred Freiberger. Directed by Ray Austin.

POLICE WOMAN, *The Trick Book* and *The Pawn Shop* (NBC/Columbia, 1976) Angie Dickinson, Earl Holliman, Ed Bernard, Charles Dierkop, Val Bisoglio. Created by Robert Collins. Screenplay by S. S. Schweitzer. Directed by Richard Benedict.

STARSKY AND HUTCH, *Starsky and Hutch on Playboy Island* (ABC, 1977) Paul Michael Glaser, David Soul, Bernie Hamilton, Antonio Fargas, Samantha Eggar. Produced by Aaron Spelling.

TALES OF THE UNEXPECTED (Anglia) *Neck*, 1977, John Gielgud; *Georgy Porgy*, 1979, John Alderton; *A Girl Can't Have Everything*, 1980, Pauline Collins.

FANTASY ISLAND, *My Fair Pharaoh* (ABC, 1980) Ricardo Montalban, Carol Lynley, Michael Ansara, Chris Capen, John Davey. Created by Gene Levitt. Produced by Aaron Spelling.

THE LOVE BOAT, *The Captain's Crush* (ABC, 1983) Delta Burke, Ron Ely, Richard Gilliland. Produced by Aaron Spelling.

THE DEAN MARTIN CELEBRITY ROAST (NBC, 1984) Dean Martin, Aaron Spelling, John Forsythe, Phyllis Diller, Angie Dickinson, Zsa Zsa Gabor.

ROSEANNE, *First Cousin, Twice Removed* (ABC, 1993) Roseanne Barr, Laurie Metcalf, John Goodman, Michael Fishman, Sara Gilbert. Screenplay by Janice Jordan. Directed by Andrew Weyman.

STAGE APPEARANCES

A DOLL'S HOUSE by Henrik Ibsen (1946, Arts Theatre, London)

FRENCH WITHOUT TEARS by Terence Rattigan (1950, Maidstone)

THE SEVENTH VEIL by Muriel and Sydney Box (1952, Q Theatre, London)

JASSY by Ronald Gow and Norah Lofts (1952, Q Theatre, London)

THE SKIN OF OUR TEETH by Thornton Wilder (1952, Q Theatre, London)

THE PRAYING MANTIS by J. L. Campbell (1954, UK tour)

CLAUDIA AND DAVID by Rose Franken (1953, Q Theatre, London)

THE LAST OF MRS CHEYNEY by Frederick Lonsdale (1979, Chichester Festival Theatre; 1981, Cambridge Theatre, London)

MURDER IN MIND by Terence Feely (1981, Yvonne Arnaud Theatre, Guildford)

PRIVATE LIVES by Noël Coward (1990–1991, Aldwych Theatre, London; 1991–1992, Broadhurst Theatre, New York, and US tour)

LOVE LETTERS by A. R. Gurney (2000, US tour)

OVER THE MOON by Ken Ludwig (2001, Yvonne Arnaud Theatre, Guildford; Theatre Royal, Bath; Old Vic, London)

FULL CIRCLE by Alan Melville (2004, UK tour)

AN EVENING WITH JOAN COLLINS (2006, UK tour)

LEGENDS! by James Kirkwood (2006–2007, Canadian and US tour)

BOOKS

AUTOBIOGRAPHY

PAST IMPERFECT (W. H. Allen, 1978; Simon and Schuster, 1984)

KATY: A FIGHT FOR LIFE (Gollancz, 1982)

SECOND ACT (Boxtree, 1996)

NOVELS

PRIME TIME (Century, 1988)

LOVE AND DESIRE AND HATE (Century, 1990)

TOO DAMN FAMOUS (Orion, 1995)

STAR QUALITY (Robson Books, 2002)

MISFORTUNE'S DAUGHTERS (Robson Books, 2004)

HEALTH AND BEAUTY

MY SECRETS (Boxtree, 1994)

MY FRIENDS' SECRETS (André Deutsch, 1999)

THE JOAN COLLINS BEAUTY BOOK (Macmillan, 1980)

JOAN'S WAY: LOOKING GOOD, FEELING GREAT (Robson, 2002)

ACKNOWLEDGEMENTS

First I must thank Julia Campion, who was truly wonderful over several months in helping me to describe Joan's schooldays at Francis Holland School in London and to track down ten of her contemporaries, all of whom generously shared their memories with me: Sally Adams, Ella Bland, Rona Blythe, Diana Hall, Charlotte Halliday, Beryl Lester, Diana Patten, Dr Penny Newall-Price, Dr Barbara Simcock and Belinda Webster. The present headmistress, Vivienne Durham, could not have been kinder, as were several other members of staff – Jeannine Addinnal, Sandy Bailey, Ron Davenport, Felicity Forde – and two delightful pupils who showed me around the school, Sophie Burstin and Valentine Miller.

I am able to describe Joan's days at RADA and her early acting career thanks to RADA's official historian, Peter Fiddick, as well as Patricia Myers, Margaret Tyzack, Doreen Hawkins, Judy Cornwell and Peter Sallis.

Others who gave me very useful interviews were Baz Bamigboye, Leslie Cavendish, Rosie de Courcy, Jaleh Falk, Tony Norcliffe, Harry O'Neill, Maryam Rokny-Owji, Belinda Selby, Bill Wiggins, Pamela Williams and Sir Allan Wright.

I am hugely indebted as always to several superbly efficient London librarians who have helped me to track down important books and articles: the staff of the British Library at St Pancras; Steve Torrington and his colleagues at the *Daily Mail*; and Steve Baker, Lee Chilvers, Paul King, Neil Edward and their colleagues at *The Times*.

Richard Webber was astonishingly generous in devoting hours to finding video tapes of Joan's rarest films for me so that I was able to watch even her first dozen movies from the early 1950s. Equally indispensable was the astonishingly comprehensive Internet Movie Database website, which lists almost every film and TV programme that any actor, director, producer or writer has made together with their full casts, crews, storylines and reviews. For the writer of any book about films and TV it is invaluable.

I owe a great deal to the authors of all the books listed hereafter in the Bibliography but especially to Garth Bardsley, whose masterly biography of Joan's second husband, Tony Newley, *Stop the World*, allowed me to describe their marriage and relationship much more fully than I would otherwise have been able to do.

Several television programmes were extremely useful: Dean Martin's 1984 *Celebrity Roast*; Court TV's *Women on Trial* recording of Joan's legal battle with her American publisher in 1996, *Random House vs Gemini Star Productions*; The Biography Channel's 1997 account of Joan's life; Melvyn Bragg's *South Bank Show* profile of Joan in November 1999; and Ruby Wax's hilarious interview with her in 2003.

I must thank Herbert Kretzmer and Standard Music Ltd for permission to quote a verse of his lovely 1974 song 'She'. And I must not forget several others whose help with particular aspects of my research was full and ungrudging: Elizabeth Chesterman, John Edwards, Lawrence Falk, Frank Johnson, Dr Alex Karidis, Wendy Leigh, John McEntee, Tony Preston, Alvin Rakoff, Don Short, Yvonne de Valera, Billy Walker, Peter Watson and Cubby Wolf. Thank you all, and especially several witnesses who talked to me on the understanding that they should remain unnamed.

BIBLIOGRAPHY

Hermione Baddeley, *The Unsinkable Hermione Baddeley* (Collins, 1984)

Garth Bardsley, *Stop the World: The Biography of Anthony Newley* (Oberon Books, 2003)

Kenneth Barrow, *On Q: Jack and Beattie de Leon and the Q Theatre* (De Leon Memorial Fund and Heritage Publications, 1992)

Marsha Lynn Beeman, *Joan Fontaine: A Bio-Bibliography* (Greenwood Press, 1994)

E. Moberly Bell, *Francis Holland School* (Waterlow & Sons, 1939)

Frank Brady, *Citizen Welles* (Hodder and Stoughton, 1990)

Melvyn Bragg, *Rich: The Life of Richard Burton* (Hodder and Stoughton, 1988)

Clark Branson, *Howard Hawks: A Jungian Study* (Capra Press, 1987)

Leslie Bricusse, *The Music Man* (Metro Books, 2006)

Michael Feeney Callan, *Richard Harris: A Sporting Life* (Sidgwick and Jackson, 1990)

Peter Carrick, *Bob Hope* (Robert Hale, 2003)

Diane Cilento, *My Nine Lives* (Viking, 2006)

Joe Collins, *A Touch of Collins* (Columbus Books, 1986)

Shaun Considine, *Barbra Streisand* (Century, 1985)

Judy Cornwell, *Adventures of a Jelly Baby* (Sidgwick & Jackson, 2005)

Susan Crimp and Patricia Burstein, *Hollywood Sisters: Jackie and Joan Collins* (Robson Books, 1989)

Jay David, *Inside Joan Collins* (Carroll & Graf, 1988)

Diana Dors, *Behind Closed Dors* (Star, 1979)

Anne Edwards, *Vivien Leigh* (W. H. Allen, 1977)

Britt Ekland, *True Britt* (Sphere, 1980)

Peter Evans, *Peter Sellers: The Man Behind the Mask* (Severn House,

1981)

William Robert Faith, *Bob Hope* (Granada, 1983)

Jocelyn Faris, *Jayne Mansfield: A Bio-Bibliography* (Greenwood Press, 1994)

Paul Ferris, *Richard Burton* (Weidenfeld and Nicolson, 1981)

Suzanne Finstad, *Natasha: The Biography of Natalie Wood* (Century, 2001)

Suzanne Finstad, *Warren Beatty: A Private Man* (Aurum, 2005)

Kate Fleming, *Celia Johnson* (Weidenfeld and Nicolson, 1991)

Joan Flory and Damien Walne, *Diana Dors* (Lennard Publishing, 1987)

Joan Fontaine, *No Bed of Roses* (W. H. Allen, 1978)

Michael Freedland, *Bing Crosby* (Chameleon, 1998)

Michael Freedland, *Linda Evans* (Weidenfeld and Nicolson, 1986)

Zsa Zsa Gabor and Gerold Frank, *My Story* (Arthur Barker, 1961)

Zsa Zsa Gabor assisted by Wendy Leigh, *One Lifetime Is Not Enough* (Headline, 1991)

Alan L. Gansberg, *Little Caesar: A Biography of Edward G. Robinson* (New English Library, 1983)

Eve Golden with Kim Kendall, *The Brief, Madcap Life of Kay Kendall* (University Press of Kentucky, 2002)

John Griggs, *The Films of Gregory Peck* (Columbus, 1988)

Larry Hagman with Todd Gold, *Hello Darlin'* (Simon and Schuster, 2001)

Peter Haining, *Bob Hope* (Foulsham, 1989)

Bill Harding, *The Films of Michael Winner* (Frederick Muller, 1978)

Warren G. Harris, *Natalie and R. J.* (Sphere, 1989)

Dennis William Hauck, *Captain Quirk* (Pinnacle Books, 1995)

Jack Hawkins, *Anything For a Quiet Life* (Elm Tree Books, 1973)

Nigel Hawthorne, *Straight Face* (Hodder and Stoughton, 2002)

Susan Hicklin, *Polished Corners 1878–1978* (Francis Holland School, 1978)

Charles Higham, *Bette: The Life of Bette Davis* (Macmillan NY, 1981)

Clive Hirschhorn, *The Films of James Mason* (LSP Books, 1975)

Ian Holm with Steven Jacobi, *Acting My Life* (Bantam, 2004)

Rick Jason, *Scrapbooks of My Mind* (Argoe Publishing, 2000)

Michael Kerbel, *Paul Newman* (Star Books, 1973)

Larry Kleno, *Kim Novak on Camera* (A. S. Barnes, 1980)

Gavin Lambert, *Natalie Wood* (Faber and Faber, 2004)

Dorothy Lamour and Dick McInnes, *My Side of the Road* (Robson Books, 1981)

Sue Lawley, *Desert Island Discussions* (Hodder and Stoughton, 1990)

Robert Levine, *Joan Collins* (Weidenfeld and Nicolson, 1985)

Roger Lewis, *The Life and Death of Peter Sellers* (Century, 1994)

Damien Love, *Robert Mitchum: Solid, Dad, Crazy* (Batsford, 2002)

James Mason, *Before I Forget* (Hamish Hamilton, 1981)

Diana Maychick and L. Avon Borgo, *Heart to Heart With Robert Wagner* (Robson Books, 1986)

David Miller, *The Complete Peter Cushing* (Reynolds and Hearn, 2005)

Gerard Molyneaux, *Gregory Peck: A Bio-Bibliography* (Greenwood Press, 1995)

Kenneth More, *Happy Go Lucky: My Life* (Robert Hale, 1959)

Kenneth More, *More or Less* (Hodder and Stoughton, 1978)

Sheridan Morley, *James Mason: Odd Man Out* (Weidenfeld and Nicolson, 1989)

Roy Moseley with Philip and Martin Masheter, *Roger Moore* (New English Library, 1985)

Michael Munn, *Trevor Howard: The Man and His Films* (Robson Books, 1989)

Suzanne L. Munshower, *Warren Beatty – Lovemaker Extraordinary* (Everest Books, 1976)

Daniel O'Brien, *Paul Newman* (Faber and Faber, 2004)

Kate O'Mara, *Vamp Until Ready* (Robson Books, 2003)

J. Roger Osterholm, *Bing Crosby: A Bio-Bibliography* (Greenwood Press, 1994)

John Parker, *The Trial of Rock Hudson* (Sidgwick and Jackson, 1990)

John Parker, *Warren Beatty: The Last Great Lover of Hollywood* (Headline, 1993)

Terence Pettigrew, *Trevor Howard* (Peter Owen, 2001)

Robert W. Pohle Jr and Douglas C. Hart, *The Films of Christopher Lee* (Scarecrow Press, 1983)

Jonathan Rigby, *Christopher Lee* (Reynolds and Hearn, 2001)

Jeffrey Robinson, *Bette Davis: Her Film and Stage Career* (Proteus Books, 1982)

Robert Ross, *The Complete Terry-Thomas* (Reynolds and Hearn, 2002)

Jeff Rovin, *Joan Collins: The Unauthorized Biography* (Bantam, 1985)

Eddie Sanderson, *Joan Collins: Portraits of a Star* (Simon and Schuster, 1987)

Margie Schultz, *Ann Sheridan: A Bio-Bibliography* (Greenwood Press, 1997)

Lee Server, *Robert Mitchum* (Faber and Faber, 2001)

Don Shepherd and Robert F. Slatzer, *Bing Crosby: The Hollow Man* (W. H. Allen, 1981)

Barbara and Scott Siegel, *Jack Nicholson* (Angus and Robertson, 1990)

Anne Sinai, *Reach For the Top: The Turbulent Life of Laurence Harvey* (Scarecrow Press, 2003)

Gus Smith, *Richard Harris* (Robert Hale, 1990)

Donald Spoto, *Elizabeth Taylor* (Little, Brown, 1995)

Robert Tanitch, *Leonard Rossiter* (Robert Royce, 1985)

David Thomson, *Warren Beatty: A Life and a Story* (Secker and Warburg, 1987)

Charles Thompson, *Bob Hope* (Thames Methuen, 1981)

Richard Todd, *In Camera* (Hutchinson, 1989)

Pamela Trescott, *Bob Hope* (W. H. Allen, 1987)

Alexander Walker, *Bette Davis* (Pavilion, 1986)

Ruth Waterbury, *Elizabeth Taylor* (Robert Hale, 1964)

Donald C. Willis, *The Films of Howard Hawks* (Scarecrow Press, 1975)

Robin Wood, *Howard Hawks* (BFI Publishing, 1968)

INDEX

Clement, Carl, 68
Clement, Dick, 166
Cleopatra (film), 72, 76, 82, 263
Clinch, Daphne, 172
Clinton, Bill, 303, 309–310
cocaine, 107, 113, 171, 175
Codron, Michael, 266
Coe, Shirley, 195, 197
Colbert, Claudette, 162, 286
Colbys, The (TV series), 213
Cole, George, 23, 35–6
Cole, Michael, 273
Coleman, Pamela, 11, 21, 38, 56
Collins, Elsie ('Elsa'; *née* Besant; Joan's mother): and Joan's childhood, 2–5, 6–7, 8, 9, 20; French holidays, 16, 21–2; and Joan's early career, 26–7, 33, 42, 59, 80; and Joan's relationships, 31, 72, 82; cancer, 85, 86, 94, 95; death, 96–7
Collins Foundation, 179
Collins, Henrietta ('Hettie'; *née* Assenheim; Joan's grandmother), 1, 4–5, 9, 34, 56, 62
Collins, Irene (*née* Korff; Joan's stepmother), 97, 107, 111, 116, 137, 245, 250
Collins, Jackie (Joan's sister): childhood and youth, 3–4, 7, 8, 10–12, 16, 21–2, 38; early career, 39–40, 55–6; on Joan's relationships, 62, 102, 248, 251–2; marriage to Wallace Austin, 81–2, 106; children, 94, 109, 122; and death of her mother, 97; marriage to Oscar Lerman, 109, 152, 276; relationship with her father, 111, 214, 251–2; writing career, 122, 140, 148, 149–50, 155, 249, 257, 332; on *Dynasty*, 170; relationship with Joan, 181, 204, 227, 241, 308–9, 327; and Joan's novels, 249–50, 258; relationship with Frank Calcagnini, 291, 310–311
Collins, Joan: birth, 1–2; childhood,

2–9; schooling 1, 5, 6, 7, 8, 9–15; at RADA, 16–20, 24–5; early film career, 22–7, 35–7, 40–42; a Rank starlet, 26, 27, 30, 32–5, 53; marriage to Maxwell Reed, 28–33, 36–8, 43, 54–5, 66, 201; relationship with Sydney Chaplin, 42–5, 46–7, 49–51, 67; arrives in Hollywood, 44–55; relationship with Arthur Loew, 50, 54, 56–8, 60–61; affair with George Englund, 66–8, 69, 70, 71–3, 75, 201; relationship with Warren Beatty, 73–89, 184; relationship with Anthony Newley, 91–2, 94–9, 201, 229–30, 268, 272; their marriage, 99–122, 126–7, 179, 222; birth of Tara, 101–2; birth of Sacha, 107; relationship with Ron Kass, 118–19, 120, 122–3, 125; their marriage, 127–30, 137, 139–40, 148, 149–50, 152, 154–5, 158, 175–9, 185–6, 188, 190–93, 202, 204; birth of Katy 125, 128; and Katy's accident, 164–7; relationship with Peter Holm, 194–9, 200–201, 202–6, 208–213, 215–16, 282; their marriage, 216–17, 219, 220–21, 225–7, 230–32, 235, 237, 242–4, 249, 250; relationship with Bill Wiggins, 232, 234–6, 238–46, 249, 252, 253, 287, 296; relationship with Robin Hurlstone, 240, 246–8, 252–3, 258–60, 263–4, 267–8, 272, 276–7, 282, 284, 287–8, 302, 305, 314–15, 318–19; and death of her father, 250–52, 256; law suit with Random House, 283–4, 291–5; awarded OBE, 299, 300; birth of grandchildren, 304–5, 330; relationship with Percy Gibson, 311, 312–13, 316–18, 319, 322–3; their marriage, 323–4, 326–7, 328, 331–2, 337, 341–2, 343, 346
Character & characteristics: ambition, 43; appearance, 8, 12–14, 19–20, 34, 52, 158, 238–9, 244–5,

Ryan, Ned, 253

St Laurent, Yves, 236
St Margaret's School, Hampstead, 132
St Wilfred's School, Brighton, 8
Salisbury, Leslie, 140
Sallis, Peter, 30
Sally Aga Khan, Princess, 323
Sanderson, Eddie, 128, 216, 217, 331
Sanderson, Elizabeth, 309
Sandersson, Madeleine (*later* Curtis), 194, 219, 231–2, 275, 282
Sangster, Robert, 267, 287, 289
Sangster, Sue, 267, 287
Santo Pietro, George, 190
Saroyan, Carol, 42
Saunders, Jennifer, 288
Sawalha, Julia, 288
Scott, Clive, 277
Scott, Ronnie, 5
Scoundrel (perfume), 205
Sea Wife (film), 19, 57–8, 201, 348–9
Seagrove, Jenny, 268
Seal, Judy, 116
Second Act (autobiography), 16, 24, 30, 250, 259, 288, 289, 290, 296–8
Segovia, 32
Seguero, Spencer, 243
Selby, Belinda, 155
Sellers, Peter, 5, 36, 89, 100, 107, 129, 131
Sessions, John, 288
Seven Thieves (film), 75–6, 349
Seventh Veil, The (Box), 30, 360
Shales, Tom, 222
Shann, Rosalie, 152, 154
Shapiro, Esther, 170, 262–3
Shapiro, Richard, 170
Sharp, Bill, 216
Shatner, William, 112–13, 183
Shearer, Norma, 53
Shepbridge, John, 44
Sheridan, Ann, 53
Sherrin, Ned, 268
Shields, Brooke, 200

Short, Don, 134
Shulman, Alexandra, 296
Shulman, Milton, 269
Silverstein, Sheldon, 194
Sim, Alastair, 23
Simcock, Barbara (*née* Truscoe), 11–12
Simmons, Maureen, 32, 39
Simon, Carly, 87
Simon and Schuster, 204, 241, 249, 267
Sims, Joan, 33, 273
Sinatra, Frank, 46, 48–9, 76, 89–90, 95, 112, 272
Sinatra, Tina, 144
Sinclair, Sir Clive, 219
Sins (TV mini-series), 211, 212, 216, 221, 222–3, 244, 356
Skeates, Anicia, 330
Skeates, Richard, 125, 329–30
Skeates, Weston, 330, 340
Skin of Our Teeth, The (Wilder), 33, 360
Skouras, Spyros, 72, 76
Small World of Sammy Lee, The (film), 95–6
Snowdon, Anthony Armstrong-Jones, Earl of, 124, 268
Snyder, Whitey, 52
Sons and Lovers (film), 76–7
Soul, David, 140
South Africa, 157, 277
South Bank Show (TV series), 46, 47, 304, 308–9
Space: 1999 (TV series), 139, 358
Spall, Timothy, 302, 303
Spectacular (perfume), 265, 286
Spectator (magazine), 302, 303, 304, 305, 306, 310, 315, 316, 323, 329, 330, 334, 340–41, 342
Spelling, Aaron, 169–70, 172, 173, 188–9, 199, 213, 215–16, 298, 308, 340
Spelling, Candy, 340
Spelling, Tori, 341
Spencer, Charles, 332
Spinetti, Victor, 115
Splendour in the Grass (film), 78–9, 81, 86, 88